Romantic Parodies,
1797–1831

The FRIEND of HUMANITY and the KNIFE-GRINDER, — Scene. The Borough in Imitation of Mr. Southey's Sapphics, — Vide. Anti-Jacobin. p.15.

An engraving by James Gillray that appeared in *The Anti-Jacobin* on 4 December 1797.

Romantic Parodies,
1797–1831

Edited by

David A. Kent and D. R. Ewen

Rutherford ● Madison ● Teaneck
Fairleigh Dickinson University Press
London and Toronto: Associated University Presses

Associated University Presses
440 Forsgate Drive
Cranbury, NJ 08512

Associated University Presses
25 Sicilian Avenue
London WC1A 2QH, England

Associated University Presses
P.O. Box 39, Clarkson Pstl. Stn.
Mississauga, Ontario,
L5J 3X9 Canada

The paper used in this publication meets the requirements
of the American National Standard for Permanence of Paper
for Printed Library Materials Z39.48-1984.

Library of Congress Cataloging-in-Publication Data

Romantic parodies, 1797–1831 / edited by David A. Kent, D. R. Ewen.
    p.   cm.
  Includes bibliographical references and index.
  ISBN 0-8386-3458-3
  1. English literature—19th century. 2. Romanticism—Great
Britain. 3. Parodies. I. Kent, David A., 1948–   . II. Ewen, D.
R., 1925–   .
PR1111.P38R66   1992
827′.708—dc20   91-55380
                                                                  CIP

Contents

6 **Contents**

Foreword: Parody and Romantic Ideology

Linda Hutcheon

"Parody is about power," write David Kent and D. R. Ewen, the editors of this volume. In our postmodern age, awash in *fin de siècle* ironies, this may come as no surprise. Today's oppositional writers and theorists—be they postcolonial, feminist, gay, or any other—argue that mimicry and parody are the complex weapons of both the oppressor and the oppressed.[1] But the parodies gathered in this collection are those of an earlier time, of the Romantic period of English literature, a time we usually think of as being well before these particular issues moved to the forefront of critical discussions. Yet, in these parodies, the variety of modes and forms, the diversity of both targets and vehicles, and the range of inferred motivations or ethos all challenge this temporal categorizing, even as they challenge any reductive notions we might have of a monolithic thing called Romantic literary discourse—and its politics.

To talk of power in this particular context is not merely to note that both liberals and conservatives at this time deployed parodic barbs, often against the same targets (alas, poor Southey). To talk of power is also to point to two extremes, two opposing poles of response, because early nineteenth-century parody is clearly used here as a tool of both reaction and reform. The long tradition of invoking parody as a retentive, conservative force used to ridicule and thus control innovation, perceived excess and aberration is well represented in this extensive collection; but so too is the equally powerful and historically validated use of parody as a form of oppositional discourse against a dominant cultural, social, or political force. After all, if parody in the Romantic period had had no teeth, so to speak, why then would we have seen the Victorian attempt to trivialize it and thus reduce its power through domestication and institutionalization? The desire to "de-fang" parody may well testify to the fear of its power, a power it shares with humor in general: what is at stake here—in addition to the specific individual issues raised by each parody—is the equation of seriousness with significance that is at the core of much of the ideology of nineteenth-century art.

These Romantic parodies, be they motivated by either reaction or reform, are always complicated beasts—complicated in terms of their intended effect, their function, and even their generic definition. No matter what the political direction of the attack, parody here is almost always aligned with satire; that is to say, parody is the literary shape taken on by social satire. Despite this close and obvious relationship, it is still necessary to insist on this distinction between the literary mode and the social intention, if for no other reason than that frequently in this collection we find parodies whose satiric target is different from its parodic vehicle: the parodies of *The Book of Common Prayer*, for instance, are not attacking that text (or Christianity), but are using the fact that parodic allusions to it will be easily recognizable to many readers in order to launch satiric attacks on other targets. This functioning of parody in conjunction with satire helps explain how, even in works in which the target and the vehicle may indeed coincide, what appears to be a limited stylistic parody can in fact sustain a broader social and political critique. The fact that parody is not the same as satire—that they are separate literary modes with separate spheres of influence—helps explain the astonishing range of ethos: this is one reason some parodies can appear to be respectful, even deferential to the parodied texts, while others seem merely playful, and still others savagely mocking. Not all parodies provide the vehicle for satire's ridiculing and ameliorative intent, even if many do.

As well as having these plural motivations, parody is also a multipurpose form of discourse. Its inherent generic complexity means that it is "literature," yes, but that it is also a form of literary criticism, enacting in its very form a kind of (often pointed) critical analysis. In addition, and in a number of different ways, parody can be seen as a form of literary history. As the editors point out in their introduction here, parodies can act as a historical index to what contemporary readers find either new and challenging or simply odd, excessive, and irritating. Here, this would include everything from a tone of moral superiority to perceived self-promotion, affectation, pretension, or obscurity—not to mention the lack of sense of humor that thus manages to turn seriousness into solemnity. Parodies also point to what, in a given historical period, readers have found even worthy of response: what was seductive and thus dangerous, perhaps, or what was deemed too silly to let go by without comment. They reveal *which* poets and works were singled out in this way and *when* their impact was felt most immediately. In short, as a form of literary history, parody is a recording of reading response, of changes in taste, fashion, interest—and ideology. As the editors insist, parody becomes the material site of "struggles for power" within the institutions of literature and culture in general.

These complexities of function, ethos, and genre help explain why parody is a literary form that has the capacity to challenge "Romantic ideology," that set of beliefs and preconceptions about the period, created in large part by Romanticism's dominant self-representations. The parodies collected in this volume work—from *inside* that ideology—to subvert the commonly accepted assumptions and orthodoxies. They both explicitly and implicitly contest what Jerome McGann has described as a process of mastering, reifying and, in general terms, simplifying of what was, in fact, a complex and contradictory history into a monolithic ideology of Romanticism—a process that has been brought about in part by the often uncritical acceptance of these self-representations by the later "clerical preservers and transmitters" of the literature of the period.[2] The presence in this collection of self-parodies, of parodies by the major Romantic poets themselves and by women writers formerly known only to their contemporaries in manuscript form, itself immediately contests any notion of the monolithic and monological by foregrounding the occulted contradictions within that ideology. Michel Foucault has argued that any network of power relations contains within itself multiple points of resistance,[3] and it would seem that these parodies mark certain of these points. As a form of intertextuality—as a text necessarily read in relation to another text—parody by definition is a mode of "parallel script,"[4] and to say that alone is to complicate one of the major founding tenets of the ideology of Romanticism: the notion of literature as unique inscription. Parody's intertextual doubleness itself, therefore, works structurally to undermine the idea not only of the unique text but also of the Romantic "ego"—the individual, unique genius—and frequently also of the attendant habit of self-obsession, self-promotion, and solipsism that is the target of much of the specific satire in this collection. In indirectly but effectively subverting this particular concept of the Romantic self, parody also managed to challenge the closely related (in both historical and structural terms) capitalist notions of literary property and the ownership rights of authors.

It is no wonder, then, that parody might be feared: fear often signals an acknowledgment of the power of challenge. That this challenge is not only launched from within, but is multiple in focus will be clear in this collection from the variety of those who take to parody and their many different reasons for doing so. The Romantic poets were the target of parodies motivated by both reaction and reform, but could themselves be said to have had much at stake in the continuance of the Romantic ideology of self—and of essential seriousness—that they and their work had helped to create. Conservative forces trying to hold onto a concept of social order founded on something beyond the individual subject appear to have discovered in parody one formally and tonally congenial way to combat that assertion of the individualistic ego and its (often condescending) self-positioning as the center of moral and political authority. Yet we must not forget that still others sought the aid of parody to vehicle a satire against what they saw as precisely this kind of conservatism.

No matter how it is used—and no matter how it is evaluated—in a structural sense, parody cannot avoid being parasitic: *parody* and *parasite* do not share their Greek root (meaning either "beside" or "against") for nothing. In a very literal sense, parodies live off other texts. And this is where the problems for later readers begin. The vehicle or parodied text has to be recognized by readers for the parody to be perceived, first of all, and then fully understood. We have to know what is being called up before we can understand the power dynamics at work—whether the motivation inferred is ridicule or reverence. It is a truism of critical thought about both parody and satire that they are forms that "date" quickly, precisely because their comprehension is tied in this manner to very particular literary, historical, social, and political contexts. Although this is undoubtedly the case, the flip side of this would be the argument that many texts have survived into the present simply because they have been parodied. The act of parodying canonizes even as it mimics; it is a gesture of imitation that, however ironically intended, is simultaneously a gesture of legitimation, ensuring some sort of continuance. Nevertheless, in reading parodies of the Romantic period today, we certainly do have to account for the loss of a classically educated readership that could easily recognize allusions and also would likely have practiced the genre, thanks to a tradition of training in the classical art of imitation. But even beyond that, for us today there are going to be gaps: there are specifics—of literary politics, of historical fact, of social practice—that will be needed for full comprehension and appreciation of the parodies of this period, like any other.

This is where the headnotes and endnotes of this collection come in, for they position both texts and authors firmly in these various contexts. In addition they point to the complexities of structural and stylistic functioning within the particular parody and to the relation of parodic vehicle to satiric target. In so doing, they underline the wide range of ethos and modes present and operating within one period, as parodies work subversively from the inside of a single ideology. And what they teach us is that, like any other, the Romantic ideology is rife with contradictions and conflicts that both belie the critical tradition's often simplifying attempts to model the period's literature and also testify to the particular and significant aesthetic, social, and political issues at stake in Romanticism. All this—and much enjoyment as well.

Introduction

Like allegory, parody has called up considerable interest among contemporary literary critics anxious to reexamine and reevaluate forms discredited by earlier schools of criticism. Parody has been recognized, to use Malcolm Bradbury's words, as "a significant mode of modernist experimentation"; indeed, "the great modernist works [Bradbury cites Joyce, Beckett, Picasso, among others] are themselves works of parody."[1] In an age obsessed with self-consciousness, when (as Bradbury also says) "the mirrors of dandyism surround us everywhere" (40), the self-consciousness of parody seems, for a number of critics, fundamental to all literature. Furthermore, parody's intertextuality, its connection to reader response theory, and its implicit critique of the creative writer and his transcendent work of art also have contributed to the attractiveness of parody to various schools of literary theory and criticism.

There have always been apologists for parody, often the editors and compilers of anthologies of parodies concerned with defending parody as "a true and legitimate branch of art," to use the words of anthologist Carolyn Wells.[2] However, prompted by the central role parody plays in twentieth-century art forms, contemporary theorists such as Margaret Rose and Linda Hutcheon, who have each recently written important books on parody, have concerned themselves with giving parody a much wider definition than had been considered by previous critics. Rose stresses, for example, that the historical and metafictional functions of parody need to be considered in addition to its stylistic dimension and "its ability to transform literary traditions."[3] Like some critics before them, both Hutcheon and Rose are anxious to distinguish parody from a host of other terms often used as synonyms for parody: especially travesty, burlesque, and pastiche, but also satire, mock-epic, plagiarism, quotation, and allusion. Hutcheon in particular draws on other art forms, including painting, music, architecture, and cinema, to support her argument that "parody is one of the major forms of modern self-reflexivity" and that modern parody has a broader "range of intent" and a wider ethos than simply mocking ridicule aimed at controlling "excesses in literary fashion."[4] At the same time, Hutcheon more than once admits—in the face of the variety of parodies, their techniques, and the fundamental ambivalence of the mode—that "there are probably no transhistorical definitions of parody possible" (10). She therefore settles on the general and neutral definition of parody as "repetition with difference" (32).

Both Hutcheon and Rose want to alter the narrow conception of parody that has dominated critical understanding until the past several years. The description of parody commonly found in literary handbooks would read like either one of the following two definitions. Parody is "a form of satire" aimed particularly at "literary follies . . . by mimicking and exaggerating foolish mannerisms and turns of thought or phrase."[5] Or, parody "explodes the pompous, corrects the well-meaning eccentric, cools the fanatical, and prevents the incompetent from achieving success."[6] These definitions describe parody as an essentially conservative force in literary tradition, fighting a rearguard action against illegitimate ideas and practices, discouraging aesthetic experimentation, and criticizing the unorthodox. The major techniques of this parody are distortion or exaggeration (which generates caricature) and substitution (of words to undercut the original, or more generally of style): these strategies create surprises for the reader and encourage a consciousness of the parodic intent. Although not denying the truth of these descriptions of parody, Hutcheon and Rose wish to enlarge the term *parody* by stressing its more inclusive range, embracing not just ridicule but also playful and respectful imitation, thereby linking parody (as Hutcheon observes, 37–38) to the notion of Renaissance imitation. This emerging critical awareness of the range of parody indicates the importance of parody in the reception history of literary texts. It also can help us to appreciate the real variety and achievement of those parodies written contemporary with the major Romantic poets.

In 1819 Robert Southey made the following observation in a letter to Walter Savage Landor:

> The swarm of imitative poets in this age is really surprising, and the success with which they imitate their models would be surprising also, if it did not prove that there can be no great difficulty in procuring what may be imitated so well. Morbid feelings, atrocious principles, exaggerated characters, and instances of monstrous and exaggerated horror, make up the fashionable compound; the more un-English, un-Christian, and immoral the better, provided it be slavered over with a froth of philosophy. I have fewer imitators than any other poet of any notoriety; the reason is, that I am less fashionable; and, perhaps also, that I am less a mannerist. To make up for this, I am favoured with more abuse than all the rest collectively. Wordsworth comes in for a very large share, and very often we go together. If my name be found in such company hereafter, it will be enough.[7]

Southey's self-revealing comments are notable for their expression of reactionary opinions and for their condemnation of the "Satanic school" of poets (as he described Byron, Shelley, and Hunt in his Preface to *A Vision of Judgement*).[8] And they are fascinating, too, for their tone and manner: defensive, smug, self-righteous, and self-justifying. But his observations are important for what they suggest about the place of parody in the Romantic period.

Most students of English Romanticism are aware of the better known collections of literary parodies published during the period, such as *The Rejected Addresses* of James and Horace Smith (1812) or *The Poetic Mirror* by James Hogg (1816). They also may recall the *Anti-Jacobin* parodies of 1797 or the two *Peter Bell* parodies published in 1819, the same year as Southey's letter quoted above. However, perhaps few would agree with Southey when he describes his age as "swarming"with "imitative poets"; yet Southey was right. There were swarms of parodies published during the Romantic period, and often they were composed by writers and gentlemen well trained in classical literature and the imitative regimen that was an integral part of their educational experience. Yet there also were parodies written by the increasing number of professional writers on behalf of a rapidly growing reading public for books, periodicals, and magazines.

Except for that major satiric achievement, Byron's *Don Juan,* the parodies written by and about the Romantic poets are the most important form that literary satire assumed in the period. The Romantics were by no means a united group, and their reciprocal animosity at times was as intense as anything hurled at them by the conservative critics alarmed at their innovations. As a young man, Southey parodied Wordsworth, and (under the pseudonym Abel Shufflebottom) he imitated that school of affected love poets known as the Della Cruscans. Coleridge, as Nehemiah Higginbottom (whose comical pseudonym Southey then imitated), parodied Charles Lamb and Charles Lloyd but also himself. A generation later (in 1819), Keats, John Hamilton Reynolds, and Shelley all parodied Wordsworth, while a short time later Byron parodied Southey in *The Vision of Judgment.* Much of Blake's genius also expressed itself through parody, although he was not sufficiently well known to be the actual object of parody until the middle of the nineteenth century. Ironically, Leigh Hunt was parodied frequently both for his poetic style and political sympathies. However, Shelley's poetry did not have a large enough audience to attract much parody, and Keats's poetry was much less well known (and almost devoid of political content) and so awaited the literary parodists of the Victorian age. In prose writing, Jane Austen—like Fielding before her and Thackeray after—began her career composing parodies: first *Love and Friendship* aimed at the epistolary tradition of sentimental novels and later *Northanger Abbey* with its critique of the popular Gothic novel. And this tradition of prose parody also is evident in the work of less celebrated writers such as William Beckford (*Modern Novel Writing,* 1796), Eaton Stannard Barrett (*The Heroine, or Adventures of Cherubina,* 1813), and William Maginn (*Whitehall; or George IV,* 1827, a parody of historical novels, especially aimed at Horace Smith's *Brambletye House,* 1826, itself an imitation of Sir Walter Scott). Inevitably, in a period so full of political, moral, and social upheaval as that of English Romanticism, we also can locate many examples of bawdy parodies, scurrilous burlesques, and vacuous travesties deservedly forgotten, including poems such as *Christa-*

bess, whose explicit immorality and lewd language have given it a reputation as one of the more vulgar and tasteless parodic works in this period. There is also a large literature of undistinguished imitations, including Horace Smith's *Horace in London* (1813), the anonymous *Posthumous Parodies and Other Pieces,* P. G. Patmore's *Rejected Articles* (1826) and his later *Imitations of Celebrated Authors* (1834). Finally, there were numerous imitations of Scott and continuations of Byron that often extended to social satire but did not parody the original author, indeed sometimes were intended as compliments.

Generally, critics of Romanticism have continued to ignore the swarms of imitative poets and poems populating the period, in part because the traditional assessment of parody as a low, insignificant literary form does persist, but also because—and it is a corollary to the first reason—parody is still seen as a parasite on the host of creative literature, and is therefore conceived of as feeding off original genius and contributing nothing creative of its own to the literary tradition. This sin has understandably been given little recognition in the criticism of Romantic literature because it is itself, at least until recently, dominated by Romantic conceptions about the nature of the poet and of literary form with their concomitant emphasis on creativity and originality.[9]

Romantic parodies are often found in the periodical literature of the time, particularly in such publications as *Blackwood's Edinburgh Magazine* and *The Satirist* (1807–1814). Parodies were produced, too, as part of a series or group called forth by a particular occasion, a tradition begun with the *Probationary Odes* (1785), supposedly written in competition for the laureateship. For example, *Rejected Addresses* was prompted by the poetry competition coincident with the rebuilding and reopening of Drury Lane Theatre. A year later, in 1813, several collections of parodies appeared at the time of Henry Pye's death and just before the appointment of Robert Southey to replace Pye as Poet Laureate (including *Accepted Addresses* and *Rejected Odes*). Here again the mock competition furnished the pretext for the parodying of popular writers of the day; *Leaves of Laurel* (published in 1813 and sometimes attributed to Byron's friend, Francis Hodgson) is one such collection. Another important parody collection published a decade later, William Frederick Deacon's *Warreniana* (1824), features another remarkable group of parodic imitations. To further confirm Southey's judgment about the swarms of imitative poets in his time, we also can find numerous parodies in obscure periodicals with such names as *The Academic. A Periodical Publication, comprising Original Essays, Reviews, Poems, etc.* or *County Constitutional Guardian and Literary Magazine.*[10] Parodies even appeared, more fugitively, in newspapers.

Many of the parodies done by the "swarm of imitative writers" in the Romantic period were, as suggested earlier, insignificant, crude, and transient, inferior verbal versions of the kinds of cartoons and caricatures being produced by graphic artists such as James Gillray, Thomas Rowlandson, and George Cruikshank during what has been regarded as a kind of golden age for caricature. These more sprightly, sometimes crude elaborations would include *Jokeby,* a burlesque on Scott's *Rokeby,* or the much shorter *Smokeby;* George Colman's *The Lady of the Wreck; or Castle Blarneygig;* or the many Byron imitations or continuations, such as *Jon Duan* or "Longinus o'er a Bottle. Canto II" by one Byronius. At their best, however, Romantic parodies provide us with contemporary critical responses to the major writers, responses marked by ideological biases which themselves were a complex mixture of social, political, moral, and aesthetic values. During the era of English Romanticism, parody was one of the major literary weapons that both the left and right wings, the liberals and conservatives, used to discredit their opponents. From Wordsworth on, the Romantics attracted parodies of striking vindictiveness. There is a distinct note of alarm in anti-Romantic parodies as if some dangerous force were at work in Romantic literature, and one that had to be stopped. It was not just the innovative or idiosyncratic style of these poets that attracted so much parody; it was the unprecedented and explicit assurance of each poet that he was right about the fundamentals of life and that society was wrong. The Romantics wanted to change their audiences, and the polemic of their work aimed at conversion. In this context, parody was often called in not to correct taste but to preserve order.

Eighteenth-century parody belongs more to the craft of burlesque. From 1753 there were numerous parodies of Gray's "Elegy," many published by the first publisher, Dodsley, and in the identical format of the original poem. But they are all tributes to Gray's poem, the author of the first (John Duncombe) apologizing reverently for his presumption. Parody was also used to describe verse directed against a target unconnected with the original poet who simply provided a celebrated model on which the attack could be based (very often a political attack). By 1865 Lewis Carroll was parodying Southey and Wordsworth in nonsense verse for humorous effects, not seriously questioning the convictions expressed by the originals. The Romantic parodies collected here differ from both their Augustan predecessors and their Victorian successors in the seriousness with which they were written and read.

The scope of Romantic parody is wide. Although most Romantic parodies take a poetic form, there are also many examples of prose parody. Parodic targets include the lengthy explanatory notes of such poets as Sir Walter Scott as well as the prefatory polemics and often convoluted syntax of Wordsworth. Interestingly, there were also parodies of literary book reviewing practices and the language of criticism found in them (for example, "Advice to a Young Reviewer" by Edward Copleston, 1807). Furthermore, there are excellent parodies of the prose style of essayists like William Hazlitt and Leigh Hunt in *Blackwood's* in the opening years of the 1820s. The attack on Hazlitt and Hunt in an article titled "Cockney Contributions for the First of April" (July 1824), for example, stands directly in the tradition of Cockney-bashing initiated seven years earlier with the series on "The Cockney School of Poetry." Egocentricity is evidently the concern of the parodist of De Quincey's *Confessions of an English Opium Eater* in the skilled essay "Confessions of an English Glutton" (published in *Blackwood's,* 1823). And of course Gothic conventions were the subject of much ridicule for many years, from the ballad parodies of "Monk" Lewis (*Tales of Wonder,* 1801) to *The Heroine* (1813) by Eaton Stannard Barrett.

Turning to poetry, we can find the entire range of the parodic ethos, from respectful through playful to scornful and satiric (Hutcheon, 6), expressed in Romantic parodies. There are parodies which focus on the style of a school of poets, be it Lake, Cockney, or Satanic. For example, in "The Bards of the Lake" (*The Satirist,* December 1809), Wordsworth, Coleridge, Southey, and Lamb (probably) are each parodied. Moreover, the article jointly condemns the group of them as a disreputable, lunatic fringe whose aberrant ideas about sharing material goods, about poetic experimentation, and about free love all demand repudiation. Parodies that focus on an individual poet rather than on a school may take one text as their primary target, as with "The Story of Doctor Pill and Gaffer Quake, after the most approved modern Style, And containing Words Worth imitation" (published in *The Satirist* in 1812). This parody follows a Wordsworth original closely, in this case "Goody Blake and Harry Gill." But the parody's adherence to a single text also illustrates that the principle of substitution, the most primitive of parodic techniques, can severely limit the parodist. An exception to this general rule occurs in the *Anti-Jacobin* parodies of Southey, where short lyrics are brilliantly imitated with no real sense of undue restrictions. Related to this approach is the parody that utilizes a popularly known text but whose parodic target is not the text used or its author but a third party, usually discussed in the text. For example, "Don Juan Unread" (1819) is a parody attacking Whiggish writers from Godwin to Moore, and especially Byron in *Don Juan,* but it does so by using the text of Wordsworth's "Yarrow Unvisited"; in fact, the original and the parody were printed by *Blackwood's* in parallel columns beside each other. The parodist, possibly William Maginn, associates political liberalism with anarchy and immorality and concludes his parody with a vision of societal upheaval, presumably the inevitable result of following the present fashionable ideas to their logical conclusion. Despite being tied to a single model, the parody succeeds, thanks to the skill of the parodist in endowing the text with energy and pointed wit. In spite of these exceptions, the most successful parodies of individual authors are usually those which try to reproduce a writer's characteristic manner by creating what might be termed a synoptic parody, perhaps (although not necessarily) containing allusions to several of the target writer's poems but not tying itself to a single pretext.

Byron was a difficult poet to parody, not to mention a dangerous one. Attacks on Byron were usually directed more at his moral and social attitudes than at his writing style. *Prodigious!!! or, Childe Paddie in London*

(1818) is a prose parody of the sentimental and Gothic novel that tries to take advantage of the popularity of *Childe Harold*, while *Don Juan, Canto the Third* (1819), possibly by Hone, turns Byron's manner and stanza to political ends (attacking the *Courier* newspaper and recalling the events at Manchester the same year). Perhaps the best parody of Byron remains "Cui Bono?" in *Rejected Addresses* (1812) in which the Smith brothers manage a superb mimicry of the Byron style as it had revealed itself by 1812. *Don Juan* spawned a large progeny of imitations, some of them censorious, as well as efforts to continue or complete Byron's poem in the same style.

Wordsworth was the Romantic poet most widely parodied by his contemporaries and apparently the only one who never wrote parodies himself. In his Preface to the second edition of *Lyrical Ballads,* Wordsworth alludes to parody as a "mode of false criticism."[11] We can also read letters written at about the same period and see his violent reaction to parodic imitations written by one Peter Bayley in his *Poems* (1803). For Wordsworth, parody is evidently a species of plagiarism, a violation both of private property and personal identity. It is perhaps no coincidence that, as Norman Fruman observes, "it was during the Romantic period that a genuine sense of authorial rights and literary property took hold."[12] Wordsworth's defensiveness about being parodied is both a measure of the seriousness with which he regarded his role and status as poet as well as an indication of how dismayed he must have become over the years as the parodies multiplied. The many parodies of Wordsworth, beginning as early as 1799 and extending right to the conventionally designated end of the Romantic period, 1832, help us to appreciate which aspects of his poetic practice and ideology stood out as distinctive, challengingly different, or simply annoying to his contemporaries. Wordsworth's particularities of description, for example, are turned by many of his parodists into a scrupulous triviality about commonplace things, and his low-life characters and poems of encounter are sometimes flippantly mocked. Furthermore, his child-like expressions of faith become either vulgar childishness or immature silliness. Hogg's two brilliant parodies in *The Poetic Mirror* transform earnest inner searchings into solipsistic, digressive delusions.

Less overtly egotistical in his poems than Wordsworth, Coleridge drew correspondingly less animosity upon himself. Parodies of his poems concentrate on individual texts rather than on the whole corpus or any consistent tone or viewpoint that might have been perceived in his writings, and the spirit is more one of playful derision in place of the fierce hostility often directed at Wordsworth. There is a movement from the political to the aesthetic, Coleridge at first being seen as a republican fanatic, but latterly as a poetic eccentric, attracted by banal or outlandish subjects, handling these with unself-critical recklessness of phrase, rhyme and rhythm, and prone to poetic miscarriage. His preoccupation with the Gothic and with the sublime were ridiculed as pretentious and perhaps as evidence of simple-mindedness.

Again unlike Wordsworth, if Coleridge read his parodists, he may well have thought they had a point.

Robert Southey, although not parodied so often as Wordsworth, was the recipient of more virulent attacks than any other Romantic writer. Southey has the distinction of being parodied by conservatives in 1797 for his republican, revolutionary, humanitarian sympathies, and—at the other end of his life and on the opposite side of the political spectrum—of being parodied by William Hone and Byron nearly 25 years later for his abandonment of all his reformist ideals. He was, for the younger generation of radicals and liberals, the prototypical turncoat, someone who had sold out to the establishment and become the enemy to change and reform. In the example of Southey, we can see parody being used as an ideological weapon of considerable force and influence, a mode lending itself to the service not just of conservatism and tradition but also, with equal or greater force, to liberalism and reform. Even in Romanticism, then, we can describe parody as a literary form not inherently conservative but rather a literary mode of service to other points of view.

Romantic parodies demonstrate that parody is about power; to parody is to assert power. In the act of mimicry the parodist achieves dominance over his model and acquires power because his imitation simultaneously appropriates the original and subverts its authority. In holding up a mirror to a particular writer, the parodist purports to disclose the artifices of language and the premises of value that constitute that writer's literary identity. In effect, a parody "deconstructs" a text to disclose the rhetorical elements that make up its supposed originality. No Romantic writer was so angrily deconstructed in this way as Southey, but nearly all of them were parodied and placed before their contemporaries.

One of the favorite and most skillful of parodies produced in the period is Byron's *Vision of Judgment,* his parody of Southey's *Vision.* Much less well known is another parody of Southey's poem, William Hone's *A New Vision* (published in 1821). Hone's literary career, particularly between 1817 and 1821, illustrates vividly how parody gradually crossed the political spectrum and became part of the arsenal of reform writers. It was Hone who, in the Preface to his 1817 printing of Southey's long supressed *Wat Tyler,* aptly summarized the position of reform-minded writers with respect to the laureate: "It is not to Mr. Southey's laying down his opinions, nor to his taking up a pension, nor to his six Epic Poems, nor to his history, nor to his philology, that we object; but we do object to his violence toward those who maintain the doctrines which he himself advocated 'in the full vigour of his incapacity'; we object to his calling on the Legislature to crush principles which he once contributed to propagate; in short, we do not object to the weakness of the man, but to the intolerance of the proselyte, and the 'malignity of the Renegado'."[13] The parodies that made Hone famous demonstrate a kind of parody that rose to greater prominence during the Victorian period. In 1817

Hone was brought to trial for publishing three blasphemous and seditious parodies: *The Sinecurist's Creed, John Wilkes's Catechism,* and *The Political Litany.* At his famous trials in December 1817 before Lord Eldon, Hone's elaborate and brilliant self-defense was aimed at justifying his practice of using elements of *The Book of Common Prayer* as the basis for his parodies. His central strategy was fundamentally the legal one of citing numerous historical and literary precedents. What he managed to argue successfully was that the form being imitated in a parody (usually a well-known text of some kind) is not necessarily the immediate object of attack and that the imitation of a particular text did not always imply criticism of the text being utilized. He was thus able to contend that he was not attacking Christianity in his liturgical parodies but rather something beyond the text: the very un-Christian character of the political powers of his day. Hone's parodies, although using what we earlier termed the most primitive of parodic techniques—substitution—still manage to convey enormous satirical power because the text used as the base, *The Book of Common Prayer,* stood next to the Bible in England as a sacred text. Even a glance at two examples from *The Late John Wilkes's Catechism of a Ministerial Member* (1817), the parody of the Creed and Lord's Prayer, will demonstrate the effectiveness of Hone's technique and explain why the government was so anxious to convict him.

As Hone's case also shows, Romantic parody reaches its height during the last part of the Regency, a time when "everyone thought they knew about stealing, whether as victims or practitioners."[14] The year 1819 saw a proliferation of parodies, the best known of which are the various *Peter Bell* parodies. England was being governed by two parodies of kingship: George III—"An old, mad, blind, despised, and dying King" (Shelley's "England in 1819"); and George IV to be—a man devoted to self-gratification who dabbled in numerous styles and modes. The Regency was, as J. B. Priestley observes, an age of extremes and of transition in which "elegance and refinement" existed beside "brutality and misery," wealth beside poverty, licentiousness beside prudery. It had "no common belief, no accepted code, no general standard of conformity."[15] Parody is an apt reflection of this age of role-playing and costume, of ostentatious dandies and vulgar improprieties, in some way the expression of political frustration. There must certainly be an analogy between upper class gentlemen dressing up like coachmen or boxers and university men donning the poetic style of poets they considered their social inferiors. Parody conveniently combined many attractive elements for Regency writers, becoming a vehicle for cynical and contemptuous criticism of political, class, and artistic enemies as well as a disguise (anonymity in addition to borrowed clothes) to protect oneself.

In an article on Romantic humor more than a decade ago, Marilyn Gaull suggests that while a period of severe ideological instability is not conducive to "the comic spirit," it does generate satire, parody, and burlesque. She later observes that "parody as an art or . . . craft comes of age as a major comic expression during the Romantic period."[16] This is not an observation that has been much affirmed in the intervening years of criticism on the Romantics. We still tend to understand parody using Romantic premises of originality or to see parody through Victorian lenses and to regard it as a relatively minor, harmless, and self-indulgent literary form, in rather the same terms as those used by Isaac Disraeli in *Curiosities of Literature:* i.e., parody as not "necessarily a corrosive satire," but as akin to "mimicry," and as a kind of "agreeable maliciousness."[17] Parody was domesticated and then institutionalized by the Victorians in such magazines as *Punch* or *Once a Week;* it often became the occasion for commentary on current events and political issues.[18] Thinking likely of Victorian parodies by writers such as J. K. Stephen (1859–1892), Riewald has remarked: "Most good parodies happen to be written out of admiration rather than distaste or contempt."[19] Victorian parody is indeed more often a matter of admiration or, in Kiremidjean's words, a "form of homage."[20] In this respect the practice of Victorian parody marks a transition from Romantic parody to that form of imitation which Hutcheon sees in twentieth-century parodies. And it is because of the work of theorists on parody, of which Hutcheon's is undoubtedly the most important to date, that this recognition is even possible.

However, Romantic parody does not fall into these generalizations quite as easily. Romantic parody is seldom a parlor game. It is rougher ideological sport, highlighting clashes of ideas, styles, and values between different generations of writers, different classes and social groups, and even between writers of the same class and generation. Flourishing in a Regency culture that worshipped the outrageous performance of role-playing dandies such as Beau Brummel or that favored the white stucco and iron railings on a typical town house facade, the act of parodying assumed that literature was the artifice of language and that literary identity was a compound of imitable roles, gestures, and habits. As with the articles and reviews found in the periodicals, Romantic parodies record struggles for power. Often complex and subtle texts, they are essential documents in the reception history of the major writers.

We are very grateful to the Faculty of Arts, York University, for providing us with funds to cover sundry expenses over several years through its program of Minor Research Grants. We wish to thank Margo Swiss for her indulgence of absence, and to commend Marlene Sherman for her patience in typing and keeping accessible our texts, especially because many of the photocopies she worked from were sometimes difficult to decipher. We are grateful to Mary Hudecki and the late Gary Macdonald for much assistance as they acquired texts for us through York University's Interlibrary Loans Office. Secretarial Services at York University also helped us immensely as we readied the manuscript for publication. The pioneering work of William

Hamilton and, more recently, the work of N. Stephen Bauer were both extremely helpful in getting our research underway. In process we have been indebted to David Groves, Donald Priestman, Roderick McGillis, Alan Osler, Jack David, and Peter McConkey for their contributions and advice. We wish to thank warmly Jerome McGann who generously took time to read the manuscript during a summer crowded with his own work. We much appreciated Antony Harrison's suggestions about aspects of our introduction. The reader for the Press, Daniel Watkins, also gave us the benefit of his very useful recommendations. We express, too, our sincere gratitude to Linda Hutcheon for her interest in our project and for her foreword to this volume. Finally, after many years of research that brought us both instruction and delight, we would like to dedicate this volume to each other.

Unless otherwise noted, we have used the first edition or printing of each text for this collection. Where asterisks appear in the text, they indicate notes by the parodists. Our references to sources are always full citations. Occasionally citations are repeated because we recognize that this collection will not always be read sequentially from beginning to end. Obvious errors in punctuation or spelling have been silently corrected.

DAVID A. KENT
D. R. EWEN

Romantic Parodies,
1797–1831

1
George Canning and John Hookham Frere, from *The Anti-Jacobin* (1797)

The Anti-Jacobin, or Weekly Examiner was published between November 1797 and July 1798. George Canning (1770–1827) and John Hookham Frere (1769–1846), two friends and conservative M.P.s, were the major figures behind this publishing enterprise. They used their periodical to attack the opposition Whigs and to support Prime Minister Pitt when French invasion threats were real and when signs of Jacobin rebellion had already been seen within the British navy.

The *Anti-Jacobin* is now remembered for its parodies of Robert Southey more than for its journalism, patriotic verse, or Latin imitations. Southey's republican sympathies in politics and his experimental meters in poetry made him especially vulnerable to conservative scorn, and the four parodies printed here accordingly attack him both politically and aesthetically.

Southey's "Inscription" concerns Henry Marten, regicide, imprisoned in Chepstow Castle for 30 years after the restoration of Charles II. The poet is sympathetic to Marten's republican ideals and associates him with the idealism of Plato and Milton. Marten was a confirmed republican but no Puritan in his private life and was described by Charles I as an "ugly whoremaster." In turn, the parody uses a sadistic murderer as the central figure. The speaker's sympathy is thus made to appear perverse and his own position to be anarchistic.

Southey's "The Widow" describes the plight of an unfortunate widow as she is pictured wandering over the downs in winter and being passed by some callous people in a "chariot." Southey's philanthropic attitude is mocked in the parody when the "Friend of Humanity" tries to use a knife-grinder's lot as evidence of the need for revolutionary reforms in society. The knife-grinder is, however, a drunken brawler and a beggar. His honesty is rewarded only by the "Friend" kicking him, peevishly angry at having the knife-grinder contradict his expectations.

Southey's "The Soldier's Wife" is a picture of misery designed to evoke the reader's pity and, ultimately, anger. "The Soldier's Friend" is, however, a subversive democrat spreading Paine's propaganda and ideas of mutiny. The second parody of Southey's original attacks the poet's writing abilities and metrical idiosyncrasies.

Southey's own poems, now the least accessible among the Romantic poets, are printed below after the parodies to allow for easy comparison.

INSCRIPTION

FOR THE DOOR OF THE CELL IN NEWGATE WHERE MRS. BROWNRIGG,[1] THE
'PRENTICE-CIDE, WAS CONFINED PREVIOUS TO HER EXECUTION

For one long Term, or e'er her trial came,
Here BROWNRIGG linger'd. Often have these cells
Echoed her blasphemies, as with shrill voice
She scream'd for fresh Geneva.[2] Not to her
Did the blithe fields of Tothill, or thy street,
St. Giles,[3] its fair varieties expand;
Till at the last in slow-drawn cart she went
To execution. Dost thou ask her crime?
SHE WHIPP'D TWO FEMALE 'PRENTICES TO DEATH,
AND HID THEM IN THE COAL-HOLE. For her mind
Shap'd strictest plans of discipline. Sage Schemes!
Such as LYCURGUS[4] taught, when at the shrine
Of the Orthyran Goddess[5] he bade flog
The little Spartans; such as erst chastised
Our MILTON, when at College. For this act
Did BROWNRIGG swing. Harsh Laws! But time shall come,
When France shall reign, and Laws be all repealed!

SAPPHICS[6]

———

THE FRIEND OF HUMANITY AND THE KNIFE-GRINDER

———

Friend of Humanity

"Needy Knife-grinder! whither are you going?
Rough is the Road, your Wheel is out of order—
Bleak blows the blast;—your hat has got a hole in't,
                    So have your breeches!

"Weary Knife-grinder! little think the proud ones,
Who in their coaches roll along the turnpike-
-road, what hard work 'tis crying all day "Knives and
                         "Scissars to grind O!"

"Tell me, Knife-grinder, how you came to grind knives?
Did some rich man tyrannically use you?
Was it the 'Squire? or Parson of the Parish?
                         Or the Attorney?

"Was it the 'Squire for killing of his Game? or
Covetous Parson for his Tythes distraining?
Or roguish Lawyer made you lose your little
                         All in a law-suit?

"(Have you not read the Rights of Man, by TOM PAINE?)
Drops of compassion tremble on my eye-lids,
Ready to fall, as soon as you have told your
                         Pitiful story."

Knife-Grinder

"Story! God bless you! I have none to tell, Sir,
Only last night a-drinking at the Chequers,
This poor old hat and breeches, as you see, were
                         Torn in a scuffle.

"Constables came up for to take me into
Custody; they took me before the Justice;
Justice OLDMIXON put me in the Parish-
                         Stocks for a Vagrant.

"I should be glad to drink your Honour's health in
A Pot of Beer, if you will give me Sixpence;
But for my part, I never love to meddle
                         With Politics, Sir."

Friend of Humanity

"*I* give thee Sixpence! I will see thee damn'd first—
Wretch! whom no sense of wrongs can rouse to vengeance—
Sordid, unfeeling, reprobate, degraded,
                         Spiritless outcast!"

(Kicks the Knife-grinder, overturns his Wheel, and exit in a transport of republican enthusiasm and universal philanthropy.)

THE SOLDIER'S FRIEND

DACTYLICS[7]

Come, little Drummer Boy, lay down your knapsack here:
I am the Soldier's Friend—here are some Books for you;
Nice clever Books, by TOM PAINE the Philanthropist.

Here's Half-a-crown for you—here are some Hand-bills too—
Go to the Barracks, and give all the Soldiers some.
Tell them the Sailors are all in a Mutiny.[8]

[*Exit Drummer Boy, with Hand-bills and Half-crown.—Manet Soldier's Friend.*]

Liberty's friends thus all learn to amalgamate,
Freedom's volcanic explosion prepares itself,
Despots shall bow to the Fasces of Liberty,[9]
    Reason, philosophy, "fiddledum diddledum,"
    Peace and Fraternity, higgledy, piggledy,
    Higgledy, piggledy, "fiddledum diddledum."

Et cetera, et cetera, et cetera.

THE SOLDIER'S WIFE

DACTYLICS

Being the quintessence of all the Dactylics that ever were, or
ever will be written
Humbly Addressed To The Author of the Above

Wearisome Sonnetteer, feeble and querulous,
Painfully dragging out thy demo-cratic lays—
Moon-stricken Sonnetteer, "ah! for thy heavy chance!"

Sorely thy Dactylics lag on uneven feet:
Slow is the Syllable which thou would'st urge to speed,
Lame and o'erburthen'd, and "screaming its wretchedness!"

+ ********************

Ne'er talk of Ears again! look at thy Spelling-book;
Dilworth and Dyche[10] are both mad at thy quantities—
DACTYLICS, call'st thou 'em?—"God help thee, silly one!"

+ My worthy friend, the Bellman, had promised to supply an additional
Stanza; but the business of assisting the Lamp-lighter, Chimney-sweeper,
&c. with Complimentary Verses for their worthy Masters and Mistresses,
pressing on him at this Season, he was obliged to decline it.

ROBERT SOUTHEY, FROM HIS *POEMS* (1797)

INSCRIPTION IV

*For the Apartment in CHEPSTOW-CASTLE where HENRY MARTEN the
Regicide was imprisoned Thirty Years*

> For thirty years secluded from mankind,
> Here Marten linger'd. Often have these walls
> Echoed his footsteps, as with even tread
> He paced around his prison: not to him
> Did Nature's fair varieties exist;
> He never saw the Sun's delightful beams,
> Save when thro' yon high bars it pour'd a sad
> And broken splendor. Dost thou ask his crime?
> He had rebell'd against the King, and sat
> In judgment on him; for his ardent mind
> Shaped goodliest plans of happiness on earth
> And peace and liberty. Wild dreams! But such
> As PLATO lov'd; such as with holy zeal
> Our MILTON worshipp'd. Blessed hopes! awhile
> From man withheld, even to the latter days,
> When CHRIST shall come and all things be fulfill'd.

THE SOLDIER'S WIFE

DACTYLICS

Weary way-wanderer languid and sick at heart
Travelling painfully over the rugged road,
Wild visag'd Wanderer! ah for thy heavy chance!

Sorely thy little one drags by thee bare-footed,
Cold is the baby that hangs at thy bending back,
Meagre and livid and screaming its wretchedness.

*Woe-begone mother, half anger, half agony,
As over thy shoulder thou lookest to hush the babe,
Bleakly the blinding snow beats in thy hagged face.

Thy husband will never return from the war again,
Cold is thy hopeless heart even as Charity—
Cold are thy famish'd babes—God help thee, widow'd One!

THE WIDOW

SAPPHICS

Cold was the night wind, drifting fast the snows fell,
Wide were the downs and shelterless and naked,
When a poor Wanderer struggled on her journey
    Weary and way-sore.

Drear were the downs, more dreary her reflections;
Cold was the night wind, colder was her bosom!
She had no home, the world was all before her,
    She had no shelter.

Fast o'er the bleak heath rattling drove a chariot,
"Pity me!" feebly cried the poor night wanderer.
"Pity me Strangers! lest with cold and hunger
    Here I should perish.

---

*This stanza was supplied by S. T. Coleridge.

"Once I had friends,—but they have all forsook me!
"Once I had parents,—they are now in Heaven!
"I had a home once—I had once a husband—
    Pity me Strangers!

"I had a home once—I had once a husband—
"I am a Widow poor and broken hearted!"
Loud blew the wind, unheard was her complaining,
    On drove the chariot.

On the cold snows she laid her down to rest her;
She heard a horseman, "pity me!" she groaned out;
Loud was the wind, unheard was her complaining,
    On went the horseman.

Worn out with anguish, toil and cold and hunger,
Down sunk the Wanderer, sleep had seiz'd her senses;
There, did the Traveller find her in the morning,
    GOD had releast her.

2
Nehemiah Higginbottom, "Sonnets, attempted in the Manner of 'Contemporary Writers'" (1797)

These parodies were published in the *Monthly Magazine* for November 1797 and were signed Nehemiah Higginbottom, a pseudonym for Coleridge. The best discussion—treating the occasion, the nature of their satire and self-parody, and the offense they caused to Southey, Lamb, and Lloyd—is by David Erdman in his article "Coleridge as Nehemiah Higginbottom" [*Modern Language Notes* 73 (1958): 569–80]. Coleridge later revised and reprinted the sonnets in *Biographia Literaria* (the version printed below). He also explained his intentions:

> "the first . . . had for its object to excite a good-natured laugh at the spirit of *doleful egotism,* and at the recurrence of favorite phrases, with the double defect of being at once trite, and licentious. The second, on low, creeping language and thoughts, under the pretence of *simplicity.* And the third, the phrases of which were borrowed entirely from my own poems, on the indiscriminate use of elaborate and swelling language and imagery."
>
> [*Biographia Literaria,* ed. James Engell and W. Jackson Bate, 2 vols. *The Collected Works of Samuel Taylor Coleridge,* 7 (Princeton: Princeton University Press, 1983), 1: 27]

Briefly, Erdman suggests that the first sonnet is more self-parody than anything, the second not a parody of Lamb but of Lloyd, and the third "a surreptitious" appropriation of an unpublished poem by Wordsworth ("Beauty and Moonlight An Ode," which became Coleridge's "Lewti").

SONNETS, ATTEMPTED IN THE MANNER OF CONTEMPORARY WRITERS

I

PENSIVE at eve on the *hard* world I mused,
And *my poor* heart was sad; so at the MOON

I gazed, and sighed, and sighed; for ah how soon
Eve saddens into night! mine eyes perused
With tearful vacancy the *dampy* grass
That wept and glitter'd in the *paly* ray:
And I *did pause me,* on my lonely way
And *mused me,* on the *wretched ones* that pass
O'er the bleak heath of sorrow. But alas!
Most of *myself* I thought! when it befel,
That the *soothe* spirit of the *breezy* wood
Breath'd in mine ear: "All this is very well,
But much of ONE thing, is for NO thing good."
Oh *my poor heart's* INEXPLICABLE SWELL!

II

TO SIMPLICITY

OH I do love thee, meek SIMPLICITY!
For of thy lays the lulling simpleness
Goes to my heart, and soothes each small distress,
Distress tho' small, yet haply great to me,
'Tis true on Lady Fortune's gentlest pad
I amble on; and yet I know not why
So sad I am! but should a friend and I
Frown, pout and part, then I am *very* sad.
And then with sonnets and with sympathy
My dreamy bosom's mystic woes I pall;
Now of my false friend plaining plaintively,
Now raving at mankind in general;
But whether sad or fierce, 'tis simple all,
All very simple, meek SIMPLICITY!

III

ON A RUINED HOUSE IN A ROMANTIC COUNTRY

And this reft house is that, the which he built,
Lamented Jack! And here his malt he pil'd,
Cautious in vain! these rats, that squeak so wild,
Squeak not unconscious of their father's guilt.
Did he not see her gleaming thro' the glade!
Belike 'twas she, the maiden all forlorn.
What tho' she milk no cow with crumpled horn,
Yet, *aye* she haunts the dale where erst she stray'd:

And *aye,* beside her stalks her amorous knight!
Still on his thighs their wonted brogues are worn,
And thro' those brogues, still tatter'd and betorn,
His hindward charms gleam an unearthly white.
Ah! thus thro' broken clouds at night's high Noon
Peeps in fair fragments forth the full-orb'd harvest-moon!

3

Robert Southey, "Inscription under an Oak" (1799)

This parody of Wordsworth by Robert Southey was published in the first volume of the *Annual Anthology* (1799). Donald G. Priestman located this parody and points out in an article ["An Early Imitation and A Parody of Wordsworth," *Notes and Queries* 26 (1979): 229–31] that it "burlesques a popular type of meditative nature poem" and, in particular, Wordsworth's "Lines Left upon a Seat in a Yew-tree" (230). The major achievement of the parody is to catch Wordsworth's sometimes judgmental and scolding tone, especially in the concluding lines where the reader's sensibility is called into question. This superior attitude is, finally, wittily embodied in the signed name (Theoderit: literally, "God he will be").

INSCRIPTION UNDER AN OAK

Here Traveller! pause awhile. This ancient Oak
Will parasol thee if the sun ride high,
Or should the sudden shower be falling fast,
Here may'st thou rest umbrella'd. All around
Is good and lovely: hard by yonder wall
The kennel stands; the horse-flesh hanging near
Perchance with scent unsavoury may offend
Thy delicate nostrils, but remember thou
How sweet a perfume to the hound it yields,
And sure its useful odours will regale
More gratefully thy philosophic nose,
Than what the unprofitable violet
Wastes on the wandering wind. Nor wilt thou want
Such music as benevolence will love,
For from these fruitful boughs the acorns fall
Abundant, and the swine that grub around,
Shaking with restless pleasure their brief tails
That like the tendrils of the vine curl up,
Will grunt their greedy joy. Dost thou not love

The sounds that speak enjoyment? Oh if not,
If thou would'st rather with inhuman ear
Hark to the warblings of some wretched bird
Bereft of freedom, sure thine heart is dead
To each good feeling, and thy spirit void
Of all that softens or ennobles man.

Theoderit

4
"S," "Joseph: An Attempt at Simplicity" (1799)

Published in *The Monthly Mirror* 7 (March 1799): 175–76, this parody (signed S.) satirizes poets like Southey who concerned themselves with the misfortunes of the poor under the guise of humanitarian sympathies. The parodist suggests that in poems such as Southey's "Hannah: A Plaintive Tale" (1797) the poet's concern is centrally with feeling pity (being "Affected"), but that he does nothing in fact to help. The parody ably mocks the plaintive tone and simplicity of style that Southey adopted in the hope of promoting benevolent behavior in society. The parodist also implies that poetry about the common man and his particular preoccupations will itself be commonplace, boring, and trite—about getting drunk, falling down, and hurting a shin. Southey's vulnerability to criticism is perhaps demonstrated by one of his prefatory comments to *English Eclogues* [quoted by William Haller, *The Early Life of Robert Southey, 1774–1803* (1917; rpt. New York: Octagon Books, 1966), 270]: "The following Eclogues, I believe, bear no resemblance to any poems in our language."

JOSEPH: AN ATTEMPT AT SIMPLICITY

In a rude hamlet,
There lives a man whose neighbors call him Joe;
Honest he is, and these his small effects:
A frisking goat—a harmless-looking sheep—
A fruitful cow—a breed of boars and sows
Which yet are pigs—an old one too to nurse them—
With a large bull-dog:—to these are also added
A three-legg'd stool, which once hath been a chair;
A pair of small-clothes, and some coarse habiliments,
Such as his humble station doth require.—
This good old man, whom now I tell you of,
Hath for some one or two score years been wedded.
His Joan is simple, and but simply skilled;
She roasts his 'tatoes, and she warms his beer,

What time the bitter frost a signal gives
For a hot supper—but of this enough.
                          It hap'd this aged swain,
Joseph, or Joe, work'd with a neighb'ring 'squire;
('Squire Thomas is the name, I think, they give him)
Now when the sun was set, and Joseph finish'd,
The worthy squire insisted on his taking
A draught of ale.—This doing, in the kitchen
With friendly chat he did amuse the servants,
While that the hours, unthought on, pass'd away;
Until, on looking at the clock, he saw
The time was half past eight. On that, he rose,
And bidding them good eve, he took his stick,
(Which from a crab-tree he had lately cut)
So, in the dark, he homeward sped his way.
The stick was useful—but, while slow he grop'd,
To keep at proper distance from the wall,
A bucket (which some careless damsel left
Before his idle neighbour, James Cole's door)
Cross'd his unwitting limbs, and—broke his shin.
                          While lately standing at his door,
To keep my best coat from the drizzling rain
I saw the bruise—
His worthy consort, Joan was his kind surgeon,
And she, in one officious hand, did hold
Brown paper steep'd in vinegar—
                          —I turn'd away,
Affected at the sight—
                                        S.

5

Robert Southey, from "The Amatory Poems of Abel Shufflebottom" (1799)

These parodies were written in 1799 as a late entry in the widespread ridiculing of the so-called Della Cruscan school of poetry, named for Robert Merry (1755–1798) who adopted the pseudonym Crusca after the Accademia Della Crusca at Florence (established 1582) to which he belonged. He and his associates (who included Mary Robinson, Mrs. Piozzi, Mr. Greathead, and Mr. Jerningham) published their pretentious, affected love poems in such magazines as *The World*. William Gifford satirizes (among others) the Della Cruscans in *The Baviad* (1794) and *The Maeviad* (1795), and even much later, in *The Rejected Addresses* (1812), the Smith brothers do the same ("Drury's Dirge" by Laura Matilda). Southey's choice of the name Shufflebottom was suggested by Coleridge's use of Higginbottom. The texts used are from volume 2 of *The Works of Robert Southey*, 10 vols. (London: Longmans, 1837–1838).

SONNET IV

THE POET EXPRESSES HIS FEELINGS RESPECTING A PORTRAIT IN DELIA'S PARLOUR

I would I were that portly Gentleman
With gold-laced hat and golden-headed cane,
Who hangs in Delia's parlour! For whene'er
From book or needlework her looks arise,
On him *converge the* SUN-BEAMS *of her eyes,*
And he *unblamed* may gaze upon MY FAIR,
And oft MY FAIR his *favour'd* form surveys.
O HAPPY PICTURE! still on HER to gaze;
I envy him! and jealous fear alarms,
Lest the STRONG *glance* of those *divinest* charms
WARM HIM TO LIVE, as in the ancient days,
When MARBLE MELTED in Pygmalion's arms.
I would I were that portly Gentleman
With gold-laced hat and golden-headed cane.

ELEGY I

THE POET RELATES HOW HE OBTAINED DELIA'S POCKET-HANDKERCHIEF

'Tis mine! what accents can my joy declare?
    Blest be the pressure of the thronging rout!
Blest be the hand so hasty of my fair
    That left the *tempting corner* hanging out!

I envy not the joy the pilgrim feels,
    After long travel to some distant shrine,
When at the relic of his saint he kneels,
    For Delia's POCKET-HANDKERCHIEF IS MINE.

When first with *filching fingers* I drew near,
    Keen hope shot tremulous through every vein;
And when the *finish'd deed* removed my fear,
    Scarce could my bounding heart its joy contain.

What though the Eighth Commandment rose to mind,
    It only served a moment's qualm to move;
For thefts like this it could not be design'd,
    The Eighth Commandment WAS NOT MADE FOR LOVE!

Here when she took the macaroons from me,
    She wiped her mouth to clean the crumbs so sweet!
Dear napkin! yes, she wiped her lips in thee!
    Lips *sweeter* than the *macaroons* she eat.

And when she took that pinch of Mocabaw,
    That made my love so *delicately* sneeze,
Thee to her Roman nose applied I saw,
    And thou are doubly dear for things like these.

No washerwoman's filthy hand shall e'er,
    SWEET POCKET-HANDKERCHIEF! thy worth profane;
For thou hast touch'd the *rubies* of my fair,
    And I will kiss thee o'er and o'er again.

6

Anonymous, "Barham Downs; or Goody Grizzle and Her Ass" (1801)

"Barham Downs" was published in *The European Magazine* 40 (September 1801): 201–2. This anonymous parody of Wordsworth is one of the earliest published attacks on *Lyrical Ballads*. It is a kind of synoptic parody that brings together features of subject and style from various ballads and desperately tries to discredit the genre and the author. The bawdy explicitness of this ballad is not uncharacteristic of contemporary caricature, as a glance at some of Gillray's illustrations featuring anal humor testifies [for example, see the 1802 print "Scientific Researches," in *The Works of James Gillray, The Caricaturist*, ed. Thomas Wright (1874; rpt. Amsterdam: Emmering, 1970), facing 292].

Dame Grizzle's unfortunate accident is certainly nothing that would occur in Wordsworth. The parodist exploits the incongruities of the subject and the language used to describe it, mocks Wordsworth's memorializing of place, and exaggerates such mannerisms of his style as repetition. The good Samaritan's rescue of woman and ass initially seems to redeem the nobility of the peasantry, but only until both go out and get drunk.

BARHAM DOWNS; OR GOODY GRIZZLE AND HER ASS

A LYRICAL BALLAD, IN THE PRESENT FASHIONABLE STILE

One winter, at the close of day,
　　Her eggs and butter sold,
Dame Grizzle took her homeward way,
　　Amidst the rain and cold.

O'er Barham-Downs, of martial fame,[1]
　　Her homeward way did pass:
Good lack! so poor was she, and lame,
　　She rode upon an ass!

The patient beast along did creep,
    A basket on each side;
O'er which the dame, her seat to keep,
    Sat with her legs astride.

The load was great, the load was great,
    For Grizzle she was big;
One basket loaded was with meat,
    And t'other with a pig.

The load was great, the road was rough,
    And much the Ass did strain;
And Grizzle, with a broom-stick tough,
    Increased the poor thing's pain.

It came to pass, it came to pass,
    Oh tale of wond'rous dole!
That Goody Grizzle and her Ass
    Fell plump into a hole.

All in a hole, all in a hole,
    Down, down they tumbled plump,
And Grizzle's nose, alas, poor soul!
    Lay close to Dapple's rump.

The Ass he kick'd, the Ass he bray'd,
    The woman loud did squall;
For much was Gammer Griz afraid,
    And painful was the fall.

Oh woe on woe! for as she lay
    Upon the Ass's back,
Struggling in vain to get away,
    She heard a dreadful crack!

And first she thought her poor, poor Ass,
    Was yielding up his breath;
"And oh! (she cried) alas! alas!
    His death will be *my* death."

And then she thought it was a ghost,
    Now prone, on each occasion,
To come from Pluto's realms per post,
    And charm the British nation.

She thought it was a modern sprite,
　　And long'd to see it pass:
"Come, Ghost! (she cried, with all her might)
　　"Come! help me and my Ass."

But ah! it was nor ghost nor groan!
　　It was a rumbling roar;
A kind of broken-winded tone
　　She ne'er had heard before.

It was—it was—oh, sad mishap!
　　The Ass in "doleful dumps,"
With whoop whoop whoop, and clap clap clap
　　Was thund'ring out his trumps!

Not wind alone, ah lack-a-day,
　　Burst forth at each explosion!
Six quarts of half-digested hay
　　Composed the od'rous lotion!

And o'er poor Grizzle's face it flew,
　　And o'er poor Grizzle's neck!
Half-choaked, she turned herself askew,
　　And lay upon her back!

Ah poor! ah, poor afflicted ass!
　　He strained—to change his station;
But every strain he made, alas!
　　Increased his crepitation!

In what a plight was Grizzle's mind!
　　The Ass her sides did kick,
And his eruptions from behind,
　　Oh, made her *vastly* sick!

Her patience gone, the poor, poor dame,
　　Tho' much she loved the creature,
Enraged by fear, and pain, and shame,
　　Oft curst his ventilator.

She opened her eyes to look around,
　　And look around did she;
She oped her eyes, and looked around,
　　But nothing could she see!

It was so dark, it was so dark,
    That, even in the sky,
Of light, oh! not a single spark
    Could Gammer Grizzle spy!

The Ass he bray'd with horrid sound;
    Dame Grizzle loud did howl;
The rain it rattled on the ground;
    The thunder it did growl;

When lo! a Heaven-directed swain,
    His mastiff dog before,
Trudging from Canterburia's plain
    To Dover's sea-laved shore,

Passed near the spot where Grizzle lay,
    And eke her ass so strong:
A lantern shed its friendly ray
    To guide his steps along.

He saw the hole, he saw the ass,
    He heard the woman bawl;
Not yet unfeeling did he pass,
    But saved her—Ass and all!

He led her to a neighbouring inn,
    Her drooping soul to cheer,
Where Grizzle she got drunk with gin,
    And he got drunk with beer.

The Jack-Ass too, dear, suffering beast!
    Was led into a stall,
Where he enjoyed of hay a feast,
    And soon forgot his fall.

And still the luckless hole is seen,
    Where Griz and Dapple fell;
And still the lotion marks the green,
    And still retains its smell;

And still is heard, in winter hoar,
    When night has banish'd day,
Poor Dapple's fundamental roar,
    And eke his fearful bray.

And still does Pity wander there,
    Her leisure hours to pass,
And still relate the wild despair
    Of Grizzle and her Ass.

For tho' Dame Grizzle did not die,
    Nor yet her Ass so strong,
Their tale deserves a tender sigh,
    And eke a tender song.
                              Rusticus

Cottage of Mon Repos, near Canterbury, Kent,
August 27, 1801

7
Peter Bayley, "The Fisherman's Wife" (1803)

"The Fisherman's Wife" was published in *Poems* (1803) by Peter Bayley. After a visit to Coleridge and Southey at Keswick, Wordsworth wrote to Scott (16 October 1803) that Southey was about to review "a Vol. of Poems by a somebody Bayley Esqr which contains a long dull Poem in ridicule of the Idiot Boy. . . ." However, Dorothy Wordsworth (on William's behalf) encouraged Coleridge in December of 1803 "to speak of the plagiarisms from other Poets: Akenside, Cowper, Bowles etc. etc." Possibly, Coleridge then wrote the review of Bayley's *Poems* that appeared in the *Annual Review* 2 (1803) in which the parodist is roundly condemned as a "literary sharper" (546), his book as "one mass of patchwork" (551), and his "petty larcenies" (550) from Wordsworth and Bowles exposed in detail. In any case, Wordsworth mentions Bayley again in a March 1804 letter to Thomas De Quincey. On this occasion he describes Bayley as "a wretched creature" and laments the "baseness" of his behavior. The whole affair, he states, "hurt me beyond measure." For quotations from the letters, see *The Letters of William and Dorothy Wordsworth,* ed. Ernest de Selincourt, 2d ed., *I: The Early Years, 1787–1805,* rev. ed. Chester L. Shaver (Oxford: Clarendon Press, 1967), 343, 352, 370, 371. For a brief but illuminating discussion of the poems and Wordsworth's reaction, see N. Stephen Bauer, "Early Burlesques and Parodies of Wordsworth," *Journal of English and Germanic Philology* 74 (1975): 559–60.

Bayley's poems are essentially imitations of Wordsworth, but "The Fisherman's Wife" does approach the status of genuine parody. Certainly Wordsworth thought it did and, as one of the first parodies to evoke the poet's scorn, it deserves inclusion here. Bayley particularly mocks Wordsworth's rural characters, his repetitious manner, and his use of questions and alliteration. After an undistinguished career as writer and editor, Bayley (b. 1778?) died on his way to the opera in January 1823.

THE FISHERMAN'S WIFE

DEDICATED TO ALL ADMIRERS OF THE FAMILIAR STYLE OF TALE-WRITING,
SO POPULAR IN 1800

The morn was fair, and fresh the breeze
That curl'd the waters as it blew,
When up rose Basil with the lark;
On the broad wave his slender bark
He launch'd, and o'er the crisp wave flew.

He sung and trimm'd his little sail,
He plied his oar both fast and strong;
And soon there came a sweeping gale,
It came, it fill'd his little sail,
And swiftly flew the boat along.

Then o'er the lake he steer'd, to gain
The creek upon the southern side;
And on that side his nets he cast,
For there, defended from the blast,
He thought his boat might safely ride.

But who is she in Basil's cot
Who sits so sad with folded arms,
Who from the window now looks out,
Now paces all the room about,
Whose face is full of her alarms?

And who but Rachel may it be?
Who may it be but Basil's wife?
The winds her cottage window shake,
Loud howls the storm along the lake,
And Rachel fears for Basil's life.

And now she calls her little child,
She calls her little daughter Jane;
And "haste thee," cries she, "to the lake;
And round thee thy close kirtle take,
For fast drives down the pelting rain.—

Oh haste thee daughter to the lake,
And look around if thou canst spy
Thy father's sail upon the wave;
And stand beneath the arching cave,
For there the bank is safe though high.

But, Jane, I charge thee, do not climb
That crag which hangs above the lake;
That rock is straight, its verge is steep,
The waters all beneath are deep;
Jane, go not thither for my sake."

Now Jane is gone to look around
If she her father's sail may spy;
And all alone her mother sits,
And looks around, and starts by fits,
As howls the tempest through the sky.

Then Rachel at her loom sat down,
Her solitary task to ply;
But soon she started from the loom,
And, restless, pac'd about the room,
And look'd abroad with anxious eye.

Strange sounds, the creatures of her fears,
Swell'd ev'ry rising gust of wind;
And in the roaring tempest's breath
She seem'd to hear the voice of Death,
And strongest terrors shook her mind.

And Rachel long remain'd alone,
With fear, suspense, and anguish wild;
And as the painful moments flew,
Her fears with every moment grew,
Nor yet return'd her darling child.

"Ah, wretch! in such a storm as this
Why sent I forth my little Jane?
Loud, loud and fearful is the blast,
And keen, and cold; and driving fast,
And pelting hard descends the rain.

What if her heedless feet should stray
Towards the steep rock's slippery verge!

What if, bewilder'd with affright,
My darling from that dreadful height
Should fall into the heaving surge!"

Thus felt the mother; and these thoughts
Almost to madness fir'd her brain;
Her fears poor Rachel would have hush'd,
But loud they cried, and forth she rush'd
Amid the storm, to seek her Jane.

Scarce did she breathe as on she ran,
And down the cottage path she flew;
And now through mingling mist and rain
She sees her little darling Jane,
And tears of joy her cheek bedew.

And now she is with her, and now
She throws her arms the child around,
Now runs on that side, now on this,
And Rachel in her present bliss
Forgets that Basil is not found.

"Where hast thou been, my darling Jane?
Hast thou look'd o'er the lake, to spy
Thy father's sail upon the wave?
Hast thou stood near the arching cave,
There where the bank is safe though high?"

Then thus made answer little Jane,
"Oh mother, on that little mound
I stood, close by the arching cave,
I saw the dashing of the wave,
It foam'd and rag'd as I look'd round;

I held me by the rock and look'd,
Nothing but water could I see,
Cold in my face did come the blast,
And in my eyes the rain so fast
Was driv'n, it almost blinded me."

And now they to the cottage come,
And Jane before the fire is plac'd;
Now Rachel's joy is calmer grown,

She muses—Now her joy is flown,
By all her former terrors chas'd.

The little Jane look'd up, she turn'd
Up to her mother's face her look;
And, while her mother sigh'd and wept,
Close to her side her darling crept,
Still looking up her hand she took.

"Mother! dear Mother! cease to weep!
My father will return anon,
At eve he'll come: beyond the lake
He waits secure, or else to take
His fish to market he is gone."*

Oh, comfort is a blessed thing!
It falls upon the mind like dew;
This simple speech of little Jane
Gave peace to Rachel's tortur'd brain,
And bade her smile serene anew.

Now less the tempest rag'd; yet still
The winds sigh'd on with sinking sound;
And now behind the waving wood
The angry sun went down like blood,
And threw a dismal gleam around.

And now behind the waving wood
At length expire his last red rays;
And bright the crackling faggots burn
For Basil when he shall return;
His cottage glows with cheerful blaze.

"Oh, Mother!" said the anxious Jane,
"He surely will return ere long—
Yes; soon my father I shall see,
And, while he smiles, upon his knee
I'll sit, and sing my artless song."

Now Rachel talks in cheerful guise,
And smiles, her little child to cheer,

---

*The simplicity of that most simple of all poets, Mr. Wordsworth himself, is scarcely more simple than the language of this stanza. Absit invidia dicto.[1]

Yet at each sound she turns her head,
And hopes she hears her husband's tread,
She struggles hardly with her fears.

'Tis dark, and still no Basil comes—
How fares the wretched Rachel now!
How may she cheer her drooping child!
(Herself with dread and anguish wild)
How may she smile! give comfort how!

Around her child her arms she threw,
Her warm tears on her child's face dropp'd;
And close she strain'd her to her breast,
Her voice by anguish was supprest,
Her breath by rising sobs was stopp'd.

At length—"Oh, Basil! wast thou here!
Wast thou but here!" at length she cried,
"Oh might I hear thy feet once more
Approaching to thy cottage door,
Or see thee sitting by my side!

Oh couldst thou hear me! but thy ears
Perhaps are deaf to human cry.
E'en now, while thus I sit and weep,
O'er thee some whelming wave may sweep,
And cold and breathless thou may'st lie.

Perhaps, thy little boat o'erset,
E'en now thou strivest with the wave:
Thou may'st be struggling near the rock
Where the steep banks thy efforts mock,
Where still some friendly hand might save."

As real Rachel's terrors paint
The thoughts that flit across her brain:
No force might hold her, forth she springs;
Those thoughts of horror lend her wings;
Alone she leaves her little Jane.

Down to the lake she goes—The wind
Yet murmurs though the storm is o'er.
Sounds of strange import swell the breeze,

As wild it murmurs through the trees,
Still the subsiding waters roar.

Thick clouds sail sullenly along;
And how may Rachel keep her way!
Unless some star with faint green light
Shines glimmering through the gloomy night,
Or the moon lends a transient ray.

Thick clouds sail on—On Rachel goes;
Nothing may turn her from her way;
Whether 'tis dark, or with green light
Some dim star glimmers through the night,
Or the moon lends a transient ray.

Up springs a breeze; the clouds sail on,
Fast o'er the face of heav'n they fly,
Swiftly they fly, and bright and clear
Between the sparkling stars appear;
The shining moon looks from the sky.

And who is she that on the rock
With hurrying pace runs to and fro?—
And now she stands, fix'd in one spot;
And o'er the lake her eye is shot,*
Her face the moon-beams plainly shew.

What may it be that rocks, and heaves
With gulphing sound? It holds her eye—
Is that her Basil's shatter'd boat?
Are those his oars that near it float?
If not, ah why that piercing cry?

Heard you that shriek? heard you that plunge?
Heard you?—And yet you could not save!
And when the morrow's sun shall gleam,
Shall the first form that meets his beam
Be Rachel breathless on the wave!

Long, long the little Jane may sit
And listen at the cottage door;

*Why not shoot, as well as "dart," according to Milton, or "hurl" an eye, according to
Cowley?2

She shall but hear the night-wind's sigh,
She shall but hear the owlet's cry,
Or distant torrent's sullen roar.

Long may she for her father look,
And long her mother hope to see;
But all that meets her longing sight
Shall be some star's pale glimm'ring light,
Or half-seen shape of waving tree.

8
Edward Copleston, "L'Allegro, A Poem" (1807)

This parody of a review appeared in the pamphlet *Advice to a Young Reviewer, with a Specimen of the Art* (1807) by Edward Copleston. Copleston was professor of poetry at Oxford (1802–1812) and provost of Oriel College from 1814. He was prompted to parody contemporary reviewing practices after his colleague Richard Mant's *Poems* (1806) was attacked in a *British Critic* notice [18 (November 1806): 559]. The *Edinburgh Review* was more kind a year later [11 (October 1807): 167–171], but Mant was still criticized for being too personal, for showing "an extraordinary occasional feebleness," and for writing for personal amusement instead of showing forth "tokens of immortality" (169–71).

Copleston's introductory remarks to his parody indicate that, like Coleridge a decade later in *Biographia Literaria,* he chiefly disagreed with the invulnerability of anonymous criticism. Described by Ian Jack in *English Literature 1815–1832* (London: Oxford University Press, 1963) as "brilliant" (471), Copleston's parody uses Milton's "L'Allegro" as the ostensible subject of review to suggest that reviewers would not know a good poet even if they read one. Complaints about the poet's lascivious imagination, the archly moralistic tone, and the perversely literal reading are all meant to be self-indicting evidence of the reviewer's blindness to real poetic merit. The writer, in trying to show off his own learning, is merely filling up pages. See Nathaniel Teich's article, "Wordsworth's Reception and Copleston's *Advice to Romantic Reviewers,*" *Wordsworth Circle* 6 (1975): 280–82.

L'ALLEGRO, A POEM. BY JOHN MILTON. NO PRINTER'S NAME.

It has become a practice of late with a certain description of people, who have no visible means of subsistence, to string together a few trite images of rural scenery, interspersed with vulgarisms in dialect, and traits of vulgar manners; to dress up these materials in a sing-song jingle, and to offer them for sale as a Poem. According to the most approved recipes, something about the heathen gods and goddesses, and the schoolboy topics of Styx and Cerberus, and Elysium, is occasionally thrown in, and the composition is complete. The stock in trade of these adventurers is in general scanty enough, and their art therefore consists in disposing it to the best advantage. But if such be the aim of the writer, it is the Critic's business to detect and defeat the imposture; to warn the public against the purchase of shop-worn goods, and tinsel wares; to protect the fair trader, by exposing the tricks of needy quacks and mountebanks; and to chastise that forward and noisy importunity, with which they present themselves to the public notice.

How far Mr. Milton is amenable to this discipline, will best appear from a brief analysis of the Poem before us. In the very opening he assumes a tone of authority, which might better suit some veteran bard than a raw candidate for the Delphic bays: for, before he proceeds to the regular process of Invocation, he clears the way by driving from his presence, with sundry hard names and bitter reproaches on her father, mother, and all the family, a venerable personage, whose age at least, and staid matron-like appearance, might have entitled her to more civil language.

> Hence loathed Melancholy;
> Of Cerberus and blackest midnight born
> In Stygian cave forlorn, &c.

There is no giving rules, however, in these matters, without a knowledge of the case. Perhaps the old lady had been frequently warned off before, and provoked this violence by continuing still to lurk about the Poet's dwelling. And, to say the truth, the reader will have but too good reason to remark, before he gets through the Poem, that it is one thing to tell the spirit of dulness to depart, and another to get rid of her in reality. Like Glendower's spirits, any one may order them away, 'but will they go, when you do order them?'[1]

But let us suppose for a moment that the Parnassian decree is obeyed, and according to the letter of the *order,* which is as precise and wordy as if Justice Shallow himself[2] had drawn it, that the obnoxious female is sent back to the place of her birth,

> ' 'Mongst horrid shapes, shrieks, sights,' &c.

at which we beg our fair readers not to be alarmed, for we can assure them they are only words of course in all poetical instruments of this nature, and mean no more than the "force and arms," and "instigation of the Devil" in a common indictment.[3] This nuisance then being abated, we are left at liberty to contemplate a character of a different complexion, "buxom, blithe, and debonair," one, who although evidently a great favourite of the Poet's, and therefore to be received with all due courtesy, is notwithstanding introduced under the suspicious description of an *alias.*

> In heaven yclep'd Euphrosyne,
> And by men, heart-easing Mirth.

Judging indeed from the light and easy deportment of this gay nymph, one might guess there were good reasons for a change of name, as she changed her residence.

But of all vices there is none we abhor more than that of slanderous insinuation; we shall therefore confine our moral strictures to the nymph's mother, in whose defence the Poet has little to say himself. Here too, as in the case of the *name,* there is some doubt: for the uncertainty of descent on the father's side having become trite to a proverb, the Author, scoring that beaten track, has left us to choose between two mothers for his favourite: and without much to guide our choice; for, whichever we fix upon, it is plain she was no better than she should be. As he seems, however, himself inclined to the latter of the two, we will even suppose it so to be.

> Or whether (as some sager sing)
> The frolic *wind that breathes the spring,*
> Zephyr with Aurora playing,
> *As he met her once a Maying;*
> There on beds of violets blue,
> And fresh-blown roses wash'd in dew, &c.

Some dull people might imagine, that the wind was more like the breath of spring, than spring the breath of the wind; but we are more disposed to question the Author's Ethics than his Physics, and accordingly cannot dismiss these May gambols without some observations.

In the first place, Mr. M. seems to have higher notions of the antiquity of the May-pole than we have been accustomed to attach to it. Or perhaps he thought to shelter the equivocal nature of this affair under that sanction. To us however, who can hardly subscribe to the doctrine that "vice loses half its evil by losing all its grossness,"[4] neither the remoteness of time, nor the gaiety of the season, furnishes a sufficient palliation. "Violets blue," and "fresh-blown roses," are to be sure more agreeable objects of the imagination than a ginshop in Wapping, or a booth in Bartholomew Fair; but in point of morality, these are distinctions without a difference: or, it may be, the cultivation of mind, which teaches us to reject and nauseate these latter objects, aggravates the case, if our improvement in taste be not accompanied by a proportionate improvement of morals.

If the reader can reconcile himself to this altitude of principle, the anachronism will not long stand in his way. Much indeed may be said in favour of this union of ancient mythology with modern notions and manners. It is a sort of chronological metaphor—an artificial analogy, by which ideas, widely remote and heterogeneous, are brought into contact, and the mind is delighted by this unexpected assemblage, as it is by the combinations of figurative language.

Thus in that elegant interlude, which the pen of Ben Johnson has transmitted to us, of the loves of Hero and Leander:—

> Gentles, that no longer your expectations may wander,
> Behold our chief actor, amorous Leander,
> With a great deal of cloth, lapp'd about him like a scarf,
> For he yet serves his father, a dyer in Puddle-Wharf;
> Which place we'll make bold with, to call it our Abydus,
> As the bank-side is our Sestos, and *let it not be denied us.*[5]

And far be it from us to deny the use of so reasonable a liberty; especially if the request be backed (as it is in the case of Mr. M.) by the craving and imperious necessities of rhyme. What man who has ever bestrode Pegasus but for an hour, will be insensible to such a claim?

> Haud ignara mali miseris succurrere disco.[6]

We are next favoured with an enumeration of the attendants of this "debonair" nymph, in all the minuteness of a German dramatis personae, or a ropedancer's hand-bill:

> Haste thee, nymph, and bring with thee
> Jest, and youthful Jollity;
> Quips, and cranks, and wanton wiles,
> Nods, and becks, and wreathed smiles,
> Such as hang on Hebe's cheek,
> And love to live in dimple sleek;
> Sport that wrinkled Care derides,
> And Laughter holding both his sides.

The Author, to prove himself worthy of being admitted of the crew, skips and capers about upon "the light fantastic toe," that there is no following him. He scampers through all the categories, in search of his imaginary beings, from Substance to Quality, and back again; from thence to Action, Passion, Habit, &c. with incredible celerity. Who, for instance, would have expected *cranks, nods, becks* and *wreathed smiles,* as part of a group, in which Jest, Jollity, Sport, and Laughter figure away as full-formed entire personages? The family likeness is certainly very strong in the two last, and if we had not been told, we should perhaps have thought the act of *deriding* as appropriate to Laughter as to Sport.

But how are we to understand the stage directions?

> *Come,* and trip it as you *go.*

Are the words used synonymously? Or is it meant that this airy gentry shall come in at a minuet step, and go off in a jig? The phaenomenon of a *tripping crank* is indeed novel, and would doubtless attract numerous spectators. But it is difficult to guess to whom among this jolly company the Poet addresses himself, for immediately after the plural appellative (you), he proceeds,

> And in *thy* right hand lead with *thee*
> The mountain nymph, sweet Liberty.

No sooner is this fair damsel introduced, but Mr. M. with most unbecoming levity, falls in love with her, and makes a request of her companion, which is rather greedy, that he may live with both of them:

> To live with her, and live with thee.

Even the gay libertine who sung, "How happy could I be with either," did not go so far as this.[7] But we have already had occasion to remark on the laxity of Mr. M.'s amatory notions.

The Poet, intoxicated with the charms of his mistress, now rapidly runs over the pleasures which he proposes to himself in the enjoyment of her society. But though he has the advantage of being his own caterer, either his palate is of a peculiar structure, or he has not made the most judicious selection. To begin the day well, he will have the *sky-lark*

> —to come in *spite of sorrow,*
> And at his window bid good morrow-

The sky-lark, if we know any thing of the nature of that bird, must come in spite of something else as well as of sorrow, to the performance of this office. In his next image the natural history is better preserved, and as the thoughts are appropriate to the time of day, we will venture to transcribe the passage, as a favourable specimen of the author's manner:

> While the Cock with lively din
> Scatters the rear of darkness thin,
> And to the stack, or the barn-door,
> Stoutly struts his dames before;
> Oft listening how the hounds and horn
> Cheerly rouse the slumbering morn,
> From the side of some hoar hill,
> Through the high wood echoing shrill.

Is it not lamentable that, after all, whether it is the Cock or the Poet that listens, should be left entirely to the reader's conjecture? Perhaps also his embarrassment may be increased by a slight resemblance of character in these two illustrious personages, at least as far as relates to the extent and numbers of their seraglio.

After a *flaming* description of sunrise, on which occasion the clouds attend in their very best liveries, the bill of fare for the day proceeds in the usual manner. Whistling ploughmen, singing milkmaids, and sentimental shepherds are always to be had at a moment's notice, and, if well grouped, serve to fill up the landscape agreeably enough. On this part of the Poem we have only to remark, that if Mr. John Milton proposeth to make himself merry with

> Russet lawns, and fallows grey,
> Where the nibbling flocks *do* stray;
> Mountains on whose barren breast
> The labouring clouds *do* often rest,
> Meadows trim with daisies pied,
> Shallow brooks, and rivers wide
> Towers and battlements, &c. &c. &c.

he will either find himself egregiously disappointed, or he must possess a disposition to merriment, which even Democritus himself might envy.[8] To such a pitch indeed does this solemn indication of joy sometimes rise, that we are inclined to give him credit for a literal adherence to the Apostolic precept, 'Is any merry, let him sing psalms.'[9]

At length however he hies away at the sound of bell-ringing, and seems for some time to enjoy the tippling and fiddling and dancing of a village wake: but his fancy is soon haunted again by spectres and goblins, a set of beings not in general esteemed the companions or inspirers of mirth.

> With stories told of many a feat,
> How fairy Mab the junkets eat;
> She was pinch'd, and pull'd, she said;
> And he, by friar's lanthern led,
> Tells how the drudging goblin sweat
> To earn his cream-bowl duly set;
> When in one night, ere glimpse of morn,
> His shadowy flail hath thresh'd the corn,
> That ten day-labourers could not end;
> Then lies him down the lubbar fiend,
> And, stretch'd out all the chimney's length,
> Basks at the fire his hairy strength;
> And crop-full out of door he flings,
> Ere the first cock his matin rings.

Mr. M. seems indeed to have a turn for this species of nursery tales and prattling lullabies; and if he will studiously cultivate his talent, he need not despair of figuring in a conspicuous corner of Mr. Newbury's shop-window;[10] unless indeed Mrs. Trimmer should think fit to proscribe those empty levities and idle superstitions, by which the world has been too long abused.[11]

From these rustic fictions we are transported to another species of *hum*.

> Tower'd cities please us then,
> And the busy hum of men,
> Where throngs of knights and barons bold
> In weeds of peace high triumphs hold,
> With *store of ladies,* whose bright eyes
> *Rain influence,* and judge the prize
> Of wit or arms, while both contend
> To win her grace, whom all commend.

To talk of the bright eyes of ladies judging the prize of wit is indeed with the poets a legitimate species of humming: but would not, we may ask, the *rain* from these ladies' bright eyes rather tend to dim their lustre? Or is there any quality in a shower of *influence,* which, instead of deadening, serves only to brighten and exhilarate? Whatever the case may be, we would advise Mr. M. by all means to keep out of the way of these knights and barons bold; for, if he had nothing but his wit to trust to, we will venture to predict, that without a large share of most undue *influence,* he must be content to see the prize adjudged to his competitors.

Of the latter part of the Poem little need be said. The Author does seem somewhat more at home when he gets among the actors and musicians, though his head is still running through Orpheus and Eurydice, and Pluto, and other sombre gentry, who are ever thrusting themselves in where we least expect them, and who chill every rising emotion of mirth and gaiety.

He appears however to be so ravished with this sketch of festive pleasures, or perhaps with himself for having sketched them so well, that he closes with a couplet, which would not have disgraced a Sternhold:[12]

> These delights if thou canst give,
> Mirth, with thee I *mean* to live.

Of Mr. M's good *intentions* there can be no doubt; but we beg leave to remind him, that in every compact of this nature there are two opinions to be consulted. He presumes perhaps upon the poetical powers he has displayed, and considers them as irresistible;—for every one must observe in how different a strain he avows his attachment now and at the opening of the Poem. Then it was,

> If I give thee honour due,
> Mirth, admit me of thy crew.

But having, it should seem, established his pretensions, he now thinks it sufficient to give notice, that he means to live with her, because he likes her.

Upon the whole, Mr. Milton seems to be possessed of some fancy and talent for rhyming; two most dangerous endowments, which often unfit men for acting an useful part in life, without qualifying them for that which is great and brilliant. If it be true, as we have heard, that he has declined advantageous prospects in business, for the sake of indulging his poetic humour, we hope it is not yet too late to prevail upon him to retract his resolution. With the help of Cocker[13] and common industry he may become a respectable scrivener;[14] but it is not all the Zephyrs, and Auroras, and Corydons, and Thyrsis's, aye, nor his junketing Queen Mab, and drudging Goblins, that will ever make him a poet.

9
George Manners, "The Bards of the Lake" (1809)

Published in *The Satirist* (December 1809): 548–56. In "Sam Spitfire; or, Coleridge in *The Satirist*" [*Bulletin of the New York Public Library* 71 (1967): 239–44], P. M. Zall attributes this article to George Manners, founding editor (1807) of *The Satirist or Monthly Meteor* (William Jerdan took his place in 1812).

This fragmentary article places a literary admirer of the Lake poets (himself an enthusiast for chivalry and romance) in the position of overhearing the poets recite their work to an appreciative audience of wives and children. They are characterized as a mad "sect" of fanatics infected with such aberrant ideas as republicanism (the communal ideals of pantisocracy), poetic experimentation, and forms of immorality (their implied endorsement of free love and "denudation"—*sans culotte* apparently taken literally). The ideal of simplicity associated with Wordsworth is turned into simple-mindedness, and Coleridge is portrayed as asinine when, in an ironic mountain-top experience, flatulence replaces the winds of inspiration. In general, then, the parodist turns liberty into the opportunity only to be vulgar and simplicity into silliness. The Lake poets are evidently a disreputable, lunatic fringe.

THE BARDS OF THE LAKE

I had been visiting the western isles of Scotland, and I was charmed with the remains which are still to be found there of the simplicity of ancient manners. My mind was full of the glories of other times, and as I crossed the highlands, I often listened with delight to some fragment of Ossian, changed rudely to the same wild notes, which those mountains had reechoed for successive centuries. Nor was I less pleased as I traversed the marches, which of old divided the sister kingdoms, with the remnants of border minstrelsy. By the time I had reached the lakes, which I had proposed to visit in my way, I could think of nothing but the minstrels and the minstrelsy of chivalry and romance. All modern poetry appeared to me to be a composition of affectation, learning, and sentimental refinement, and a hundred other things, with which in fact poetry had nothing to do.—I was not a little delighted, therefore, arriving at the beautiful village of Ambleside, to learn that a brotherhood of modern bards had established themselves there, whose opinions of poetry exactly coincided with mine, and who regulated their practice accordingly. I did not enquire very particularly into the tenets of this sect, being certain that as simplicity and nature were their object, they must be right, by whatever means they attained them. I had very fortunately, on the evening of my arrival the means of judging of their success; and the impression which their impassioned enunciation of their unrivalled strains made upon me is indelible.

I was walking by the side of the neighbouring lake, in company with a friend who had lived some time in the vicinity. As I could think of nothing but the bards, I asked him a thousand questions about them. He was very eloquent in praise of the blameless virtue and pastoral simplicity of their lives, and the admirable harmony that subsisted between them. I was not displeased to hear so fair an account of their private virtues, but it was of their poetry that I wished to speak.

We had just reached the summit of a gentle eminence, and were descending the other side, when in the little vale beneath us, which commanded a beautiful view of the lake, we perceived seated in the grass a groupe of men, women, and children; and in the midst of the groupe stood one, who by the energy of his action appeared to be reciting; but he had concluded, and sat down, before we were near enough to hear what he said.

"Behold the bards and their wives and their children!" exclaimed my friend; "they are rehearsing some of their new poems: this is a frequent custom with them: we will sit down at the foot of yonder beech; where we shall be near enough to hear them: they will not heed us."

While he spoke, another of the bards arose, and took his station in the midst of the groupe.[1] My friend whispered me, that he had composed some famous *lyrical ballads* and was proceeding to descant on his genius, when the bard began, first announcing his subject to be,

THE HERMIT AND THE SNAIL

A hermit walk'd forth from his cell one day,
And he met a snail across his way,
And thus to the snail did the hermit say,
    'Silly snail!'

"Is it thy love thou goest to meet,
To woo her in her green retreat?
No—thou hast horns upon thy head,
Thou art already married,
    Silly snail!"

I was charmed with the original simplicity of this elegant little composition, to which I did not know what appellation to apply, or in what class of poetry to place it. I perceived that it gave much satisfaction to the brotherhood of bards, though the ladies seemed not altogether to approve the indirect satire contained in it. I had scarcely finished copying it into my book of memoranda, when another bard[2] started from his seat, and with a violent bound dashed into the middle of the circle. He seemed to labour with all the inspiration of poetry, and to be agitated by some mighty thoughts. For some time he spoke not; and meanwhile my friend took occasion to inform me, that this bard had published some odes which were supposed to be very fine, but they were too sublime for vulgar comprehension. He had also written an elegy to an ass, which was more level to its subject, but it was on the ode he prided himself. He had formerly, he said, been of Cambridge, but enlisted as a private of dragoons: he had often been known to harangue his comrades on themes of liberty, and had endeavoured to inspire them with the free spirit of the citizens of the ancient republics, to which he was enthusiastically devoted. His learning, which was various and classical, had astonished his officers, and on his real circumstances and quality being in consequence discovered, he had quitted the service. He still however, dreams of nothing but liberty, continued my friend, and talks of nothing but freedom. Not long ago, he read lectures on poetry at a fashionable institution,[3] but, whether— At that instant the bard, without announcing his subject, which, however, it was afterwards agreed to entitle *The Breeches*, burst forth with the utmost vehemence into the following short ode.

BREECHES

AN ODE

On some high mountain's rugged top sublime,
    Where mortal tyrant never trod,
Through all the rounds of time,
    Free as the unpolluted clod
Fain would I sit *bare breech'd!* most fitly so,
    That the free wind might blow.

It's welcome rude, changing the native hue
Of those unclothed parts from red to blue,
    And every rainbow tint and dye,
    Making sweet variety.
I love such honest freedom, better far
Than the false sunshine of the court, or smile
    Of fickle beauty earn'd by slavish suit,
    Keeping the free thought mute,
In bondage vile
As slaves of Turkey are.

    Breeches are masks, which none would wear,
    If all were honest, all were fair!
    Naked truth needs no disguise,
    Falsehood then in breeches lies,

Therefore I love them not;
But him most honest hold, who's most a *sans culotte*.

When thus bare-breech'd on high,
Upon the mountain's top 'mid purer air,
   Thinking sublimer thoughts I lie,
Ask you, what I do there?
Why, I would say, and I would sing
   Whate'er to sing or say I list,
   Till that 'the winds in wonder whist'[4]
Listen'd to my minstrelsing.
   And when ended was my strain,—
   I'd walk down again!

I was no less delighted with this inimitable production itself than with the effect it seemed to have on those to whom it was immediately addressed. The countenances of the female part of the groupe were lit up with a wonderful expression of intelligence and animation: and so powerfully did it seem to work on the minstrel brotherhood, that from some preparatory motions, I began to suspect that a general denudation was about to take place; but this inclination was repressed by the ladies. It was some time before the violent sensation excited by the Breeches Ode had subsided, so that I had sufficient time to complete my copy of this also, before another bard arose.

The next that ventured into the circle, stepped forward with rather a *sheepish* air: my friend was not able to satisfy my curiosity to know the name of this bard; for he told me there were two so much alike, one with all the meekness of a *Lamb*, and the spirit of the other so much *a-lloy'd*, that he could never tell them apart.[5] However it was one of them, he was certain, and it was of little consequence which; "They are," said he, *"par nobile fratrum," "Arcades ambo," "cantare pares;"*[6] he was running on with a hundred other scraps of Latin, when I stopped him, for I perceived the bard addressed himself to speak—

"The subject of my verse," said he, "is *The Witch and the Stocking, a Ballad*.[7] But after the breeches of my friend, I fear my stocking scarce will fit you."

They all laughed right merrily at this wit, and the bard began:

THE WITCH AND THE STOCKING

A Ballad

An old wither'd hag all alone was sitting,
   At the door of her lowly shed,
Worsted hose her bony fingers were knitting,
   And she was clothed in a cloak of red.

And 'twas the fearfuliest sight to see
        That could be seen, alack!
The old wither'd hag in her tatter'd red rag,
        For the red was patched with black!

'Now goody, now goody what are you about?'
        I cried as I came near,
But she took no heed, of me, indeed
        Just as if she didn't hear.

But she said her say, and mumbled away,
        As no one had been by,
And she look'd like a witch, if she dropp'd a stitch,
        And cried, 'worse luck for I.'

And I marked the goose quill by her side
        In which her needle was placed,
And I thought of the goose from whence it came,
        And the witch had a savoury taste.

But whilst I ponder'd how my thoughts,
        Mote best resolved be,
The old wither'd hag in her patch'd red rag,
        Most strangely vanish'd from me,

For she rose from her seat, and walk'd into her shed,
        As another old woman would do,
When a witch might as well have walk'd on her head,
        Or on a broom-stick flew.

And never, oh never have I seen,
        Ever since that terrible day
The old wither'd hag in her black and red rag
        Or the stocking she bore away!

This ballad was received with great applause, and much praised for its amiable simplicity both of subject and manner, and the fidelity with which it conformed to the most approved ancient models. The children, I perceived, particularly admired it, and they hung round the bard's knees, and kissed him very affectionately when he had concluded; thanking him for his pretty story, and telling him it was just like what they read in their pretty gilt story books. He seemed much flattered by this proof of the success with which he had cultivated simplicity.

I had scarcely completed my transcript of the ballad, when my friend eagerly directed my attention to the group. "We are indeed fortunate this evening," said he, "the chief bard I see, is about to recite some of his verses. You have heard of him before. It is he that used to write *Epics* in less time than common geniusses do *Impromptus*, till he found it so easy a thing that he thought Epics beneath him, a *degraded sort of thing,* and so he wrote some large works, printed like verse, to which neither he nor any body else, has yet been able to give a proper name."[8] His idea of harmony of versification is rather singular, he asserts that "harshness is essential to harmony," and that the finest harmony is composed of a number of discords arranged in a peculiar manner.[9] This gives a very strange effect of his verse, and those that are unaccustomed to it, think it the oddest, maddest thing in the world; but to such as like it, it is no doubt very agreeable. He has besides a strong predilection for particular ejaculations, and benedictions, which he scatters through his poetry very plentifully; and he is so liable to be borne away from his subject by the vigor of his imagination, that if he begins with one thing, he is sure to end with another. But this is genius, this is inspiration. Hark! he speaks!!

"My theme is HARMONY," said the bard, "and I sing it in dithyrambics invented by myself."[10]

DITHYRAMBICS
OR HARMONY

Ah woe the while! God help me! lack a day!
    The goodly times of HARMONY,
Whose various measures linked with strange mystery
    Could woo the charmed soul to sweet oblivion
Of the many miseries of this bad world,
    Are all gone by. The soul of verse
Is chain'd and trammell'd, hacknied to the pace
    Of baby in a go-cart, or the dull jade
That still goes round and round
    In the blank circle of a mill, the mill-horse,
Most hapless one! the thought of thee doth make me sad
    Sad even to every sorrow, for doubtless
There was a time when thou wert joyous,
    When thou did'st frisk and bound upon the plain right
    merrily;
Or in the dusky wood or hazel'd copse
    Did'st woo thy equine loves, dappled or bay,
Or brown, or sorrel, pyebald, roan, or black,
    Or richer chestnut, if barbarous man had spar'd
The power to love:—but thou art now, verily,
    A miserable object; thy bones do shew
Through thy dry hairless skin most villainously;
    Thy master is most pitiless! God help thee, toiling one,[11]
The thought of thee has drawn me from my theme,
    Which was of harmony; but a tale of pity
Told in harmonious numbers doth as well,
    And the tear of the soft-eyed maid shall consecrate my
    verse.

A gentle murmur of approbation followed the close of the song of the bard, like a * * * * * * * * * *[12]

10

Anonymous, "Lines originally intended to have been inserted in the last Edition of Wordsworth's Poems" (1811)

This anonymous parody (published 1 June 1811 in *The Satirist:* 488) mocks Wordsworth's poems of encounter by inverting the typical pattern in which the poet learns something important from a solitary figure he has met (e.g., "Resolution and Independence"). Here, instead, the poet is led to offer homely advice to an old drunk of the lower classes. The sing-song rhythm and rhyme help to emphasize the triviality of the experience as well as the childishness of the moral.

LINES ORIGINALLY INTENDED TO HAVE BEEN INSERTED IN THE LAST EDITION OF WORDSWORTH'S POEMS

I

I met an old man on the road,
    His name was Robert Lake;[1]
Old man, said I, how do you do?
    He said his tooth did ache.

II

I think, good Sir, he cried in grief,
    My tooth's not worth a pin;
But now and then to get relief
    I fill my mouth with gin.

III

You fill your mouth with gin, said I,
    Your face too doth denote
That, now and then, by way of change,
    You pour it down your throat.

IV

Indeed 'tis not a goodly drink,
    It fills the mind with doubt;
And if your tooth doth ache, I think
    You'd better have it out.

V

So to his tooth a string I tied,
    And pull'd right strong, forsooth;
The old man held tight by the post,
    And soon out came his tooth.

VI

The pain immediately took wing,
    No ghost e'er vanished quicker;
"Ho," quoth the man, "a bit of string
    Is better far than liquor."

11
Anonymous, "Review Extraordinary" (1812)

Published anonymously in *The Satirist* (September 1812), this parody mocks the inflated rhetoric of literary reviews in contemporary periodicals. The fundamental joke in the parody—that it is the review of a book with blank pages—is meant to expose the formula-ridden quality of reviews with their grand generalizations stated in balanced antitheses.

REVIEW EXTRAORDINARY

Mr. Satirist,

Though I imagine you are not in the habit of receiving REVIEWS from unknown correspondents, yet, I flatter myself, the obvious impartiality of that which I now send, to *say nothing of the importance of its subject,* will induce you to depart from your usual rule, and give it a place in your valuable Magazine.

I am,

Yours, &c.

A PURE CRITIC

Poetry may be said to delight in fiction: creation, as the word implies, is its chief object. Soaring on the wings of fancy and imagination, new worlds and new beings present themselves to the poet's phrenzied view. To the *realities* he adds all the possibilities of existence, and, unsatisfied *pedestribus historiis* with plain narrations,[1] in which only human actors and human exploits are exhibited, he enriches his scene and interests the reader by the introduction of preternatural beings. Homer could not sing the contentions between the Grecian and Dardan hosts, at the siege of Troy, without elevating his subject by associating divinities with heroes, and forcing the gods themselves to bear a part in the mighty conflict. He employed the popular superstitions of his age to impart a grandeur and solemnity to his theme, selecting from the mythology which then prevailed the machinery of his immortal Iliad.

The divinities of Greece having been transported to, and worshipped at, Rome, the Latin epic poets were forced to adopt the machinery, as well as to follow the plans, of Homer—they had little left except to be servile copyists of this great original: but when the Muses began to be courted by our northern ancestors, poetry was obliged to have recourse for its machinery to new superstitions, and to substitute Gothic demons for Grecian deities: Odin and Thor superseded Jupiter and Mars. In this we are of opinion poetry sustained no loss. Nothing is perhaps more truly adapted to its genius than the Gothic fictions and manners. The military institutions and customs of chivalry, united with the gloomy theology and fables of the north, which included a system of magic, enchantment, and prodigy, opened a spacious field to the epic adventurer. The old romances, though they wanted powers to cultivate it to perfection, serve to demonstrate to the discerning critic its extensive *capabilities*. Ariosto, Tasso, and our Spenser, have employed them to singular advantage; and had Homer flourished in the Gothic age, the supposition is not extravagant, that he might have produced a work superior to the Iliad itself, as he would certainly have found more unlimited scope for his genius. In the refined gallantry and military fanaticism of this period, there was more of the tender as well as of the terrific, and more to engage the softer affections of the heart, as well as to harrow up the soul, than the civil and religious state of ancient Greece presented to his observation, or to his fancy.

We have been led to make these observations, *not from what is found in the work before us,* but from the circumstances of no effort having been made to enrich its pages from these sources. Its claim to public approbation rests not on the exploits of the heroes of antiquity; it is derived from the exertions of those who have *figured* in modern times. Saying this, however, we do not wish to be understood to assert that its pages are occupied with the frivolous occurrences of modern life, or with the insipid anecdotes of fashionable folly, which have of late swelled almost every new publication. If, however, it has not those deeds of "high emprize,"[2] of which the lovers of romance are so much enamoured, sung in never dying strains, and if it cannot boast of that fashionable chit-chat which is so ardently admired by the readers of modern novels, on the other hand it avoids that disgusting bombast which frequently attends an attempt to celebrate the former, and that atrocious slander which is too generally the characteristic of the latter. If it is to be censured as wanting that animating fire and fascinating vivacity usually sought for in works of that description to which we have alluded, it possesses nothing that can be regarded as insulting to common sense, nothing to put female delicacy out of countenance.

This work is understood to be compiled by Mr. Hoffman, a gentleman *well known* in the *literary* world, and who has been for some time regarded, if not as a rising, at least as a *stationary,* genius.[3] The present is, certainly not his *greatest* work; but we are happy to say, that, comparing it with his former productions of the *same cast,* we cannot discover that there is any *falling off.*

While we bear testimony to the merits of this work, as in no way offending against the purest morality, we cannot but admit that there are parts which, in our opinion, would admit of considerable improvement. It however affords us no small satisfaction to find that one work, at least, has been produced in the present day, which, besides being recommended by the circumstance of its being not only free from nonsense and immorality, but wholly exempt from those errors of style which too frequently disfigure even works of merit; from the beginning to the end we have not been able to discover one fault in grammar, or even in punctuation. Its pages are not sullied by one improper, nor even by one inelegant, expression. We cannot say that it is recommended to us by all the fire of Walter Scott; but if it has not the beauties of his style, it is happily free from its defects, and, much as we may regret the want of its harmony, we are in a very considerable degree consoled by the absence of its affectation.

We cannot conclude without observing, that this work is in an eminent degree entitled to the praise of consistency, and this of itself is no common merit. No statements are made at the end, which are at variance with any thing contained in the early part of this book. Nothing is advanced to influence the thoughtless, or to mislead the ignorant. In no part are we disgusted with an assumption of importance, or of superior information, which is not warranted by facts. It is never attempted to baffle the under-standing by an affectation of mystery. We are never perplexed by a series of asterisks, dashes, or initial and final letters, significantly marked in italics. Its contents are in no part unintelligible or even doubtful; but the work is in every part *fair, clear,* and perfectly *plain.* With such claims to approbation, possessing merits so great, and with no faults but of omission, this produc-tion, though not all that could be wished, is still of considerable value; and we have no hesitation in recommending it as more harmless than most modern works of fiction, and as a performance which, if it does not enrapture, does not offend; if it does not convulse with laughter, does not disgust with ribaldry; and if it does not please with novelty of thought, does not excite distaste from impotent attempts at dazzling conceits. Its errors are few, trivial, and unimportant; its beauties, numerous as its leaves, apparent, and perfectly original.—The uniformity of its style is unbroken by plagiarism or quotation, and what some hypercritics might challenge as sameness or insipidity is amply compensated by its purity, entire connexion, fidelity to its subject, adherence to truth, clearness of conception, and delicacy of execu-tion.—These praises are not undeserved; these plaudits not exaggerated; for, reader, the object of this critique is—A BLANK BOOK.

12
James and Horace Smith, from *Rejected Addresses* (1812)

Written by the brothers James (1775–1839) and Horace Smith (1779–1849) and published anonymously in 1812, *Rejected Addresses* is undoubtedly the best known collection of parodies published in the period. A great popular success in its own day, the volume went through sixteen printings in seven years. The identity of the authors—who wrote the parodies in the space of six weeks—was not long in leaking out, although never explicitly acknowledged.

The occasion for the Smiths' undertaking was the impending reopening of Drury Lane Theatre and a competition that had been established to celebrate this event with an inaugural ode. When none of the one hundred and twelve addresses submitted to the committee was found to be acceptable, Lord Byron was approached to compose an address and he complied. The actual addresses, or rather forty-two of them, were published under the title of *The Genuine Rejected Addresses* after *Rejected Addresses* had already appeared. The *Quarterly Review* (September 1812) described the Smiths' collection as having been "executed with great humour, discrimination, and good taste" (117). The longer, more detailed review by Francis Jeffrey in the *Edinburgh Review* ranked the volume with the *Anti-Jacobin* parodies and even allowed that it might demonstrate "a still more exquisite talent of imitation, with powers of poetical composition that are scarcely inferior" (20 November 1812: 434).

Barbara Garlitz has explained, in her article "The Baby's Debut: The Contemporary Reaction to Wordsworth's Poetry of Childhood" [*Boston University Studies in English* 4 (1960): 85–94], how the poet's exalted view of the child violated his society's accepted perception of childhood, and how critics had been complaining for years about "his mawkish affectations of childish simplicity and nursery stammering" (as the *Edinburgh Review* puts it, 438). Appropriately, then, the Smith parody of Wordsworth ("The Baby's Debut") features a destructive and disobedient little girl as its major character. The girl is vaguely similar to the girl in "We Are Seven," while the Smiths have aped the rhyme and rhythm of their poem from Wordsworth's "Ruth." In spite of being himself a victim of one of the parodies, Byron praised the volume in a letter to John Murray (17 October 1812) as "by far the best thing of the kind since the Rolliad . . . altogether I very much admire the perform-

ance & wish it all success" [*Byron's Letters and Journals,* ed. Leslie A.
Marchand (London: John Murray, 1973), vol. 2, 1810–1812, 228]. The parody
of Byron, "Cui Bono?", demonstrates a superb mimicry of his style (including diction, phrasing, and antitheses) and of the attitudes of gloomy pessi-
mism, melancholy, and condescending scorn that he adopted in his poetry
and which he made fashionable.

"The Rebuilding," the parody of Southey, dramatized what the classically
educated reader perceived as the pretentious and obfuscating qualities of the
future laureate's mythologizing imagination. The metrical irregularities
clearly look back to the republican hysteria of Southey's past as well as to his
metrical experiments. The spoof on epic catalogues in this parody is nicely
complemented by various mock-heroic touches in "A Tale of Drury Lane,"
the parody of Scott. For example, battle descriptions are turned into scenes
of firefighting in disreputable districts of London. The rambling, digressive
manner of "Playhouse Musings" suggests slyly that incoherence is a defining
quality of Coleridge's conversation poems. In contrast to Byron, Coleridge
reacted angrily in a letter to Southey (13 February 1813); he called the parody
"a trifle" and described it as "contemptible." In public, the *Edinburgh
Review* simply termed it "unquestionably Lakish" (445).

The text below is the first edition of 1812 (although it was later revised). The
occasional note that features quotation marks designates notes added to the
18th edition (1833) by the Smith brothers. The most sustained piece of
criticism on the collection is the Ph.D. thesis by Dennis H. Sigmon, *"Rejected Addresses" and the Art of Poetic Parody* [*DAI* 37 (April 1977), 6514–
A].

THE BABY'S DEBUT
by W.W.

Thy lisping prattle and thy mincing gait,
All thy false mimic fooleries I hate,
For thou art Folly's counterfeit, and she
Who is right foolish hath the better pleas;
Nature's true Ideot I prefer to thee.
                                          —Cumberland[1]

[*Spoken in the character of Nancy Lake, a girl eight
years of age, who is drawn upon the stage in a child's
chaise, by Samuel Hughes, her uncle's porter.*]

My brother Jack was nine in May,
And I was eight on new year's day;
    So in Kate Wilson's shop
Papa, (he's my papa and Jack's)

Bought me, last week, a doll of wax
 And brother Jack a top.

Jack's in the pouts, and this it is,
He thinks mine came to more than his,
 So to my drawer he goes,
Takes out the doll, and, Oh, my stars!
He pokes her head between the bars,
 And melts off half her nose!

Quite cross, a bit of string I beg,
And tie it to his peg top's peg,[2]
 And bang, with might and main,
Its head against the parlour door:
Off flies the head, and hits the floor,
 And breaks a window pane.

This made him cry with rage and spite:
Well, let him cry, it serves him right.
 A pretty thing, forsooth!
If he's to melt, all scalding hot,
Half my doll's nose, and I am not
 To draw his peg top's tooth!

Aunt Hannah heard the window break,
And cried, "O naughty Nancy Lake!
 "Thus to distress your aunt:
"No Drury Lane for you to day!"
And while papa said, "Pooh, she may!"
 Mama said "No she shant!"

Well, after many a sad reproach,
They got into a hackney coach,
 And trotted down the street.
I saw them go: one horse was blind,
The tails of both hung down behind,
 Their shoes were on their feet.

The chaise in which poor brother Bill
Used to be drawn to Pentonville,[3]
 Stood in the lumber room:
I wiped the dust from off the top,
While Molly mopp'd it with a mop,
 And brush'd it with a broom.

My uncle's porter, Samuel Hughes,
Came in at six to black the shoes,
   (I always talk to Sam:)
So what does he, but takes, and drags
Me in the chaise along the flags,[4]
   And leaves me where I am.

My father's walls are made of brick,
But not so tall, and not so thick,
   As these; and, goodness me!
My father's beams are made of wood,
But never, never half so good,
   As these that now I see.

What a large floor! 'tis like a town!
The carpet, when they lay it down,
   Wont hide it, I'll be bound;
And there's a row of lamps, my eye!
How they do blaze! I wonder why
   They keep them on the ground.

At first I caught hold of the wing,
And kept away; but Mr. Thing-
   umbob, the prompter man,
Gave with his hand my chaise a shove,
And said, Go on, my pretty love,
   Speak to 'em little Nan.

You've only got to curtsey, whisp-
er, hold your chin up, laugh and lisp,
   And then you're sure to take:
I've known the day when brats not quite
Thirteen got fifty pounds a night,
   Then why not Nancy Lake?[5]

But while I'm speaking, where's papa?
And where's my aunt? and where's mama?
   Where's Jack? Oh, there they sit!
They smile, they nod, I'll go my ways,
And order round poor Billy's chaise,
   To join them in the pit.

And now, good gentlefolks, I go
To join mama, and see the show;

So, bidding you adieu,
I curtsey, like a pretty miss,
And if you'll blow to me a kiss,
I'll blow a kiss to you.

[*Blows a kiss, and exit.*]

CUI BONO?[1]
BY LORD B.

I

Sated with home, of wife, of children tired,
The restless soul is driven abroad to roam;
Sated abroad, all seen, yet nought admired,
The restless soul is driven to ramble home;
Sated with both, beneath new Drury's dome
The fiend Ennui awhile consents to pine,
There growls, and curses, like a deadly Gnome,
Scorning to view fantastic Columbine,[2]
Viewing with scorn and hate the nonsense of the Nine.

II

Ye reckless dupes, who hither wend your way,
To gaze on dupes who meet an equal doom,
Pursuing pastimes glittering to betray,
Like falling stars in life's eternal gloom,
What seek ye here? Joy's evanescent bloom?
Woe's me! the brightest wreaths she ever gave
Are but as flowers that decorate a tomb,
Man's heart, the mournful urn o'er which they wave,
Is sacred to despair, its pedestal the grave.

III

Has life so little store of real woes,
That here ye wend to taste fictitious grief?
Or is it that from truth such anguish flows
Ye court the lying drama for relief?
Long shall ye find the pang, the respite brief,
Or if one tolerable page appears
In folly's volume, 'tis the actor's leaf,
Who drives his own by drawing others' tears,
And raising present mirth, makes glad his future years.

IV

Albeit how like young Betty doth he flee!
Light as the mote that daunceth in the beam,
He liveth only in man's present 'ee,
His life a flash, his memory a dream,
Oblivious down he drops in Lethe's stream:[3]
Yet what are they, the learned and the great?
Awhile of longer wonderment the theme!
Who shall presume to prophecy *their* date,
Where nought is certain, save th' uncertainty of fate?

V

This goodly pile upheav'd by Wyatt's toil,[4]
Perchance than Holland's edifice more fleet,[5]
Again red Lemnos' artisan may spoil[6];
The fire alarm, and midnight drum may beat,
And all be strewed ysmoking at your feet.
Start ye? Perchance Death's angel may be sent
Ere from the flaming temple ye retreat,
And ye who met on revel idlesse bent
May find in Pleasure's fane your grave and monument.

VI

Your debts mount high—ye plunge in deeper waste,
The plaintiff calls—no warning voice ye hear;
The plaintiff sues—to public shews ye haste;
The bailiff threats—ye feel no idle fear[7];
Who can arrest your prodigal career?
Who can keep down the levity of youth?
What sound can startle age's stubborn ear?
Who can redeem from wretchedness and ruth
Men true to falsehood's voice, false to the voice of truth?

VII

To thee, blest saint! who doff'd thy skin to make
The Smithfield rabble leap from theirs with joy,[8]
We dedicate the pile—arise! awake!—
Knock down the muses, wit and sense destroy,
Clear our new stage from reason's dull alloy,
Charm hobbling age, and tickle capering youth
With cleaver, marrow bone, and Tunbridge toy[9];
While, vibrating in unbelieving tooth,[10]
Harps twang in Drury's walls, and make her boards a booth.

VIII

For what is Hamlet, but a hare in march?
And what is Brutus, but a croaking owl?
And what is Rolla? Cupid steep'd in starch,
Orlando's helmet in Augustine's cowl.[11]
Shakespear, how true thine adage, "fair is foul"[12];
To him whose soul is with fruition fraught,
The song of Braham is an Irish howl,[13]
Thinking is but an idle waste of thought,
And nought is every thing, and every thing is nought.

IX

Sons of Parnassus! whom I view above,
Not laurel crown'd, but clad in rusty black,
Not spurring Pegasus through Tempe's grove,
But pacing Grub-street on a jaded hack.[14]
What reams of foolscap, while your brains ye rack,
Ye mar to make again! for sure, ere long,
Condemned to tread the bards time-sanction'd track,
Ye all shall wail in poverty your wrong,
And reproduce in rags the rags ye blot in song.

X

So fares the bard who sings in fashion's train,
He toils to starve, and only lives in death;
We slight him till our patronage is vain,
Then round his skeleton wind laurel wreath,
And o'er his bones a balmy requiem breathe—
Oh! with what tragic horror would he start
(Could he be conjur'd from the grave beneath)
To find the stage again a Thespian cart,[15]
And elephants and colts down trample Shakespear's art.

XI

Hence, pedant Nature! with thy Grecian rules,
Centaurs (not fabulous) those rules efface.
Back, sister muses, to your native schools;
Here booted grooms usurp Apollo's place,
Hoofs shame the boards that Garrick used to grace;
The play of limbs succeeds the play of wit;
Man yields the drama to the Houynim race,
His prompter spurs, his licencer the bit,
The stage a four in hand, a jockey club the pit.

XII

Is it for these ye rear this proud abode?
Is it for these your superstition seeks
To build a temple worthy of a god,
To laud a monkey, or to worship leeks?
Then be the stage, to recompence your freaks,
A motley chaos, jumbling age and ranks,
Where Punch, the lignum vitae Roscius, squeaks,[16]
And Wisdom weeps, and Folly plays his pranks,
And moody Madness laughs, and hugs the chain he clanks.

THE REBUILDING
BY R. S.

———————

—per audaces nova dithyrambos
Verba devolvit, numerisque fertur
Lege solutis.

Horace[1]

———————

Spoken by a Glendoveer.[2]

I am a blessed Glendoveer;
'Tis mine to speak and yours to hear.

———————

Midnight, yet not a nose
From Tower-hill to Piccadilly snored!
Midnight, yet not a nose
From Indra drew the essence of repose![3]
See with what crimson fury,
By Indra fann'd, the god of fire ascends the walls
of Drury;
The tops of houses, blue with lead,
Bend beneath the landlord's tread;
Master and 'prentice, serving man and lord,
Nailor and taylor,
Grazier and brazier,
Thro' streets and alleys pour'd,
All, all abroad to gaze,

And wonder at the blaze.
Thick calf, fat foot, and slim knee,
Mounted on roof and chimney,[4]
The mighty roast, the mighty stew
To see;
As if the dismal view
Were but to them a Brentford jubilee.[5]

Vainly, all radiant Surya, sire of Phaeton,
(By Greeks call'd Apollo)[6]
Hollow
Sounds from thy harp proceed;
Combustible as reed,
The tongue of Vulcan licks thy wooden legs:
From Drury's top, dissever'd from thy pegs,
Thou tumblest,
Humblest,
Where late thy bright effulgence shone on high;
While, by thy somerset excited, fly
Ten million
Billion
Sparks from the pit to gem the sable sky.

Now come the men of fire to quench the fires,
To Russel Street see Globe and Atlas flock,
Hope gallops first, and second Rock;
On flying heel,
See Hand in Hand
O'ertake the band,[7]
View with what glowing wheel
He nicks
Phoenix;
While Albion scampers from Bridge-street Black-
friars,
Drury Lane! Drury Lane!
Drury Lane! Drury Lane!
They shout and they hollow again and again.
All, all in vain!
Water turns steam;
Each blazing beam
Hisses defiance to the eddying spout;
It seems but too plain that nothing can put it out;
Drury Lane! Drury Lane!
See, Drury Lane expires!

Pent in by smoke-dried beams, twelve moons or more,
Shorn of his ray,
Surya in durance lay:
The firemen heard him shout,
But thought it would not pay
To dig him out.
When lo! terrific Yamen, lord of hell,
Solemn as lead,
Judge of the dead,
Sworn foe to witticism,
By men call'd criticism,
Came passing by that way:
Rise! cried the fiend, behold a sight of gladness,
Behold the rival theatre,
I've set O.P. at her,[8]
Who, like a bull-dog bold,
Growls and fastens on his hold;
The many headed rabble roar in madness:
Thy rival staggers; come and spy her
Deep in the mud as thou art in the mire.

So saying, in his arms he caught the beaming one,
And crossing Russel Street,
He placed him on his feet,
'Neath Covent Garden dome. Sudden, a sound
As of the bricklayers of Babel rose:
Horns, rattles, drums, tin trumpets, sheets of copper,
Punches and slaps, thwacks of all sorts of sizes,
From the knobb'd bludgeon to the taper switch,
Ran echoing round the walls: paper placards
Blotted the lamps, boots brown with mud the benches:
A sea of heads roll'd roaring in the pit;
On paper wings O.P.s
Reclin'd in letter'd ease;
While shout and scoff,
Ya! ya! off! off!
Like thunderbolt on Surya's eardum fell,
And seem'd to paint
The savage oddities of Saint
Bartholomew in hell.

Tears dimm'd the god of light;
Bear me back, Yamen, from this hideous sight,
Bear me back, Yamen, I grow sick,

Oh! bury me again in brick;
Shall I on New Drury tremble,
To be O.P.'d like Kemble?[9]
No,
Better remain by rubbish guarded,
Than thus hubbubish groan placarded:
Bear me back, Yamen, bear me quick,
And bury me again in brick.
Obedient Yamen
Answer'd, Amen,
And did
As he was bid.

There lay the buried god, and Time
Seem'd to decree eternity of lime:
But pity, like a dew-drop, gently prest
Almighty Veshnoo's adamantine breast:[10]
He, the preserver, ardent still
To do whate'er he says he will,
From South-hill urged his way,
To raise the drooping lord of day.
All earthly spells the busy one o'erpower'd;
He treats with men of all conditions,
Poets and players, tradesmen and musicians;
Nay, even ventures
To attack the renters,
Old and new:
A list he gets
Of claims and debts,
And deems nought done while aught remains to do.
Yamen beheld, and wither'd at the sight;
Long had he aim'd the sun beam to controul
For light was hateful to his soul:
Go on, cried the hellish one, yellow with spite;
Go on, cried the hellish one, yellow with spleen;
Thy toils of the morning, like Ithaca's queen,[11]
I'll toil to undo every night.

Ye sons of song, rejoice!
Veshnoo has still'd the jarring elements,
The spheres hymn music:
Again the god of day
Peeps forth with trembling ray,
And pours at intervals a strain divine.

I have an iron yet in the fire, cried Yamen;
The vollied flame rides in my breath,
My blast is elemental death;
This hand shall tear their paper bonds to pieces;
Ingross your deeds, assignments, leases,
My breath shall every line erase
Soon as I blow the blaze.

The lawyers are met at the Crown and Anchor,[12]
And Yamen's visage grows blanker and blanker.
The lawyers are met at the Anchor and Crown,
And Yamen's cheek is a russety brown.
Veshnoo, now thy work proceeds;
The solicitor reads,
And, merit of merit!
Red wax and green ferret
Are fix'd at the foot of the deeds!

Yamen beheld, and shiver'd;
His finger and thumb were cramped;
His ear by the flea in't was bitten,
When he saw by the lawyer's clerk written,
Seal'd and deliver'd,
Being first duly stamped.

Now for my turn, the demon cries, and blows
A blast of sulphur from his mouth and nose;
Ah! bootless aim! the critic fiend!
Sagacious Yamen, judge of hell,
Is judged in his turn;
Parchment won't burn!
His schemes of vengeance are dissolv'd in air,
Parchment won't tear!!

Is it not written in the Himakoot book,
(That mighty Baly from Kehama took)
"Who blows on pounce
"Must the Swerga renounce"?[13]
It is! it is! Yamen, thine hour is nigh;
Like as an angel claws an asp,
Veshnoo has caught him in his mighty grasp,
And hurl'd him, in spite of his shrieks and his squalls,
Three times as high as Meru mountain,[14]
Which is

Ninety-nine times as high as St. Paul's.
Descending, he twisted like Levi the Jew,
Who a durable grave meant
To dig in the pavement
Of Monument-yard[15];
To earth by the laws of attraction he flew,
And he fell, and he fell,
To the regions of hell;
Nine centuries bounced he from cavern to rock,
And his head as he tumbled, went nickety knock,
Like a pebble in Carisbrook well.[16]

Now Veshnoo turn'd round to a capering varlet,
Array'd in blue and white and scarlet,
And cried, Oh! brown of slipper as of hat,
Lend me, Harlequin, thy bat:
He seiz'd the wooden sword, and smote the earth,
When lo! upstarting into birth,
A fabric, stately to behold,
Outshone in elegance the old,
And Veshnoo saw, and cried, Hail, playhouse mine!
Then bending his head, to Surya he said,
Go mount yon edifice,
And shew thy steady face
In renovated pride,
More bright, more glorious than before!
But ah! coy Surya still felt a twinge,
Still smarted from his former singe,
And to Veshnoo replied,
In a tone rather gruff,
No, thank you! one tumble's enough!

A TALE OF DRURY LANE
BY W. S.

Thus he went on, stringing one extravagance upon another, in the style his books of chivalry had taught him, and imitating as near as he could their very phrase.

—Don Quixote[1]

To be spoken by Mr. Kemble in a suit of the Black Prince's armour borrowed from the Tower.

Survey this shield all bossy bright;
These cuisses twain behold;
Look on my form in armour dight
Of steel inlaid with gold:
My knees are stiff in iron buckles,
Stiff spikes of steel protect my knuckles.
These once belong'd to sable prince,
Who never did in battle wince;
With valour tart as pungent quince,
    He slew the vaunting Gaul:
Rest there awhile, my bearded lance,
While from green curtain I advance
To yon foot lights, no trivial dance,
And tell the town what sad mischance
    Did Drury Lane befal.

THE NIGHT

On fair Augusta's[2] towers and trees
Flitted the silent midnight breeze,
Curling the foliage as it past,
Which from the moon-tipp'd plumage cast
A spangled light like dancing spray,
Then reassum'd its still array:
When as night's lamp unclouded hung,
And down its full effulgence flung,
It shed such soft and balmy power,
That cot and castle, hall and bower,
And spire and dome, and turret height,
Appear'd to slumber in the light.
From Henry's chapel, Rufus' hall,[3]
To Savoy, Temple, and St. Paul,
From Knightsbridge, Pancras, Camden Town,
To Redriff, Shadwell, Horsleydown,
No voice was heard, no eye unclosed,
But all in deepest sleep reposed.[4]
They might have thought, who gazed around,
Amid a silence so profound
    It made the senses thrill,
That 'twas no place inhabited,

But some vast city of the dead,
    All was so hush'd and still.

THE BURNING

As chaos which, by heavenly doom,
Had slept in everlasting gloom,
Started with terror and surprize,
When light first flash'd upon her eyes:
So London's sons in nightcap woke,
    In bedgown woke her dames,
For shouts were heard mid fire and smoke
And twice ten hundred voices spoke,
    "The Playhouse is in flames."
And lo! where Catherine Street extends
A fiery tail its lustre lends
    To every window pane:
Blushes each spout in Martlet Court,
And Barbican, moth eaten fort,[5]
And Covent Garden kennels sport,
    A bright ensanguin'd drain;
Meux's new brewhouse shows the light,
Rowland Hill's chapel, and the height
    Where patent shot they sell:[6]
The Tennis Court, so fair and fall,
Partakes the ray, with Surgeons' Hall,[7]
The ticket porters' house of call,
Old Bedlam, close by London Wall,
Wright's shrimp and oyster shop withal,
    And Richardson's Hotel.

Nor these alone, but far and wide
Across the Thames's gleaming tide,
To distant fields the blaze was borne,
And daisy white and hoary thorn
In borrowed lustre seem'd to sham
The rose or red sweet Wil-li-am.
    To those who on the hills around
    Beheld the flames from Drury's mound,
As from a lofty altar rise;
    It seem'd that nations did conspire,
    To offer to the god of fire
Some vast stupendous sacrifice!

The summon'd firemen woke at call,
And hied them to their stations all.
Starting from short and broken snooze,
Each sought his pond'rous hobnail'd shoes,
But first his worsted hosen plied,
Plush breeches next in crimson dyed,
     His nether bulk embraced;
Then jacket thick of red or blue,
Whose massy shoulder gave to view
The badge of each respective crew,
     In tin or copper traced.
The engines thunder'd thro' the street,
Fire-hook, pipe, bucket, all complete,
And torches glared, and clattering feet
     Along the pavement paced.

And one, the leader of the band,
From Charing Cross along the Strand,
Like stag by beagles hunted hard,
Ran til he stopp'd at Vin'gar Yard.[8]
The burning badge his shoulder bore,
The belt and oil-skin hat he wore,
The cane he had his men to bang,
Show'd foreman of the British gang.
His name was Higginbottom; now
'Tis meet that I should tell you how
     The others came in view:
The Sun, the London, and the Rock,
The Pelican, which nought can shock,
Th' Exchange, where old insurers flock,
     The Eagle, where the new[9];
With these came Rumford, Bumford, Cole,
Robins from Hockley in the Hole,
Lawson and Dawson, cheek by jowl,
Crump from St. Giles's Pound:
Whitford and Mitford join'd the train,
Huggins and Muggins from Chick Lane,[10]
And Clutterbuck, who got a sprain
     Before the plug was found.[11]
Scroggins and Jobson did not sleep,
But ah! no trophy could they reap,
For both were in the Donjon Keep
     Of Bridewell's gloomy mound!

E'en Higginbottom now was posed,
For sadder scene was ne'er disclosed;
Without, within, in hideous show,
Devouring flames resistless glow,
And blazing rafters downward go,
And never halloo "heads below!"
    Nor notice give at all:
The firemen, terrified, are slow
To bid the pumping torrent flow,
    For fear the roof should fall.
Back, Robins, back! Crump, stand aloof!
Whitford, keep near the walls!
Huggins, regard your own behoof,
For lo! the blazing rocking roof
    Down, down in thunder falls!

An awful pause succeeds the stroke,
And o'er the ruins volumed smoke,
Rolling around its pitchy shroud,
Conceal'd them from th' astonish'd crowd.
At length the mist awhile was clear'd,
When lo! amid the wreck uprear'd
Gradual a moving head appear'd,
    And Eagle firemen knew,
'Twas Joseph Muggins, name rever'd
    The foreman of their crew.
Loud shouted all in signs of woe,
"A Muggins to the rescue, ho!"
    And pour'd the hissing tide:
Meanwhile the Muggins fought amain,
And strove and struggled all in vain,
For rallying but to fall again,
    He totter'd, sunk, and died!

Did none attempt, before he fell,[12]
To succour one they lov'd so well?
Yes, Higginbottom did aspire
(His fireman's soul was all on fire,)
    His brother chief to save;
But ah! his reckless generous ire
    Serv'd but to share his grave!
Mid blazing beams and scalding streams,
Thro' fire and smoke he dauntless broke,

Where Muggins broke before.
But sulphury stench and boiling drench
Destroying sight o'erwhelm'd him quite,
    He sunk to rise no more.
Still o'er his head, while Fate, he braved,
His whizzing water-pipe he waved;
"Whitford and Mitford ply your pumps,
"You Clutterbuck, come stir your stumps,
"Why are you in such doleful dumps?
"A fireman and afraid of bumps!
"What are they fear'd on, fools? 'od rot'em!"
Were the last words of Higginbottom.[13]

THE REVIVAL

Peace to his soul! new prospects bloom
And toil rebuilds what fires consume!
Eat we and drink we, be our ditty,
"Joy to the managing committee."
Eat we and drink we, join to rum
Roast beef and pudding of the plum;
Forth from thy nook John Horner come,
With bread of ginger brown thy thumb,
    For this is Drury's gay day:
Roll, roll thy hoop, and twirl thy tops,
And buy to glad thy smiling chops,
Crisp parliament with lollypops
    And fingers of the Lady.[14]
Didst mark, how toil'd the busy train
From morn to eve, till Drury Lane
Leap'd like a roebuck from the plain?
Ropes rose and sunk, and rose again,
    And nimble workmen trod;[15]
To realize bold Wyatt's plan
Rush'd many a howling Irishman,
Loud clatter'd many a porter can,
And many a ragamuffin clan,
    With trowel and with hod.

Drury revives! her rounded pate
Is blue, is heavenly blue with slate;
She "wings the midway air" elate,[16]
    As magpie, crow, or chough;
White paint her modish visage smears,

Yellow and pointed are her ears,
No pendent portico appears
Dangling beneath, for Whitbread's shears[17]
    Have cut the bauble off.

Yes, she exalts her stately head,
And, but that solid bulk outspread,
Oppos'd you on your onward tread,
And posts and pillars warranted
That all was true that Wyatt said,
You might have deem'd its walls so thick,
Were not compos'd of stone or brick,
But all a phantom, all a trick,
Of brain disturb'd and fancy sick,
So high it soars, so vast, so quick.

PLAYHOUSE MUSINGS
BY S.T.C.

————————

Ille velut fidis arcana sodalibus olim
Credebat libris; neque si male cesserat, usquam
Decurrens alio, neque si bene.

                                    —Horace[1]

————————

My pensive public, wherefore look you sad?
I had a grandmother, she kept a donkey
To carry to the mart her crockery ware,
And when that donkey look'd me in the face,[2]
His face was sad! and you are sad, my Public!

    Joy should be yours: this tenth day of October
Again assembles us in Drury Lane.
Long wept my eye to see the timber planks
That hid our ruins; many a day I cried
Ah me! I fear they never will rebuild it!
Till on one eve, one joyful Monday eve,
As along Charles Street I prepar'd to walk,
Just at the corner, by the pastry cook's,
I heard a trowel tick against a brick.
I look'd me up, and strait a parapet,

Uprose at least seven inches o'er the planks.
Joy to thee, Drury! to myself I said,
He of Blackfriars Road who hymn'd thy downfal
In loud Hosannahs,[3] and who prophecied
That flames like those from prostrate Solyma[4]
Would scorch the hand that ventur'd to rebuild thee,
Has proved a lying prophet. From that hour,
As leisure offer'd, close to Mr. Spring's
Box office door, I've stood and eyed the builders;
They had a plan to render less their labours.
Workmen in elder times would mount a ladder
With hodded heads, but these stretch'd forth a pole
From the wall's pinnacle, they placed a pulley
Athwart the pole, a rope athwart the pulley,
To this a basket dangled; mortar and bricks
Thus freighted, swung securely to the top,
And in the empty basket workmen twain
Precipitate, unhurt, accosted earth.

Oh! 'twas a goodly sound to hear the people
Who watch'd the work, express their various thoughts!
While some believed it never would be finish'd,
Some on the contrary believed it would.

I've heard our front that faces Drury Lane,
Much criticised; they say 'tis vulgar brick work,
A mimic manufactory of floor cloth.
One of the morning papers wish'd that front
Cemented like the front in Brydges Street;
As it now looks they call it Wyatt's Mermaid,
A handsome woman with a fish's tail.

White is the steeple of St. Bride's in Fleet Street,
The Albion (as its name denotes) is white;
Morgan and Saunders' shop for chairs and tables
Gleams like a snow-ball in the setting sun;
White is Whitehall. But not St. Bride's in Fleet Street,
The Spotless Albion, Morgan, no, nor Saunders,
Nor white Whitehall is white as Drury's face.

Oh, Mr. Whitbread! fie upon you, sir!
I think you should have built a colonnade.
When tender Beauty, looking for her coach,
Protrudes her gloveless hand, perceives the shower,

And draws the tippet closer round her throat,
Perchance her coach stands half a dozen off,
And, ere she mounts the step, the oozing mud
Soaks thro' her pale kid slipper. On the morrow
She coughs at breakfast, and her gruff papa
Cries, "there you go! this comes of playhouses!"
To build no portico is penny wise:
Heaven grant it prove not in the end pound foolish!

Hail to thee, Drury! Queen of Theatres!
What is the Regency in Tottenham Street,
The Royal Amphitheatre of Arts,
Astley's Olympic, or the Sans Pareil,
Compared with thee?[5] Yet when I view thee push'd
Back from the narrow street that christen'd thee,
I know not why they call thee Drury Lane.

Amid the freaks that modern fashion sanctions,
It grieves me much to see live animals
Brought on the stage. Grimaldi has his rabbit,
Laurent his cat, and Bradbury his pig;
Fie on such tricks![6] Johnson, the machinist
Of former Drury, imitated life
Quite to the life. The elephant in Blue Beard,
Stuff'd by his hand, wound round his lithe proboscis
As spruce as he who roar'd in Padmanaba.[7]
Nought born on earth should die. On hackney stands
I reverence the coachman who cries "Gee,"
And spares the lash. When I behold a spider
Prey on a fly, a magpie on a worm,
Or view a Butcher with horn-handled knife,
Slaughter a tender lamb as dead as mutton,
Indeed, indeed, I'm very, very sick!

[*Exit hastily.*]

13

Francis Hodgson, from *Leaves of Laurel* (1813)

Leaves of Laurel was published in London in 1813. The title page reads "Collected and Edited by Q. Q. and W. W." It is attributed to Francis Hodgson (1781–1852), a close friend of Byron from about 1807. See Rev. James T. Hodgson, *Memoir of the Rev. Francis Hodgson, B.D.: Scholar, Poet, and Divine* (1878; rpt. New York: AMS Press, 1977), 1: 264–66. For a contrary opinion, see Leslie Marchand's article on Byron and Hodgson in *The Evidence of Imagination: Studies of Interactions Between Life and Art in English Romantic Literature*, ed. Donald H. Reiman, Michael C. Jaye, and Betty T. Bennett (New York: New York University Press, 1978), 285–311.

The death of Henry Pye in 1813 (Poet Laureate since 1790) was the occasion for this group of parodies. Like the *Probationary Odes for the Laureateship* prompted by the appointment of Thomas Warton, Jr. to the post in 1785, *Leaves of Laurel* purportedly contains poems by various rivals competing for the honor of the laureateship. The poets gather at the modern version of Helicon, Sadler's Wells, and their poems are judged by the well-known contemporary clown, Grimaldi. As the prefatory note (not reprinted here) suggests, in addition to ridiculing the mannerisms of several popular poets the collection has a major satiric target in the laureateship itself. The position was seldom distinguished by the poetry of its holders and, particularly in the eighteenth century, the appointment had been usually governed solely by political considerations. For the somewhat tangled story of how Southey received the appointment in 1813, see Kenneth Hopkins, *The Poets Laureate* (London: Bodley Head, 1954), 130–37. Some transitional material and parodies of Campbell, Rogers, and Lewis have been omitted from the text printed here.

"Good night to the Laureat! but since he's no more,"
Said old Saul,*[1] " 'tis but foolish his fate to deplore";

---

*Great confusion has arisen in Grub and other streets from the similarity of name in two of the rival candidates for the Laurel. We fear that we shall not lessen the mystery by our delicate mode of printing the appellatives S—y and S—y. Rumor, however, now mentions the younger Ambigu as the favourite. It is added (what the public will be delighted to hear) that the ode is to be abolished; and that another sinecure (which may not be so delightful) is to be added to the list by

"Perchance *I* may catch the proud cloak he lets fall"—
"Perchance *I* may catch"—said the rhyming-men all,
And re-echoed the sigh that was breath'd by old Saul.
There was C—b—ll, and R—g—s, and wild W—l—r S—tt,
And B—r—n, and S—th—y, and who was there not?
Each determined his foe *hors de combat* to put,
And to win the one hundred and sweet malmsey butt.[4]
Oh whence this strange fervour?—the surgeons, 'tis said,
Sacrilegiously curious, have cut up the dead;
(As the critics the living)—and *now* ask you why?
"He sets the birds singing who opens the P—e."

The judge was Grimaldi[5]: in hardier times,
A chamberlain dared to decide upon rhymes,
With the aid of Delpini[6]*;—more modest we're grown,
And the judge of this cause is Grimaldi alone.
At the Wells of Old Sadler,[7] where Islington Spa**
Has ceas'd her scorbutic frequenters to draw,
As at Wells of old Helicon, dwelt the high judge,
And would not one step from his dwelling-place budge.
Therefore C—b—ll, and R—g—s, and wild W—l—r S—tt,
And B—r—n, and S—th—y, and God knows who not,
In the Pentonville Stages together repair,[8]
To submit their bold verse to the great critic there.

It was noon; and fierce August remorselessly gave
His cloudless effulgence to wood and to wave;
On a ship o'er thy water, thou New-River-Head!
Whose poop burnt with gold, sate the censor so dread:
Little boats at its side held the poets so gay,
And each grew impatient to flourish away . . .

---

the Laureatship. What will Mr. Banks say to this?[2] Will he insist on the restoration of the Ode?
Phoebus forbid!—The Town would then indeed exclaim with Shenstone—

> "My *Banks* will be furnish'd with bees
> "Whose music invites you to sleep—" &c.[3]

*See the "Probationary Odes."
**Still called *New* Tunbridge Wells.

THE LAY OF THE LAST LAUREAT
BY W.S.

"The summer day throws dying fire
"From Stanmore's height, from Harrow's spire;*[9]
"Fair Headstone's** lowlands swiftly fade
"In gathering mist and closing shade;
"And, Cardinal! the pensive hour
"Sheds sadness on thy ruin'd bower.
"Dim flits the bat o'er Harrow-weald,
　　"And owl hoots hoarse in Pinner-field:[10]
" 'Tis darker yet, and yet more still,
"By watery vale, and wooded hill;
"Like baby hush'd on mother's breast,
"Meek nature droops, and sinks to rest.
　　"The moon, half-hid, and half-display'd,
"Shows like warm blush of Highland maid;
"But, redder as it gleams through Heaven,
"Blushes like sinner unforgiven.
"Why sleeps it thus on new rais'd grave?
"Minstrel! it sleeps, thy pride to save.
"Go, ponder o'er that solemn sight,
"Go, ponder by the red moon-light,
"And read such aweful warning right!
"That grave is emblem of distress
"To dreaming child of happiness;
"That grave thy wandering step will guide,
"In winter, or in summer tide;
"That grave will bid thee put aside
"(Aside, proud bard, for ever put!)
"Both 100£ and malmsey butt.
"Oh! follow such monition high,
"And, Minstrel, say not—"I am P—e!"
" 'Tis grand," quoth Grimaldi, " 'tis wondrously grand,
"But it runs, I should think, rather easy in hand;
"Yet I know not how boundless that spirit may be,
"Which can only be great when 'tis perfectly free."
　　But say who is He that advances so fast,
He has almost obscur'd the renown of the last?

---

*The topographical imagination of the poet, here reciting, has actually transported him from the New River Head to a summer-house in the neighbourhood of Stanmore; and he is now depicting the rural objects around him with the utmost accuracy.
**Cardinal Wolsey had a house at Headstone.

MAN WAS MADE TO MOURN[11]
BY L—d B.

"Where is the breath of P—e? forever blown
"O'er the wide welkin, and to nothing turn'd!
"He, who once made the listening Court his own,
"His courtly incense now in vain has burn'd.
"Can all, by saint, sage, sophist, taught or learn'd,*
"Refill this empty P—e?—or raise his crust?
"Thus perish false and true; thus, all inurn'd
"In one sad nothingness, return they must
"To dust, from whence they rose, to dull, dark,** dirty dust.
"Wherefore deride my melancholy rhyme?
"Why scoff at sorrow's scroll?—for what is man?
"A baseless bubble on the tide of time!
"His fast how long, his feast how short in span,
"Bairam three days to four weeks Rhamazan!"***[13]
"Blind beetle, spiteful spider, phantom frail,
"What are thy ways? how speeds thy proudest plan?
"All that thou fear'st shall hap, thou hop'st shall fail,
"And Taedium's self shall tire to tell thy twice-told tale.
      "Where is the Laureat progeny of yore,
"Yclept illustrious in their little day?
"They blazed like wills of wisp, and were no more—
"Elkanah, Bayes himself, have passed away,[14]
"Albeit they drank like us this vital ray!
"We too, eftsoons, shall wear oblivion's rust,
"Like those, who, whilome, in close coffin lay—
"Weak, wandering, worthless man! say what thy trust?
"When dust is all in all, and all in all is dust!"****[15]

---

*The poet here seems to have stolen from himself—See C—de H—d—

    "Can all saint, sage, or sophist ever writ,
    "People this lonely tow'r, this tenement refit?"

[canto II, stanza 6]

**Quere *"Deathly Dust?"* Shakespeare has *"dusty death."* Why should not adjectives and substantives change sides and back again, in the Dance of Death? Note by the Author.
But, indeed, the whole thought may have been suggested by the well-known epitaph on Eleanor Bachelor—

    "Now here she doth lie, and make a dirt pie," &c.[12]

***Our Turkish readers will be pleased with this allusion. To others we would observe, that the said fast and feast are of the proportional durations above-mentioned.
****The Author seems to have borrowed (what few have to lend, and fewer still would borrow) an inimitable burlesque upon himself in this passage.

HUSH A BYE! BABY BYE!
BY W.W.

"A child so small, I cannot tell
   "How small she was indeed,
"Met me, while walking in the dell,
   "That's nigh to Pinner mead.
"She pull'd me by the coat; and oh!
"She look'd, as if she wish'd I'd go,
"Where stood a cottage in the lane
"That borders upon Pinner plain.
"I went with her—and then she said,
"The Poet Laureat, P—e, is dead."
"Ah me! I answer'd sad; and so
"We reach'd the little house of woe.
   "The wicker gate was open'd wide,
"The flowers were trodden down beside;
"It look'd, as if some friend had past
"Eager on P—e to look his last.
"I know not—but I heav'd a sigh—
"The little child stood weeping by.

   "We enter'd at the cottage door,
"And saw the man who was no more.
"That child—I never will forsake her—
"Though sneer'd at by the undertaker"—

With a pitiful sob here the story broke off,
And hard-hearted they felt who were tempted to scoff;
There was something so good in the bard, yet so silly,
That you lov'd him and laugh'd at him too, willy nilly.
   And hark! here's another! whose drawl makes you doubt,
If he's preaching, or praying, or what he's about.

THE RESURRECTION TRAGEDY
BY S. T. C.

   "A poisonous tree's the laurel; yet can bear
"Fruit much more fam'd than apple or than pear:
"Therefore, perhaps, it was esteem'd by P—e—
"And yet, on second thoughts, I know not why.
"Though laurel leaves the conqueror's brow adorn,
"Though laurel leaves by conquering bards are worn,

"With laurel leaves did Donellan destroy
"Sir Theodosius Boughton, yet a boy.[16]
"In human things how closely does alloy
"Mingle with purest gold! this proverb's force
"Is shown, too clearly, by my own remorse;
"Remorse I *daily* feel, for having rais'd
"The fame of actors, whom I *weekly** prais'd.
"And yet, reviving from its deathlike rest,
"R—m—e, so long by Sh—r—d—n** supprest,[17]
"Shall hail me father, spite of the fool's jest;
"Spite of stage-faults, in closet read, shall bear
"Fruit sweeter far than apple or than pear,
"Mellow renown!—but still, perforce, I dread
"These poisonous bays; still wish them on my head.
"How win the prize? the drawback how avoid?
"What thing on earth is perfectly enjoy'd?
"Yon centipede, indeed"————————***

THE BLESSING OF A SINECURE
BY R. S.

"Daylight! and yet no sleep?
"O'er Sadler's Wells so deep,
"O'er Islington's exalted spire,
"O'er Pentonville, the festal fire
"Streams on the blazing town from every station,
"And heightens Victory's Illumination.
"No falling rain-drop damps
"The lustre of the lamps;
"To thee, the MIGHTY-ONE of Spain,[19] they shine,
"And all this blaze of stateliness is thine.
"Fast fled the French o'er valley and o'er mountain,
"Nearly was King Joe shot by Captain Wyndham:[20]
"Proudly wast thou exhibited in England,
    "Staff of the Marshal!****[21]
"Horns! horns! around the Square—
"What do these horns declare?

---

*Other MSS. read *"weakly."* See the Preface to R—m—e.
**Must not this gentleman feel some remorse for having suppressed R—m—e so long? Quere by the Author.
***See R—m—e. The judge is so struck with the beauty of this allusion, which he remembers to have heard on the Stage, that he cannot help interrupting the author with his usual note of approbation, *"nice, nice!"* and, before the perfect enjoyments of the centipede can be described, the poet is overwhelmed by another of the Lake or Water fraternity. This, therefore, is another instance of the involuntary Aposiopesis.[18]
****At Vauxhall!!!

"Loud as Orlando's horn from Roncevaux,
"From the same vales the Fall of France they blow!
"Hear them! thou modern Charlemagne! oh hear!
"Though Dresden now is not so near
"To Bloomsbury-Square, as Paris on that day,
"To Fontarabia!
    "Joy, joy to Wellington,
    "The glorious Wellington,
"Joy!—in the passes of the Pyrenees,
"Passes that never saw such passings through as these,
"Where hollow winds with mountain echoes sport,
"Soult has been vanquish'd at Jean Pied de Port.[22]
"Thy 27th and 28th, July!
"Swell'd the loud battle's cry;
    "Till, when the harvest moon in youth appear'd,
    "Abisbal's Condè, who no Frenchman fear'd,
"Succour'd brave Rowland Hill,[23]
"Yet mask'd thy towers, Pamplona! still—
    "—How much more calm is Pinner green!
    "There P—e's untimely tomb is seen,
    "Tomb of the green in age,
"Tomb of the TUNEFUL-ONE!—who still could sing
"To Britain's Queen, to Britain's King,
"Of annual praise a page."

14
Eaton Stannard Barrett, from *The Heroine, or Adventures of Cherubina* (1813)

Published in 1813, *The Heroine, or Adventures of Cherubina* was written by Eaton Stannard Barrett (1786–1820), about whom not a great deal is known. A native of Cork, Barrett studied law but apparently was never called to the bar. He did write a number of political satires as well as the less successful *The Hero; or, the Adventures of a Night* (1817), another compendium of parodic scenes from various Gothic novels.

In this period, with the exception of Jane Austen's *Northanger Abbey*, *The Heroine* is probably the best parody of the Gothic novel to appear, although it also contains satiric glances at features of the sentimental novel. Jane Austen herself was " 'much amused' " by it [quoted by Archibald Shepperson, *The Novel in Motley* (Cambridge, Mass.: Harvard University Press, 1936), 171]. A second edition appeared in 1814, a third in 1815, and the first American edition also in 1815.

In brief, Cherry Wilkinson is the bored young woman of ordinary but prosperous circumstances who, infected by the novels she has been reading, determines to become a "heroine" and so turn her life into romantic adventure. The epistolary structure of the narrative allows Barrett to parody numerous Gothic motifs. He even identified some of the writers mocked by providing a list in the second edition. It would, however, be impossible to identify all Barrett's allusions without (as Shepperson observes) reconstructing the circulating libraries of the day. Eventually, the heroine comes to recognize "the value of living in the real world" [Paul Lewis, "Laughing at Fear: Two Versions of the Mock Gothic," *Studies in Short Fiction* 15 (1978): 411] and accepts the sensible Stuart as her husband.

THE HEROINE

LETTER I

Ah! my good Governess, guardian of my youth, must I behold you no more? Descending to breakfast, must I no more see your melancholy features

101

shrouded by your umbrageous cap; a novel in the one hand, a cup in the other, and tears springing from your eyes, at the tale too tender, or at the tea too hot? Must I no longer wander with you, through painted meadows, and by purling rivulets? Motherless, am I bereft of my more than mother, at the sensitive age of fifteen? What though papa caught the Butler kissing you in the pantry? What though he turned you by the venerable shoulder, out of the house? I am well persuaded that the kiss was maternal, not amorous, and that the interesting Butler, Simon Snagg, is your son.

Perhaps you married in early life, and without the knowledge of your parents. A gipsy stole the rosy pledge of your love; and, at length, you have recognized him by some improbable concurrence of events. Happy, happy mother!

Happy too, perhaps, in being cast upon the world, unprotected and de-famed; while I am doomed to endure the security of a home, and the dullness of an unimpeached reputation. For me, there is no hope whatever of being reduced to despair. Alas, I must waste my health, bloom, and youth, in a series of uninterrupted prosperity.

It is not, my friend, that I wish for ultimate unhappiness, but that I am anxious to suffer present sorrow, with the hope of securing future felicity: an improvement, you will own, on the system of other girls, who, to enjoy the passing moment, run the risk of being wretched ever after. Have not all persons their favourite pursuits, and do not all brave fatigue, vexation, and calumny, for the purpose of accomplishing them? One woman aspires to be a beauty, another a title, a third a bel esprit; and in effecting these objects, health is sacrificed, reputation tainted, and peace of mind destroyed. Now my ambition is to be a Heroine, and how can I hope for success, unless I, too, suffer privations and inconveniences? Besides, have I not far greater merit, in getting a husband by sentiment, adventure, and melancholy, than by dress-ing, gadding, dancing, and singing? For heroines are just as much on the alert to get husbands, as other young ladies; and in truth, I would never voluntarily undergo misfortunes, were I not certain that matrimony would be the last of them. But even misery itself has its consolations and advantages. It makes one, at least, look interesting, and affords an opportunity for ornamental murmurs. Besides, it is the mark of a refined mind. Only fools, children, and savages, are happy.

With these sentiments, no wonder I feel discontented at my present mode of life. Such an insipid routine, always, always, always the same. Rising with no better prospect than to make breakfast for papa. Then 'tis, "Good mor-row, Cherry," or "is the paper come, Cherry?" or "more cream, Cherry," or "what shall we have for dinner, Cherry?" At dinner, nobody but a farmer or the parson; and nothing talked but politics and turnips. After tea I am made sing some fal lal la of a ditty, and am sent to bed, with a "Good night, pretty miss," or "sweet dear." The clown!

Now instead of this, just conceive me a child of misery, in a castle, a convent, or a cottage; becoming acquainted with the hero by his saving my life—I beautifully confused,—"Good Heaven, what an angel!" cries he—then—sudden love on both sides—in two days my hand kissed. Embarrassments—my character suspected—a quarrel—a reconciliation—fresh embarrassments.—O Biddy, what an irreparable loss to the public, that a victim of thrilling sensibility, like me, should be thus idling her precious time over the common occupations of life!—prepared as I am, too, by a course of novels (and you can bear witness that I have read little else), to embody and ensoul those enchanting reveries, which I indulge, and which really constitute almost the whole happiness of my life.

That I am not deficient in the qualities requisite for a heroine, is indisputable. I know nothing of the world, or of human nature; and every one says I am handsome. My form is tall and aerial, my face Grecian, my tresses flaxen, my eyes blue and sleepy. Then, not only peaches, roses, and Aurora, but snow, lilies, and alabaster, may, with perfect propriety, be applied to a description of my skin. I confess I differ from other heroines in one point. They, you may remark, are always unconscious of their charms; whereas, I am, I fear, convinced of mine, beyond all hope of retraction.

There is but one serious flaw in my title to Heroine—the mediocrity of my lineage. My father is descended from nothing better than a decent and respectable family. He began life with a thousand pounds, purchased a farm, and by his honest and disgusting industry, has realized fifty thousand. Were even my legitimacy suspected, it would be some comfort; since, in that case, I might hope to start forth, at one time or other, the daughter of some plaintive nobleman, who lives retired, and occasionally slaps his forehead.

Another subject perplexes me. It is my name; and what a name—Cherry! It reminds one so much of plumpness and ruddy health. Cherry—better be called Pine-apple at once. There is a green and yellow melancholy in pineapple, that is infinitely preferable. I wonder whether Cherry could possibly be an abbreviation of CHERUBINA. 'Tis only changing y into ubina, and the name becomes quite classic. Celestina, Angelina, Seraphina, are all of the same family. But Cherubina sounds so empyrean, so something or other beyond mortality; and besides I have just a face for it. Yes, Cherubina I am resolved on being called, now and evermore.

But you must wish to learn what has happened here since your departure. I was in my boudoir, reading the Delicate Distress, when I heard a sudden bustle below, and "Out of the house, this moment," vociferated by my father.[1] The next minute he was in my room with a face like fire.

"There!" cried he, "I knew what your famous romances would do for us at last."

"Fie!" said I, playfully spreading my fingers over his face. "Don't frown so, but tell me what these famous romances have done?"

"Only a kissing match between the Governess and the Butler," answered he. "I caught them at the sport in the pantry."

I was petrified. "Dear Sir," said I, "you must mistake."

"No such thing," cried he. "The kiss was too much of a smacker for that.—Egad, it rang through the pantry, like the smash of twenty plates. But she shall never darken my doors again, never. I have just packed the pair of wrinkled sweet-hearts off together; and what is better, I have ordered all the novels in the house, to be burnt, by way of purification. They talk so much of flames, that I suppose they will like to feel them." He spoke, and ran raging out of the room.

Adieu, then, ye dear romances, adieu for ever. No more shall I sympathize with your heroines, while they faint, and blush, and weep, through four half-bound octavos. Adieu, ye Edwins, Edgars, and Edmunds; ye Selinas, Evelinas, Malvinas: ye inas all adieu! The flames will consume you all. The melody of Emily, the prattle of Annette, and the hoarseness of Ugo, will all be confounded in one indiscriminate crackle. The Casa and Castello will blaze with equal fury; nor can the virtue of Pamela save you; nor Wolmar charmed to see his wife swooning; nor Werter shelling peas and reading Homer, nor Charlotte cutting bread and butter for the children.[2]

Write to me, my friend, and advise me in this emergency! Alas! I am torn with grief at the destruction of my romance, and the discharge of my loved governess, who was not even permitted to take and receive a hysterical farewell. Adieu.

Cherubina

LETTER XVI

O Biddy, I have ascertained my genealogy! I am—but I must not anticipate. Take the particulars.

Having secured a comfortable bed at Jerry's, and eaten something, I repaired in a coach to the Pantheon[3]; and that faithful Irishman escorted me thither.

But I must first describe my Tuscan dress. It was a short petticoat of pale green, and a boddice of white silk; the sleeves were loose, and tied up at the shoulders, with ribbons and bunches of flowers. My hair, which fell in ringlets on my neck, was also ornamented with flowers, and with a rural hat of wheaten straw.

Fearfully and anxiously, I entered the assembly. Such a multitude of grotesque groups as presented themselves! Clowns, harlequins, nuns, devils; all talking and none listening. The clowns were happy in being called fools, the harlequins were as awkward as clowns, the nuns were impudent, and the devils well-conducted.

Too much agitated to support my character, I hastened into a recess, and there awaited the arrival of the ancient vassal.

In a few minutes a mask approached. It was an old man. His infirm figure leaned upon a staff, a palsy shook his venerable locks, and his garments had all the quaintness of antiquity.

For some minutes he stood gazing on me with earnestness; and at length, heaving a heavy sigh, he thus broke into tremulous utterance.

"A-well-a-day! how the antique tears do run adown my wrinkled cheeks; for well I wis, thou beest herself—the Lady Cherubina De Willoughby, the long-lost daughter of mine honoured mistress."

"And you," cried I, starting from my seat, "you are the ancient and loyal vassal!"

"Now by my truly, 'tis even so," said he.

I could have hugged the obsolete old man to my heart.

"Welcome, welcome, much respected menial!" cried I, grasping his hand. "But tell me at once all about it;—all about my family; and I will be the making of your fortune: dear good old man, depend upon it I will."

"Now by my fay," said he, "I will say forth my say. I am ycleped Whylome Eftsoones, and I was accounted comely when a younker. Good my lady, I must tell unto thee a right pleasant and quaint saying of a certain nun touching my face."

"For pity's sake," cried I, "pass it over."

"Certes, my lady," said he. "Well, I was first taken, as a bonny page, into the service of thy great grandfather's fader's brother; and I was in at the death of these four generations; till lastly, I became seneschal unto thine honoured fader, Lord De Willoughby. His lordship married the Lady Hysterica Belamour, and thou wast the sole issue of that ill-fated union.

"Soon after my birth, thy noble father died of an apparition. Returning, mickle dolorous, from his funeral, I was stopt, on a common, by a tall figure, with a mirksome cloak, and a flapped hat. I shook grievously, ne in that ghastly dreriment wist how myself to bear.

"Anon, he threw aside his disguise, and I beheld—Lord Gwyn! Lord Gwyn who was ywedded unto the sister of Lord De Willoughby, the Lady Eleanor."

"Then Lady Eleanor Gwyn is my own aunt!" cried I.

"Thou sayest truly," replied he. " 'My good Eftsoones,' whispered Lord Gwyn to me, 'know you not that my wife, Lady Eleanor Gwyn, would enjoy all the extensive estates of her brother, Lord De Willoughby, if his child, the little Cherubina, were no more?'

" 'I trow, ween, and wote, 'tis as your Lordship saith,' answered I.

"His Lordship then put into mine hand a stiletto.

" 'Eftsoones,' said he, 'if this dagger be planted in the heart of a child, it will grow, and bear a golden flower!'

"He spake, and incontinently took to striding away from me, in such wise, that maulgre and albe, I gan make effort after him, nathlesse and algates did child Gwyn forthwith flee from mine eyne."

"Bless me!" cried I, quite provoked, "I cannot understand half you say.

And what do you mean by Child Gwyn? Surely his Lordship was no suckling."

"In good old times," answered Eftsoones, "childe signified a noble youth; and it is coming into fashion again. For instance, there is Childe Harold."

"Then," said I, "there is 'second childishness;' and I fancy there will be 'mere oblivion.' But if possible, finish your tale in more modern language."

"I will endeavour," said he. "Tempted by this golden flower, I stole you from your mother, secreted you at the house of a peasant, and bribed him to rear you as his own daughter. I then told Lord Gwyn that I had dispatched you; and the golden flower he gave me, was a silver shilling!

"When the dear lady, your mother, missed you, she became insane, executed the most elegant outrages on society; and having plucked the last hair from her own head, ran into the woods, and has never been found since."

"Dear sainted sufferer," exclaimed I.

"I heard no more of the peasant or of you," continued Eftsoones, "till a few days ago, when the peasant sent for me. I went. He was dying. Such a scene! He confessed, that he had sold you to one farmer Wilkinson, about thirteen years before; who purchased you on speculation."

"Yes," cried I, "on the speculation of a reward from Lord Gwyn for assassinating me. I have a parchment which ascertains the fact."

"What! beginning with 'THIS INDENTURE'?" cried Eftsoones.

"Yes," said I, "and then, 'for and in consideration of——'

" 'Doth grant, bargain, release——' " cried he.

" 'Possession, and to his heirs and assigns' " cried I.

"Hurra, hurra, hurra!" cried he, taking a stiff frisk; "your title is as clear as the sun; and I hereby and thereby hail you Lady Cherubina de Willoughby, rightful heiress of all the territory that now appertaineth, or that may hereinafter appertain unto the House of De Willoughby."

"Wonderful! most wonderful!" cried I. "Oh, I am the happiest, happiest creature living!"

"Now listen," said he. "Lady Gwyn, (for his Lordship is long dead) resides at this moment, on your own estate. I have a carriage in waiting: we will set off together this very night——"

"This very moment!" cried I; but just as I spoke, a Domino came forward, took off its mask, and I beheld Stuart. The moment he saluted me, Whylome Eftsoones slunk away. . . .

LETTER XXXV

"GRACIOUSNESSOSITY!" cried Dame Ursulina, as she brought breakfast this morning, "there is the whole castle in such a fluster; and such hammering and clamouring, and paddling at all manner of possets,[4] to make much of the fine company, that are coming down here to-day."

"Heavens!" exclaimed I, "when will my troubles cease? Doubtless this fine company are a most dissolute set. An amorous Verezzi, an insinuating Cavigni, an abandoned Orsino; besides some lovely Voluptuary, some fascinating Desperado, who plays the harp, and poisons by the hour."[5]

"La, not at all," said the Dame. "There are none but old Sir Charles Grandison, and his lady, Miss Harriet Byron, that was;—old Mr. Mortimer Delville, and his lady, Miss Cecilia, that was;—and old Lord Mortimer, and his lady, Miss Amanda, that was.[6]

"Santa Maria!" cried I. "Why those are all heroes and heroines!"

" 'Pon my conversation, and as I am true maiden, so they are," said she. "And we shall have such tickling and pinching; and fircumdandying, and cherrybrandying, and the genteel poison of bad wine; and the Warder blowing his horn, and the Baron in his scowered armour, and I in the most rustling silk I have. And Philippo, the butler, meets me coming along a dark passage. 'Oddsboddikins,' says he, 'mayhap I should know the voice of that silk?' 'Oddspittikins,' says I, 'peradventure thou should'st;' and then he catches me round the neck, and——"

"There, there!" cried I, "you distract me."

"Marry come up!" muttered she. "Some people think some people—— Marry come up, quotha!" And this frumpish old woman sailed out of the chamber in a great fume.

I sat down to breakfast, astonished at what I had just heard. Harriet Byron, Cecilia, Amanda, and their respective consorts, all alive and well! Oh, could I get but one glimpse of them, speak ten words with them, I should die content. I was interrupted by the return of Dame Ursulina.

"The Baron," said she, "has just left the castle, to consult physicians about his periodical madness, and government about a peace with France. So my young mistress, the Lady Sympathina, has sent me to tell you, that she will visit you, during his absence."

I felt infinitely delighted at this information, and I prepared for an interview of congenial natures; nor was I long kept in suspense. Hardly had the Dame disappeared, when the door opened again, and a tall, thin, lovely girl flew into the room. Her yellow ringlets hung round her pale face, like a mist round the moon. She ran forward, took both my hands, and stood gazing on my features.

"Ah," said she, "what wonder Montmorenci should be captivated by these charms! No, I will not, cannot take him from you. He is your's, my friend. Marry him, and leave me to the solitude of a cloister."

"Never!" cried I. "Ah, Madam, ah, Sympathina, your magnanimity amazes, transports me. Yes, my friend; your's he shall, he must be; for you love him, and I hate him."

"Hate him!" cried she; "and wherefore? Ah, what a form is his, and ah, what a face! Locks brown as cinnamon; eyes half dew, half lightning; lips like a casket of jewels, loveliest when open——."

"And teeth like the Sybil's books," said I; "for two of them are wanting."

"Ah," cried she, "why should his want of teeth prevent you from marrying him? Are all his charms in his teeth, as all Sampson's strength was in his hair?"

"Upon my honour," said I, "I would not marry him, if he had five hundred teeth. But you, my friend, you shall marry him, in spite of his teeth."

"Then," cried she; "my father will torture you to death!"

"And so will you," said I, "if you do not marry Montmorenci."

"But if I do," said she, "I shall torture him."

"Then happen what may," said I, "some of us must be tortured."

"My torture were sweet," said she, "for it would be in the cause of justice."

"Mine were sweeter," said I; "for it would be in the cause of generosity."

"Is it generosity," said she, "to spurn the man who loves you?"

"Is it justice," said I, "to make me marry the man whom I do not love?"

"Ah, my friend," said she, "you may surpass me in repartee, but never shall you conquer me in magnanimity."

"Then, let us swear an eternal friendship," said I.

"I swear!" cried she.

"I swear!" cried I.

We rushed into each other's arms.

"And now," said she, when the first transports had subsided, "how do you like being a Heroine?"

"Above all things in the world," said I.

"And how do you prosper at the profession?" asked she.

"It is not for me to say," answered I. "Only this, that ardour and assiduity are not wanting on my part."

"Of course, then," said she, "you shine in the requisite qualities. Do you blush well?"

"As well as can be expected," said I.

"Because," said she, "blushing is my *chef d'oeuvre*. I blush one tint and three-fourths, with joy; two (including forehead and bosom), with modesty; and four, with love to the points of my fingers. My father once blushed me against the Dawn, for a tattered banner to a rusty poniard."

"And who won?" said I.

"It was play or pay," replied she; "so the morning turning out misty, we had no sport; but I fainted, which was as good, if not better. Are you much addicted to fainting?"

"A little," said I.

"'Pon honour?"

"Well, ma'am, to be honest, I am afraid I have never fainted yet; but at a proper opportunity, I flatter myself—"

"Nay, love," said she, "do not be distressed about the matter. If you weep well, 'tis a good substitute. Do you weep well?"

"Extremely well, indeed," said I.

"Come then," cried she, "we will weep on each other's necks." And she flung her arms about me. We remained some moments, in motionless endearment.

"Are you weeping?" said she, at length.

"No, ma'am," answered I.

"Ah, why don't you?" said she.

"I can't, ma'am," said I; "I can't."

"Ah, do," said she.

"Upon my word, I can't," said I: "sure I am trying all I possibly can. But, bless me, how desperately you are crying. Your tears are running down my back, boiling hot. Excuse me, ma'am, you will give me my death of cold." And I gently disengaged myself from her.

"Ah, my fondling," said she, "tears are my sole consolation. Ofttimes I sit and weep, I know not why; and then I weep to find myself weeping. Then, when I can weep, I weep at having nothing to weep at; and then, when I have something to weep at, I weep that I cannot weep at it. This very morning, I bumpered a tulip with my tears, while reading a dainty ditty, which I must now repeat.

"The moon had just risen, as a lover stole from his mistress. A sylph guarded her parting sigh through the deserts of air, and bathed in its moisture, and enhaled its odours. As he flew over the ocean, he saw a sea-nymph sitting on the shore, and singing the fate of a shipwreck, that appeared at a distance. Her instrument was her own long and blue tresses, which she had strung across rocks of coral. The sparkling spray struck them, and made sweet music. He saw, he loved, he hovered over her. But invisible, how could he attract her eyes? Incorporeal, how could he touch her? Even his voice could not be heard by her, amidst the dashing of the waves, and the melody of her ringlets. The sylphs, pitying his miserable state, exiled him to an arboret of blossoms.—There he droops his unused pinions, dips his ethereal pen in dewy moonshine, and writes his love on the bell of a lily."

This tale led us to talk of moonshine. We moralized upon the uncertainty of it, and of life; discussed sighs, and agreed that they were charming things; enumerated the various kinds of tresses—flaxen, golden, chestnut, amber, sunny, jetty, carroty; and I suggested two new epithets—sorrel hair, and narcissine hair. Such a flow of soul as came from our rosy lips!

At last she rose to depart.

"Now, my love," said she, "I am in momentary expectation of Sir Charles Grandison, Mortimer Delville, and Lord Mortimer, with their amiable wives. Will you permit them to visit you this evening, and give you some good advice respecting your present predicament?"

I grasped at the proposal eagerly; and she flitted out of the chamber with a promissory smile.

What an angel is this Sympathina! Her face has the contour of a Madona, and the sensibility of a Magdalen. Her voice languishes like the last accents of a dying maid. Her sigh is melodious, her oh is sublime, and her ah is beautiful.

Adieu

LETTER XL

I have now so far recovered my bodily health, that I am no longer confined to my room; while the good Stuart, by his lively advice and witty reasoning, more complimentary than reproachful, and more insinuated than expressed, is perfecting my mental reformation.

He had lately put Don Quixote into my hands; and on my returning it to him, with a confession of the benefit which I derived from it, the conversation naturally ran upon romances in general. He thus delivered his sentiments.

"I do not protest against the perusal of fictitious biography altogether; for many works of this kind may be read without injury, and some with advantage. Novels such as the Vicar of Wakefield, Cecilia, O'Donnel, the Fashionable Tales, and Coelebs, which draw man as he is, imperfect, instead of man as he cannot be, superman, are both instructive and entertaining. Romances, such as the Mysteries of Udolpho, the Italian, and the Bravo of Venice, which address the imagination alone, are often captivating, and seldom detrimental.[7] But unfortunately, so seductive is the latter class of composition, that people are apt to become too fond of it, and to neglect more useful books. This, however, is not the only evil. Romances, indulged in extreme, act upon the mind like inebriating stimulants; first elevate, and at last enervate it. They accustom it to admire ideal scenes of transport and distraction; and to feel disgusted with the vulgarities of living misery. They likewise incapacitate it from encountering the turmoils of active life; and teach it erroneous notions of the world, by relating adventures too improbable to happen, and depicting characters too perfect to exist.

"In a country where morals are on the decline, sentimental novels always become dissolute. For it is their province to represent the prevalent opinions; nay, to run forward and meet the coming vice, and to sketch it with an exaggerating and prophetic pencil. Thus, long before France arrived at her extreme vicious refinement, her novels had adopted that last master-stroke of immorality, which wins by the chastest aphorisms, while it corrupts by the most alluring pictures of villainy. Take Rousseau, for instance. What St. Preux is to Heloise, the book is to the reader.[8] The lover fascinates his mistress with his honourable sentiments, till she cannot resist his criminal advances. The book infatuates the reader, till, in his admiration of its morality, he loses all horror of its licentiousness. It may be said, that an author ought to pourtray seductive vice, for the purpose of unmasking its arts, and thus of warning the young and inexperienced. But let it be recollected, that though familiarity with voluptuous descriptions may improve our prudence, it must undermine our delicacy; and that while it teaches the reason to resist, it entices the passions to yield. Rousseau, however, painted the scenes of a brothel, merely that he might talk the cant of a monastery; and thus has undone many an imitating miss or wife, who began by enduring the attempts of the libertine that she might speak sentimentally, and act virtuously; and ended by falling a victim to them, because her heart had become entangled, her head bewildered, and her principles depraved.

"But I am happy, that in this country there has arisen an improved order of sentimental novels; which, gratifying our reason more than our imagination, and interesting us, not so much by the story as by the morality, are at once a test and a source of national virtue. Foremost among this superior class, I would rank Rasselas and A Picture of Society.[9]

"Still, however, most of our native novels indulge in a certain strain of overwrought and useless, if not pernicious sentimentality; and I will add, that your principles, which have hitherto been formed upon such books alone, appear, at times, a little perverted by their influence. It should now, therefore, be your object to counteract these bad effects, with some more enlightened line of reading; and, as your present views of life are drawn merely from romances; and as even your manners are vitiated by them, I would likewise recommend your mixing much in the world, that you may learn practical morality, and fit yourself for the social duties."

With this opinion my father coincided: the system has already commenced, and I now pass my time both usefully and agreeably. Morality, history, languages, and music, occupy my mornings; and my evenings are enlivened by balls, operas, and familiar parties.

Stuart, my counsellor and my companion, sits beside me, guides, encourages, endears my studies, applauds my progress, and corrects my mistakes. Indeed, he has to correct them often; for I still retain some taints of my former follies and affectations. My postures are sometimes too picturesque, my phrases too flowery, and my sentiments too exotic.

Adieu

15
Anonymous, "The Universal Believer" (1815)

This poem, supposedly by Byron in imitation of Thomas Moore, appeared in an unidentified newspaper in 1815 and was acquired by the British Museum in 1960. Although the parody's model is Moore's "The Catalogue," the speaker dramatizes himself with all the characteristics of the Byronic hero (restless, libidinous, iconoclastic, self-pitying, uncommitted). Yet the poem also implies that Byron was both parasite and con man. This "Universal Believer" believes in everything at one time or another, but finally believes in nothing except himself. He moves rapidly from French philosophy through Islamic hedonism to a conversion to Judaism (at least in terms of his collaboration with Isaac Nathan; see note below). The parody thus encapsulates Byron's poetic career to date and portrays it as a series of unstable enthusiasms.

THE UNIVERSAL BELIEVER;
BY Lord Byr*n,

*in imitation of his friend Tommy M**re,*
Tune—"Come tell me, says Rosa."

I

"Come, tell me," says J*RS*Y,[1] one midnight at whist,
    And she trumped me the moment she spoke,
"Come riddle my riddle, come tell me the list
    "Of the creeds you have sworn to and broke."
"Believe me, my syren," I bowing reply'd,
    "Truth and title but seldom agree;
"But I'll try and remember how often I've ly'd,
    "And my *lying* shall finish with thee.

II

"First philosophy touch'd me, and, all in a flame,
    "About reason I ventur'd to prance,

"Till I fancy'd that I could leap up the old game,
    "And caper like rascals in France,[2]
"But the world was so darken'd, the age was so cool,
    "That one half couldn't find out my light;
"T'other sneer'd at my brains, called me more knave than fool;
    "And I think, on my soul, they were right.

III
"Then sicken'd of Frenchmen to Turkey I flew,
    "By *ennui* and poverty driven,
"For my purse was but light, love, before I kiss'd you,
    "And a rope's but a rough way to heaven:
"So I learn'd to mount trowsers,[3] and soak in sherbet,
    "Toy'd with Mufti's, pressed Houries Elysian,
"Made salams, lov'd harams,[4] rather lik'd Mahomet;
    "Tho' for life I shall curse Circumcision.

IV
"Then of freaks sadly tir'd, and lost in a fog
    "Of systems, old, middle and new,
"I turn'd my loose legs to the first synagogue,
"And at present I'm fix'd in—the Jew!
"So of critics and scissars no longer in dread,
    "Thou thy Byr*n a Rabbi shalt see,
"By libel and Psalmody earning my bread
    "And rhyming for Nathan and thee."[5]

16

James Hogg, from *The Poetic Mirror* (1816)

Published in 1816, this volume originated in James Hogg's idea for an anthology of contemporary poets. The proceeds would have been used to support his establishment at Eltrive Farm, Yarrow, which had been given to him for a nominal rent by the Duke of Buccleuch. The scheme fell apart when Scott refused to contribute, but Hogg went on to create the anthology anyway by imitating the major writers he had hoped to include. The collection is one of the major achievements in Romantic parody and has been variously described as "brilliant" by Douglas Gifford [*James Hogg:* (Edinburgh: The Ramsay Head Press, 1976), 63] and "ingenious" by Nelson Smith [*James Hogg* (Boston: Twayne, 1980), 118].

In "The Flying Tailor" Hogg demonstrates his mastery of Wordsworth's idiom by turning the experience of reading into a frustrating excursion through labyrinthine, syntactical patterns, annoying repetitions, elaborate digressions, and Miltonic inversions. The object of attack is essentially Wordsworth's sensibility—the errant and associative imagination too "apt to perceive in slightest circumstances / Mysterious meaning." The mock-heroic impulse, in which grand manner and trivial substance are juxtaposed, is even more devastatingly evident in "James Rigg." The description of the quarryman's mental state just as an explosion blinds him is a remarkable instance of parodic hyperbole. The poem itself is cast in the form of an encounter between the egocentric poet and James Rigg. As with the leech gatherer of "Resolution and Independence," so too Rigg is elevated (or inflated) to an exalted spiritual status, the poet praising the man's "unconquerable spirit" and his eloquence. While obliquely engaged in self-promotion, the poet actually reveals himself to be conceited, trivial, and tiresome. Unable to stop himself, the poet (after indecorously turning to breakfast from his memories of Rigg) simply breaks off in mid-simile.

"Isabelle" is a parody of Coleridge's poetic habits as they are especially displayed in "Christabel." The parody lacks a strong plot or story and seems to be based on a popular tale or possibly a superstition about the dead rising that Hogg probably imbibed during his childhood. The incompleteness as well as the attention to atmosphere both suggest "Christabel" as the model, and the identification is specifically supported by other references: for example, the yelping whelp, the question-answer rhetoric of an often naive narrator, and the mock exactitude of the numerous references to counting. The last of Hogg's parodies from *The Poetic Mirror* included here is "The Curse of the Laureate." This parody seems meant to convey an impression of Southey as a morally confused but vindictive man who is stubbornly convinced of his own poetic worth and of the critical injustice he has suffered repeatedly. The poem focuses on Southey's vituperative condemnation of that critical judge of *The Edinburgh Review,* Francis Jeffrey, and concludes with a lengthy, hysterical cursing fit. The efficacy of the exercise is, however, effectively undercut by the fact that it is only the fabrication of Southey's dream-vision.

FURTHER EXTRACT FROM "THE RECLUSE," A POEM.

THE FLYING TAILOR.

IF ever chance or choice thy footsteps lead
Into that green and flowery burial-ground
That compasseth with sweet and mournful smiles
The church of Grasmere,—by the eastern gate
Enter—and underneath a stunted yew,
Some three yards distant from the gravel-walk,
On the left-hand side, thou wilt espy a grave,
With unelaborate headstone beautified,
Conspicuous 'mid the other stoneless heaps
'Neath which the children of the valley lie.
There pause—and with no common feelings read
This short inscription—"Here lies buried
The Flying Tailor, aged twenty-nine!"
　　　Him from his birth unto his death I knew,
And many years before he had attain'd
The fulness of his fame, I prophesied
The triumphs of that youth's agility,
And crown'd him with that name which afterwards
He nobly justified—and dying left
To fame's eternal blazon—read it here—
"The Flying Tailor!"
　　　　　It is somewhat strange

That his mother was a cripple, and his father
Long way declined into the vale of years
When their son Hugh was born. At first the babe
Was sickly, and a smile was seen to pass
Across the midwife's cheek, when, holding up
The sickly wretch, she to the father said,
"A fine man-child!" What else could they expect?
The mother being, as I said before,
A cripple, and the father of the child
Long way declined into the vale of years.

But mark the wondrous change—ere he was put
By his mother into breeches, Nature strung
The muscular part of his economy
To an unusual strength, and he could leap
All unimpeded by his petticoats,
Over the stool on which his mother sat
When carding wool, or cleansing vegetables,
Or meek performing other household tasks.
Cunning he watch'd his opportunity,
And oft, as house-affairs did call her thence,
Overleapt Hugh, a perfect whirligig,
More than six inches o'er th' astonish'd stool.
What boots it to narrate,[2] how at leap-frog
Over the breech'd and unbreech'd villagers
He shone conspicuous? Leap-frog do I say?
Vainly so named. What though in attitude
The Flying Tailor aped the croaking race
When issuing from the weed-entangled pool,
Tadpoles no more, they seek the new-mown fields,
A jocund people, bouncing to and fro
Amid the odorous clover—while amazed
The grasshopper sits idle on the stalk
With folded pinions and forgets to sing.
Frog-like, no doubt, in attitude he was;
But sure his bounds across the village green
Seem'd to my soul—(my soul for ever bright
With purest beams of sacred poesy)—
Like bounds of red-deer on the Highland hill,
When, close-environed by the tinchel's chain,[3]
He lifts his branchy forehead to the sky,
Then o'er the many-headed multitude
Springs belling half in terror, half in rage,

And fleeter than the sunbeam or the wind
Speeds to his cloud-lair on the mountain-top.

No more of this—suffice it to narrate,
In his tenth year he was apprenticed
Unto a Master Tailor by a strong
And regular indenture of seven years,
Commencing from the date the parchment bore,
And ending on a certain day, that made
The term complete of seven solar years.
Oft have I heard him say, that at this time
Of life he was most wretched; for, constrain'd
To sit all day cross-legg'd upon a board,
The natural circulation of the blood
Thereby was oft impeded, and he felt
So numb'd at times, that when he strove to rise
Up from his work he could not, but fell back
Among the shreds and patches that bestrew'd
With various colours, brightening gorgeously,
The board all round him[4]—patch of warlike red
With which he patched the regimental-suits
Of a recruiting military troop,
At that time stationed in a market town
At no great distance—eke of solemn black
Shreds of no little magnitude, with which
The parson's Sunday-coat was then repairing,
That in the new-roof'd church he might appear
With fitting dignity—and gravely fill
The sacred seat of pulpit eloquence,
Cheering with doctrinal point and words of faith
The poor man's heart, and from the shallow wit
Of atheist drying up each argument,
Or sharpening his own weapons only to turn
Their point against himself, and overthrow
His idols with the very enginery
Reared 'gainst the structure of our English Church.

Oft too, when striving all he could to finish
The stated daily task, the needle's point,
Slanting insidious from th' eluded stitch,
Hath pinched his finger, by the thimble's mail
In vain defended, and the crimson blood
Disdain'd the lining of some wedding-suit;

A dismal omen! that to mind like his,
Apt to perceive in slightest circumstance
Mysterious meaning, yielded sore distress
And feverish perturbation, so that oft
He scarce could eat his dinner—nay, one night
He swore to run from his apprenticeship,
And go on board a first-rate man-of-war,
From Plymouth lately come to Liverpool,
Where, in the stir and tumult of a crew
Composed of many nations, 'mid the roar
Of wave and tempest, and the deadlier voice
Of battle, he might strive to mitigate
The fever that consumed his mighty heart.

But other doom was his. That very night
A troop of tumblers came into the village,
Tumbler, equestrian, mountebank,—on wire,
On rope, on horse, with cup and balls, intent
To please the gaping multitude, and win
The coin from labour's pocket—small perhaps
Each separate piece of money, but when join'd
Making a good round sum, destined ere long
All to be melted, (so these lawless folk
Name spending coin in loose debauchery)
Melted into ale—or haply stouter cheer,
Gin diuretic,[5] or the liquid flame
Of baneful brandy, by the smuggler brought
From the French coast in shallop many-oar'd,
Skulking by night round headland and through bay,
Afraid of the King's cutter, or the barge
Of cruising frigate, arm'd with chosen men,
And with her sweeps across the foamy waves
Moving most beautiful with measured strokes.

It chanced that as he threw a somerset
Over three horses (each of larger size
Than our small mountain-breed) one of the troop
Put out his shoulder, and was otherwise
Considerably bruised, especially
About the loins and back. So he became
Useless unto that wandering company,
And likely to be felt a sore expense
To men just on the eve of bankruptcy,
So the master of the troop determined

To leave him in the workhouse, and proclaim'd
That if there was a man among the crowd
Willing to fill his place and able too,
Now was the time to show himself. Hugh Thwaites[6]
Heard the proposal, as he stood apart
Striving with his own soul—and with a bound
He leapt into the circle, and agreed
To supply the place of him who had been hurt.
A shout of admiration and surprise
Then tore heaven's concave, and completely fill'd
The little field, where near a hundred people
Were standing in a circle round and fair.
Oft have I striven by meditative power,
And reason working 'mid the various forms
Of various occupations and professions,
To explain the cause of one phenomenon,
That, since the birth of science, hath remain'd
A bare enunciation, unexplain'd
By any theory, or mental light
Stream'd on it by the imaginative will,
Or spirit musing in the cloudy shrine,
The Penetralia of the immortal soul.
I now allude to that most curious fact,
That 'mid a given number, say threescore,
Of tailors, more men of agility
Will issue out, than from an equal show
From any other occupation—say
Smiths, barbers, bakers, butchers, or the like.

Let me not seem presumptuous, if I strive
This subject to illustrate; nor, while I give
My meditations to the world, will I
Conceal from it, that much I have to say
I learnt from one who knows the subject well
In theory and practice—need I name him?
The light-heel'd author of the Isle of Palms,
Illustrious more for leaping than for song.[7]

First, then, I would lay down this principle,
That all excessive action by the law
Of nature tends unto repose. This granted,
All action not excessive must partake
The nature of excessive action—so
That in all human beings who keep moving,

Unconscious cultivation of repose
Is going on in silence. Be it so.
Apply to men of sedentary lives
This leading principle, and we behold
That, active in their inactivity,
And unreposing in their long repose,
They are, in fact, the sole depositaries
Of all the energies by others wasted,
And come at last to teem with impulses
Of muscular motion, not to be withstood,
And either giving vent unto themselves
In numerous feats of wild agility,
Or terminating in despair and death.

    Now, of all sedentary lives, none seems
So much so as the tailor's.—Weavers use
Both arms and legs, and, we may safely add,
Their bodies too, for arms and legs can't move
Without the body—as the waving branch
Of the green oak disturbs his glossy trunk.
Not so the Tailor—for he sits cross-legg'd,
Cross-legg'd for ever! save at time of meals,
In bed, or when he takes his little walk
From shop to alehouse, picking, as he goes,
Stray patch of fustian, cloth, or cassimere,[8]
Which, as by natural instinct, he discerns,
Though soil'd with mud, and by the passing wheel
Bruised to attenuation 'gainst the stones.

    Here then we pause—and need no farther go,
We have reach'd the sea-mark of our utmost sail.
Now let me trace the effect upon his mind
Of this despised profession. Deem not thou,
O rashly deem not, that his boyish days
Past at the shop-board, when the stripling bore
With bashful feeling of apprenticeship
The name of Tailor, deem not that his soul
Derived no genial influence from a life,[9]
Which, although haply adverse in the main
To the growth of intellect, and the excursive power,
Yet in its ordinary forms possessed
A constant influence o'er his passing thoughts,
Moulded his appetences and his will,
And wrought out, by the work of sympathy,

Between his bodily and mental form,
Rare correspondence, wond'rous unity!
Perfect—complete—and fading not away.
While on his board cross-legg'd he used to sit,
Shaping of various garments, to his mind
An image rose of every character
For whom each special article was framed,
Coat, waistcoat, breeches. So at last his soul
Was like a storehouse, filled with images,
By musing hours of solitude supplied.
Nor did his ready fingers shape the cut
Of villager's uncouth habiliments
With greater readiness, than did his mind
Frame corresponding images of those
Whose corporeal measurement the neat-mark'd paper
In many a mystic notch for ay retain'd.
Hence, more than any man I ever knew,
Did he possess the power intuitive
Of diving into character. A pair
Of breeches to his philosophic eye
Were not what unto other folks they seem,
Mere simple breeches, but in them he saw
The symbol of the soul—mysterious, high
Hieroglyphics! such as Egypt's Priest
Adored upon the holy Pyramid,
Vainly imagined tomb of monarchs old,
But raised by wise philosophy, that sought
By darkness to illumine, and to spend
Knowledge by dim concealment—process high
Of man's imaginative, deathless soul.
Nor, haply, in th' abasement of the life
Which stern necessity had made his own,
Did he not recognise a genial power
Of soul-ennobling fortitude. He heard
Unmoved the witling's shallow contumely,
And thus, in spite of nature, by degrees
He saw a beauty and a majesty
In this despised trade, which warrior's brow
Hath rarely circled—so that when he sat
Beneath his sky-light window, he hath cast
A gaze of triumph on the godlike sun,
And felt that orb, in all his annual round,
Behold no happier nobler character
Than him, Hugh Thwaites, a little tailor-boy.

Thus I, with no unprofitable song,
Have, in the silence of th' umbrageous wood,
Chaunted the heroic youthful attributes
Of him the Flying Tailor. Much remains
Of highest argument, to lute or lyre
Fit to be murmur'd with impassion'd voice;
And when, by timely supper and by sleep
Refresh'd, I turn me to the welcome task,
With lofty hopes,—Reader, do thou expect
The final termination of my lay.
For, mark my words,—eternally my name
Shall last on earth, conspicuous like a star
'Mid that bright galaxy of favour'd spirits,
Who, laugh'd at constantly whene'er they publish'd,
Survived the impotent scorn of base Reviews,
Monthly or Quarterly, or that accursed
Journal, the Edinburgh Review, that lives
On tears, and sighs, and groans, and brains, and blood.

STILL FURTHER EXTRACT
FROM
"THE RECLUSE," A POEM

JAMES RIGG

On Tuesday morn, at half-past six o'clock,
I rose and dress'd myself, and having shut
The door o' the bed-room still and leisurely,
I walk'd down stairs. When at the outer door
I firmly grasp'd the key that ere night-fall
Had turn'd the lock into its wonted niche
Within the brazen implement, that shone
With no unseemly splendour,—mellow'd light,
Elicited by touch of careful hand
On the brown lintel; and th' obedient door,
As at a potent necromancer's touch,
Into the air receded suddenly,
And gave wide prospect of the sparkling lake,
Just then emerging from the snow-white mist
Like angel's veil slow-folded up to heaven.
And lo! a vision bright and beautiful

Sheds a refulgent glory o'er the sand,
The sand and gravel of my avenue!
For, standing silent by the kitchen-door,
Tinged by the morning sun, and in its own
Brown natural hide most lovely, two long ears
Upstretching perpendicularly, then
With the horizon levell'd—to my gaze
Superb as horn of fabled Unicorn,
Each in its own proportions grander far
Than the frontal glory of that wandering beast,
Child of the Desart! Lo! a beauteous Ass,
With panniers hanging silent at each side!
Silent as cage of bird whose song is mute,
Though silent yet not empty, fill'd with bread
The staff of life, the means by which the soul
By fate obedient to the powers of sense,
Renews its faded vigour, and keeps up
A proud communion with the eternal heavens.
Fasten'd to a ring it stood, while at its head
A boy of six years old, as angel bright,
Patted its neck, and to its mouth applied
The harmless thistle that his hand had pluck'd
From the wild common, melancholy crop.

Not undelightful was that simple sight,
For I at once did recognize that ass
To be the property of one James Rigg,
Who for the last seven years had managed,
By a firm course of daily industry,
A numerous family to support, and clothe
In plain apparel of our shepherd's grey.
On him a heavy and calamitous lot
Had fallen. For working up among the hills
In a slate-quarry, while he fill'd the stone,
Bored by his cunning with the nitrous grain,
It suddenly exploded, and the flash
Quench'd the bright lustre of his cheerful eyes
For ever, so that now they roll in vain
To find the searching light that idly plays
O'er the white orbs, and on the silent cheeks
By those orbs unillumined calm and still.

Quoth I, I never see thee and thy ass,
My worthy friend, but I methinks behold

The might of that unconquerable spirit,
Which, operating in the ancient world
Before the Flood, when fallen man was driven
From paradise, accompanied him to fields
Bare and unlovely, when the sterile earth
Oft mock'd the kindly culture of the hand
Of scientific agriculture—mock'd
The shepherd's sacrifice, and even denied
A scanty pittance to the fisherman,
Who by the rod or net sought to supply
His natural wants from river or from mere.
Blind were these people to the cunning arts
Of smooth civility—men before the Flood,
And therefore in the scriptures rightly call'd
Antediluvians!
    While this I spake
With wisdom, that industrious blind old man,
Seemingly flatter'd by those words of mine,
Which, judging by myself, I scarcely think
He altogether understood, replied,
While the last thistle slowly disappear'd
Within the jaws of that most patient beast:
"Master!" quoth he,—and while he spake his hat
With something of a natural dignity
Was holden in his hand—"Master," quoth he,
"I hear that you and Mrs. Wordsworth think
Of going into Scotland, and I wish
To know if, while the family are from home,
I shall supply the servants with their bread,
For I suppose they will not all be put
Upon board-wages."
    Something in his voice,
While thus he spake, of simplest articles
Of household use, yet sunk upon my soul,
Like distant thunder from the mountain-gloom
Wakening the sleeping echoes, so sublime
Was that old man, so plainly eloquent
His untaught tongue! though something of a lisp,
(Natural defect,) and a slight stutter too
(Haply occasion'd by some faint attack,
Harmless, if not renew'd, of apoplex)
Render'd his utterance most peculiar,
So that a stranger, had he heard that voice
Once only, and then travell'd into lands

Beyond the ocean, had on his return,
Met where they might, have known that curious voice
Of lisp and stutter, yet I ween withal
Graceful, and breathed from an original mind.

Here let me be permitted to relate,
For sake of those few readers who prefer
A simple picture of the heart to all
Poetic imagery from earth or heaven
Drawn by the skill of bard,—let me, I say,
For sake of such few readers, be permitted
To tell, in plain and ordinary verse,[1]
What James Rigg first experienced in his soul,
Standing amid the silence of the hills,
With both the pupils of his eyes destroyed.

When first the loud explosion through the sky
Sent its far voice, and from the trembling rocks
That with an everlasting canopy
O'ershadow Stickle-Tarn[2] the echoes woke,
So that the mountain-solitude was filled
With sound, as with the air! He stood awhile,
Wondering from whence that tumult might proceed,
And all unconscious that the blast had dimm'd
His eyes for ever, and their smiling blue
Converted to a pale and mournful grey.
Was it, he thought, some blast the quarrymen
Blasted at Conniston, or in that vale,
Called from its huge and venerable yew,
Yewdale? (though other etymologists
Derive that appellation from the sheep,
Of which the female in our English tongue
Still bears the name of ewe.) Or did the gun
Of fowler, wandering o'er the heathery wilds
In search of the shy gor-cock,[3] yield that voice
Close to his ear, so close that through his soul
It rolled like thunder? or had news arrived
Of Buonaparte's last discomfiture,
By the bold Russ, and that great heir of fame
Blucher,[4] restorer of the thrones of kings?
And upon Lowood bowling-green did Laker
Glad of expedient to beguile the hours,
Slow moving before dinner, did he fire
In honour of that glorious victory,

The old two-pounder by the wind and rain
Rusted, and seemingly to him more old
Than in reality it was, though old,
And on that same green lying since the days
Of the last landlord, Gilbert Ormathwaite,
Name well-remember'd all the country round,
Though twenty summer suns have shed their flowers
On the green turf that hides his mortal dust.
Or was it, thought he, the loud signal-gun
Of pleasure-boat, on bright Winander's wave,
Preparing 'gainst some new antagonist
To spread her snowy wings before the wind,
Emulous of glory and the palmy wreath
Of inland navigation? graceful sport!
It next perhaps occurr'd to him to ask,
Himself, or some one near him, if the sound
Was not much louder than those other sounds,
Fondly imagined by him,—and both he,
And that one near him, instantly replied,
Unto himself, that most assuredly
The noise proceeded from the very stone,
Which they two had so long been occupied
In boring, and that probably some spark,
Struck from the gavelock[5] 'gainst the treacherous flint,
Had fallen amid the powder, and so caused
The stone t' explode, as gunpowder will do,
With most miraculous force, especially
When close ramm'd down into a narrow bore,
And cover'd o'er with a thin layer of sand
To exclude the air, else otherwise the grain,
Escaping from the bore, would waste itself
In the clear sky, and leave the bored stone
Lying unmoved upon the verdant earth,
Like some huge creature stretch'd in lazy sleep[6]
Amid the wilderness,—or lying dead
Beneath the silence of the summer sun.

    This point establish'd, he was gently led
By the natural progress of the human soul,[7]
Aspiring after truth, nor satisfied
Till she hath found it, wheresoever hid,
(Yea even though at the bottom of a well,)
To enquire if any mischief had been done

By that explosion; and while thus he stood
Enquiring anxiously for all around,
A small sharp boy, whose task it was to bring
His father's breakfast to him 'mid the hills,
Somewhat about eleven years of age,
Though less than some lads at the age of eight,
Exclaim'd—"Why, father, do you turn the white
Of your eyes up so?" At these simple words
Astonishment and horror struck the souls
Of all the quarrymen, for they descried,
Clear as the noon-day, that James Rigg had lost
His eyesight, yea his very eyes were lost,
Quench'd in their sockets, melted into air,
A moisture mournful as the cold dim gleam
Of water sleeping in some shady wood,
Screen'd from the sunbeams and the breath of heaven.

On that he lifted up his harden'd hands,
Harden'd by sun, and rain, and storm, and toil,
Unto the blasted eye-balls, and awhile
Stood motionless as fragment of that rock
That wrought him all his woe, and seem'd to lie,
Unwitting of the evil it had done,
Calm and serene, even like a flock of sheep,
Scatter'd in sunshine o'er the Cheviot-hills.[8]
I ween that, as he stood in solemn trance,
Tears flow'd from him who wept not for himself,
And that his fellow-quarrymen, though rude
Of soul and manner, not untouchingly
Deplored his cruel doom, and gently led
His footsteps to a green and mossy rock,
By sportive Nature fashion'd like a chair,
With seat, back, elbows,—a most perfect chair
Of unhewn living rock! There, hapless man,
He moved his lips, as if he inly pray'd,
And clasp'd his hands and raised his sightless face
Unto the smiling sun, who walk'd through heaven,
Regardless of that fatal accident,
By which a man was suddenly reduced
From an unusual clear long-sightedness
To utter blindness—blindness without hope,
So wholly were the visual nerves destroyed.
"I wish I were at home!" he slowly said,

"For though I ne'er must see that home again,
"I yet may hear it, and a thousand sounds
"Are there to gladden a poor blind man's heart."

    He utter'd truth,—lofty, consoling truth!
Thanks unto gracious Nature, who hath framed
So wondrously the structure of the soul,[9]
That though it live on outward ministry,
Of gross material objects, by them fed
And nourish'd, even as if th' external world
Were the great wet-nurse of the human race,[10]
Yet of such food deprived, she doth not pine
And fret away her mystic energies
In fainting inanition; but, superior
To the food she fed on, in her charge retains
Each power, and sense, and faculty, and lives,
Cameleon-like, upon the air serene
Of her own bright imaginative will,
Desiderating nothing that upholds,
Upholds and magnifies, but without eyes
Sees—and without the vestige of an ear
Listens, and listening, hears—and without sense
Of touch (if haply from the body's surface
Have gone the sense of feeling) keenly feels,
And in despite of nose abbreviate
Smells like a wolf—wolf who for leagues can snuff
The scent of carrion, bird by fowler kill'd,
Kill'd but not found, or little vernal kid
Yean'd[11] in the frost, and soon outstretch'd in death,
White as the snow that serves it for a shroud.

    Therefore James Rigg was happy, and his face
Soon brighten'd up with smiles, and in his voice
Contentment spoke most musical; so when
The doctor order'd his most worthy wife
To loose the bandage from her husband's eyes,
He was so reconciled unto his lot,
That there almost appear'd to him a charm
In blindness—so that, had his sight return'd,
I have good reason to believe his happiness
Had been thereby scarcely at all increased.

    While thus confabulating with James Rigg,
Even at that moment when such silence lay

O'er all my cottage, as by mystic power
Belonging to the kingdom of the ear,
O'erthrew at once all old remembrances—
Even at that moment, over earth, and air,
The waving forest, and the sleeping lake,
And the far sea of mountains that uplifted
Its stately billows through the clear blue sky,
Came such a sound, as if from her dumb trance
Awaken'd Nature, starting suddenly,
Were jealous of insulted majesty,
And sent through continent and trembling isle
Her everlasting thunders. Such a crash
Tore the foundations of the earth, and shook
The clouds that slumber'd on the breast of heaven!
It was the parlour-bell that suddenly
An unknown hand had rung. I cast my eyes
Up the long length of bell-rope, and I saw
The visible motion of its iron tongue,
By heaven I *saw* it tinkling. Fast at first,
O most unearthly fast, then somewhat slower,
Next very slow indeed, until some four
Or half-a-dozen minutes at the most,
By Time's hand cut from off the shorten'd hour,
It stopp'd quite of itself—and idly down,
Like the sear leaf upon th' autumnal bough[12]
Dangled! * * * * * * * *

ISABELLE

Can there be a moon in heaven to-night,
That the hill and the grey cloud seem so light?
The air is whiten'd by some spell,
For there is no moon, I know it well;
On this third day, the sages say,
('Tis wonderful how well they know,)
The moon is journeying far away,
Bright somewhere in a heaven below.

    It is a strange and lovely night,
A greyish pale, but not white!
Is it rain, or is it dew,
That falls so thick I see its hue?
In rays it follows, one, two, three,

Down the air so merrily,
Said Isabelle, so let it be!

Why does the Lady Isabelle
Sit in the damp and dewy dell
Counting the racks of drizzly rain,
And how often the Rail cries over again?
For she's harping, harping in the brake,
Craik, craik—Craik, craik.
Ten times nine, and thrice eleven;—
That last call was an hundred and seven.[1]
Craik, craik—the hour is near—
Let it come, I have no fear!
Yet it is a dreadful work, I wis,
Such doings in a night like this!

Sounds the river harsh and loud?
The stream sounds harsh, but not loud.
There is a cloud that seems to hover,
By western hill the church-yard over,
What is it like?—'Tis like a whale[2];
'Tis like a shark with half the tail,
Not half, but third and more;
Now 'tis a wolf, and now a boar;
Its face is raised—it cometh here;
Let it come—there is no fear.
There's two for heaven, and ten for hell,[3]
Let it come—'tis well—'tis well!
Said the Lady Isabelle.

What ails that little cut-tail'd whelp,
That it continues to yelp, yelp?
Yelp, yelp, and it turns its eye
Up the tree and half to the sky,
Half to the sky and full to the cloud,
And still it whines and barks aloud.
Why I should dread I cannot tell;
I see it in yon falling beam—
Is it a vision, or a dream?
It is no dream, full well I know,
I have a woful deed to do!
Hush, hush, thou little murmurer;
I tell thee hush—the dead are near!

If thou knew'st all, poor tailless whelp,
Well might'st thou tremble, growl, and yelp;
But thou know'st nothing, hast no part,
(Simple and stupid as thou art)
Save gratitude and truth of heart.
But they are coming by this way
That have been dead for a year and a day;
Without challenge, without change,
They shall have their full revenge!
They have been sent to wander in woe
In the lands of flame, and the lands of snow;
But those that are dead
Shall the green sward tread,
And those that are living
Shall soon be dead!
None to pity them, none to help!
Thou may'st quake, my cut-tail'd whelp!

There are two from the grave
That I fain would save.
Full hard is the weird[4]
For the young and the brave!
Perchance they are rapt in vision sweet,
While the passing breezes kiss their feet;
And they are dreaming of joy and love!—
Well, let them go—there's room above.

There are three times three, and three to these,
Count as you will, by twos or threes!
Three for the gallows, and three for the wave,
Three to roast behind the stone,
And three that shall never see the grave
Until the day and the hour are gone!
For retribution is mine alone!
The cloud is redder in its hue,
The hour is near, and vengeance due;
It cannot, and it will not fail,—
'Tis but a step to Borrowdale![5]
Why shouldst thou love and follow me,
Poor faithful thing? I pity thee!

Up rose the Lady Isabelle,
I may not of her motion tell,
Yet thou may'st look upon her frame;

Look on it with a passing eye,
But think not thou upon the same,
Turn away, and ask not why;
For if thou darest look again,
Mad of heart and seared of brain,
Thou shalt never look again!

What can ail that short-tail'd whelp?
'Tis either behind or far before,
And it hath changed its whining yelp
To a shorten'd yuff—its little core
Seems bursting with terror and dismay,
Yuff, yuff,—hear how it speeds away.
Hold thy peace, thou yemering thing,
The very night-wind's slumbering,
And thou wilt wake to woe and pain
Those that must never wake again.

Meet is its terror and its flight,
There's one on the left and two on the right!
But save the paleness of the face,
All is beauty, and all is grace!
The earth and air are tinged with blue;
There are no footsteps in the dew;
Is this to wandering spirits given,
Such stillness on the face of heaven?
The fleecy clouds that sleep above,
Are like the wing of beauteous dove,
And the leaf of the elm-tree does not move!
Yet they are coming! and they are three!
Jesu! Maria! can it be?

THE CONCLUSION

Sleep on, fair maiden of Borrowdale!
Sleep! O sleep! and do not wake!
Dream of the dance, till the foot so pale,
And the beauteous ancle shiver and shake;
Till thou shalt press, with feeling bland,
Thine own fair breast for lover's hand.
Thy heart is light as summer breeze,
Thy heart is joyous as the day;
Man never form of angel sees,
But thou art fair as they!

So lovers ween, and so they say,
So thine shall ween for many a day!
The hour's at hand, O woe is me!
For they are coming, and they are three!

THE CURSE OF THE LAUREATE

Carmen Judiciale[1]

I

IN vale of Thirlemere,[2] once on a time,
    When birds sung sweet and flowers were in the spring,
While youth and fancy wanton'd in their prime,
    I laid me down in happy slumbering;
The heavens in balmy breezes breathed deep,
My senses all were lull'd in grateful, joyous sleep.

II

Sleep had its visions—fancy all unsway'd
    Revelled in fulness of creative power:
I ween'd that round me countless beings stray'd,
    Things of delight, illusions of an hour;
So great the number of these things divine,
Scarce could my heart believe that all the imps were mine.

III

Yet mine they were, all motley as they moved;
    Careless I viewed them, yet I loved to view;
The world beheld them, and the world approved,
    And blest the train with smiles and plaudits due:
Proud of approval, to myself I said,
From out the group I'll chuse, and breed one favourite maid.

IV

Joan I chose,[3] a maid of happy mien;
    Her form and mind I polished with care;
A docile girl she proved, of moping vein,
    Slow in her motions, haughty in her air;
Some mention'd trivial blame, or slightly frown'd;
Forth to the world she went, her heavenly birth it own'd.

V

The next, a son, I bred a Mussulman[4];
    With creeds and dogmas I was hard bested,[5]

For which was right or wrong I could not tell,
    So I resolved my offspring should be bred
As various as their lives—the lad I loved,
A boy of wild unearthly mien he proved.

VI

Then first I noted in my mazy dream
    A being scarcely of the human frame,
A tiny thing that from the north did seem,
    With swaggering, fuming impotence he came;
I fled not, but I shudder'd at his look:
Into his tutelage my boy he took.[6]

VII

Each principle of truth and purity,
    And all that merited the world's acclaim,
This fiend misled—nor could I ever free
    From his destroying grasp my darling's fame;
But yet I could not ween that heart of gall
Could be a foe to one, whose heart beat kind to all.

VIII

My third, a Christian and a warrior true,
    A bold adventurer on foreign soil,
And next, his brother, a supreme Hindu,[7]
    I rear'd with hope, with joy, and painful toil.
Alas! my hopes were vain! I saw them both
Reft by an emmet!—crush'd before a moth!

IX

Still could I not believe this vengeful spite,
    For in his guise a speciousness appear'd;
My bitterness of heart I feigned light;
    But wholly as he urged my next I reared;
He said of all the gang he was the best,[8]
And wrung his neck before mine eyes in jest.

X

From that time forth, an independent look,
    A bold effrontery I did essay;
But of my progeny no pains I took,
    Like lambs I rear'd them for the lion's prey;
And still as playful forth they pass'd from me,
I saw them mock'd and butcher'd wantonly.

XI

'Just heaven!' said I, 'to thy awards I bow,
        For truth and vengeance are thine own alone;
Are these the wreaths thou deignest to bestow
        On bard, whose life and lays to virtue prone,
Have never turn'd aside on devious way?
Is this the high reward, to be of fools the prey?'

XII

A laugh of scorn the welkin seem'd to rend,
        And by my side I saw a form serene;
'Thou bard of honour, virtue's firmest friend,'
        He said, 'canst thou thus fret? or dost thou ween
That such a thing can work thy fame's decay?
Thou art no fading bloom—no flow'ret of a day!

XIII

'When his o'erflowings of envenom'd spleen
        An undistinguish'd dunghill mass shall lie,
The name of SOUTHEY, like an evergreen,
        Shall spread, shall blow, and flourish to the sky;
To Milton and to Spenser next in fame,
O'er all the world shall spread thy laurell'd name.'

XIV

'Friend of the bard,' I said, 'behold thou hast
        The tears of one I love o'er blushes shed;
Has he not wrung the throb from parent's heart,
        And stretch'd his hand to reave my children's bread?⁹
For every tear that on their cheeks hath shone,
O may that Aristarch with tears of blood atone!'¹⁰

XV

'If cursing thou delight'st in,' he replied,
        'If rage and execration is thy meed,
Mount the tribunal—Justice be thy guide,
        Before thee shall he come his rights to plead;
To thy awards his fate forthwith is given,
Only, be justice thine, the attribute of heaven.'

XVI

Gladly I mounted, for before that time
        Merit had crown'd me with unfading bays.
Before me was brought in that man of crime,

Who with unblushing front his face did raise;
But when my royal laurel met his sight,
He pointed with his thumb, and laughed with all his might.

XVII

Maddening at impudence so thorough-bred,
    I rose from off my seat with frown severe,
I shook my regal sceptre o'er his head—
    'Hear, culprit, of thy crimes, and sentence hear!
Thou void of principle! of rule! of ruth!
Thou renegade from nature and from truth!

XVIII

'Thou bane of genius!—party's sordid slave!
    Mistaken, perverse, crooked is thy mind!
No humble son of merit thou wilt save,
    Truth, virtue, ne'er from thee did friendship find;
And while of freedom thou canst fume and rave,
Of titles, party, wealth, thou art the cringing slave!

XIX

'Thou hast renounced Nature for thy guide,
    A thousand times hast given thyself the lie,
And raised thy party-curs to wealth and pride,
    The very scavengers of poetry.
Thy quibbles are from ray of sense exempt,
Presumptuous, pitiful, below contempt!

XX

'Answer me, viper! here do I arraign
    Thy arrogant, self-crowned majesty!
Hast thou not prophesied of dole and pain,
    Weakening the arms of nations and of me?
Thou foe of order!—Mercy lingers sick—
False prophet! Canker! Damned heretic!'

XXI

Then pointing with my sceptre to the sky,
    With vehemence that might not be restrain'd,
I gave the awful curse of destiny!
    I was asleep, but sore with passion pain'd.
It was a dreadful curse; and to this day,
Even from my waking dreams it is not worn away.

The Curse[11]

May heaven and earth,
And hell underneath,
Unite to ensting thee
In horrible wrath.
May scorning surround thee,
And conscience astound thee,
High genius o'erpower,
And the devil confound thee.
The curse be upon thee
In pen and in pocket,
Thy ink turn to puddle,
And gorge in the socket;
Thy study let rats destroy,
Vermin and cats annoy,
Thy base lucubrations
To tear and to gnaw,
Thy false calculations
In Empire and Law.
The printers shall harass,
The devils shall dun thee,
The trade shall despise thee,
And C—t—e shun thee.[12]
The judge shall not hear thee,
But frown and pass by thee,
And clients shall fear thee,
And know thee, and fly thee!
I'll hunt thee, I'll chase thee,
To scorn and deride thee,
The cloud shall not cover,
The cave shall not hide thee;
The scorching of wrath
And of shame shall abide thee,
Till the herbs of the desert
Shall wither beside thee.
Thou shalt thirst for revenge
And misrule, as for wine,
But genius shall flourish!
And royalty shine!
And thou shalt remain
While the Laureate doth reign,
With a fire in thy heart,

And a fire in thy brain,
And Fame shall disown thee
And visit thee never,
And the curse shall be on thee
For ever and ever!

17
William Hone, from his Parodies on *The Book of Common Prayer* (1817)

Among the most notorious of the period, several parodies of the *BCP* were written and published by William Hone (1780–1842) in January and February of 1817. Hone held vigorously to his reformist principles and, for about seven years, tirelessly attacked the government (including the extravagant Prince Regent) for its rampant corruption and for excluding the "people" from a share in political power. Hone's parodies of the *BCP*—"The Bullet 'Te Deum'," "The Canticle of the Stone," "The Late John Wilkes's Catechism of a Ministerial Member" (all printed below), "The Sinecurist's Creed," and "The Political Litany"—had to be withdrawn on 22 February, however, as a renewal of government repression and censorship was threatened and then enacted. In the wake of the suspension of *habeas corpus,* Hone was taken into custody on 3 May and held for two months. He was eventually brought to trial in December 1817 to face charges that his parodies had brought the Christian religion into ridicule.

Hone was tried on three successive days (18, 19, and 20 December), a different parody being used by the prosecution each day as the government desperately sought his conviction. Hone spoke each day for six or seven hours in his own defense, and he was acquitted by the jury on all three counts. His victory was hailed widely by the reformists, and a large dinner was held in his honor at which money was raised to meet all the expenses he had incurred. In *Freedom of the Press: An Annotated Bibliography* (Evanston: Southern Illinois University Press, 1968), Ralph McCoy (336) indicates that about 100,000 additional copies of the parodies were sold after the trial had brought public attention to them.

THE BULLET
TE DEUM,

with the

CANTICLE
OF
THE STONE[1]

Imprimatur

F. Rabelais

There shall be read distinctly, with an audible voice, the Leading Article of the Courier,[2] (except there be other LESSONS appointed by the Treasury for that Day:) he that readeth, so standing and turning himself, as he may best be heard of all such as are present. And after that, shall be said or sung, in English, daily through the week, as followeth:—

Te Deum Laudamus

WE praise thee O Stone: we acknowledge thee to be a Bullet.
All the Corruptionists doth worship thee: the Placegiver everlasting.
To thee all Placemen cry aloud: the Treasury, and all the Clerks therein.
To thee Pensioners and Sinecurists: continually do cry,
Bullet, Bullet, Bullet: from thee our power floweth.
Borough-mongers and Lords in waiting: are full of thy two holes a quarter of an inch apart.
The glorious company of the Chinese Eating Room: praise thee.
The goodly fellowship of the Pavilion:[3] praise thee.
The noble army of Tax Commissioners: praise thee.
The pure Legitimates throughout all the world: doth acknowledge thee,
The Saviour of an expiring Ministry.
Thou art the Trick of Tricks: O Bullet.
Thou art the everlasting prop: of the Ministry.
When they took upon them to call thee a Bullet: they did not abhor the public shame.
When they had failed to overcome the sharpness of Truth: thou didst open the Kingdom to the leaven of new deceivers.
We believe that thou art a pretext: for rejecting Reform.
We therefore pray thee help the Lord of the Bedchamber: but appear not unto him for his memory's sake.
O Bullet, save the Ministry: for thou alone art their heritage.

Keep them in place: and they will call thee Bullet for ever.

Day by day: the Courier doth magnify thee;

And it worshippeth thy name: every night without end.

Vouchsafe, O Bullet: to keep us this year without Reform.

O Bullet, have mercy upon us: have mercy upon us.

O Bullet, keep Reform afar from us: as our trust is in thee.

O Bullet, in thee have we trusted: let the Reformists for ever be confounded.

[*Here endeth the Bullet Te Deum.*]

THE
CANTICLE
OF
THE STONE

*Which may, or may not, be sung or said immediately
after* Te Deum Laudamus

Benedicite omnia, &c.

O ALL ye workers of Corruption, bless ye the Stone: praise it, and *magnify* it as a Bullet for ever.

O most chaste, most pious, most magnificent, and gracious Prince, who alone workest great marvels: magnify it for ever.

O thou Private Secretary, Secretary Extraordinary, and Privy Seal: magnify it for ever.

O thou Chancellor and Keeper of the Great Seal of the Duchy: magnify it for ever.

O thou Vice Admiral, Lord Warden of the Stannaries,[4] and Steward of the Duchy: magnify it for ever.

O ye Lords and Grooms of the Bedchamber: magnify it for ever.

O ye Sticks in waiting: magnify it for ever.

O ye Lords of the Treasury: magnify it for ever.

O ye Solicitors to the Treasury: magnify it for ever.

O ye Tailors and Accoutrement Makers to the Household Troops, whose dress hath not been altered during ten entire days last past: magnify it for ever.

O ye Sword Cutlers, Helmet Makers, Epaulette Makers, Feather Makers, Buttonhole Stitchers, and cunning Workmen in Embroidery: magnify it for ever.

O ye Dames to Hertford and Jersey, and Mother St. Ursula and the Eleven Thousand Virgins: magnify it for ever.[5]

O ye One hundred and Nine Chaplains in Ordinary, whose names are written in the Royal Kalendar: magnify it for ever.

O ye Makers and Manufacturers of Sham Plots: magnify it for ever.

O thou eldest Son of Impudence, George Cunning,[6] who didst transform the foot of an old Stocking with a few Bullets, into a waggon load of Ammunition: magnify it for ever.

O ye Old Cabbage Dog Rose,[7] and the Managers and Directors of Saving Banks: magnify it for ever.

O ye admirers of Louis the Desired, and Ferdinand the Beloved:[8] magnify it for ever.

O ye who believe the People have nothing to do with the Laws but to obey them: magnify it for ever.

O ye who are arrayed in purple and fine linen; who toil not, neither do ye spin: magnify it without end, for ever and ever.

Now to the Right Honourable Lord ELLENBOROUGH, Sir John Silvester, and Mr. Justice Hicks,[9] be committed the entire disposal of the Lives and Liberties of the People of England at this time and for ever hereafter. *Amen.*

[Here endeth the Canticle.]

THE LATE
JOHN WILKES'S
CATECHISM
OF A
MINISTERIAL MEMBER

A CATECHISM,
THAT IS TO SAY,

An Instruction, to be learned of every Person before he be brought to be confirmed a Placeman or Pensioner by the Minister.[1]

Question

What is your Name?

Answer. Lick Spittle.

Q. Who gave you this Name?

A. My Sureties[2] to the Ministry, in my Political Change, wherein I was made a Member of the Majority, the Child of Corruption, and a Locust to devour the good Things of this Kingdom.

Q. What did your Sureties then for you?

A. They promise and vow three things in my Name. First, that I should renounce the Reformists and all their Works, the pomps and vanity of Popular Favour, and all the sinful lusts of Independence. Secondly, that I should believe all the Articles of the Court Faith. And thirdly, that I should keep the Minister's sole Will and Commandments, and walk in the same, all the days of my life.
Q. Dost thou not think that thou art bound to believe and to do as they have promised for thee?
A. Yes verily, and for my own sake, so I will; and I heartily thank our heaven-born Ministry, that they have called me to this state of elevation, through my own flattery, cringing, and bribery; and I shall pray to their successors to give me their assistance, that I may continue the same unto my life's end.
Q. Rehearse the Articles of thy Belief.
A. I believe in GEORGE, the Regent Almighty, Maker of New Streets and Knights of the Bath,[3]

And in the present Ministry, his only choice, who were conceived of Toryism, brought forth of WILLIAM PITT, suffered loss of Place under CHARLES JAMES FOX, were execrated, dead, and buried. In a few months they rose again from their minority; they re-ascended to the Treasury benches, and sit at the right hand of a little man in a large wig[4]; from whence they *laugh* at the Petitions of the People, who pray for Reform, and that the sweat of their brow may procure them Bread.

I believe that King James the Second was a legitimate Sovereign, and that King William the Third was not; that the Pretender was of the right line, and that George the Third's Grandfather was not; that the dynasty of Bourbon is immortal; and that the glass in the eye of Lord James Murray, was not Betty Martin.[5] I believe in the immaculate purity of the Committee of Finance, in the independence of the Committee of Secresy, and that the Pitt System is everlasting. Amen.
Q. What dost thou chiefly learn in these Articles of thy Belief?
A. First, I learn to forswear all conscience, which was never meant to trouble me, nor the rest of the tribe of Courtiers. Secondly, to swear black is white, or white black, according to the good pleasure of the Ministers. Thirdly, to put on the helmet of impudence, the only armour against the shafts of patriotism.
Q. You said that your Sureties did promise for you, that you should keep the Minister's Commandments: tell me how many there be?
A. Ten.
Q. Which be they?

Answer
The same to which the Minister for the time being always obliges all his creatures to swear, I the Minister am the Lord thy liege, who brought thee out of Want and Beggary, into the House of Commons.

I. Thou shalt have no other Patron but me.

II. Thou shalt not support any measure but mine, nor shalt thou frame clauses of any bill in its progress to the House above, or in the Committee beneath, or when the mace is under the table, except it be mine. Thou shalt not bow to Lord COCHRANE,[6] nor shake hands with him, nor any other of my real opponents; for I thy Lord am a jealous Minister, and forbid familiarity of the Majority, with the Friends of the People, unto the third and fourth cousins of them that divide against me; and give places, and thousands and tens of thousands, to them that divide with me, and keep my Commandments.

III. Thou shalt not take the Pension of thy Lord the Minister in vain; for I the Minister will force him to accept the Chilterns that taketh my Pension in vain.

IV. Remember that thou attend the Minister's Levee day[7]; on other days thou shalt speak for him in the House, and fetch and carry, and do all that he commandeth thee to do; but the Levee day is for the glorification of the Minister thy Lord: In it thou shalt do no work in the House, but shall wait upon him, thou, and thy daughter, and thy wife, and the Members that are within his influence; for on other days the Minister is inaccessible, but delighteth in the Levee day; wherefore the Minister appointed the Levee day, and chatteth thereon familiarly, and is amused with it.

V. Honour the Regent and the helmets of the Life Guards, that thy stay may be long in the Place, which thy Lord the Minister giveth thee.

VI. Thou shalt not call starving to death murder.

VII. Thou shall not call Royal gallivanting adultery.

VIII. Thou shalt not say, that to rob the Public is to steal.

IX. Thou shalt bear false witness against the People.

X. Thou shalt not covet the People's applause, thou shalt not covet the People's praise, nor their good name, nor their esteem, nor their reverence, nor any reward that is theirs.

Q. What doest thou chiefly learn by these Commandments?

A. I learn two things—my duty towards the Minister, and my duty towards myself.

Q. What is thy duty towards the Minister?

A. My duty towards the Minister is, to trust him as much as I can; to fear him; to honour him with all my words, with all my bows, with all my scrapes, and all my cringes; to flatter him; to give him thanks; to give up my whole soul to him; to idolize his name, and obey his word; and serve him blindly all the days of his political life.

Q. What is thy duty towards thyself?

A. My duty towards myself is to love nobody but myself, and to do unto most men what I would not they should do unto me; to sacrifice to my own interest even my father and mother; to pay little reverence to the King, but to compensate that omission by my servility to all that are put in authority under him; to lick the dust under the feet of my superiors, and to shake a rod of iron over the backs of my inferiors; to spare the People by neither word or deed; to observe neither truth nor justice in my dealings with them; to bear them malice and hatred in my heart and where their wives and properties are concerned, to keep my body neither in temperance, soberness, nor chastity, but to give my hands to picking and stealing, and my tongue to evil speaking and lying, and slander of their efforts to defend their liberties and recover their rights; never failing to envy their privileges, and to learn to get the Pensions of myself and my colleagues out of the People's labour, and to do my duty in that department of public plunder unto which it shall please the Minister to call me.

Q. My good Courtier, know this, that thou art not able of thyself to preserve the Minister's favour, nor to walk in his Commandments, nor to serve him, without his special protection; which thou must at all times learn to obtain by diligent application. Let me hear, therefore, if thou canst rehearse the Minister's Memorial.

Answer

Our Lord who art in the Treasury, whatsoever be thy name, thy power be prolonged, thy will be done throughout the empire, as it is in each session. Give us our usual sops, and forgive us our occasional absences on divisions; as we promise not to forgive them that divide against thee. Turn us not out of our Places; but keep us in the House of Commons, the land of Pensions and Plenty; and deliver us from the People. Amen.

Q. What desirest thou of the Minister in this Memorial?

A. I desire the Minister, our Patron, who is the disposer of the Nation's overstrained Taxation, to give his protection unto me and to all Pensioners and Placemen, that we may vote for him, serve him, and obey him, as far as we find it convenient; and I beseech the Minister that he will give us all things that be needful, both for our reputation and appearance in the House and out of it; that he will be favourable to us, and forgive us our negligences; that it will please him to save and defend us, in all dangers of life and limb, from the People, our natural enemies; and that he will help us in fleecing and grinding them; and this I trust he will do out of care for himself, and our support of him through our corruption and influence; and therefore I say Amen. So be it.

Q. How many Tests hath the Minister ordained?

A. Two only, as generally necessary to elevation; (that is to say) Passive Obedience and Bribery.

Q. What meanest thou by this word Test?

A. I mean an outward visible sign of an inward intellectual meanness, ordained by the Minister himself as a pledge to assure him thereof.

Q. How many parts are there in this Test?

A. Two; the outward visible sign, and the inward intellectual meanness.

Q. What is the outward visible sign or form of Passive Obedience?

A. Dangling at the Minister's heels, whereby the person is degraded beneath the baseness of a slave, in the character of a Pensioner, Placeman, Expectant Parasite, Toadeater, or Lord of the Bedchamber.

Q. What is the inward and intellectual meanness?

A. A death unto Freedom, a subjection unto perpetual Thraldom: for being by nature born free, and the children of Independence, we are hereby made children of Slavery.

Q. What is required of persons submitting to the Test of Passive Obedience?

A. Apostacy, whereby they forsake Liberty; and faith, whereby they stedfastly believe the promises of the Minister, made to them upon submitting to that Test.

Q. Why was the Test of Bribery ordained?

A. For the continual support of the Minister's influence, and the feeding of us, his needy creatures and sycophants.

Q. What is the outward part or sign in the Test of Bribery?

A. Bank notes, which the Minister hath commanded to be offered by his dependants.

Q. Why then are beggars submitted to this Test, when by reason of their poverty they are not able to go through the necessary forms?

A. Because they promise them by their Sureties; which promise, when they come to lucrative offices, they themselves are bound to perform.

Q. What is the inward part, or thing signified?

A. The industry and wealth of the People, which are verily and indeed taken and had by Pensioners and Sinecurists, in their Corruption.

Q. What are the benefits whereof you are partakers thereby?

A. The weakening and impoverishing the People, through the loss of their Liberty and Property, while our wealth becomes enormous, and our pride intolerable.

Q. What is required of them who submit to the Test of Bribery and Corruption?

A. To examine themselves, whether they repent them truly of any signs of former honour and patriotism, stedfastly purposing henceforward to be faithful towards the Minister; to draw on and off like his glove; to crouch to him like a spaniel; to purvey for him like a jackall; to be as supple to him as Alderman Sir WILLIAM TURTLE; to have the most lively faith in the Funds, especially in the Sinking Fund[8]; to believe the words of Lord CASTLEREAGH alone; to have remembrance of nothing but what is in the Courier; to hate MATTHEW WOOD, the present Lord Mayor, and his second Mayoralty, with all our heart, with all our mind, with all our soul, and with all our strength; to admire Sir JOHN SILVESTER, the Recorder, and Mr. JOHN LANGLEY[9]; and to be in charity with those only who have something to give.

[*Here endeth the Catechism.*]

18
John Keats, "The Gothic Looks Solemn" (1817)

Keats's playful parody of Wordsworth was written while Keats was in Oxford with Benjamin Bailey and working on *Endymion*. It was enclosed in a letter of September 1817 to Reynolds with remarks about the style of some Wordsworth poems being like "school exercises" [*The Letters of John Keats 1814–1821*, ed. Hyder E. Rollins, 2 vols. (Cambridge, Mass.: Harvard University Press, 1958), 1: 151–52]. The same year Keats wrote his sonnet "Nebuchadnezzar's Dream," a parody of the Book of Daniel praising William Hone and attacking his prosecutors.

THE GOTHIC LOOKS SOLEMN

1

The Gothic looks solemn,
The plain Doric column
Supports an old bishop and crosier;
The mouldering arch,
Shaded o'er by a larch,
Stands next door to Wilson the Hosier.

2

Vicè—that is, by turns,—
O'er pale faces mourns
The black tassell'd trencher and common hat;
The chantry boy sings,
The steeple-bell rings,
And as for the Chancellor—*dominat*.

3

There are plenty of trees,
And plenty of ease,
And plenty of fat deer for parsons;
And when it is venison,
Short is the benison,—
Then each on a leg or thigh fastens.

19
Anonymous, "The Old Tolbooth" (1818)

"The Old Tolbooth" was published 16 May 1818 in *The Letter-Box*, no. 14: 199–208, and signed J. F. This anonymous parody may have originated in Wordsworth's comments about marauding geologists in the Lake District (*The Excursion* 3.173ff), or in the following comment in the Preface to the second edition of *Lyrical Ballads* [*The Poetical Works of Wordsworth*, rev. ed. Ernest de Selincourt (London: Oxford University Press, 1950)]: "The remotest discoveries of the Chemist, the Botanist, or Mineralogist will be as proper objects of the Poet's art. . . ." (738). The parody essentially attacks Wordsworth's "waking dreams" and flights of fancy as irresponsible self-obsession rather than genuine poetic inspiration. The poet's evident fascination with his own thoughts and experience is maintained only at the cost of contact with reality. The parodist effectively embodies this narcissism in the tortured structure of articulation: the suspended syntactical constructions; the repeated use of parentheses (even parentheses within parentheses); the frequent digressions into irrelevancies; the annoyingly intrusive moralizing; and the use of a specialized, esoteric vocabulary (here, of minerals). In addition to preciosity of style, the parody further buries its ostensible subject (Wordsworth's encounter with an old soldier in an Edinburgh street) under lines of philosophizing, sentimental reflections, classical allusions, and meditations on rocks. In its exaggeration and satiric skill, "The Old Tolbooth" rivals Hogg's parodies and may even be denser in its allusiveness.

THE OLD TOLBOOTH[1]

> . . . "Egyptian Thebes,
> Tyre, by the margin of the sounding waves,
> Palmyra, central in the desert, fell."
>
> —Wordsworth[2]

———

That bell ('twas Giles's clock that toll'd the hour)
Hath ever unto me a pleasant sound;
For, when it swings ding-dong, I shut my eyes,

And straight transport myself unto the lake,
The still blue lake of beauteous Windermere,
And fancy that the spirit of the sound
Which meets my ear, comes borne from out the tower
Of the old church, high toppling o'er the trees,
Whose branchy arms hang in the dimpling wave,
Kissing the source from whence their freshness springs.
And then I stoop (O! fond Enthusiast)
Upon the pebbl'd margin, to admire
The varied fragments of the min'ral world;
Floetz, trap and schistus; wakke and porphyry,
Magnesian limestone, secondary rock;
('Mong which we reckon coal, in French—charbon)
Granite, and other schists of primitive
Formation; quartose and schistoze sandstone,
Of finest grain, arranged in thin laminae—
Such as great Humboldt found in Iconouzo.[3]
And then I bring all fresh into my mind,
The grotto rais'd in days of thoughtless happiness,
Glancing and glitt'ring in the borrow'd spoils
Of half the German's (Werner is the name)
Nomenclature'—'twixt whom and Hutton's school
Exist such literary bickerings.[4]
O then I'm happy as an Eastern king,
While thus I flounder in the unebbing tide
That laves the palace of Imagination,
Till, with uncivil shove, some vulgar wight,
Mayhap a porter, wakes me from my dream,
And then I find that Windermere is gone,
And village tow'r and pebbl'd margin all.
     Such were my waking dreams—my musing thoughts,
(For I do love to muse) as towards the shop
Of Arch'bald Constable I mov'd along,
Fully resolv'd to find most grievous fault
With Francis Jeffrey, whose unjust reviews[5]
Deal out damnation, as a grocer deals
His sauded sugar, by the hundred weight[6];
But just as I had got within some feet
(If I may judge by moderated measure,
Methinks, five feet, three inches and a half)
Of the aforesaid shop, a whirlwind of dust
Came whizzing down the street, and, with great force
Of particles minute, drove full against
My yellow waistcoat; and my breeches drab;

Unlike that show'r of vegetative gold
Which Mr. Thomson, from the banks of Tweed,
Affirms th'autumnal orchards pour amain.[7]
This was a show'r had almost made me sneeze,
And well nigh clos'd those visual orbs of light,
Through which, transmitted, the prismatic rays
(Sir Isaac's bright discovery) there collect
In one unbroken focus—a spec'lum
That back reflects the objects to our sense,
Causing us to see temples and cobblers stalls,
And domes imperial, and the peasant's cot.
  Wishing to know the cause of this same dust,
(For causes, it is said, precede effects)
I pass'd the shop I had resolv'd to enter;
And seeing on the other side of the way,
An ancient vet'ran in a long red coat,
With hat cock'd o'er his brow, and round his neck
A Belcher handkerchief; at sight of which,
I puzzled me to find a reason why
He lack'd a leathern stock which soldiers wear——[8]
I understood, though 'twas some days thereafter,
That that particular band in which he was,
Had no restrictions on the score of cravats,
Each wearing what he chose.
      I cross'd the street,
Accosting him in terms of friendly warmth,
(Rais'd by the long red coat and black cockade,
For such, thought I, all George's soldiers wear)
To know from whence arose those clouds of dust.
Turning upon me with a smiling look,
Such as Lavater could have well defin'd,[9]
He said, "your honour, 'tis the *Old Tolbooth,*
From which proceeds the dust you talk of."
"Are then the prisoners," I quick replied,
"Become unruly, that they, thus uncheck'd,
Send forth their dusty volumes through our streets,
Making day night,—emblem of their dark deeds?"
He smil'd again—but 'twas in such a sort,
As if he thought me ignorant indeed,
And little vers'd in what concern'd the town,
Which Sir John Carr compares to Grecian Athens,[10]
"No Sir," said he, "but may I be so bold
As ask, if you're a stranger in this place?"
Glad of this question, I replied, "You're right—

My name is W—ds—th, dear to all the nine
A poet to my trade, and that self man
Whom if you read the Edinbro' Review,
You will discover founder of the sect,
Which Frank denom'nates *Lakers,* from the place
Where we our lonely residence have fix'd."
At this the honest vet'ran with his hands—
His sun-burnt hands stretch'd tow'rd the empyreal vault
(At that same moment free from threat'ning cloud)
Exclaim'd, "The Lakers! don't know such a corps—
Most likely a militia term'd local;
Who, in the price and fulness of their hearts,
Stand forth the guardians of our sea-girt isle.
I like such nobleness—here, here I stand,
John Kennedy* by name, who, oft as danger lours,
With this good axe, yclep'd Lochaber, dares
The prentice youths, and all the rotten stench
Of cats a twelvemonth dead—thrown from the grip
Of floury Baxter—Salamander swain!"[11]
    I held my head aside, and wept—yea, wept,
To see in one so bent with age and toil,
So much unbending patriotic zeal:
And as I grasp'd his horny fist, and shook
The very powder from his well curl'd-locks,
I swore by Styx, such conduct far surpass'd
The vaunted deeds of hectoring Trojan Hector.
    Pray, what was Hector, if I may but ask?
The fleshless phantom of old Homer's brain—
A rude and boisterous savage—one whose soul
Was like his beard—matted and dry—
And all begrim'd (if snuff was then in fashion)
With beggars brown, and that called Irish blackguard.
But here, by storms of circumstance unshaken,
And subject neither to the gout nor ache,
Stands one in all the energy of grace,
Unborrow'd of the sun—(which sun, some think
The centre of our system; dispensing
Life and heat, and vegetative power,
And light, and every other blessing, which
An *Intelligence abstract* for wisest[12]
Reasons, deigns to shed upon—within
The bosom of our oblate spheroid.)

---

*A well-known character in the late City guard.

Here, I say, stands one, whose antique corps,
Although the ridicule of reg'lar troops,
Has often stood the brunt of civil broils,
And birth-day burgherings—whose boney limbs,
Cas'd in their ample cuisse of scarlet cloth,
And spatterdash of what was black when new,[13]
Wade on to glory through a sea of puddle!
        Involuntarily I turned round,
And found the subject of my meditations
Slow pacing up the street. His sun-burnt hands
Were clasp'd behind his back, where hung what seem'd
A bayonet—(a weapon in the use of which
Much good (if killing Gallic slaves be good)
Was done in the peninsular campaign;
When Joseph Bonaparte—a man of wax,
Presum'd to occupy the Spanish throne.)[14]
I followed after, (Kennedy to wit)
And when I would again have spoken to him,
Puff comes a cloud of mortar in my eyes—
My mouth, my very nostrils had their share;
To cleanse out which took by St Giles's clock
Six minutes and a quarter—for be't known
The bell was tolling half past one o'clock,
Exactly as the dust clogg'd up my eyes,
And when I found my sight I ey'd the dial plate,
And found 'twas to a moment when I've said.
        My eyes being brightened, I beheld, till then
Unnotic'd, the cause of all this hubbub and confusion—
Here stood a pallisade
Of rotten joists, to fence from harm the lieges,
There lay the rubbish of two cent'ries growth,
Consisting of old weather-eaten stone,
And lumps of mortar—some as hard as stones;
And broken fragments of the fatal tree,
Whereon had hung villains of blackest dye—
Murd'rers and thieves, and traitors to their king,
Misguided men! to virtue strangers ever!
Humanity may prompt a tear for those
Whom one *faux pas,* or (anglice) false step,
Has caus'd the fatal gibbet to jut forth:
But justice—blended justice with her sword
Swoops off the tear, and lo! 'tis gone for ever!!!!!!!!
        "Oh! what a feast is here, my worthy John,
And fitting food for frantic contemplation?"

I said—and stumbled o'er a stone, which once
Had been (in technical masonic phrase)
A Rybet,*—This small incident to some[15]
Would ne'er have wak'd a thought of good or ill.
But far, far different with me I ween!
The tinyest atom in the moral world
Engenders in my breast most pleasing dreams.
The falling of a pin upon the floor
Stirs up the cauldron of my boiling wit,
Whence foams the steam of my luxuriant fancy,
Bedazzling the world with its fantasies.
For scarcely had I sprung upon my feet,
Than quite as quick began within my brain
To spring a thousand images of woe,
Treading each other heels, as Shakespeare says,
And bursting through their cellular abodes,
That they might perch upon my quill's sharp point,
In semblance to what follows:
                         "Thou Rybet!
Quarried from out the bowels of Craigleith,
Or Ravelston[16]; or any other mine
In the vicinity of this good town,
Whither sage builders, men of square and rule,
Resort, to chuse out blocks fit for the use
Of Lintel, chimney-top, or portico.
Oh! what a tale were thine, wert thou endow'd
With faculty of speech, and could converse
In dialectic style, (such as was held
By Socrates—that man of bull dog phiz,
Whom Aristophanes in *Nubibus,*
Baptis'd the Attic jester—and whose dad,
Old Sophroniscus was a marble cutter,
Dwelling hard by the Acropolis, where stood
The Temple of Minerva, dear to owls,
And this same Sophroniscus, it would seem
Took to his bed a lady midwife-bred.
So say Diogenes Laertius;
Confirmed too by Xenophon, who in
His *Memorabilia* repeats the tale)[17]
But ah thou can'st not, I am loth to say,
Yet may I fancy that thou talk'st to me
With most miraculous organ, Rybet!

Stones used in building the sides of windows, are so called.

I hear thee tell of many sigh and groan,
And lonely pray'r for blessed Liberty,
And anxious look toward the mid-day sun,
That shone in broken rays along thy side,
Playing in mockery on the cold damp floor,
Where, stretch'd along, the wretched prisoner lay,—
And I can fancy that thou speak'st to me
Of wretched wife clasp'd in a husband's arms,
Who ere the next day's sun had sunk to rest,
Has been the inmate of another world,—
And I can picture me, their haggard looks
Of anguish and despair, and piercing shrieks,
When they have snatch'd their farewell kiss,
And groan'd in agony upon their babes—
Their fated orphans—sharers of the guilt
That dooms their father to a shameful end;—
Aye, guilt!—will not the world point its finger
And exclaim—"There goes a robber's children!"
Oh! I am sick at heart to think of this,
And know it true as text of Holy Writ!"
        What great effects do spring from little causes!
Witness the fore-going extacies sublime,
And doleful cogitations. Their parent
An old stone, which, as I said before, mechanics
Call a rybet—explained, as you would see,
In a short note below—Italic-wise;
So Newton, glorious sage! beneath the shade
Of Pippin-tree, (engrafted on the trunk
Of that, whose fruit makes famous cyder)
By the mere circumstance of one of those
Same trees dropping a pippin on his nob,
Which rais'd a knob, or hard protuberance
Thereon, he set to work with altitude
And observation due, in consonance
With mathematic rules, tangents and sines,
Rhombs, parabolic curves, paralaxes,
And the Rule of Three—(which said rule is one
I've found extremely useful to find out
The price of tatoes and so forth) proving
Even to a demonstration, that the laws
Of gravitation and attraction, hinge
Reciprocally on one another.
And all this eminent, this goodly fruit,
Of Newton's mighty mind sprung from

The fruit of an old Pippin-tree—by Jove!
 Most courteous reader, by the help of Heaven,
I had essay'd with all due def'rence
To thy utmost patience, to have giv'n
An essay metaphysical, upon
The moral fitness of the Calton jail,[18]
In form of a desultory dialogue;
The principal prolocutor in which,
Had been my rev'rend friend from Athole hills—[19]
"The vagrant merchant bending neathe his load,"
But, on a fresh concoction of ideas,
It seem'd to me more fit and profitable,
That it be woove as weft, or rather woof,
Within my web poetic forthcoming,
Entituled *"An Excursion to the Lakes."*
In five thick volumes, royal quarto,
Till then, my gentle friends, I take my leave.
 Hoping you'll live t' enjoy my proffer'd feast,
Cull'd from the mystic categ'ries of Kant,
And Jacob Behmen, I remain your friend,[20]
And cat'rer to your pleasures,

WM. W—DS—TH.
October 1817.—J.F.

20
Thomas Love Peacock, from *Nightmare Abbey* (1818)

Thomas Love Peacock (1785–1866) has often been described as a "major parodist," as by Marilyn Gaull in *English Romanticism: The Human Context* (New York: Norton, 1988), 245. But too often critics use the term *parody* merely as an alternative to "burlesque" or "lampoon"—and not only with reference to Peacock. In *His Fine Wit: A Study of Thomas Love Peacock* (Berkeley: University of California Press, 1970), Carl Dawson states (5–6) that "except briefly in 'The Four Ages of Poetry,' he [Peacock] never managed a good parody of Wordsworth." In fact he never attempted a parody of Wordsworth, and the passage to which Dawson refers ("Poetical genius is the finest of all things," and so on) is a facetious summary of the attitudes Peacock believed to underlie the writings of "that egregious confraternity of rhymesters, known by the name of the Lake Poets." Similarly, although Peacock mocks certain features of Coleridge's thought and personality in *Nightmare Abbey* and elsewhere, he does not parody the poetry, for which he had a great admiration. See his sympathetic and analytic defense of "Christabel" and "Kubla Khan" in *An Essay on Fashionable Literature*.

Peacock's books elude classification, scarcely even qualifying as novels, but if they had to be categorized it would be as comedies of ideas satirizing a wide range of nineteenth-century obsessions and intellectual fashions. In other narratives his targets include democratic government, social progress, the new science of economics, and the artistic pretensions of the *nouveaux riches*. In *Nightmare Abbey* his major target is the Romantic poets.

No short extracts could do justice to the wit and inventiveness, or to what Shelley called the "chastity," of Peacock's writing, but, for the benefit of anyone who has not yet enjoyed that pleasure, the following are offered as inducements. These extracts feature Peacock's satire at its closest to parody.

(FROM CHAPTER II)

He now became troubled with the *passion for reforming the world.*[1] He built many castles in the air, and peopled them with secret tribunals, and bands of illuminati, who were always the imaginary instruments of his projected regeneration of the human species. As he intended to institute a perfect republic, he invested himself with absolute sovereignty over these mystical dispensers of liberty. He slept with Horrid Mysteries[2] under his pillow, and dreamed of venerable eleutherarchs[3] and ghastly confederates holding midnight conventions in subterranean caves. He passed whole mornings in his study, immersed in gloomy reverie, stalking about the room in his nightcap, which he pulled over his eyes like a cowl, and folding his striped calico dressing-gown about him like the mantle of a conspirator.

'Action,' thus he soliloquised, 'is the result of opinion,[4] and to new-model opinion would be to new-model society. Knowledge is power; it is in the hands of a few, who enjoy it to mislead the many, for their own selfish purposes of aggrandisement and appropriation. What if it were in the hands of a few who should employ it to lead the many? What if it were universal, and the multitude were enlightened? No. The many must be always in leading-strings; but let them have wise and honest conductors. A few to think, and many to act; that is the only basis of perfect society. So thought the ancient philosophers: they had their esoterical and exoterical doctrines. So thinks the sublime Kant, who delivers his oracles in language which none but the initiated can comprehend. Such were the views of those secret associations of illuminati, which were the terror of superstition and tyranny, and which, carefully selecting wisdom and genius from the great wilderness of society, as the bee selects honey from the flowers of the thorn and the nettle, bound all human excellence in a chain, which, if it had not been prematurely broken, would have commanded opinion, and regenerated the world.'

Scythrop proceeded to meditate on the practicability of reviving a confederation of regenerators. To get a clear view of his own ideas, and to feel the pulse of the wisdom and genius of the age, he wrote and published a treatise,[5] in which his meanings were carefully wrapt up in the monk's hood of transcendental technology, but filled with hints of matter deep and dangerous, which he thought would set the whole nation in a ferment; and he awaited the result in awful expectation, as a miner who has fired a train awaits the explosion of a rock. However, he listened and heard nothing; for the explosion, if any ensued, was not sufficiently loud to shake a single leaf of the ivy on the towers of Nightmare Abbey; and some months afterwards he received a letter from his bookseller, informing him that only seven copies had been sold, and concluding with a polite request for the balance.

Scythrop did not despair. 'Seven copies,' he thought, 'have been sold. Seven is a mystical number, and the omen is good. Let me find the seven purchasers of my seven copies, and they shall be the seven golden candlesticks with which I will illuminate the world.'

* * * * *

(FROM CHAPTER V)

A parcel was brought in for Mr Listless; it had been sent express. Fatout was summoned to unpack it; and it proved to contain a new novel, and a new poem, both of which had long been anxiously expected by the whole host of fashionable readers; and the last number of a popular Review, of which the editor and his coadjutors were in high favour at court, and enjoyed ample pensions for their services to church and state. As Fatout left the room, Mr Flosky entered, and curiously inspected the literary arrivals.

MR FLOSKY

(Turning over the leaves.) 'Devilman, a novel.'[6] Hm. Hatred—revenge—misanthropy—and quotations from the Bible. Hm. This is the morbid anatomy of black bile.—'Paul Jones,[7] a poem.' Hm. I see how it is. Paul Jones, an amiable enthusiast—disappointed in his affections—turns pirate from ennui and magnanimity—cuts various masculine throats, wins various feminine hearts—is hanged at the yard-arm! The catastrophe is very awkward, and very unpoetical.—'The Downing Street Review.' Hm. First article—An Ode to the Red Book,[8] by Roderick Sackbut,[9] Esquire. Hm. His own poem reviewed by himself. Hm-m-m.

*   *   *   *   *

(FROM CHAPTER VI)

MR FLOSKY

I pity the man who can see the connection of his own ideas. Still more do I pity him, the connection of whose ideas any other person can see. Sir, the great evil is, that there is too much commonplace light in our moral and political literature; and light is a great enemy to mystery, and mystery is a great friend to enthusiasm. Now the enthusiasm for abstract truth is an exceedingly fine thing, as long as the truth, which is the object of the enthusiasm, is so completely abstract as to be altogether out of the reach of the human faculties; and, in that sense, I have myself an enthusiasm for truth, but in no other, for the pleasure of metaphysical investigation lies in the means, not in the end; and if the end could be found, the pleasure of the means would cease. The mind, to be kept in health, must be kept in exercise. The proper exercise of the mind is elaborate reasoning. Analytical reasoning is a base and mechanical process, which takes to pieces and examines, bit by bit, the rude material of knowledge, and extracts therefrom a few hard and obstinate things called facts, every thing in the shape of which I cordially hate. But synthetical reasoning, setting up as its goal some unattainable abstraction, like an imaginary quantity in algebra, and commencing its course with taking for granted some two assertions which cannot be proved, from the union of these two assumed truths produces a third assumption, and so on in infinite series, to the unspeakable benefit of the human intellect. The beauty of this process is, that at every step it strikes out into two branches, in a compound ratio of ramification; so that you are perfectly sure of losing your way, and keeping your mind in perfect health, by the perpetual exercise of an interminable quest; for these reasons I have christened my eldest son Emanuel Kant Flosky.[10]

THE REVEREND MR LARYNX

Nothing can be more luminous.

THE HONOURABLE MR LISTLESS

And what has all that to do with Dante, and the blue devils?

MR HILARY

Not much, I should think, with Dante, but a great deal with the blue devils.

MR FLOSKY

It is very certain, and much to be rejoiced at, that our literature is hag-ridden. Tea has shattered our nerves; late dinners make us slaves of indigestion; the French Revolution has made us shrink from the name of philosophy, and has destroyed, in the more refined part of the community (of which number I am one), all enthusiasm for political liberty. That part of the *reading public*[11] which shuns the solid food of reason for the light diet of fiction, requires a perpetual adhibition of *sauce piquante* to the palate of its depraved imagination. It lived upon ghosts, goblins, and skeletons (I and my friend Mr. Sackbut served up a few of the best), till even the devil himself, though magnified to the size of Mount Athos, became too base, common, and popular, for its surfeited appetite. The ghosts have therefore been laid, and the devil has been cast into outer darkness, and now the delight of our spirits is to dwell on all the vices and blackest passions of our nature, tricked out in a masquerade dress of heroism and disappointed benevolence; the whole secret of which lies in forming combinations that contradict all our experience, and affixing the purple shred of some particular virtue to that precise character, in which we should be most certain not to find it in the living world; and making this single virtue not only redeem all the real and manifest vices of the character, but make them actually pass for necessary adjuncts, and indispensable accompaniments and characteristics of the said virtue.

*   *   *   *   *

(FROM CHAPTER VIII)

MARIONETTA

I must apologise for intruding on you, Mr Flosky; but the interest which I—you—take in my cousin Scythrop—

MR FLOSKY

Pardon me, Miss O'Carroll; I do not take any interest in any person or thing on the face of the earth; which sentiment, if you analyse it, you will find to be the quintessence of the most refined philanthropy.

MARIONETTA

I will take it for granted that it is so, Mr Flosky; I am not conversant with metaphysical subtleties, but—

MR FLOSKY

Subtleties! my dear Miss O'Carroll. I am sorry to find you participating in the vulgar error of the *reading public,* to whom an unusual collocation of words, involving a juxtaposition of antiperistatical ideas, immediately suggests the notion of hyperoxysophistical paradoxology.[12]

MARIONETTA

Indeed, Mr Flosky, it suggests no such notion to me. I have sought you for the purpose of obtaining information.

MR FLOSKY *(SHAKING HIS HEAD)*

No one ever sought me for such a purpose before.

MARIONETTA

I think, Mr Flosky—that is, I believe—that is, I fancy—that is, I imagine—

MR FLOSKY

The TOUTESTI, the *id est,* the *cioè,* the *c'est à dire,* the *that is,* my dear Miss O'Carroll, is not applicable in this case—if you will permit me to take the liberty of saying so. Think is not synonymous with believe—for belief, in many most important particulars, results from the total absence, the absolute negation of thought, and is thereby the sane and orthodox condition of mind; and thought and belief are both essentially different from fancy, and fancy, again, is distinct from imagination. This distinction between fancy and imagination is one of the most abstruse and important points of metaphysics. I have written seven hundred pages of promise[13] to elucidate it, which promise I shall keep as faithfully as the bank will its promise to pay.

MARIONETTA

I assure you, Mr Flosky, I care no more about metaphysics than I do about the bank; and, if you will condescend to talk to a simple girl in intelligible terms—

MR FLOSKY

Say not condescend! Know you not that you talk to the most humble of men, to one who has buckled on the armour of sanctity, and clothed himself with humility as with a garment?

MARIONETTA

My cousin Scythrop has of late had an air of mystery about him, which gives me great uneasiness.

MR FLOSKY

That is strange: nothing is so becoming to a man as an air of mystery. Mystery is the very key-stone of all that is beautiful in poetry, all that is sacred in faith, and all that is recondite in transcendental psychology. I am writing a ballad which is all mystery; it is 'such stuff as dreams are made of,'[14] and is, indeed, stuff made of a dream; for, last night I fell asleep as usual over my book, and had a vision of pure reason. I composed five hundred lines in my sleep[15]; so that, having had a dream of a ballad, I am now officiating as my own Peter Quince, and making a ballad of my dream, and it shall be called Bottom's Dream, because it has no bottom.[16]

*　*　*　*　*

(FROM CHAPTER XI)

MR CYPRESS

I have no hope for myself or for others. Our life is a false nature; it is not in the harmony of things; it is an all-blasting upas, whose root is earth, and whose leaves are the skies which rain their poison-dews upon mankind. We wither from our youth; we gasp with unslaked thirst for unattainable good; lured from the first to the last by phantoms—love, fame, ambition, avarice—all idle, and all ill—one meteor of many names, that vanishes in the smoke of death.[17]

*   *   *   *   *

ALL

A song from Mr Cypress.

MR. CYPRESS *SUNG*—

There is a fever of the spirit,
    The brand of Cain's unresting doom,[18]
Which in the lone dark souls that bear it
    Glows like the lamp in Tullia's tomb:[19]
Unlike that lamp, its subtle fire
    Burns, blasts, consumes its cell, the heart,
Till, one by one, hope, joy, desire,
    Like dreams of shadowy smoke depart.

When hope, love, life itself, are only
    Dust—spectral memories—dead and cold—
The unfed fire burns bright and lonely,
    Like that undying lamp of old:
And by that drear illumination,
    Till time its clay-built home has rent,
Thought broods on feeling's desolation—
    The soul is its own monument.

MR GLOWRY

Admirable. Let us all be unhappy together.

21
D. M. Moir, "The Rime of the Auncient Waggonere" (1819)

"The Rime of the Auncient Waggonere" was published in *Blackwood's* in February 1819. David Macbeth Moir (1798–1851), known as Delta (Δ), was a physician and a regular contributor to the periodical. Moir's humorous parody of Coleridge's well-known narrative is notable for its witty use of a marginal gloss, which summarizes the action or comments ironically on it (sometimes it even contradicts the text). Together with a noticeable coarsening of the original and introducing some bursts of rhetoric, Moir sends up Coleridge for his pedantic attachment to the past (as the archaisms indicate) as well as his use of specific numbers (as in the miscounting of ribs in Part Third). The parodist especially exploits the principle of substitution in satirizing the original; a drunken goose replaces the albatross, bailiffs are used instead of spirits, and physical action is emphasized wherever possible over psychological effects. Scottish slang and colloquialisms complete the conspiracy to undermine the original poem's sublimity.

THE RIME OF THE AUNCIENT WAGGONERE

PART FIRST

An auncient waggonere stoppeth ane tailore going to a wedding, whereat he hath been appointed to be best manne, and to take a hand in the casting of the slippere.

IT is an auncient Waggonere,
  And he stoppeth one of nine:—[1]
"Now wherefore dost thou grip me soe
With that horny fist of thine?"

The waggonere in mood for chate, and admits of no excuse.

"The bridegroom's doors are opened wide,
  And thither I must walke;
Soe, by youre leave, I muste be gone,
  I have noe time for talke!"

The tailore seized with the ague.

Hee holds him with his horny fist—
  "There was a wain," quothe hee,
"Hold offe, thou raggamouffine tykke,"
  Eftsoones his fist dropped hee.

163

He listeneth like a three
yeares and a half child.

Hee satte him downe upon a stone,
  With ruefulle looks of feare;
And thus began this tippsye manne,
  The red nosed waggonere.

The appetite of the
tailore whetted by the
smell of cabbage.

"The wain is fulle, the horses pulle,
  Merrilye did we trotte
Alonge the bridge, alonge the road,
  A jolly crewe, I wotte:"—
And here the tailore smotte his breaste,
  He smelte the cabbage potte!

The waggonere in talkinge
anent Boreas,[2] maketh bad
orthographye.

"The nighte was darke, like Noe's arke,
  Oure waggone moved alonge;
The hail pour'd faste, loude roared the
    blaste,
  Yet stille we moved alonge;
And sung in chorus, 'Cease loud Borus,'
  A very charminge songe.

Their mirthe interrupted;

" 'Bravoe, bravissimoe,' I cried,
  The sounde was quite elatinge;
But, in a trice, upon the ice,
  We heard the horses skaitinge.

And the passengers
exercise themselves in the
pleasant art of swiminge,
as doeth also their prog,
to witte, great store of
colde roasted beef; item,
ane beef-stake pye; item,
viii choppines of
usquebaugh.[3]

"The ice was here, the ice was there,
  It was a dismale mattere,
To see the cargoe, one by one,
  Flounderinge in the wattere!

"With rout and roare, we reached the shore,
  And never a soul did sinke;
But in the rivere, gone for evere,
  Swum our meate and drinke.

The waggonere hailethe
ane goose with ane novelle
salutatione.

"At lengthe we spied a goode grey goose,
  Thorough the snow it came;
And with the butte ende of my whippe,
  I hailed it in Goddhis name.

"It staggered as it had been drunke,
  So dexterous was it hitte;
Of broken boughs we made a fire,
  Thomme Loncheone roasted itte."—

The tailore impatient to
be gone, but is forcibly
persuaded to remain.

"Be done, thou tipsye waggonere,
  To the feaste I must awaye."—
The waggonere seized him bye the coatte,
  And forced him there to staye,

> Begginge, in gentlemanlie style,
> Butte halfe ane hours delaye.

PART SECOND

The waggonere's bowels
yearn towards the sunne.

> "The crimsone sunne was risinge o'ere
> The verge of the horizon;
> Upon my worde, as faire a sunne
> As ever I clapped eyes onne.

The passengers throwe the
blame of the goose
massacre on the innocente
waggonere.

> " ' 'Twill bee ane comfortable thinge,'
> The mutinous crewe 'gan crye;
> ' 'Twill be ane comfortable thinge,
> Within the jaile to lye;
> Ah! execrable wretche,' saide they,
> 'Thatte caused the goose to die!'

The sunne sufferes ane
artificial eclipse, and
horror follows, the same
not being mentioned in the
Belfaste Almanacke.

> "The day was drawing near itte's close,
> The sunne was well nighe settinge;
> When lo! it seemed, as iffe his face
> Was veiled with fringe-warke-nettinge.

Various hypotheses on the
subject, frome which the
passengers draw wronge
conclusions.

> "Some saide itte was ane apple tree,
> Laden with goodlye fruite,
> Somme swore itte was ane foreigne birde,
> Some said it was ane brute;
> Alas! it was ane bumbailiffe,[4]
> Riding in pursuite!

Ane lovelye sound
ariseth; ittes effects
described.

> "A hue and crye sterte uppe behind,
> Whilke smote oure ears like thunder,
> Within the waggone there was drede,
> Astonishmente and wonder.

The passengers throw
somersets.

> "One after one, the rascalls rane,
> And from the carre did jump;
> One after one, one after one,
> They felle with heavye thump.

> "Six miles ane houre theye offe did scoure,
> Like shippes on ane stormye ocean,
> Theire garments flappinge in the winde,
> With ane shorte uneasy motion.

The waggonere
complimenteth the
bumbailiffe with ane
Mendoza.[6]

> "Their bodies with their legs did flye,
> Theye fled withe feare and glyffe[5];
> Whye star'st thoue soe?—With one goode blow,
> I felled the bumbailiffe."

PART THIRD

"I feare thee, auncient waggonere,
   I feare thy hornye fiste,
For itte is stained with gooses gore,
   And bailiffe's blood, I wist.

The tailore meeteth
Corporal Feare.

"I fear to gette ane fisticuffe
   From thy leathern knuckles brown",
With that the tailore strove to ryse—
   The waggonere thrusts him down.

"Thou craven, if thou mov'st a limbe,
   I'll give thee cause for feare;"—
And thus went on, that tipsye man,
   The red-billed waggonere.

The bailiffe complaineth
of considerable
derangement of his animal
economye.

"The bumbailiffe so beautiful!
   Declared itte was no joke,
For, to his knowledge, both his legs
   And fifteen ribbes were broke.

Policemen, with their
lanthernes, pursue the
waggonere.

"The lighte was gone, the nighte came on,
   Ane hundrede lantherns sheen,
Glimmerred upon the kinge's highwaye.
   Ane lovelye sighte I ween.

" 'Is it he,' quoth one, 'is this the manne,
   I'll laye the rascalle stiffe;'
With cruel stroke the beak he broke
   Of the harmless bumbailiffe.

steppeth 20 feete in
imitatione of the
Admirable Crichtoun.[7]

"The threatening of the saucye rogue
   No more I coulde abide.
Advancing forthe my goode right legge,
   Three paces and a stride,
I sent my lefte foot dexteriously
   Seven inches thro' his side.

Complaineth of foul play,
and falleth down in ane
trance.

"Up came the seconde from the vanne;
   We had scarcely fought a round,
When someone smote me from behinde,
   And I fell down in a swound:

One acteth the parte of
Job's comfortere.

"And when my head began to clear,
   I heard the yemering crew—
Quoth one, 'this man hath penance done,
   And penance more shall do.' "

PART FOURTH

The waggonere maketh ane
shrewd observation.

"Oh! Freedom is a glorious thing!—
    And, tailore, by the bye,
I'd rather in a halter swing,
    Than in a dungeon lie.

The waggonere tickleth
the spleen of the jailer,
who daunces ane Fandango.[8]

"The jailere came to bringe me foode,
    Forget it will I never,
How he turned uppe the white o' his eye,
    When I stuck him in the liver.

Rejoicethe in the
fragrance of the aire.

"His threade of life was snapt; once more
    I reached the open streete;
The people sung out 'Gardyloo'[9]
    As I ran down the streete.
Methought the blessed air of heaven
    Never smelte so sweete.

Dreadeth Shoan Dhu,[10] the
corporal of the guarde.

"Once more upon the broad highwaye,
    I walked with feare and drede;
And every fifteen steppes I tooke
    I turned about my heade,
For feare the corporal of the guarde
    Might close behind me trede!

"Behold upon the western wave,
    Setteth the broad bright sunne:
So I must onward, as I have
    Full fifteen miles to runne;—

The waggonere taketh
leave of the tailore,

"And should the bailiffes hither come
    To aske whilke waye I've gone,
Tell them I took the othere road,"
    Said hee, and trotted onne.

to whome ane small
accidente happeneth.
Whereupon followeth the
morale very proper to be
had in minde by all
members of the Dilettanti
Society[11] when they come
over the bridge at these
houres. Wherefore let
them take heed and not lay
blame where it lyeth nott.

The tailore rushed into the roome,
    O'erturning three or foure;
Fractured his skulle against the walle,
    And worde spake never more!!

MORALE

Such is the fate of foolish men,
The danger all may see,
Of those, who list to waggoneres,
And keepe bade companye.

22
Anonymous, "Pleasant Walks: A Cockney Pastoral" (1819)

This poem was published in the *Literary Journal* of 20 March 1819 and reprinted in *Keats Reviewed by His Contemporaries,* ed. Lewis M. Schwartz (Metuchen, N.J.: The Scare Crow Press, 1973), 152–55. This anonymous parody ably mocks Leigh Hunt as a vain, self-conscious aesthete whose preoccupation with beauty appears effeminate and whose poetry is marred by irregular measures, chattiness, sentimentality, an excess of 'y' adjectives, and an abundance of tasteless images. The parody also takes aim at Keats who continued to be associated by critics with Hunt long after their friendship had waned. The parodist also manages to suggest that the Cockney poets practice a debased pastoral and that they lack due respect for such predecessors as Pope.

PLEASANT WALKS: A COCKNEY PASTORAL

In the manner of Leigh Hunt, Esq.

" 'Tis well I see the beautiful of things"
—*Myself*[1]

'Tis well I see the beautiful of things,
Else, K—, there thousands are who wouldn't see
Scarce any thing, in this most stupid age,
Worth calling poetry.
Aye, and it's well, too, I do not engage
To any niceties of *measure* in my rhyme,
Because, such beautiful thoughts as I,
At times, let fly,
Would, were they confin'd,
Before and behind
By your silky Pope-like tethers, be,
Like over-fondled children—ill and rickety.[2]

You know, K., I sometimes use your little lines
That drop,
In this short manner, like a rotten prop
From under a bunch of streaky woodbines,
Letting the whole beautiful superstructure
Of my flowers poetical,
Whate'er I cull,
Fall smack adown upon the muddy ground,
Scattering, all o'er every where around,
Their perfumes into air!
Wonder ye?—poo! now none of your scurvy jokes—
I cannot bear to do like other folks.
What! waste my time in *measurings* and *rules?*
Let Byron, Scott, and Campbell—precious fools!
Be, to such things, mere mercenary tools.
'Tis well for *them* to trim old-maidish wings,
But *I* can see—"the beautiful of things."

Listen, (if Nature's loveliness ought bind ye)
Whom kindred wanderings have brought behind me,
And I will map ye out some pleasant walks,
O'er furrowy lands, and green grass banks,
Where Nature hath dropt her wild, unpolish'd showers,
And bought up heaps of wild unpolish'd flowers,
And unfurl'd,
The glorious forest world.
How nice it is to stray all among brooks,
In dark green nooks,
That, hid in their drowsy windings, snore,
In their stuff'd up, rushy, weedy beds,
Dreamingly: how sweet to see
The glib eel, nibbling hastily
The newly-caught worm, held by her neck fast,
Making his summer breakfast:
Or hear the hoarse frog,
In the reedy bog,
Singing the poor worm's elegy.
How sweet to stroll up chequer'd lanes and highways,
(Provided they are bye-ways)
To feel the soft come-o'er-ye-breeze, that dreads,
As 'twere, to touch your hatty heads,
Lest it should ruffle your curly locks,
And fling your beavers
Into the unaccommodating, saucy rivers;—

A sweet breeze, that won't set you in the stocks
Of coughy colds, and still-limb'd catarrhs,
And such-like stay-at-home wars,
As we, in playing life's poor game at loo,[3]
Are subject to!

And O! to ramble all about some heath—
A lovely one—(and not
One like Hampstead's up-and-down pathy spot)
To take, as 'twere a pill, a breath
Of nutmeg-smelling air, cutting, like knife,
From off our lungs the city's filthy soot,
And smoke to boot;
So as to bless,
And raise to liveliness,
With freshening draughts, the nauseous-cup of life;
Especially where the sun-toasted gypsies,
Hang out, all over the branched trees,
Their sunny draperies
Because, in our ramblings, we
Like good company.
Like you this plumage of my muse's wings?
Ah! *I* can see the "beautiful of things."
Do you not like where a dark wood covers,
With her leafy hood all things, and hovers
Above some up-hill and down-dale track,
(The sun in your face, and the wind in your back,)
To go, and see the industrious pig root up
The buried acorn, where the oaks shoot up,
Making itself "green head-dresses,"
And "leafy wildernesses,"
Lovely dryad!—and the "young-eyed" lambs
That walk by their dams,
With their milk-white dresses,
And their light prettinesses,
And feet that go skipity-skip![4]
And the sage cow,
That munches the drooping newly-clad bough,
Hanging its fresh'ning leaves o'er her head
And her back's glossy red;
O! these *are* objects for Castalian springs![5]
But *I,* you know, can see "the beautiful of things!"
Stop!—there's something of the gypsies, O dear,[6]
I forgot to mention: I'll do it here.

Like not ye to sit with them and chat,
And all that,
(Beneath the over-hanging bunchy leaves,)
With that enlighten'd, independent few!
I love it, K—, and so, I think, do you;
For theirs, look ye,
Whom kindred fancies have brought after me,
Is, like the quiv'ring blown-off leaves
On which they tread, real unpolluted liberty,
That never grieves!
And love ye not to walk where flings
Some old wind-mill her muttering flys about?
Or like ye, where some white-wash'd farms peep out,
To hear the clapping of the old hens' wings,
Where the quick wind, round the hay-stack sings
A delicious tune,
In the month of June,
When the sun pops out,
And spreads, all about
The cornfields' yellow dress,
His yellower loveliness?
And, O! to hear the rural ding-a-dings,
Where the sweet little old village church up springs
Its dumpy spire, becrown'd
With tall trees, and ivy-bound!—
Don't, don't I paint the—*"the beautiful of things?"*

Beppo[7]

23
John Hamilton Reynolds, *Peter Bell* (1819)

Published in 1819, this parody by John Hamilton Reynolds is the best known of several parodies of Wordsworth published the same year and one of the best known parodies in the entire period. The *Literary Gazette* of 10 April 1819 had announced the imminent appearance of a new Wordsworth poem, *Peter Bell,* and Reynolds promptly seized the opportunity of composing this parody, some have said in five hours' time, others say in the course of a day. Reynolds luckily borrowed the rhyme scheme from "The Idiot Boy" and (accidentally hitting the rhyme scheme of Wordsworth's poem) thereby manage to suggest even more forcefully the utter predictability of Wordsworth's art.

The parody charges Wordsworth with arrogance and presumptuousness, with having sold his loyalties to conservative political principles (the poem ends with an echo of the Anglican liturgy), and with a distastefully smug tone of moral superiority in both verse and prose. Reynolds suggests that Wordsworth has existed for too long in his own isolated world of fanciful pastoral characters and that these beings, together with the poet's vacuous, homely poetry, belong in the graveyard of contemporary art. The repeated reference to the poet's so-called "labours" may derive from a Wordsworth letter to Reynolds three years earlier after the young poet had sent the elder a copy of *The Naiad* (1816) and solicited poetic advice. Wordsworth responded to Reynolds by telling him that his poem was too long and his "Fancy . . . too luxuriant" [*The Letters of Wiliam and Dorothy Wordsworth, III: The Middle Years, 1812–1820,* part 2, rev. ed. Mary Moorman and Alan G. Hill (Oxford: Clarendon Press, 1970), 345–46]. This letter of 28 November 1816 begins its conclusion with the following observation by Wordsworth: "I am gratified by your favourable opinion of my labours."

Coleridge was initially perplexed by the appearance of Reynolds's poem and wrote to the publishers (Taylor and Hessey). They clarified the matter by sending him a copy of the parody together with an explanatory letter, and Coleridge subsequently confessed: "I laughed heartily at *all the prose,* notes included. . . ." [Quoted and discussed in H. C. Shelley, *Literary By-Paths in*

Old England (Boston: Little, Brown, 1909), 241]. In contrast, Wordsworth's reaction to being parodied is summarized in his sonnet, "On the Detraction Which followed the publication of a certain poem" (1820).

PREFACE

It is now a period of one-and-twenty years since I first wrote some of the most perfect compositions (except certain pieces I have written in my later days) that ever dropped from poetical pen. My heart hath been right and powerful all its years. I never thought an evil or a weak thought in my life. It has been my aim and my achievement to deduce moral thunder from butter-cups, daisies*, celandines, and (as a poet, scarcely inferior to myself, hath it) "such small deer."[2] Out of sparrows' eggs I have hatched great truths, and with sextons' barrows have I wheeled into human hearts, piles of the weight-iest philosophy.[3] I have persevered with a perseverance truly astonishing, in persons of not the most pursy purses;—but to a man of my inveterate morality and independent stamp, (of which Stamps I am proud to be a Distributor)[4] the sneers and scoffings of impious Scotchmen, and the neglect of my poor uninspired countrymen, fall as the dew upon the thorn, (on which plant I have written an immortal stanza or two) and are as fleeting as the spray of the waterfall, (concerning which waterfall I have composed some great lines which the world will not let die.)[5]—Accustomed to mountain solitudes, I can look with a calm and dispassionate eye upon that fiend-like vulture-souled, adder-fanged critic, whom I have not patience to name, and of whose Review I loathe the title, and detest the contents.[6]—Philosophy has taught me to forgive the misguided miscreant, and to speak of him only in terms of patience and pity. I love my venerable Monarch and the prince Regent**. My Ballads are the noblest pieces of verse in the whole range of English poetry: and I take this opportunity of telling the world I am a great man. Mr. Milton was also a great man. Ossian was a blind old fool. Copies of my previous works may be had in any numbers, by application at my publisher.

Of PETER BELL I have only thus much to say: it completes the simple system of natural narrative, which I began so early as 1798. It is written in that pure unlaboured style, which can only be met with among labourers;—and I can safely say, that while its imaginations spring beyond the reach of the most imaginative, its occasional meaning occasionally falls far below the

---

*A favourite flower of mine. It was a favourite with Chaucer, but he did not understand its moral mystery as I do.

"Little Cyclops, with one eye."
Poems by M.E.[1]

**Mr. Vansittart, the great Chancellor of the Exchequer, is a noble character:—and I consecrate this note to that illustrious financier.[7]

meanest capacity. As these are the days of counterfeits*, I am compelled to caution my readers against them, "for such are abroad."[9] However, I here declare this to be the true Peter; this to be the old original Bell. I commit my Ballad confidently to posterity. I love to read my own poetry**: it does my heart good.

W. W

N.B. The novel of Rob Roy is not so good as my poem on the same subject.[11]

PETER BELL

1.
It is the thirty-first of March,[12]
A gusty evening—half past seven;
The moon is shining o'er the larch,
A simple shape—a cock'd-up arch,
Rising bigger than a star,
Though the stars are thick in heaven.

2.
Gentle moon! how canst thou shine
Over graves and over trees,
With as innocent a look
As my own grey eye-ball*** sees,
When I gaze upon a brook?

3.
Od's me! how the moon doth shine:
It doth make a pretty glitter,
Playing in the waterfall;

---

*The white Doe of Rylstone is not of my writing. If it be a serious imitation of my style, I venerate the author; but if it be meant as a joke against me,—I cannot but weep at its remorseless cruelty. I neither know the tragic *Doe*, nor am I acquainted with the tragic *Buck*,—though both these poetical creatures have of late piteously moaned over their buffettings of fortune—. "But let the stricken *deer* go weep," as Bacon philosophically hath it.[8]

**
> "Often have I sigh'd to measure
> By myself a lonely pleasure,
> Sigh'd to think I read a book
> Only read perhaps by me."
> Poems.i.249[10]

***My eyes are grey. Venus is said to have had grey eyes. Grey eyes please me well,—being, as a friend of mine finely saith, "beautiful exceedingly."[13]

As when Lucy Gray doth litter
Her baby-house with bugles small.[14]

4.

Beneath the ever blessed moon
An old man o'er an old grave stares,
You never look'd upon his fellow;
His brow is covered with grey hairs,
As though they were an umbrella.

5.

He hath a noticeable look*,
This old man hath—this grey old man;
He gazes at the graves, and seems,
With over waiting, over wan,
Like Susan Harvey's** pan of creams.

6.

'Tis Peter Bell—'tis Peter Bell,
Who never stirreth in the day;
His hand is wither'd—he is old!
On Sundays he is us'd to pray,
In winter he is very cold***.

7.

I've seen him in the month of August,
At the wheat-field, hour by hour,
Picking ear,—by ear,—by ear,—
Through wind,—and rain,—and sun,—and shower,
From year,—to year,—to year,—to year.

8.

You never saw a wiser man,
He knows his Numeration Table;
He counts the sheep of Harry Gill****,
Every night that he is able,
When the sheep are on the hill.

---

*"A noticeable man with large grey eyes."
           Lyrical Ballads.[15]
**Dairy-maid to Mr. Gill.
***Peter Bell resembleth Harry Gill in this particular: "His teeth they chatter, chatter, chatter," I should have introduced this fact in the text, but that Harry Gill would not rhyme. I reserve this for my blank verse.
****Harry Gill was the original proprietor of Barbara Lewthwaite's pet-lamb; and he also bred Betty Foy's celebrated pony, got originally out of a Night-mare, by a descendant of the great Trojan horse.

9.

Betty Foy—*My* Betty Foy,
Is the aunt of Peter Bell;
And credit me, as I would have you,
Simon Lee was once his nephew,
And his niece is Alice Fell*.

10.

He is rurally related;
Peter Bell hath country cousins,
(He had once a worthy mother)
Bells and Peters by the dozens,
But Peter Bell he hath no brother.

11.

Not a brother owneth he,
Peter Bell he hath no brother;
His mother had no other son,
No other son e'er call'd her mother;
Peter Bell hath brother none.

12.

Hark! the church-yard brook is singing
Its evening song amid the leaves;
And the peering moon doth look
Sweetly on that singing brook,
Round** and sad as though it grieves.

13.

The little leaves on long thin twigs
Tremble with a deep delight,
They do dance a pleasant rout,
Hop and skip and jump about
As though they all were craz'd to night.

14.

Peter Bell doth lift his hand,
That thin hand, which in the light
Looketh like to oiled paper;

---

*Mr. Sheridan, in his sweet poem of the Critic, supplies one of his heroes with as singularly clustering a relationship.[16]
**I have here changed the shape of the moon, not from any poetical heedlessness, or human perversity, but because man is fond of change, and in this I have studied the metaphysical varieties of our being.

Paper oiled,—oily bright,—
And held up to a waxen taper.

15.

The hand of Peter Bell is busy,
Under the pent-house[17] of his hairs;
His eye is like a solemn sermon;
The little flea severely fares,
'Tis a sad day for the vermin.

16.

He is thinking of the Bible—
Peter Bell is old and blest;
He doth pray and scratch away,
He doth scratch, and bitten, pray
To *flee* away, and be at rest.

17.

At home his foster child is cradled—
Four brown bugs are feeding there*;
Catch as many, sister Ann,
Catch as many as you can* *[19]
And yet the little insects spare.

18.

Why should blessed insects die?
The flea doth skip o'er Betty Foy,
Like a little living thing:
Though it hath not fin or wing,
Hath it not a moral joy?

19.

I the poet of the mountain,
Of the waterfall and fell,
I the mighty mental medlar,[20]
I the lonely lyric pedlar,
I the Jove of Alice Fell,

---

*I have a similar idea in my Poem on finding a Bird's Nest:—

"Look! *five* blue eggs are gleaming there."[18]

But the numbers are different, so I trust no one will differ with the numbers.
**I have also given these lines before; but in thus printing them again, I neither tarnish their value, not injure their novelty.

20.

I the Recluse—a gentle man*;
A gentle man—a simple creature,
Who would not hurt, God shield the thing,
The merest, meanest May-bug's wing,
Am tender in my tender nature.

21.

I do doat on my dear wife,
On the linnet, on the worm,
I can see sweet written salads
Growing in the Lyric Ballads,
And always find them green and firm.

22.

Peter Bell is laughing now,
Like a dead man making faces;
Never saw I smile so old,
On face so wrinkled and so cold,
Since the Idiot Boy's grimaces.

23.

He is thinking of the moors,
Where I saw him in his breeches;
Ragged though they were, a pair
Fit for a grey old man to wear;
Saw him poking,—gathering leeches.**

24.

And gather'd leeches are to him,
To Peter Bell, like gather'd flowers;
They do yield him such delight,
As roses poach'd from porch at night,
Or pluck'd from oratoric*** bowers.

---

*See my Sonnet to Sleep:—

"I surely not a man ungently made."[21]

**See my story of the Leech-gatherer, the finest poem in the world,—except this.
***"Ah!" said the Briar, "Blame me not."
Waterfall and Eglantine.
Also, —
"The Oak a Giant and a Sage, /
His neighbour thus address'd."[22]

25.

How that busy smile doth hurry
O'er the cheek of Peter Bell;
He is surely in a flurry,
Hurry skurry—hurry skurry,
Such delight I may not tell.

26.

His stick is made of wilding wood,
His hat was formerly of felt,
His duffel cloak of wool is made,[23]
His stockings are from stock in trade,
His belly's belted with a belt.

27.

His father was a bellman once,
His mother was a beldame old;
They kept a shop at Keswick Town,
Close by the Bell, (beyond the Crown),
And pins and peppermint they sold.

28.

He is stooping now about
O'er the grave-stones one and two;
The clock is now a striking eight,
Four more hours and 'twill be late,
And Peter Bell hath much to do.

29.

O'er the grave-stones three and four,
Peter stoopeth old and wise;
He counteth with a wizard glee
The graves of all his family,
While the hooting owlet cries.

30.

Peter Bell, he readeth ably,
All his letters he can tell;
Roman W,—Roman S,[24]
In a minute he can guess,
Without the aid of Dr. Bell.[25]

31.

Peter keeps a gentle pony,
But the pony is not here;

Susan who is very tall*,
And very sick and sad withal,
Rides it slowly far and near.

32.

Hark! the voice of Peter Bell,
And the belfry bell is knelling;
It soundeth drowsily and dead,
As though a corse th' "Excursion" read;
Or Martha Ray her tale was telling.

33.

Do listen unto Peter Bell,
While your eyes with tears do glisten:
Silence! his old eyes do read
All, on which the boys do tread
When holidays do come—Do listen!

34.

The ancient Marinere lieth here,
Never to rise, although he pray'd,—
But all men, all, must have their fallings;
And, like the Fear of Mr. Collins**
He died "of sounds himself had made."27

35.

Dead mad mother,—Martha Ray,
Old Matthew too, and Betty Foy,
Lack-a-daisy! here's a rout full;
Simon Lee whose age was doubtful***,
Simon even the Fates destroy.

---

*"*Long Susan* lay deep lost in thought."
        The Idiot Boy
**See what I have said of this man in my excellent supplementary *Preface*.27
***I cannot resist quoting the following lines, to shew how I preserve my system from youth to age. As Simon was, so he is. And one and twenty years have scarcely altered (except by death) that cheerful and cherry-cheeked Old Huntsman. This is the truth of Poetry.

> "In the sweet shire of Cardigan,
>   Not far from pleasant Ivor-hall;
> An old man dwells—a little man—
>   I've heard he once was tall;
> Of years he has upon his back,
>   No doubt, a burthen weighty;
> He says he is threescore and ten,
>   But others say he's eighty."

These lines were written in the summer of 1798, and I bestowed great labour upon them.28

36.

Harry Gill is gone to rest,
Goody Blake is food for maggot;
They lie sweetly side by side,
Beautiful as when they died;
Never more shall she pick faggot.

37.

Still he reads, and still the moon
On the church-yard's mounds doth shine;
The brook is still demurely singing,
Again the belfry bell is ringing,
'Tis nine o'clock, six, seven, eight, nine!

38.

Patient Peter pores and proses
On, from simple grave to grave;
Here marks the children snatch'd to heaven.
None left to blunder "we are seven;"—
Even Andrew Jones* no power could save.

39.

What a Sexton's work** is here,
Lord! the Idiot Boy is gone;
And Barbara Lewthwaite's fate the same,
And cold as mutton is her lamb;
And Alice Fell is bone by bone.[30]

40.

Stephen Hill is dead and buried,
Reginald Shore is crumbling—crumbling,
Giles Fleming—Susan Gale—alas![31]
Death playeth in the church-yard grass
His human nine-pins—tumbling—tumbling.

41.

But Peter liveth well and wisely,
For still he makes old Death look silly,
Like those sage ducks of Mrs. Bond,

---

*Andrew Jones was a very singular old man.—See my Poem,
        "I hate that Andrew Jones—he'll breed," &c.[29]
**"Let thy wheelbarrow alone, &c." See my poem to a Sexton.

Who, not of killing over fond,
Turn a deaf ear to dilly, dilly.[32]

42.
And tears are thick with Peter Bell,
Yet still he sees one blessed tomb;
Tow'rds it he creeps with spectacles,
And bending on his leather knees
He reads the *Lake*iest Poet's doom.

43.
The letters printed are by fate,
The death they say was suicide;
He reads—"Here lieth W.W.
Who never more will trouble you, trouble you:"
The old man smokes who 'tis that died.[33]

44.
Go home, go home—old Man, go home;
Peter, lay thee down at night,
Thou art happy, Peter Bell,
Say thy prayers for Alice Fell,
Thou hast seen a blessed sight.

45.
He quits that moon-light yard of skulls,
And still he feels right glad, and smiles
With moral joy at that old tomb;
Peter's cheek recalls its bloom,
And as he creepeth by the tiles,
He mutters ever—"W.W.
Never more will trouble you, trouble you."

Here Endeth The Ballad of Peter Bell

SUPPLEMENTARY ESSAY

I BEG leave, once for all, to refer the Reader to my previous Poems, for illustrations of the names of the characters, and the severe simplicity contained in this affecting Ballad. I purpose, in the course of a few years, to write laborious lives of all the old people who enjoy sinecures in the text, or are pensioned off in the notes, of my Poetry. The Cumberland Beggar is dead. He could not crawl out of the way of a fierce and fatal post chaise, and so fell a sacrifice to the Philosophy of Nature. I shall commence the work in heavy quarto, like the Excursion, with that "old, old Man," (as the too joyous Spenser saith.)[34]—If ever I should be surprised into a second edition of my whole Poems, I shall write an extra-supplementary Essay on the principles of simple Poetry. I now conclude, with merely extracting (from my own works) the following eloquent and just passage (my Prose is extremely good) contained in the two volumes lately published, and not yet wholly disposed of:—

"A sketch of my own notion of the Constitution of Fame has been given; and as far as concerns myself, I have cause to be satisfied,—The love, the admiration, the indifference, the slight, the aversion, and even the contempt, with which these Poems have been received, knowing, as I do, the source within my own mind, from which they have proceeded; and the labour and pains which, when labour and pains appeared needful, have been bestowed upon them,—must all, if I think consistently, be received as pledges and tokens, bearing the same general impression though widely different in value;—they are all proofs that for the present time I have not laboured in vain; and afford assurances, more or less authentic, that the products of my industry will endure."

Lyrical Ballads, vol. 1.368

24
D. M. Moir, "Christabel, Part Third" (1819)

This parody was published in *Blackwood*'s 5 (June 1819): 286–91. In his review of " 'Christabel'; 'Kubla Khan, A Vision'; 'The Pains of Sleep' " (1816) in *The Examiner* (2 June 1816), Hazlitt complained that Coleridge had omitted from the published version of Christabel certain lines that help the reader identify Geraldine as a witch (Hazlitt knew the poem in manuscript). The resulting obscurity, Hazlitt states, involves both "dishonesty" and "affectation" on the author's part. He also observed that "There is something disgusting at the bottom of his subject, which is but ill glossed over by a veil of Della Cruscan sentiment and fine writing. . . ." ["Mr. Coleridge's Christabel" rpt. in *The Complete Works of William Hazlitt,* ed. P. P. Howe (London: Dent, 1930–1934), vol. 19.32, 34]. The suggestion that there was perhaps something obscene about the poem was picked up by reviewers and parodists alike. One result was J. Duncombe's vulgar parody *Christabess* (1816); another was the tamer, yet more effective "Christabel, Part Third." Its author was first assumed to be William Maginn, whose usual pen name was Morgan Odoherty, but others have since suggested David Macbeth Moir [for example, see the discussion in Arthur H. Nethercot, *The Road to Tryermaine* (1939; rpt. New York: Russell & Russell, 1962), 35–36; or *The Fraserian Papers of the late William Maginn,* ed. R. Skelton Mackenzie (New York: Redfield, 1857), 5. xxxi].

The parody is hardly a narrative, because essentially nothing happens beyond a dog moaning, a clock telling the hour, and a cow lowing. Rather it is intended to be a revelation of the author's state of mind which is (from the parodist's point of view and in the confession of the opening line) "mad." Part of Coleridge's irrationality is the idea that sleep and dreams can reveal truth. The parodist also satirizes his stance as a priest of the esoteric and as a poet of atmospheric effects. Coleridge's attachment to archaisms, numbers, rhetorical devices such as repetition and questions, and Gothic accoutrements (including the fashionable vampirism) are all exaggerated effectively in verse of highly irregular meter. At the end Christabel, pregnant with an illegitimate child, goes off to get drunk and the parodist implies that the reader may very well have to do the same.

LETTER FROM MR. ODOHERTY, ENCLOSING THE THIRD PART OF CHRISTABEL

My Dear Editor,

I need not say how much obliged to you I am for your kind recommendation of my poems to the notice of the public. Such liberality does you credit, and "I verily believe promotes your sale." Nothing can more decidedly prove the degraded state of our periodical criticism, than this fact, that not one review, but your own incomparable one, has so much as alluded to the existence of my poetry. What Mr. Gifford[1] can mean by such neglect of a man of at least equal genius with himself, I leave him to explain to the world, when and how he can—as for Mr. Jeffrey, the well-known difference of our political sentiments sufficiently accounts for his silence.[2] The Monthly Reviewers hate me because I am not a Unitarian, nor dissenter of any kind, and the British Critic looks down upon me because I am neither an Oxonian nor a Cantab. Of the notice of "Maga" I am not very ambitious, having been long tired of old women, and I do trust should my muse ever be buried, Colburn will not suffer that vampyre, Dr. Polidori, to suck her blood.[3] To you, therefore, my sweet editor, my undivided gratitude is due, and it shall be expressed in a way most conducive to your interests. You must have observed with regret, that many of our best living poets leave their greatest works in an unfinished state. It is my intention to finish these works for them, for I never could, at any period of my life, bear to think that any thing should be left but half done. I have accordingly finished Mr. Coleridge's Christabel, and what was a still more laborious task, Mr. Wordsworth's Excursion. If Lord Byron does not publish Don Juan speedily, I will, for I have written him, and he is very restless in my desk. I have likewise ready for the press, a thick octavo of "Plays on the Passions," which, if Miss Joanna Baillie[4] does not bestir herself, shall infallibly be out before the fall of the leaf. In short, I wish, like the celebrated Macvey Napier, Esq., to become a SUPPLEMENTARY GENIUS, and while he undertakes to render complete all the rest of human knowledge, permit me to do the same service to poetry.[5] I have sent you the third part of Christabel, per my friend the "Bagman,"[6] who, so far from being a fool, as one of your critics averred, is next to our friend D, one of the sharpest blades in Glasgow. You will receive a bale of the Excursion by the waggon very soon.—Yours, for ever and a day.

                                                              Morgan Odoherty

Archie Cameron's College, Glasgow.[7]
    4th June.

                              Christabel

                  The Introduction to Part the Third
Listen! ye know that I am mad,

And ye will listen!—wizard dreams
    Were with me!—all is true that seems!—
From dreams alone can truth be had—
In dreams divinest lore is taught,
For the eye, no more distraught,
Rests most calmly, and the ear,
    Of sound unconscious, may apply
Its attributes unknown, to hear
    The music of philosophy!
Thus am I wisest in my sleep,
For thoughts and things, which day-light brings,
    Come to the spirit sad and single,
But verse and prose, and joys and woes
    Inextricably mingle,
When the hushed frame is silent in repose!
Twilight and moonlight, mist and storm,
Black night, and fire-eyed hurricane,
And crested lightning, and the snows
That mock the sunbeams, and the rain
Which bounds on earth with big drops warm,
All are round me while I spell
The legend of sweet Christabel!

CHRISTABEL, PART THIRD

Nine moons have waxed, and the tenth, in its wane,
Sees Christabel struggle in unknown pain!
—For many moons was her eye less bright,
For many moons was her vest more tight,
And her cheek was pale, save when, with a start,
The life blood came from the panting heart,
And fluttering, o'er that thin fair face
Past with a rapid nameless pace,
And at moments a big tear filled the eye,
And at moments a short and smothered sigh
Swelled her breast with sudden strain,
Breathed half in grief, and half in pain,
For her's are pangs, on the rack that wind
The outward frame and the inward mind.
—And when at night she did visit the oak,
She wore the Baron's scarlet cloak,
(That cloak which happy to hear and to tell
Was lined with the fur of the leopard well,)
And as she wandered down the dell

None said 'twas the lady Christabel.—
Some thought 'twas a weird and ugsome elf,[8]
Some deemed 'twas the sick old Baron himself,
Who wandered beneath the snowy lift
To count his beads in solemn shrift—
(For his shape below was wide to see
All bloated with the hydropsie.)
Oh! had her old father the secret known,
He had stood as stark as the statue of stone
That stands so silent, and white, and tall,
At the upper end of his banquet hall!

    Am I asleep or am I awake?
In very truth I oft mistake,
As the stories of old come over my brain,
And I build in spirit the mystic strain;—
Ah! would to the virgin that I were asleep!
But I must wake, and I must weep!
    Sweet Christabel, it is not well
That a lady, pure as the sunless snow
That lies so soft on the mountain's brow,
That a maiden of sinless chastity
In childbirth pangs should be doomed to die,
Or live with a name of sorrow and shame,
And hear the words of blemish and blame!
—For the world that smiles at the guilt of man,
Places woman beneath its ban;
Alas, that scandal thus should wreak
Its vengeance on the warm and weak,
That the arrows of the cold and dull
Should wound the breast of the beautiful!

    Of the things that be did we know but half,
Many, and many would weep, who laugh!
Tears would darken many an eye,
Or that deeper grief, (when its orb is dry,
When it cannot dare the eye of day),
O'er the clouded heart would sway,
Till it crumbled like desert dust away!
But here we meet with grief and grudge,
And they who cannot know us, judge!
Thus, souls on whom good angels smile,
Are scoffed at in our world of guile—
Let this, Ladie, thy comfort be;

Man knows not us, good angels know
The things that pass in the world below;
And scarce, methinks, it seems unjust,
That the world should view thee with mistrust,
For who that saw that child of thine
Pale Christabel, who could divine
That its sire was the Ladie Geraldine?

But in I rush, with too swift a gale,
Into the ocean of my tale!
Not yet young Christabel, I ween,
Of her babe hath lighter been.
—'Tis the month of the snow and the blast,
And the days of Christmas mirth are past,
When the oak-roots heaped on the hearth blazed bright,
Casting a broad and dusky light
On the shadowy forms of the warriors old,
Who stared from the wall, most grim to behold—
On shields where the spider his tapestry weaves,
On the holly boughs and the ivy leaves,
The few green glories that still remain
To mock the storm and welcome the rain,
Brighter and livelier mid tempest and shower,
Like a hero in the battle hour!—
Brave emblems o'er the winter hearth,
They cheered our fathers' hours of mirth!—

Twelve solar months complete and clear
The magic circle of the year!
Each (the ancient riddle saith)
Children, two times thirty, hath!
Three times ten are fair and white,
Three times ten are black as night,
Three times ten hath Hecate,
Three times ten the God of day;
Thus spoke the old hierophant
(I saw her big breast swelling pant)
What time, I dreamed, in ghostly wise
Of Eleusinian mysteries,[9]
For I am the hierarch
Of the mystical and dark—
And now, if rightly I do spell
Of the lady Christabel,
She hates the three times ten so white,

And sickens in their searching light,
And woe is hers—alas! alack!
She hates the three times ten so black—
As a mastiff bitch doth bark,
I hear her moaning in the dark!—

'Tis the month of January,
Why lovely maiden, light and airy,
While the moon can scarcely glow,
Thro' the plumes of falling snow,
While the moss upon the bark
Is withered all, and damp, and dark,
While cold above the stars in doubt
Look dull, and scarcely will stay out,
While the snow is heavy on beechen bower
And hides its name-sake, the snow-drop flower,
Why walk forth thus mysteriously?
Dear girl, I ask thee seriously.
Thy cheek is pale, thy locks are wild—
Ah, think, how big thou art with child!—
Tho' the baron's red cloak thro' the land hath no fellow,
Thou should'st not thus venture without an umbrella!

Dost thou wander to the field of graves
Where the elder its spectral branches waves?
And will thy hurried footsteps halt
Where thy mother sleeps in the silent vault?
Where the stranger pauses long to explore
The emblems quaint of heraldic lore,
Where tho' the lines are tarnished and dim,
Thy mother's features stare gaunt and grim,
And grinning skull, and transverse bone,
And the names of warriors dead and gone
Mark Sir Leoline's burial stone;
Thither go not, or I deem almost
That thou wilt frighten thy mother's ghost!

Or wilt thou wend to the huge oak-tree,
And, kneeling down upon thy knee,
Number the beads of thy rosary?
Nine beads of gold and a tenth of pearl,
And a prayer with each, my lovely girl,
Nine, and one, shalt thou record,
Nine to the virgin and one to the Lord!

The pearls are ten times one to behold,
And ten times nine are the beads of gold;
Methinks 'tis hard of the friar to ask
On a night like this so weary a task!

'Tis pleasant—'tis pleasant, in summer time,
In the green wood to spell the storied rhyme,
When the light winds above 'mong the light leaves are singing,
And the song of the birds thro' your heart is ringing,
'Tis pleasant—'tis pleasant, when happily humming
To the flowers below the blythe bee is coming!—
When the rivulet coy, and ashamed to be seen,
Is heard where it hides 'mong the grass-blades green,
When the light of the moon and each sweet starry islet
Gives a charm more divine to the long summer twilight,
When the breeze o'er the blossomy hawthorn comes cheerful,
'Tis pleasant—with heart—ah, how happy!—tho' fearful,
With heaven-beaming eyes, where tears come, while smiles glisten
To the lover's low vows in the silence to listen!
   'Tis pleasant too, on a fine spring day
   (A month before the month of May)
   To pray for a lover that's far away!
   But, Christabel, I cannot see
   The powerful cause that sways with thee
   Thus, with a face all waxen white,
   To wander forth on a winter night.

The snow hath ceased, dear lady meek,
But the light is chill and bleak!—
And clouds are passing swift away
Below the moon so old and gray—
The crescent moon, like a bark of pearl,
That lies so calm on the billowy whirl;—
   Rapidly—rapidly
      With the blast,
   Clouds of ebony
      Wander fast,
And one the maiden hath fixed her eyes on,
Hath pass'd o'er the moon, and is near the horizon!
   Ah Christabel, I dread it, I dread it,
      That the clouds of shame
   Will darken and gather
      O'er the maiden's name,
   Who chances unwedded
   To give birth to a child, and knows not its father!

One—Two—Three—Four—Five—Six—Seven—Eight—Nine—Ten—
Eleven!—
Tempest or calm—moonshine or shower,
The castle clock still tolls the hour,
And the cock awakens, and echoes the sound,
And is answered by the owls around—
And at every measured tone
You may hear the old baron grunt and groan;
'Tis a thing of wonder, and fright, and fear,
The mastiff-bitch's moans to hear—
And the aged cow in her stall that stands
And is milked each morning by female hands
(That the baron's breakfast of milk and bread
May be brought betimes to the old man's bed
Who often gives, while he is dressing,
His Christabel a father's blessing)
That aged cow, as each stroke sounds slow,
Answers it with a plaintive low!
And the baron old, who is ill at rest,
Curses the favourite cat for a pest—
For let him pray, or let him weep,
She mews thro— all the hours of sleep—
Till morning comes with its pleasant beams,
And the cat is at rest, and the baron dreams!

    Let it rain, however fast,
    Rest from rain will come at last,
    And the blaze that strongest flashes
    Sinks at last, and ends in ashes!
    But sorrow from the human heart
    And mists of care will they depart?
    I know not, and cannot tell,
    Saith the lady Christabel—
    But I feel my bosom swell!

In my spirit I behold
A lady—call her firm, not bold—
    Standing lonely by the burn
—Strange feelings thro' her breast and brain
Shoot with a sense of madness and pain.
    Ah Christabel return, return,
Let me not call on thee in vain!
Think, lady dear, if thou art drowned
That thy body will be found,

What anguish will thy spirit feel,
When it must to all reveal
What the spell binds thee to conceal!
How the baron's heart will knock 'gainst his chest
When the stake is driven into thy breast,
When thy body to dust shall be carelessly flung,
And over the dead no dirge be sung,
No friend in mourning vesture dight,
No lykewake sad[10]—no tapered rite!—

Return, return thy home to bless,
　　Daughter of good Sir Leoline;
In that chamber a recess
　　Known to no other eye than thine,
　　Contains the powerful wild-flower wine
That often cheer'd thy mother's heart,
Lady, lovely as thou art
Return, and ere thou dost undress
And lie down in thy nakedness
Repair to thy secret and favourite haunt
And drink the wine as thou art wont!
Hard to uncork and bright to decant.

My merry girl—she drinks—she drinks,
　　Faster she drinks and faster,
My brain reels round as I see her whirl,
She hath turned on her heel with a sudden twirl;—
　　Wine, wine is a cure for every disaster,
For when sorrow wets the eye
Yet the heart within is dry,
Sweet maid upon the bed she sinks—
May her dreams be light, and her rest be deep!
Good angels guard her in her sleep!

25

John Wilson Lockhart, from *Benjamin the Waggoner* (1819)

In place of John Hamilton Reynolds, John Wilson Lockhart has been suggested by Jack Gohn as the possible author of this lengthy parody ["Who wrote 'Benjamin the Waggoner'? An Inquiry," *Wordsworth Circle* 8 (1977): 69–74], but no certain identification of the writer has been made. The parody appeared in 1819 after Wordsworth's poem *(The Waggoner)* was advertised in the *London Literary Gazette* for 22 May. As Gohn explains, the pattern initiated by the earlier *Peter Bell* parody was followed. Reynolds used the form of "The Idiot Boy" in his *Peter Bell;* the author of *Benjamin the Waggoner* uses *Peter Bell* as his parodic model.

Benjamin the Waggoner is itself encumbered by a long introduction and a long section of notes. The selection presented here should indicate the primary objects of attack: the parodist's view of Wordsworth's egotism, of his concern with moralizing about, and describing closely, essentially trivial events and objects, and of his digressive and unexpected shifts of subject which render his narrative dangerously incoherent. An asterisk indicates a note by the parodist at the end of the text.

BENJAMIN
THE
WAGGONER

> O Reader! had you in your mind
>   Such store as silent thought can bring,
> O gentle Reader, you would find
>   A Tale in every thing.
>
> What more I have to say is short,
>   I hope you'll kindly take it;
> It is no Tale; but should you think,
>   Perhaps a Tale you'll make it.

Simon Lee[1]

194

Another tale in verse I'll sing,
Another after that I'll drag on;
Now tell me, BESS, I prithee tell,
Shall it be of the Potter Bell,
Or Benjamin who drives the Waggon?   (5)

The Potter Peter Bell you choose,
The Potter who had scarce a rag on;
We'll leave, then, till another time,
That merry tale, in serious rhyme,
Of Benjamin who drives the Waggon.   (10)

Where left we off, my pretty BESS?
My pretty BESS, where left we off?
Peter Bell was on his knees,
And there we'll leave him, if you please,
Though the place is rather rough.   (15)

I'm seated on my chair so easy,
I'm seated on my easy chair,
'Tis a chair I'm sure would please ye,
The covering is of good horse hair;
Only it sometimes tears one's breeches!   (20)

But nothing is without a moral—
Breeches decay, and so do we—
We decay—we who wear 'em—
They decay—the chairs that tear'em—
Now you may a moral see.   (25)
• • • • • • •
'Tis sweet to sit at river side;
'Tis sweet to sit close by the brink;
To throw a stone in—see bubbles up,
Running like inverted cup;
And then the stone, to see it sink.   (65)

And as the little stone is sinking,
To see the fishes turn aside,*
How they do wag their little tails!
And move their little fins like sails,
And skim along in swimming pride.   (70)

O, that men would learn to mark
The little—little—little beauties,
Which I do see in field or hill,

In river, or in where I will;
O, that men would mind their duties!   (75)

To gaze upon a fallow field;
To see a worm turned up with harrow;
To look upon a blade of grass—*
A duck—a goose—a pig—an ass—
Manure that's wheel'd in a wheelbarrow.   (80)

To mark the little things of Nature;
To see the little naughty flies
Making their loves upon the window,
Never thinking that they sin do;
For me—I always shut my eyes.   (85)

I'd have this world a moral world—
How better far't would be than riches;
Naughty flies I always loathe;
My hens in petticoats I'd clothe,
I keep my cocks in breeches.   (90)

The reader knows I love "Excursions,"
To right or left, as it may hap,
If he should like a road that's straight,
For me he better had not wait,
* * * * * * nap.*——   (95)

O, the Moon it is a lovely Moon!
And she is a lovely Moon to me;
Just sixteen times, in parts before,
I've used her name—sixteen—no more—
Count them, and then you'll see.*   (100)

I love the words which run so easy—
Boat and float—and you and do—
Ass and grass make pretty rhyme;
Boat, I've used it many a time,
And ass—times just forty-two.*——   (105)
• • • • • • •
There's something in a glass of ale,
There's something in good sugar-candy;[2]
And when a man is getting old,
And when the weather's getting cold,
There's something in a glass of brandy.   (220)

There's something in Gambado's horse,[3]
There's something in a velocipede;
That's the horse I'd like the best,
On it your book may easy rest,
And he who runs may read.

I wish it had a pair of wings,
And like the Arab, a little peg;
I'd instant lay across my leg,
And rising up to other spheres,[4]
No more should critics vex my ears.   (230)

And now I *have* a velocipede,
And now I have the little peg,
And now I've fix'd upon its wings,
And bidding adieu to earthly things,
I lift—and lay across my leg.   (235)

Now I rise, and away we go,
My little hobby-horse and me;
And now I'm near the planet Venus,
Nothing seems to be between us,
Not a bit of earth I see.   (240)

Away we go—my horse and I,
Kicking and prancing midst the stars;
To leave the earth is quite refreshing,
I did not think it such a blessing,
And now I'm near the planet Mars.   (245)

At every world I touch, I ask
If they have poets dwelling there?
They answer yes—and not a few,
Poets of all sorts—critics too,
Enough of both, and some to spare.—   (250)

Now I pounce o'er Gallia's land,
Now I see the land of posies;
Now swift I turn the little peg,
And ere you've time to shew a leg,
I'm happy in the land of Noses.   (255)

Happy, happy, happy people!
Happy, ignorant of law;

Honest, kind, and mild, and good—
Only they stole a piece of wood,
And would have stol'n all they saw.—   (260)

There is the music of the spheres—
There is the music of the woods—
There's music in the ripling streams
When glancing in the moonlight beams;
There's music in the roaring floods.   (265)

There's music in a poultry yard;
There's music in a grunting hog—
An owl—a duck—an ass—a goose—
A dozen little pigs let loose;
There's music in a croaking frog.   (270)

How sweet to listen to the sounds
Of rustic noise, and health, and labour:
How better far than hirdy-girdy,
Play'd in town by beggar sturdy;
How sweet the dance, the pipe and tabor.——   (275)

Now Peter he oft thought of marrying,
Marrying as you and I might marry;
So popp'd the question to the widow,
Who answered ——————.   (280)

Happy was Peter and the widow,
(And happy was the widow's ass),
Though children she had at first but seven;
They had four more—in all eleven.—   (285)

But what is this which o'er our heads,
And round about is nearer gaining?
There is a rustling 'mong the leaves,
The vicar's wife scream'd loudly, Thieves!
But soon we found,—'twas only raining.   (290)

Says I, let's leave our rustic seat,
And let us leave the large stone table,
And come into my little study;
And by a fire both warm and ruddy,
I'll tell you tales as long's I'm able.   (295)

So up we rose, in number nine,
And off we set, some slow, some fast,
With little Bess, and all the rest;
They were first in who ran the best,
But, as I limp'd, I was the last.   (300)

The Vicar slept—the Vicar snored—
And starting, cried, "Another flagon!
"Where am I?—Oh!"—and quite confus'd,
He said he had been much amus'd
With Benjamin who drives the Waggon.   (305)

To hear the Vicar I was wroth,
Was full of fury as a dragon;
And then, methought, twas much the same;
The Tale's the thing, whate'er the name,
Whether of Bell, or Ben the Waggon—er.   (310)

Juliet says, a Rose by any
Other name, would smell as sweet;
So, whether my Tale is Peter Bell,
Or Benjamin—'tis just as well;
It will not fail * * *   (315)

NOTES

NOTE V (1.67)

"To see the fishes turn aside."

I believe Mr. Hogg (I wish he would change name) had a similar line in his 'Queen's Wake,'

'The little fishes turn'd aside;'

but he cannot deem an apology requisite from me, for I only speak of *my own little fishes.* See my Note to the Daisy.

NOTE VIII (1.78)

"To look upon a blade of grass."

It is truly surprising how intelligent every flower and animal is, which dwells around me.—Animal did I say? Ah, my dear little donkies! little do you deserve the epithet; less, far less, than those bipeds who sip punch, and sip tea, and sit in parlours "all silent and all damn'd."[5]

> "Could father Adam open his eyes,
> And see this sight beneath the skies,
> He's wish to close them again—"
>   *Myself.*

It is supposed that father Adam has been blind ever since his fall—for 'twas a great fall. This is a new, but a fine idea.

The reader must long since have observed how my little daises, my pansies, my cuckoos, my butterflies, and my donkies talk to me,—dear little creatures!—'I love you all.' As a worthy representative in the city said to his constituents—'I love you all.' N.B. 'Twas "Love's Labour Lost" with him.

Let the reader judge for himself what a delightful society we form in the country.

> 'Much *converse* do I find in thee.'
>   *To a Butterfly.*
> 'I heard a stock-dove sing or say.'
>   *Moods of my own Mind.*
> 'This the cuckoo cannot *tell*.'
> 'The pansy at my feet
> 'Doth the same line *repeat*.'
> 'Flowers *laugh* before thee on their beds.'
> 'Thou a flower of *wiser wits*.'
> 'Sweet *silent* creature!'
>   *To a Daisy.*
> 'But then he is a horse *that thinks*.'
>   Idiot Boy.
> 'Yet for his life he *cannot* tell
> What he has got upon his back.'
>   *Ditto.*
> 'Shame on you! cried my little boat.'
>   *Peter Bell.*

NOTE XI (1.95)

——"NAP"——

The reader must be satisfied with this word at present—and as it is not the first time I have bestowed it upon him, I hope he will not complain—use is everything—

> 'Do not complain of what you now endure,
> Custom will give you ease, or time a cure.'

This is consoling enough.—N.B. I often write the last word of my line first—for, come what may before it, the last words must rhyme, and I find them the most difficult.

NOTE XIII (1.100)

"Count them, and then you'll see."

If the reader will take this trouble, I believe he will find it correct.

NOTE XIV (1.105)

And ass—times just fortytwo."

See note above.[6]

BY THE SAME AUTHOR,

AND SHORTLY TO BE HAD OF ALL THE BOOKSELLERS

MY MOTHER'S DUCKLINGS,

AN AFFECTING TALE IN VERSE, AND FOUNDED UPON FACT.

In the above will be related the melancholy death of a couple of little ducklings, caused by keeping their tails too long up in the air while feeding in a pool of water, whereby they were most lamentably drowned.

It is purposed to extend the above work to six volumes, in which will be pourtrayed the distinguishing propensities, instincts, habits, and language of those interesting amphibious fowls; the whole to conclude with a most melancholy ditty, which the Old Duck sung or said, on learning the fate of her offspring—taken in shorthand, as she was uttering it, by a Cuckoo.

Early next spring, the same author hopes to indulge the Public (to whom he is much indebted for their great display of patience, and takes this mode of acknowledging it) with his long-promised long Poem of 'The Cat and the Fiddle.'

> ' 'Tis a pretty baby treat,
> Nor I deem for me unmeet;
> Here, for neither babe or me,
> Other play-mates can I see.'   *Myself.*[7]

It will be endeavoured to compress the above Poem into as little space as possible, and the Author hopes to do it in two volumes quarto.

A few volumes royal quarto, with numerous illustrative engravings, will be struck off for Subscribers only.

The subsequent Parts of Peter Bell will be brought forward as speedily as possible, which will contain the particulars of Peter's Life, from his Marriage with the Widow to that period in which he joins the Company he saw in the parlour,

> 'All silent and all damn'd.'

The other favourite works of the Author—'The Silent Cricket,' 'The Thinking Pony,' 'The Speaking Cuckoo,' 'The Whispering Leaf,' 'The Laughing Flowers,' and 'The Scornful Boat,' to be had of all the Booksellers in Christendom, having been translated into all the modern Languages.

26
John Hamilton Reynolds, *The Dead Asses* (1819)

Published in July or August 1819, *The Dead Asses* is another of the four lengthy parodies of Wordsworth written in 1819. There is no evidence that John Hamilton Reynolds authored this parody in addition to his earlier *Peter Bell* but, as George Marsh observed ["The *Peter Bell* Parodies of 1819," *Modern Philology* 40 (1943): 274], *The Dead Asses* is much more likely the work of Reynolds than *Benjamin the Waggoner,* often attributed to Reynolds.

Although *The Dead Asses* captures something of the arrogant tone in many of Wordsworth's critical statements (in addition to mocking his hypersensitivity and self-absorption), Coleridge also is a target of the parodist. Both *Christabel* and "To a Young Ass" furnish evidence with which the parodist satirizes Coleridge's excessive sympathy with all living things. The parodist turns Coleridge into someone asinine but, in the concluding lines, Wordsworth becomes the ass itself.

PREFACE

The poem of the DEAD ASSES, which is here offered to the public, hath been dictated by impulses of no ordinary nature; its design and execution afford me ample satisfaction, and I know that the reader is prepared to value the work before him as highly as I do.

Towards the elucidation of my preface, I may inform him that the following Poem, (which shall be lucid* and speak for itself,) records the premature death of two steady and industrious *Donkies.*

Very few themes, indeed, could so powerfully call forth the genuine rhymes of a simple and "unlettered Muse"[1] as that which I have chosen; and I rejoice that I have chosen it, for it seems to be one peculiarly adapted to my powers. *My* pen alone could do justice to the narration of an incident in itself as severely pathetic and sympathetically simple.

---

*To be lucid is a quality usually wanting in my verses, according to the critics and my enemies.

And here I shall be pardoned for enlarging on the merits of that truly picturesque and sedate animal, the Ass.

As a poet and as a man, I stand deeply indebted to him, and, with candour, I acknowledge that he hath contributed to render my verses immortal.

I need not say that the Ass is frequently conspicuous in my writings: it hath been my delight to pourtray him, and for the most part, as becomes his humble nature, humbly and naturally, in the back ground. *Here,* however, he comes nearer to the view: like Morland, I have brought him to the front of my canvass, where, although a dead Ass, he shall live as long as the Literature of my country shall endure, and perhaps not longer.[2]

But in thus speaking of myself and Morland, I cannot help adverting to the great superiority which Poetry maintains over Painting.

For as the painter's hand is the sole agent of the painter's soul, as soon as that hand is motionless, so soon does the agency cease; and *then* the fame of the artist depends on the physical force, or resisting power of his colours and his canvass.

Not so the Bard.—A thousand agencies (and each susceptible of continual renovation) are at work to cherish his beloved effusions. They may exist either in the memory of his friends, orally delivered from age to age, or in their manuscripts, or in the types of the printer; which last is the most permanent agency, and that which I, who possess a confidence in my own impulses,* have ever employed.[3]

Need I any longer insist on the simple beauty of my performances, in preference to the tinsel and fustian of more ornamental writers?[4] I would fain form the taste of the age, for I am the child and the poet of nature. I am moreover, a critical judge of my own compositions, and I pronounce them all to be, without exception or qualification, the most perfect things in our language; but in the *Dead Asses* may be traced the perfection of my art.——Surely *it* is imperishable.

The critics will declare it to be a not imperishable production; but their criticism will fall like the lash on a Dead Ass, harmless and unheeded. They will inveigh against the irregularity in my metre and the inequality of my stanzas: but those who are more conversant with me will discern that, as my mind hath been variously agitated, my verses have been variously methodized, and will discover an inexpressible charm in this sweet and natural variety.

After these warm, but faithful commendations, the reader will be anxious to pass on from a Preface, which I have extended to a considerable length, under the conviction that my prose is equal in excellence to my poetry.

He will find subjoined an extract from one of the daily journals, (some of which daily journals I am in the daily habit of perusing). It simply relates a

---

*I have said full as much in my preface to PETER BELL, and I repeat it to persuade the world, if possible, that the faith I repose in my own impulses is a well-founded one.

simple fact, and it will acquaint him that my Poem has for its argument, (as a Writer, scarcely my inferior, hath it,) "an ower true tale."[5]

W. W.

"On Friday last two Donkies were found in Joiner's Wood, tied with chaise-reins to the shrubs, completely starved to death, having devoured every edible substance within reach.

"It is supposed that they were stolen, and fixed by some villains, who have been since apprehended, and consequently left the wretched animals to perish thus miserably."

New Times, Wednesday, July 21, 1819.

THE
DEAD ASSES

1.

There are things that make me weep,
Things that happen every day,
But the thoughtless and the gay
Of such, alas! no reckoning keep:
I cannot smile as others can,—
For at this moment while I'm speaking,
Death and danger sure are wreaking
Vengeance on the race of man;

2.

On the race of man and beast,
Fishes, birds, and insects too;
To feel and pity is the least
That a gentle man can do.

3.

But I do more than others do,—
My soul is kind.—A heartless lout
Has got no heart; but when I see
A bug, I let him run about;
(Rats and mice may run about.)
I could never kill a flea.[6]

4.

I could never break a head,
I at school would never fight,
The others jeered; and cousin Ned
Told me I was very right.

5.

And I would never learn to fish,
Although 'twas uncle Isaac's wish,[7]
Except sometimes a bit of bread
I fastened to a bit of thread;
(Little fishes should be fed.)
Wormless hook and hookless string
Make it quite another thing;
Then no worms, no fishes bleed.
I am very kind indeed.

6.

Though Donkies are not good for bait,
Yet it is of them I sing;
Donkies twain that perish'd late,
Fastened by a tether string,
Fastened by a fastening:
Fastened that they might not go.
They were starved to death, I ween.
Backwards, forwards, to and fro,
Donkies that were very lean.

7.

The village clock had stricken three.
My watch was only half-past two,
But village watches can't agree,
Village children seldom do;
(Time was nearly right by me,)
The village clocks were not agreed,*
But all of them were rather late,
Peter Bell's was half past eight,—
His was very wrong indeed.

---

*It may be worth while to quote a case which came under my own notice, where a country clock was probably wrong,—

" 'Tis scarcely afternoon,—
The Minster-clock has just struck two,
And yonder is the moon."
Lucy Gray.—Lyrical Ballads, vol. ii, p. 72, Edit. 1805.

8.

Stop and listen!—One! two! three!
Village chimes come cheerily
Sailing up the summer gale,
Chimes from village churches sail
Upon the light breeze merrily.

9.

The wind is going rustle! rustle!
It is shaking something near:
The wind is in a mighty bustle—
And is it in a bush?
From the day that I was born
I've been very quick to hear,
Whether it sweepeth a field of corn,
Or shaketh but a rush.

10.

I am not so quick to see,—*8
What is this that clatters so?
Am I near some gallows-tree,
Where murderer dangleth to and fro?
I have got no optic-glasses—
Shield us well!—I may not stay,—
And what is this that strikes my shoe?
But lo! against my feet there lay
A pair of lifeless Asses!

11.

Lifeless Asses, by the rood!
Fixed, and stark, and thin, and grey,
As if they had been dead a day,—
Like the children in the wood,
As innocent and young as they.

12.

A bird hath lately left the bodies,
A bird hath flown to yonder tree;
Is it a robin gone to bring
Some leaves to make their covering?

---

*This passage will call to the reader's mind the opening of the 3d Book of "Paradise Lost," where as great a bard makes a similar allusion.

Is it a robin that I see
Rising now upon the wing?

13.

Was it a robin that I saw?
Was it a pigeon or a daw?
I could tell if I heard it sing.—
I have heard, and well I know
That it is nought but carrion crow.

14.

Are not these two dark grey bags
That the wind is whistling in?
They are like old clothesmen's rags,
Grey great coats that once have been.

15.

All the flesh is fairly gone,
For it is dried in noon-day sun;
But the ribs are very plain,
I can count them one by one,
Let me count them once again.[9]

16.

Now let me count the other side,
And *there* the flesh is fairly dried,
But where the Donkey's flesh should be,
Between each rib, so well I hide
My little finger, none can see
That I have got a little finger;
And yet I have, though none can tell,
I can count them very well.

17.

And what is this that makes the ground
Free from grass, where grass has been?
It is closely shaven round,
Like a closely shaven chin.[10]

18.

All the grass is gone away,
Nought but dust and mould appear;
The very roots are cropped away
In a circle round them here.

19.
Is it a rope that binds them so?
For they are fastened to the ground;
And they have wandered to and fro,
As far as this would let them go,
Round and round, round and round.

20.
But why did they not gnaw their tether,
Strung to the ground and strung together?
Though the tether were of chain,
I would have gnawed with might and main;
Though the tether were of leather,
I would have bitten it through and through;
Though the rope were very tough,
I would have bitten it quite in two;
But Donkies have not sense enough.

21.
They have not had a decent death.—
There was a blind horse in a mill,
Round and round, and round and round.
I stop and pity him, but still
His keeper keeps his old horse bound.

22.
But when the day's declining sun
Shews that his daily work is done,
He hath a manger and a stall,
And wholesome food to feed withal;
And when at last he fails in breath,
He hath a sweet and decent death.

23.
Now I have viewed this Donkey well,
And by his cropped ears I can tell
That very often I have seen
His figure pacing on the green,
Which skirts the road that leads you down
From Ambleside to Keswick-town.*

---

*At no great distance from this very spot, rises GREAT HOW, a single and conspicuous hill, and the scene of an elegant ballad called "Rural Architecture."

Lyrical Ballads, 2. 163.

24.

His back was once so stout and strong,
Meet to support a heavy load;
Meat he bore from butcher's shelf,
And now he's meat for crows himself;
Meet to support a heavy load,
Blithe but silent on the road,
Mute but cheerfully along.

25.

And see he hath a chafed side,
Grazed with the panniers here and there,
Which sheweth like a trunk of hair,
Just where the cordage hath been tied.

26.

An old grey trunk that may have been
Some two or three score years, not more,
Upon the road, from inn to inn,
From house to house, from door to door.

27.

Ah me! how dull his eye doth seem,
Half-shut beneath his honest brow,
'Twas once so bright and fresh, I ween,
As some brown pebble, richly seen
Transparent through a trembling stream,——
But more like all-spice now.[11]

28.

I wish that little Bess were here,[12]
For she has got a necklace made
Of spicy beads, both great and small,
And she would say, as I have said,
That his brown eye is like them all.[13]

29.

How calm and solemn doth he look:
And yet he is not like the Fly

That died of cold in Germany,*
No friend or brother being nigh,
He is not like that little fly.

30.

But I am one who dearly love
The children of the field and grove,**
Both flies and donkies, every one,
And joy to think he was not left,
Of brother and of friend bereft,[14]
To perish all alone.

31.

The other hath more perfect form—
They have not cropped his ear away,
But though it resteth perfect here,
The pivot of his skull is gone,
And now his long and dark left ear
Hath nothing left to roll upon.***

---

*See lines written in Germany on one of the coldest days of the century.—Lyrical Ballads, 2.146.

Of a freezing Fly.

"See his spindles sink under him, foot, leg, and thigh,
His eye-sight and hearing are lost;
Between life and death his blood freezes and thaws,
And his two pretty pinions of blue dusky gauze
Are glued to his sides by the frost.

No brother, no friend has he near him—while I"—

But in the contrast between myself and the Fly the balance is so greatly in my own favour, that it would seem like egotism to continue the stanza.
**"Here's a fly, a disconsolate creature, perhaps,
A child of the field or the grove."
See the Poem just quoted.
***I have here pursued a beautiful allusion contained in my own PETER BELL.
The few, who have not had the happiness to peruse that simple effusion, will pardon me for inserting, in this place, the passage in question.

"All, all is silent; rocks and woods
All still and silent—far and near;
Only the Ass, with motion dull,
Upon the pivot of his skull
Turns round his long left ear.

Thought Peter, what can mean all this?
Some ugly witchcraft must be here.
Once more the Ass, with motion dull,
Upon the pivot of his skull
Turn'd round his long left ear."

Peter Bell, p. 32.

32.

And see he has a little eye,
For carrion crow hath taken some;
Now I know that it waiteth nigh,
And scanneth me full carefully,
For when I go, the crow will come.

33.

But let me think before I go,
A goodly thought concerning me,
Which is, that if it might be so,
I, "the Recluse," henceforth would be,
Like a dead Ass in face and mien,
So calm, and gentle, and serene.*

---

*A similar allusion, and one as striking may be found in a "Fragment" in the Lyrical Ballads.

"For calm and gentle is his mien,
Like a *dead boy* he is serene."

27
Percy Bysshe Shelley, *Peter Bell The Third* (1819)

Shelley's parody of Wordsworth's *Peter Bell* was written in late October 1819. He had read Hunt's review earlier in the year (*Examiner,* 2 May 1819), but it is "very likely" [so argues Jack Gohn, "Did Shelley Know Wordsworth's 'Peter Bell'?" *Keats-Shelley Journal* 28 (1979): 24] that he began the parody only after reading the poem itself. Shelley's attitude toward Wordsworth was highly ambivalent, as a letter to Peacock the previous year (25 July 1818) shows:

> What a beastly and pitiful wretch that Wordsworth! That such a man should be a poet! I can compare him with no one but Simonides, that flatterer of Sicilian tyrants, and at the same time the most natural and tender of lyric poets.
> [*Letters of Percy Bysshe Shelley,* ed. F. L. Jones (Oxford: Clarendon Press, 1964), 2. 26]

Shelley's parody especially condemns Wordsworth's Methodist view of humanity as hopelessly depraved and, above all, the social consequence of such a view, political passivity. The Peter Bell in Shelley's poem is a figure of the poet Wordsworth—an artist who has prostituted his creativity to win the establishment's favor. The poem remained unpublished until Mary Shelley somewhat apologetically introduced it into the second edition of Shelley's *Poetical Works* (1839), from which the text here used is taken. An earlier parody of Wordsworth by Shelley is discussed by Mary A. Quinn ["Shelley's 'Verses on the Celandine': An Elegaic Parody of Wordsworth's Early Lyrics," *Keats-Shelley Journal* 36 (1987): 88–109].

Peter Bell The Third
By Miching Mallecho, Esq.

Is it a party in a parlour,
Crammed just as they on earth
    were crammed,
Some sipping punch—
    some sipping tea,
But, as you by their faces see,
All silent, and all——damned!
    Peter Bell, by W. Wordsworth.[1]

Ophelia: What means this, my lord?
Hamlet: Marry, this is Miching Mallecho; it means mischief.

Shakespeare.[2]

DEDICATION
TO THOMAS BROWN, ESQ., THE YOUNGER, H.F.[3]

Dear Tom—Allow me to request you to introduce Mr. Peter Bell to the respectable family of the Fudges; although he may fall short of those very considerable personages in the more active properties which characterize the Rat and the Apostate,[4] I suspect that even you, their historian, will confess that he surpasses them in the more peculiarly legitimate qualification of intolerable dulness.

You know Mr. Examiner Hunt[5]; well—it was he who presented me to two of the Mr. Bells. My intimacy with the younger Mr. Bell naturally sprung from this introduction to his brothers. And in presenting him to you, I have the satisfaction of being able to assure you that he is considerably the dullest of the three.

There is this particular advantage in an acquaintance with any one of the Peter Bells, that if you know one Peter Bell, you know three Peter Bells; they are not one, but three; not three but one. An awful mystery, which after having caused torrents of blood, and having been hymned by groans enough to deafen the music of the spheres, is at length illustrated to the satisfaction of all parties in the theological world, by the nature of Mr. Peter Bell.

Peter is a polyhedric Peter, or a Peter with many sides. He changes colours like a cameleon, and his coat like a snake. He is a Proteus of a Peter. He was at first sublime, pathetic, impressive, profound; then dull; then prosy and dull; and now dull—O, so very dull! it is an ultra-legitimate dulness.

You will perceive that it is not necessary to consider Hell and the Devil as supernatural machinery. The whole scene of my epic is in "this world which is"—So Peter informed us before his conversion to *White Obi*—[6]

—The world of all of us, *and where
We find our happiness, or not at all.*[7]

Let me observe that I have spent six or seven days in composing this sublime piece; the orb of my moonlike genius[8] has made the fourth part of its revolution round the dull earth which you inhabit, driving you mad, while it has retained its calmness and its splendour, and I have been fitting this its last phase "to occupy a permanent station in the literature of my country."[9]

Your works, indeed, dear Tom, sell better; but mine are far superior. The public is no judge; posterity sets all to rights.

Allow me to observe that so much has been written of Peter Bell, that the present history can be considered only, like the Iliad, as a continuation of

that series of cyclic poems, which have already been candidates for bestow-
ing immortality upon, at the same time that they receive it from, his character
and adventures. In this point of view, I have violated no rule of syntax in
beginning my composition with a conjunction; the full stop which closes the
poem continued by me, being, like the full stops at the end of the Iliad and
Odyssey, a full stop of a very qualified import.

Hoping that the immortality which you have given to the Fudges, you will
receive from them; and in the firm expectation, that when London shall be an
habitation of bitterns, when St. Paul's and Westminster Abbey shall stand,
shapeless and nameless ruins, in the midst of an unpeopled marsh; when the
piers of Waterloo-Bridge shall become the nuclei of islets of reeds and osiers,
and cast the jagged shadows of their broken arches on the solitary stream,
some transatlantic commentator will be weighing in the scales of some new
and now unimagined system of criticism, the respective merits of the Bells
and the Fudges, and their historians; I remain, dear Tom, Yours sincerely

Miching Mallecho.

December 1, 1819.

P.S.—Pray excuse the date of place; so soon as the profits of this publication come in, I mean to hire lodgings in a more respectable street.[10]

PROLOGUE

Peter Bells, one, two and three,
O'er the wide world wandering be.—
First, the antenatal Peter,[11]
Wrapt in weeds of the same metre,
The so long predestined raiment
Clothed, in which to walk his way meant
The second Peter; whose ambition
Is to link the proposition,
As the mean of two extremes—
(This was learnt from Aldric's themes)[12]
Shielding from the guilt of schism
The orthodoxal syllogism;
The First Peter—he who was
Like the shadow in the glass
Of the second, yet unripe,
His substantial antitype.—
Then came Peter Bell the Second,
Who henceforward must be reckoned
The body of a double soul,
And that portion of the whole

Without which the rest would seem
Ends of a disjointed dream.—
And the Third is he who has
O'er the grave been forced to pass
To the other side, which is,—
Go and try else,—just like this.

Peter Bell the First was Peter
Smugger, milder, softer, neater,
Like the soul before it is
Born from *that* world into *this.*
The next Peter Bell was he,
Predevote, like you and me,
To good or evil as may come;
His was the severer doom,—
For he was an evil Cotter,
And a polygamic Potter.
And the last is Peter Bell,
Damned since our first Parents fell,
Damned eternally to Hell—
Surely he deserves it well!

PART THE FIRST

DEATH

And Peter Bell, when he had been
  With fresh-imported Hell-fire warmed,
Grew serious—from his dress and mien
'Twas very plainly to be seen
  Peter was quite reformed.

His eyes turned up, his mouth turned down;
  His accent caught a nasal twang;
He oiled his hair, there might be heard
The grace of God in every word
  Which Peter said or sang.   10

But Peter now grew old, and had
  An ill no doctor could unravel;
His torments almost drove him mad;—
Some said it was a fever bad—
  Some swore it was the gravel.[13]

His holy friends then came about,
    And with long preaching and persuasion,
Convinced the patient that, without
The smallest shadow of a doubt,
    He was predestined to damnation.   20

They said—"Thy name is Peter Bell;
    Thy skin is of a brimstone hue;
Alive or dead—aye, sick or well—
The one God made to rhyme with hell;
    The other, I think, rhymes with you."

Then Peter set up such a yell!—
    The nurse, who with some water gruel
Was climbing up the stairs, as well
As her old legs could climb them—fell,
    And broke them both—the fall was cruel.   30

The Parson from the casement leapt
    Into the lake of Windermere—
And many an eel—though no adept
In God's right reason for it—kept
    Gnawing his kidneys half a year.

And all the rest rushed through the door,
    And tumbled over one another,
And broke their skulls.—Upon the floor
Meanwhile sat Peter Bell, and swore,
    And cursed his father and his mother;   40

And raved of God, and sin, and death,
    Blaspheming like an infidel;
And said, that with his clenched teeth,
He'd seize the earth from underneath,
    And drag it with him down to Hell.

As he was speaking came a spasm,
    And wrenched his gnashing teeth asunder;
Like one who sees a strange phantasm
He lay,—there was a silent chasm
    Between his upper jaw and under.   50

And yellow death lay on his face;
    And a fixed smile that was not human

Told, as I understand the case,
That he was gone to the wrong place:—
    I heard all this from the old woman.

Then there came down from Langdale Pike
    A cloud, with lightning, wind and hail;
It swept over the mountains like
An ocean,—and I heard it strike
    The woods and crags of Grasmere vale.   60

And I saw the black storm come
    Nearer, minute after minute;
Its thunder made the cataracts dumb[14];
With hiss, and clash, and hollow hum,
    It neared as if the Devil was in it.

The Devil *was* in it:—he had bought
    Peter for half-a-crown; and when
The storm which bore him vanished, nought
That in the house that storm had caught
    Was ever seen again.   70

The gaping neighbours came next day—
    They found all vanished from the shore:
The Bible, whence he used to pray,
Half scorched under a hen-coop lay;
    Smashed glass—and nothing more!

PART THE SECOND

THE DEVIL

The Devil, I safely can aver,
    Has neither hoof, nor tail, or sting;
Nor is he, as some sages swear,
A spirit, neither here nor there,
    In nothing—yet in everything.   80

He is—what we are; for sometimes
    The Devil is a gentleman;
At others a bard bartering rhymes
For sack[15]; a statesman spinning crimes;
    A swindler, living as he can;

A thief, who cometh in the night,
  With whole boots and net pantaloons,
Like some one whom it were not right
To mention;—or the luckless wight
  From whom he steals nine silver spoons.   90

But in this case he did appear
  Like a slop-merchant from Wapping,[16]
And with smug face, and eye severe,
On every side did perk and peer
  Till he saw Peter dead or napping.

He had on an upper Benjamin[17]
  (For he was of the driving schism)
In the which he wrapt his skin
From the storm he travelled in,
  For fear of rheumatism.   100

He called the ghost out of the corse;—
  It was exceedingly like Peter,—
Only its voice was hollow and hoarse—
It had a queerish look of course—
  Its dress too was a little neater.

The Devil knew not his name and lot,
  Peter knew not that he was Bell:
Each had an upper stream of thought,
Which made all seem as it was not;
  Fitting itself to all things well.[18]   110

Peter thought he had parents dear,
  Brothers, sisters, cousins, cronies,
In the fens of Lincolnshire;
He perhaps had found them there
  Had he gone and boldly shown his

Solemn phiz[19] in his own village;
  Where he thought oft when a boy
He'd clomb the orchard walls to pillage
The produce of his neighbour's tillage,
  With marvellous pride and joy.   120

And the Devil thought he had,
  'Mid the misery and confusion

Of an unjust war, just made
A fortune by the gainful trade
Of giving soldiers rations bad—
    The world is full of strange delusion.

That he had a mansion planned
    In a square like Grosvenor-square,
That he was aping fashion, and
That he now came to Westmorland   130
    To see what was romantic there.

And all this, though quite ideal,—
    Ready at a breath to vanish,—
Was a state not more unreal
Than the peace he could not feel,
    Or the care he could not banish.

After a little conversation,
    The Devil told Peter, if he chose,
He'd bring him to the world of fashion
By giving him a situation   140
    In his own service—and new clothes.

And Peter bowed, quite pleased and proud,
    And after waiting some few days
For a new livery—dirty yellow
Turned up with black—the wretched fellow
    Was bowled to Hell in the Devil's chaise.

PART THE THIRD

HELL

Hell is a city much like London—
    A populous and a smoky city;
There are all sorts of people undone,
And there is little or no fun done;   150
    Small justice shown, and still less pity.

There is a Castles,[20] and a Canning,
    A Cobbett, and a Castlereagh;
All sorts of caitiff corpses planning,

All sorts of cozening for trepanning[21]
    Corpses less corrupt than they.

There is a ***,[22] who has lost
    His wits, or sold them, none knows which;
He walks about a double ghost,
And though as thin as Fraud almost—   160
    Ever grows more grim and rich.

There is a Chancery Court; a King;
    A manufacturing mob; a set
Of thieves who by themselves are sent
Similar thieves to represent;
    An Army; and a public debt.

Which last is a scheme of paper money,
    And means—being interpreted—
Bees, "keep your wax—give us the honey,
And we will plant, while skies are sunny,   170
    Flowers, which in winter serve instead."

There is great talk of revolution—
    And a great chance of despotism—
German soldiers—camps—confusion—
Tumults—lotteries—rage—delusion—
    Gin—suicide—and methodism.

Taxes too, on wine and bread,
    And meat, and beer, and tea, and cheese,
From which those patriots pure are fed,
Who gorge before they reel to bed   180
    The tenfold essence of all these.

There are mincing women, mewing,
    (Like cats, who *amant miserè,*)[23]
Of their own virtue, and pursuing
Their gentler sisters to that ruin,
    Without which—what were chastity?

Lawyers—judges—old hobnobbers
    Are there—bailiffs—chancellors—
Bishops—great and little robbers—
Rhymesters—pamphleteers—stock-jobbers—   190
    Men of glory in the wars,—

Things whose trade is, over ladies
   To lean, and flirt, and stare, and simper,
Till all that is divine in woman
Grows cruel, courteous, smooth, inhuman,
   Crucified 'twixt a smile and whimper.

Thrusting, toiling, wailing, moiling,
   Frowning, preaching—such a riot!
Each with never-ceasing labour,
Whilst he thinks he cheats his neighbour,   200
   Cheating his own heart of quiet.

And all these meet at levees;—
   Dinners convivial and political;—
Suppers of epic poets;—teas,
Where small talk dies in agonies;—
   Breakfasts professional and critical;

Lunches and snacks so aldermanic
   That one would furnish forth ten dinners,
Where reigns a Cretan-tongued[24] panic,
Lest news Russ, Dutch, or Alemannic   210
   Should make some losers, and some winners

At conversazioni—balls—
   Conventicles—and drawing-rooms—
Courts of law—committees—calls
Of a morning—clubs—book-stalls—
   Churches—masquerades—and tombs.

And this is Hell—and in this smother
   All are damnable and damned;
Each one damning, damns the other;
They are damned by one another,   220
   By none other are they damned.

'Tis a lie to say, "God damns!"
   Where was Heaven's Attorney General
When they first gave out such flams?[25]
Let there be an end of shams,
   They are mines of poisonous mineral.

Statesmen damn themselves to be
   Cursed; and lawyers damn their souls

To the auction of a fee;
Churchmen damn themselves to see   230
   God's sweet love in burning coals.

The rich are damned, beyond all cure,
   To taunt, and starve, and trample on
The weak and wretched; and the poor
Damn their broken hearts to endure
   Stripe on stripe, with groan on groan.

Sometimes the poor are damned indeed
   To take,—not means for being blessed,—
But Cobbett's snuff, revenge; that weed
From which the worms that it doth feed   240
   Squeeze less than they before possessed.

And some few, like we know who,
   Damned—but God alone knows why—
To believe their minds are given
To make this ugly Hell a Heaven;
   In which faith they live and die.

Thus, as in a town, plague-stricken,
   Each man be he sound or no
Must indifferently sicken;
As when day begins to thicken,   250
   None knows a pigeon from a crow,—

So good and bad, sane and mad,
   The oppressor and the oppressed;
Those who weep to see what others
Smile to inflict upon their brothers;
   Lovers, haters, worst and best;

All are damned—they breathe an air,
   Thick, infected, joy-dispelling:
Each pursues what seems most fair,
Mining like moles, through mind, and there   260
Scoop palace-caverns vast, where Care
   In throned state is ever dwelling.[26]

PART THE FOURTH

SIN

Lo, Peter in Hell's Grosvenor-square,
  A footman in the devil's service!
And the misjudging world would swear
That every man in service there
  To virtue would prefer vice.

But Peter, though now damned, was not
  What Peter was before damnation.
Men oftentimes prepare a lot   270
Which ere it finds them, is not what
  Suits with their genuine station.

All things that Peter saw and felt
  Had a peculiar aspect to him;
And when they came within the belt
Of his own nature, seemed to melt,
  Like cloud to cloud, into him.

And so the outward world uniting
  To that within him, he became
Considerably uninviting   280
To those, who meditation slighting,
  Were moulded in a different frame.

And he scorned them, and they scorned him;
  And he scorned all they did; and they
Did all that men of their own trim
Are wont to do to please their whim,
  Drinking, lying, swearing, play.

Such were his fellow-servants; thus
  His virtue, like our own, was built
Too much on that indignant fuss   290
Hypocrite Pride stirs up in us
  To bully out another's guilt.

He had a mind which was somehow
  At once circumference and centre
Of all he might or feel or know;

Nothing went ever out, although
    Something did ever enter.

He had as much imagination
    As a pint-pot;—he never could
Fancy another situation
From which to dart his contemplation,
    Than that wherein he stood.

Yet his was individual mind,
    And new created all he saw
In a new manner, and refined
Those new creations, and combined
    Them, by a master-spirit's law.

Thus—though unimaginative—
    An apprehension clear, intense,
Of his mind's work, had made alive
The things it wrought on; I believe
    Wakening a sort of thought in sense.

But from the first 'twas Peter's drift
    To be a kind of moral eunuch,
He touched the hem of nature's shift,
Felt faint—and never dared uplift
    The closest, all-concealing tunic.

She laughed the while, with an arch smile,
    And kissed him with a sister's kiss,
And said—"My best Diogenes,
I love you well—but, if you please,
    Tempt not again my deepest bliss.

" 'Tis you are cold—for I, not coy,
    Yield love for love, frank, warm and true;
And Burns, a Scottish peasant boy—
His errors prove it—knew my joy
    More, learned friend, than you.

"Bocca baciata non perde ventura
    Anzi rinnuova come fa la luna:—[27]
So thought Boccaccio, whose sweet words might cure a
Male prude, like you, from what you now endure, a
    Low-tide in soul, like a stagnant laguna."

300

310

320

330

Then Peter rubbed his eyes severe,
    And smoothed his spacious forehead down,
With his broad palm;—'twixt love and fear,
He looked, as he no doubt felt, queer,
    And in his dream sate down.

The Devil was no uncommon creature;
    A leaden-witten thief—just huddled
Out of the dross and scum of nature;   340
A toad-like lump of limb and feature,
    With mind, and heart, and fancy muddled.

He was that heavy, dull, cold thing,
    The spirit of evil well may be:
A drone too base to have a sting;
Who gluts, and grimes his lazy wing,
    And calls lust, luxury.

Now he was quite the kind of wight
    Round whom collect, at a fixed aera,
Venison, turtle, hock, and claret,—   350
Good cheer—and those who come to share it—
    And best East Indian madeira!

It was his fancy to invite
    Men of science, wit, and learning,
Who came to lend each other light;
He proudly thought that his gold's might
    Had set those spirits burning.

And men of learning, science, wit,
    Considered him as you and I
Think of some rotten tree, and sit   360
Lounging and dining under it,
    Exposed to the wide sky.

And all the while, with loose fat smile,
    The willing wretch sat winking there,
    Believing 'twas his power that made
That jovial scene—and that all paid
    Homage to his unnoticed chair.

Though to be sure this place was Hell;
    He was the Devil—and all they—

What though the claret circled well,   370
And wit, like ocean, rose and fell?—
Were damned eternally.

PART THE FIFTH

GRACE

Among the guests who often staid
　　Till the Devil's petits-soupers,
A man there came,[28] fair as a maid,
And Peter noted what he said,
　　Standing behind his master's chair.

He was a mighty poet—and
　　A subtle-souled psychologist;
All things he seemed to understand,   380
Of old or new—of sea or land—
　　But his own mind—which was a mist.

This was a man who might have turned
　　Hell into Heaven—and so in gladness
A Heaven unto himself have earned;
But he in shadows undiscerned[29]
　　Trusted,—and damned himself to madness.

He spoke of poetry, and how
　　"Divine it was—a light—a love—
A spirit which like wind doth blow   390
As it listeth, to and fro;
　　A dew rained down from God above.

"A power which comes and goes like dream,
　　And which none can ever trace—
Heaven's light on earth—Truth's brightest beam."
And when he ceased there lay the gleam
　　Of those words upon his face.

Now Peter, when he heard such talk,
　　Would, heedless of a broken pate,
Stand like a man asleep, or baulk   400
Some wishing guest of knife or fork,
　　Or drop and break his master's plate.

At night he oft would start and wake
  Like a lover, and began
In a wild measure songs to make
On moor, and glen, and rocky lake,
  And on the heart of man.[30]

And on the universal sky—
  And the wide earth's bosom green,—
And the sweet, strange mystery   410
Of what beyond these things may lie,
  And yet remain unseen.

For in his thought he visited
  The spots in which, ere dead and damned,
He his wayward life had led;
Yet knew not whence the thoughts were fed,
  Which thus his fancy crammed.

And these obscure remembrances
  Stirred such harmony in Peter,
That whensoever he should please,   420
He could speak of rocks and trees
  In poetic metre.

For though it was without a sense
  Of memory, yet he remembered well
Many a ditch and quick-set fence;
Of lakes he had intelligence,
  He knew something of heath, and fell.

He had also dim recollections
  Of pedlars tramping on their rounds;
Milk-pans and pails; and odd collections   430
Of saws, and proverbs; and reflections
  Old parsons make in burying-grounds.

But Peter's verse was clear, and came
  Announcing from the frozen hearth
Of a cold age, that none might tame
The soul of that diviner flame
  It augured to the Earth.

Like gentle rains, on the dry plains,
  Making that green which late was grey,

Or like the sudden moon, that stains   440
Some gloomy chamber's window panes
    With a broad light like day.

For language was in Peter's hand,
    Like clay, while he was yet a potter;
And he made songs for all the land,
Sweet both to feel and understand,
    As pipkins late to mountain Cotter.[31]

And Mr.——, the bookseller,[32]
    Gave twenty pounds for some;—then scorning
A footman's yellow coat to wear,   450
Peter, too proud of heart, I fear,
    Instantly gave the Devil warning.

Whereat the Devil took offence,
    And swore in his soul a great oath then,
"That for his damned impertinence,
He'd bring him to a proper sense
    Of what was due to gentlemen!"——

PART THE SIXTH

DAMNATION

"O that mine enemy had written
    A book!"—cried Job:[33]—a fearful curse:
If to the Arab, as the Briton,   460
'Twas galling to be critic-bitten:—
    The Devil to Peter wished no worse.

When Peter's next new book found vent,
    The Devil to all the first Reviews
A copy of it slily sent
With five-pound note as compliment,
    And this short notice—"Pray abuse."

Then *seriatim,* month and quarter,
    Appeared such mad tirades.—One said—
"Peter seduced Mrs. Foy's daughter,   470
Then drowned the mother in Ullswater,
    The last thing as he went to bed."

Another—"Let him shave his head!
 Where's Dr. Willis?[34]—Or is he joking?
What does the rascal mean or hope,
No longer imitating Pope,
 In that barbarian Shakespeare poking?"

One more, "Is incest not enough?
 And must there be adultery too?
Grace after meat? Miscreant and Liar!   480
Thief! Blackguard! Scoundrel! Fool! Hell-fire
 Is twenty times too good for you.

"By that last book of yours WE think
 You've double damned yourself to scorn;
We warned you whilst yet on the brink
You stood. From your black name will shrink
 The babe that is unborn."

All these Reviews the Devil made
 Up in a parcel, which he had
Safely to Peter's house conveyed.   490
For carriage, ten-pence Peter paid—
 Untied them—read them—went half mad.

"What!"—cried he, "this is my reward
 For nights of thought, and days of toil?
Do poets, but to be abhorred
By men of whom they never heard,
 Consume their spirits' oil?

"What have I done to them?—and who
 Is Mrs. Foy? 'Tis very cruel
To speak of me and Emma so!   500
Adultery! God defend me! Oh!
 I've half a mind to fight a duel.

"Or," cried he, a grave look collecting,
 "Is it my genius, like the moon,
Sets those who stand her face inspecting,
That face within their brain reflecting,
 Like a crazed bell-chime, out of tune?"

For Peter did not know the town,
 But thought, as country readers do,

For half a guinea or a crown,   510
He bought oblivion or renown
   From God's own voice in a review.

All Peter did on this occasion
   Was, writing some sad stuff in prose.
It is a dangerous invasion
When poets criticise; their station
   Is to delight, not pose.

The Devil then sent to Leipsic fair,
   For Born's translation of Kant's book[35];
A world of words, tail foremost, where   520
Right—wrong—false—true—and foul—and fair,
   As in a lottery-wheel are shook.

Five thousand crammed octavo pages
   Of German psychologics,—he
Who has *furor verborum*[36] assuages
Thereon, deserves just seven months' wages
   More than will e'er be due to me.

I looked on them nine several days,
   And then I saw that they were bad;
A friend, too, spoke in their dispraise,—   530
He never read them;—with amaze
   I found Sir William Drummond[37] had.

When the book came, the Devil sent
   It to P. Verbovale, Esquire,[38]
With a brief note of compliment,
By that night's Carlisle mail. It went,
   And set his soul on fire.

Fire, which *ex luce praebens fumum*,[39]
   Made him beyond the bottom see
Of truth's clear well—when I and you Ma'am,   540
Go, as we shall do, *subter humum*,[40]
   We may know more than he.

Now Peter ran to seed in soul
   Into a walking paradox;
For he was neither part nor whole,

Nor good, nor bad—nor knave nor fool,
   Among the woods and rocks

Furious he rode, where late he ran,
   Lashing and spurring his tame hobby;
Turned to a formal puritan,   550
A solemn and unsexual man,—
   He half believed *White Obi*.

This steed in vision he would ride,
   High trotting over nine-inch bridges,
With Flibbertigibbet,[41] imp of pride,
Mocking and mowing by his side—
A mad-brained goblin for a guide—
   Over corn-fields, gates, and hedges.

After these ghastly rides, he came
   Home to his heart, and found from thence   560
Much stolen of its accustomed flame;
His thoughts grew weak, drowsy, and lame
   Of their intelligence.

To Peter's view, all seemed one hue;
   He was no whig, he was no tory;
No Deist and no Christian he;—
He got so subtle, that to be
   Nothing, was all his glory.

One single point in his belief
   From his organisation sprung,   570
The heart-enrooted faith, the chief
Ear in his doctrines' blighted sheaf,
   That "happiness is wrong;"

So thought Calvin and Dominic[42];
   So think their fierce successors, who
Even now would neither stint nor stick
Our flesh from off our bones to pick,
   If they might "do their do."

His morals thus were undermined:—
   The old Peter—the hard, old Potter   580
Was born anew within his mind;
He grew dull, harsh, sly, unrefined,
   As when he tramped beside the Otter.[43]

In the death hues of agony
   Lambently flashing from a fish,[44]
Now Peter felt amused to see
Shades like a rainbow's rise and flee,
   Mixed with a certain hungry wish.

So in his Country's dying face
   He looked—and lovely as she lay,   590
Seeking in vain his last embrace,
Wailing her own abandoned case,
   With hardened sneer he turned away:

And coolly to his own soul said;—
   "Do you not think that we might make
A poem on her when she's dead:—
Or, no—a thought is in my head—
   Her shroud for a new sheet I'll take.

"My wife wants one.—Let who will bury
   This mangled corpse! And I and you,   600
My dearest Soul, will then make merry,
As the Prince Regent did with Sherry,—
   Ay—and at last desert me too."[45]

And so his Soul would not be gay,
   But moaned within him; like a fawn
Moaning within a cave, it lay
Wounded and wasting, day by day,
   Till all its life of life was gone.

As troubled skies stain waters clear,
   The storm in Peter's heart and mind   610
Now made his verses dark and queer:
They were the ghosts of what they were,
   Shaking dim grave-clothes in the wind.

For he now raved enormous folly,
   Of Baptisms, Sunday-schools, and Graves,
'Twould make George Colman[46] melancholy,
To have heard him, like a male Molly,[47]
   Chaunting those stupid staves.

Yet the Reviews, who heaped abuse
   On Peter while he wrote for freedom,   620

So soon as in his song they spy,
The folly which soothes tyranny,
   Praise him, for those who feed 'em.

"He was a man, too great to scan;—
   A planet lost in truth's keen rays:—
His virtue, awful and prodigious;—
He was the most sublime, religious,
   Pure-minded Poet of these days."

As soon as he read that, cried Peter,
   "Eureka! I have found the way   630
To make a better thing of metre
Then e'er was made by living creature
   Up to this blessed day."

Then Peter wrote odes to the Devil;—
   In one of which[48] he meekly said:
"May Carnage and Slaughter,
Thy niece and thy daughter,
May Rapine and Famine,
Thy gorge ever cramming,
   Glut these with living and dead!   640

   "May death and damnation,
   And consternation,
Flit up from hell with pure intent!
   Slash them at Manchester,[49]
   Glasgow, Leeds and Chester;
Drench all with blood from Avon to Trent.

   "Let thy body-guard yeomen
   Hew down babes and women,
And laugh with bold triumph till Heaven be rent,
   When Moloch in Jewry,   650
   Munched children with fury,
It was thou, Devil, dining with pure intent."

PART THE SEVENTH

DOUBLE DAMNATION

The Devil now knew his proper cue.—
  Soon as he read the ode, he drove
To his friend Lord MacMurderchouse's[50]
A man of interest in both houses,
  And said:—"For money or for love,

"Pray find some cure or sinecure,[51]
  To feed from the superfluous taxes,
A friend of ours—a poet—fewer   660
Have fluttered tamer to the lure
  Than he." His Lordship stands and racks his

Stupid brains, while one might count
  As many beads as he had boroughs,—
At length replies; from his mean front,
Like one who rubs out an account,
  Smoothing away the unmeaning furrows:

"It happens fortunately, dear Sir,
  I can. I hope I need require
No pledge from you, that he will stir   670
In our affairs;—like Oliver,[52]
  That he'll be worthy of his hire."

These words exchanged, the news sent off
  To Peter, home the Devil hied,—
Took to his bed; he had no cough,
No doctor,—meat and drink enough,—
  Yet that same night he died.

The Devil's corpse was leaded down;
  His decent heirs enjoyed his pelf,[53]
Mourning-coaches, many a one,   680
Followed his hearse along the town:—
  Where was the Devil himself?

When Peter heard of his promotion,
  His eyes grew like two stars for bliss:
There was a bow of sleek devotion,

Engendering in his back; each motion
   Seemed a Lord's shoe to kiss.

He hired a house,[54] bought plate, and made
   A genteel drive up to his door,
With sifted gravel neatly laid,—   690
As if defying all who said,
   Peter was ever poor.

But a disease soon struck into
   The very life and soul of Peter—
He walked about—slept—had the hue
Of health upon his cheeks—and few
   Dug better—none a heartier eater.

And yet a strange and horrid curse
   Clung upon Peter, night and day,
Month and month the thing grew worse,   700
And deadlier than in this my verse,
   I can find strength to say.

Peter was dull—he was at first
   Dull—O, so dull—so very dull!
Whether he talked, wrote, or rehearsed—
Still with this dulness was he cursed—
   Dull—beyond all conception—dull.

No one could read his books—no mortal,
   But a few natural friends, would hear him;
The parson came not near his portal;   710
His state was like that of the immortal
   Described by Swift[55]—no man could bear him.

His sister, wife, and children yawned,
   With a long, slow, and drear ennui,
All human patience far beyond;
Their hopes of Heaven each would have pawned,
   Any where else to be.

But in his verse, and in his prose,
   The essence of his dulness was
Concentred and compressed so close,   720
'Twould have made Guatimozin[56] doze
   On his red gridiron of brass.

A printer's boy, folding those pages,
    Fell slumbrously upon one side;
Like those famed seven who slept three ages.[57]
To wakeful frenzy's vigil rages,
    As opiates, were the same applied.

Even the Reviewers who were hired
    To do the work of his reviewing,
With adamantine nerves, grew tired;—   730
Gaping and torpid they retired,
    To dream of what they should be doing.

And worse and worse, the drowsy curse
    Yawned in him, till it grew a pest—
A wide contagious atmosphere,
Creeping like cold through all things near;
    A power to infect and to infest.

His servant-maids and dogs grew dull;
    His kitten, late a sportive elf,
The woods and lakes, so beautiful,   740
Of dim stupidity were full,
    All grew dull as Peter's self.

The earth under his feet—the springs,
    Which lived within it a quick life,
The air, the winds of many wings,
That fan it with new murmurings,
    Were dead to their harmonious strife.

The birds and beasts within the wood,
    The insects, and each creeping thing,
Were now a silent multitude;   750
Love's work was left unwrought—no brood
    Near Peter's house took wing.

And every neighbouring cottager
    Stupidly yawned upon the other:
No jack-ass brayed; no little cur
Cocked up his ears;—no man would stir
    To save a dying mother.

Yet all from that charmed district went
    But some half-idiot and half-knave,

Who rather than pay any rent,   760
Would live with marvellous content,
    Over his father's grave.

No bailiff dared within that space,
    For fear of the dull charm, to enter;
A man would bear upon his face,
For fifteen months in any case,
    The yawn of such a venture.

Seven miles above—below—around—
    This pest of dulness holds its sway;
A ghastly life without a sound;   770
To Peter's soul the spell is bound—
    How should it ever pass away?

28
William Maginn, "Don Juan Unread" (1819)

This poem was published in *Blackwood*'s in November 1819. The author may have been William Maginn (1794–1842), although the initials after the prefatory letter (M. N.) might suggest otherwise. This parody is based on Wordsworth's "Yarrow Unvisited" (it was first printed in parallel columns beside its model) and uses the idea of refusing to go in a suggested direction prominent in that poem. The parody vigorously censures "Whiggish" writers from Godwin to Moore, but it especially condemns Byron's *Don Juan*. In the eyes of some members of the conservative establishment, that poem and its kindred set a dangerous precedent. Thus political liberalism is libellously associated with anarchy and immorality. The parody concludes with a vision of social upheaval, presumably the inevitable result of following the present fashions to their logical conclusion.

Mr. Editor,

I composed the following poem on Tuesday-night last, between the hours of eleven and twelve o'clock, during a sound sleep, into which I had fallen while in the act of attempting to peruse Constable's Magazine.[1] While I slept I was busily employed in versifying, and should, I am sure, have composed much more, but that I unfortunately threw the Magazine off the table upon my foot, which instantly awaked me. A half-hundred could not have descended with more weight, a circumstance which proves how very heavy the articles contained in that work must be; and I feel the effects of it yet. I send my lines merely as a psychological curiosity like Kubla Khan. It is a remarkable fact, that a poem of Mr. Wordsworth's, *"Yarrow Unvisited,"* bears a resemblance to this of mine; how to account for this coincidence I know not.—I remain, Sir, your humble servant,

M. N.

DON JUAN UNREAD

Of Corinth Castle we had read
    The amazing Siege unravelled,
Had swallowed Lara and the Giaour,
    And with Childe Harold travelled;
And so we followed cloven-foot*
    As faithfully as any,
Until he cried, "Come turn aside
    And read of Don **Giovanni."

"Let Whiggish folk, *frae* Holland House,[2]
    Who have been lying, prating,
Read Don Giovanni, 'tis their own,
    A child of their creating!
On jests profane they love to feed,***
    And there they are—and many:
But we, who link not with the crew,
    Regard not Don Giovanni.

"There's Godwin's daughter, Shelley's wife,
    A writing fearful stories;[3]
There's Hazlitt, who, with Hunt and Keats
    Brays forth in Cockney chorus;
There's pleasant Thomas Moore, a lad
    Who sings of Rose and Fanny;****
Why throw away those wits so gay
    To take up Don Giovanni.

"What's Juan but a shameless tale,
    That bursts all rules asunder?
There are a thousand such elsewhere
    As worthy of your wonder."
Strange words they seem'd of slight and scorn;
    His Lordship look'd not *canny*;*****

---

*A recollection of the usual accoutrement of the prince of the air, to whose service the poem of Don Juan is devoted, will account for this epithet being applied to its author.

**Italice for Juan, which is Hispanice for John.

***Witness the subscription for Hone as a reward for parodying the Lord's Prayer, &c. in which list the Duke of Bedford, Lord Sefton, and many other Whig leaders, figured conspicuously.

****"Come, tell me, says Rosa, as kissing and kissed," &c. and "Sweet Fanny of Timmol," with many other equally edifying little *pieces*.

*****Scotice for—I do not exactly know what—but it signifies something pleasant, comfortable, knowing, snug, or the like.

And took a pinch of snuff, to think
    I flouted Don Giovanni.

"O! rich," said I, "are Juan's rhymes,
    And warm its verse in flowing!
Fair crops of blasphemy it bears,
    But we will leave them growing,
In *Pindar's strain, in prose of Paine,[4]
    And many another Zanny,[5]
As gross we read, so where's the need,
    To wade through Don Giovanni.

"Let Colburn's town-bred cattle snuff
    The filths of Lady Morgan,[6]
Let Maturin to amorous themes
    Attune his barrel organ![7]
We will not read them, will not hear
    The parson or the granny;**
And, I dare say, as bad as they
    Or worse, is Don Giovanni.

"Be Juan then unseen, unknown!
    It must, or we may rue it;
We may have virtue of our own;
    Ah! why should we undo it?
The treasured faith of days long past,
    We still shall prize o'er any;
And we shall grieve to hear the gibes
    Of scoffing Don Giovanni.

"When Whigs with freezing rule shall come,
    And piety seem folly;
When Cam and Isis*** curbed by Brougham,[8]
    Shall wander melancholy;
When Cobbett, Wooler, Watson, Hunt,[9]
    And all the swinish many,
Shall rough-shod ride**** o'er church and state,
    Then hey! for Don Giovanni."[11]

---

*Peter to wit.

**Vulgariter for grandmother, not that I mean to assert that Lady M. *is* a grandmother, but to insinuate, that as she is old enough to be one, she has a fair claim to the title.

***Rivers, on the banks of which certain Universities much indebted to the learned jurisconsult mentioned in the text for his kind attention to their interests, are seated.

****"We shall ride roughshod over Carlton House."—Speech of all the talents through the mouthpiece of Lord—, on hearing of the assassination of Mr. Percival.[10]

29
David Carey, "The Water Melon" (1820)

This rhythmically clever poem was apparently written by David Carey (1782–1824), a Whig journalist in London and the author of several volumes of poetry. Published in *The Beauties of the Modern Poets* (1820), which Carey also edited, this poem is not so much a parody of a particular Wordsworthian model as a satire on the poet's habit of moralizing about sometimes trite objects or inconsequential experiences in nature. The joke about Wordsworth's drinking of water may have its origin in the 1815 Preface in which he describes himself as "a water drinker" [*The Poetical Works of Wordsworth*, ed. Ernest de Selincourt (London: Oxford University Press, 1950), 756], or in poems such as "The Waggoner" (line 60) or "To The Daisy," which contains the following lines: "But now my own delights I make,— / My thirst at every rill can slake. . . ." (5–6). The notion of drinking water is presumably a jibe at Wordsworth's status as a "Lake" poet and his adopted stance of moral purity, but the tradition of the water drinking bard (in contrast to the wine drinking poet) reaches back to Milton (see "Elegia Sexta") and beyond.

THE WATER MELON

'TWAS noon, and the reapers reposed on the bank,
    Where our rural repast had been spread,
Beside us meander'd the rill where we drank,[1]
    And the green willow wav'd o'er our head;
Lucinda, the Queen of our rustical treat,[2]
    With smiles, like the season, auspicious,
Had render'd the scene and the banquet more sweet—
    But, oh! the dessert was delicious.

A Melon, the sweetest that loaded the vine,
    The kind-hearted damsel had brought;
Its crimson core teem'd with the richest of wine,
    "How much like her kisses!"—I thought.

And I said, as its nectarous juices I quaff'd,
    "How vain are the joys of the vicious!
No tropical fruit ever furnish'd a draught
    So innocent, pure, and delicious."

In the seeds which embellished this red juicy core,
    An emblem of life we may view;
For human enjoyments are thus sprinkled o'er
    With specks of an ebony hue;
But if we are wise to discard from the mind,
    Every thought and affection that's vicious,
Like the seed-speckled core of the melon, we'll find,
    Each innocent pleasure delicious.

30

William Maginn and Others, from " 'Luctus' on the Death of Sir Daniel Donnelly, Late Champion of Ireland" (1820)

Prize fighting was an enormously popular sport during the Regency period. Sir Daniel Donnelly, said to have been knighted by George IV, was the Irish champion who died prematurely on 18 February 1820; he was well known for his love of food, drink, gambling, and women. Boxing inspired one of Hazlitt's memorable essays ("The Fight," published in *The New Monthly Magazine* for February 1822), and it was often the subject of articles in *Blackwood's* (*Boxiana* had been serialized in the journal since 1818). Therefore, in the May 1820 issue Donnelly's death became the occasion for a "luctus" or public expression of grief featuring the parodied poems of contemporary poets, including Byron and Wordsworth. Wordsworth's prose and poetry are both parodied by John Wilson ("Christopher North") for the usual qualities disliked by the *Blackwood's* reviewers: excessive self-concern, the convoluted and suspended syntax, tiresome egocentricity, and the poet's effeminate sensibility.

LETTER FROM MR. W. W. TO MR. CHRISTOPHER NORTH

Dear Sir,

Had it not been one of the deepest convictions of my mind, even from very early youth, that there was something in periodical literature radically and essential wrong, *in rerum naturâ,* as Bacon Lord Verulam has wisely observed of a subject somewhat different,[1] I should certainly, before the commencement of the present portion of time, have sent divers valuable communications unto your Miscellany. For, concerning both the matter and manner of Blackwood's Edinborough Magazine, it hath fallen to my lot in life, on six, eight, or ten different occasions—some of them not without their importance, considered in relation to the ordinary on-goings of the world which we inhabit, and others of them, peradventure, utterly and thoroughly worthless;—I say, that it hath fallen to my lot in life to hear the Work, of which you are the Editor, spoken of in words of commendation and praise. It appeareth manifest, however, that to form a philosophical, that is, a true character of a work published periodically, it behoveth a man to peruse the whole series of the above-mentioned work seriatim, that is, in continuous and uninterrupted succession, inasmuch as that various articles, on literature, philosophy, and the fine arts, being by their respective authors left unfinished in one number, are mayhap brought to a conclusion in a second— nay, peradventure, continued in a second, and even a third—yea, often not finished until a tenth, and after the intervention of divers Numbers free wholly and altogether from any discussion on that specific subject, but composed, it may be, either of nobler or of baser matter. Thus, it often fareth ill with one particular Number of a periodical work—say for June or January—because, that although both the imaginative and reasoning faculties may be manifested and bodied forth visibly and palpably, so that, as I have remarked on another occasion, they may "lie like surfaces,"[2] nevertheless, if there shall be the intervention of a chasm of time between the first portion of the embodied act and the visible manifestation of the second—or again, between the second and third, and so on according to any imaginable or unimaginable series,—then I aver, that he will greatly err, who, from such knowledge of any work, (that is, a periodical work, for indeed it is of such only that it can be so predicated,) shall venture to bestow or to inflict upon it a decided and permanent character, either for good or for evil. Thus, for example, I have observed in divers Numbers of Blackwood's Edinborough Magazine, sarcasms rather witty than wise, in my apprehension, directed against myself, on the score of the Lyrical Ballads, and my Quarto Poem entitled the Excursion. In other Numbers again—I cannot charge my memory for what months or in what year, nor indeed is it of vital importance to this question—methinks I have read disquisitions on my poetry, and on those great and immutable principles in human nature on which it is built, and in virtue of which I do not feel as if I were arrogating to myself any peculiar gift of prophecy, when I declare my belief that these my poems will be immortal;—I repeat, that in such and such Numbers I have perused such and such articles and compositions, in which I have not been slow to discern a fineness of tact and a depth of thought and feeling not elsewhere to be found, unless I be greatly deceived, in the criticism of this in many things degenerate, because too intellectual age. Between the folly of some Numbers, therefore, and the wisdom of others—or in other words of still more perspicuous signification, between the falsehood of one writer, and the truth of another, there must exist many shades by which such opposite extremes are brought, without a painful sense of contrariety, before the eyes of what Mr. Coleridge has called the "Reading Public."[3] Of all such shades—if any such there be—I am wholly unapprised—because I see the work but rarely, as I have already observed, for I am not, to the best of my recollection, a subscriber to the Kendal Book-Club; such institutions being, in small towns, where the spirit of literature is generally bad in itself and fatally misdirected, conducted upon a principle, or rather a want of principle, which cannot be too much discommended.

The upshot of the whole is this, that it is contrary both to my theory and my practice to become a regular contributor to any periodical work whatsoever, forasmuch as such habits of composition are inimical to the growth and sanity of original genius, and therefore unworthy of him who writes for "all time" except the present.

Nevertheless, it hath so happened, that in seasons prior to this, I have transmitted to the Editors of divers periodical Miscellanies, small portions of large works, and even small works perfect in themselves; nor, would it be altogether consistent with those benign feelings which I am disposed to cherish towards your Miscellany, as a Periodical that occasionally aimeth at excellence, and may even, without any flagrant violation of truth, be said occasionally to approximate thereto, to withhold from it such slight marks of my esteem, as, upon former occasions, I have not scrupled to bestow upon others haply less worthy of them. I therefore send you first, an Extract from my Great Poem on my Own Life, and it is a passage which I have greatly elaborated;—and, secondly, Sir Daniel Donnelly, a Ballad, which, in the next edition of my works, must be included under the general class of "Poems of the Imagination and the Affections."

EXTRACT FROM MY GREAT AUTO-BIOGRAPHICAL POEM

It is most veritable,—that sage law
Which tells that, at the wane of mightiness,
Yea even of colossal guilt, or power
That, like the iron man by poets feign'd,[4]
Can with uplifted arm draw from above
The ministering lightnings, all insensible
To touch of other feeling, we do find
That which our hearts have cherish'd but as fear,
Is mingled still with love; and we must weep
The very loss of that which caus'd our tears.—
Ev'n so it happeneth when Donnelly dies.
Cheeks are besullied with unused brine,
And eyes disguis'd in tumid wretchedness,
That oft have put such seeming on for him,
But not at Pity's bidding!—Yea, even I,
Albeit, who never "ruffian'd" in the ring,

Nor know of "challenge," save the echoing hills;
Nor "fibbing," save that poesy doth feign[5];
Nor heard his fame, but as the mutterings
Of clouds contentious on Helvellyn's side,
Distant, yet deep, agnize[6] a strange regret,
And mourn Donnelly—Honourable Sir Daniel:—
(Blessings be on them, and eternal praise,
The Knighter and the Knighted.)—Love doth dwell
Here in these solitudes, and our corporal clay
Doth for its season bear the self-same fire,
Impregnate with the same humanities,
Moulded and mixed like others.
                           I remember,
Once on a time,—'twas when I was a boy,
For I was childish once, and often since
Have, with a cheerful resignation, learnt
How soon the boy doth prophecy the man,—
I chanced, with one whom I could never love,
Yet seldom left, to thread a thorny wood,
To seek the stock-doves' sacred domicile;—
Like thieves, we did contend about our crime,
I and that young companion. Of that child
His brief coevals still had stood in awe,
And Fear did do him menial offices,
While Silence walk'd beside, and word breath'd none.
Howbeit, mine arm, which oft in vassal wise
Had borne his satchel, and but ill defended
From buffets, half in sport, half tyrannous,
With which I was reguerdon'd,—chanced prevail.
   His soul was then subdued, and much and sore
He wept, convulsive; nay, his firm breast heav'd,
As doth the bosom of the troublous lake
After the whirlwind goeth; and so sad
Did seem the ruins of his very pride,
I could not choose but weep with him,[7] so long
We sobb'd together, till a smile 'gan dry
The human rain, and he once more was calm;—
For sorrow, like all else, hath end. Albeit,
Those tears, however boyish, were more fit,
Since nature's self did draw them from their source,
Than aught that cunning'st poet can distil
By potent alchemy, from human eye,
To consecrate Donnelly's grave. Even so;
For they discours'd with a dumb eloquence,

Beyond the tongue of dirge or epitaph,
Of that which passeth in man's heart, when Power,
Like Babylon, hath fall'n, and pass'd away.

SIR DANIEL DONNELLY—A BALLAD

I came down to breakfast—And why all this sobbing,
This weeping and wailing? I hastily cried;
Has Grimalkin,[8] my boy, ta'en away your tame Robin?
Has Duckling, or Pullet, or White Coney died?

'Twas thus the short list of his Joys I ran over,
While the tears were fast coursing down Timothy's face,[9]
And strove the small darling his red cheek to cover.—
What is this?—thought my soul—Is it grief or disgrace?

I looked on the Courier, my weekly newspaper,[10]
For I felt that the cause of his sorrow was there;
So quick is grief's eye that no word can escape her—
"Dead is Daniel, the hero of Donnybrooke fair!"[11]

Anonymous, "The Nose-Drop: A Physiological Ballad" (1821)

This parody was published in *The Academic: A Periodical Publication, comprising Original Essays, Reviews, Poems, &c.* [1.1 (15 January 1821): 15–20], a short-lived periodical produced in Liverpool. The poetic text has been printed in *The Wordsworth Circle*, 2, no. 3 (Summer 1971): 92–98, in which Robert Mortenson cites almost twenty Wordsworth poems directly alluded to by the parodist. The complete parody, including the "Preface by the Author" and "Note, by the Editor," is printed below.

The first section of prose deftly subverts Wordsworth's theories by substituting low-life terms in the middle of very Wordsworthian statements or within actual quotations from the poet's prose (the Preface to the second edition of *Lyrical Ballads* especially). The effect is to ridicule the poet's claims, to expose his sense of self-importance and evident egotism, as well as to attack his levelling of critical distinctions (such as that between prose and poetry), which classically minded critics believed was important.

Next, with its masterly handling of tone, the editor's note charitably kills Wordsworth off in the manner of Lucy while simultaneously suggesting that the poor man was either demented or senile. The poem that follows portrays the poet as a simpleton whose misplaced precision and whose discovery of the nose-drop are all too typical of his revelations of meaning in nature. There are glances at Coleridge as well, especially "The Ancient Mariner," in lines 20, 45, and 63, for example.

THE NOSE-DROP: A PHYSIOLOGICAL BALLAD BY THE LATE W. W.

"Difficile est proprie communia dicere."[1]

Hor. *Epist. ad Pison.*

———————

PREFACE BY THE AUTHOR

The following Poem, which I have endeavoured to fit for filling permanently a station in the Literature of my Country, was written upon the same system which I first promulged in the Preface to my Lyrical Ballads, and which I have ever since preserved throughout the whole range of my poetry. The pervading spirit of this system is, that all composition, whether in prose or in verse, requires one and the same language; and, consequently, that a poem, even of the most elevated character, is good in exact proportion as it approximates to the language of prose. Hence I have taken as much pains to avoid what is usually called *poetic diction,* as others ordinarily take to produce it; and, restricting myself from the use of those cut-and-dry figures of speech which have long been regarded as the common inheritance of poets, I have converted their Parnassus into a nursery, and exchanged the winged Pegasus for a hobbyhorse, and the mantle of the Muse for the bib and tucker of a baby. Another principle of this system is the selection of subjects and incidents from low and rustic life—for the sentiment should give importance to the action and situation, and not the action and situation to the sentiment;—and, accordingly, sextons and leech-gatherers, spades,[2] plates, and porringers have been my ordinary themes. These I have described throughout, as far as was possible, with the most rigid adherence to nature and truth; and even in the few instances in which, by way of contrast, I have taken an opposite course, I have made my horses *think,* asses *grin,*[3] &c. &c. with a proper regard to probability. The greater part of readers, accustomed to the inane phraseology of writers who have deluged the land with Oriental tales in verse and other extravagancies, may, probably, consider this style of composition as mean and ludicrous; but the select few, whose judgment can be confidently relied upon, will, I believe, agree with me in preferring a daffodil or periwinkle, a sparrow or buzzard-cock, to all the roses and enamoured bulbuls of the Garden of Gul.[4] To say the truth,—taste and understanding, in these matters, belong exclusively to those who sojourn in rural seclusion. There is something in the atmosphere of towns, which blunts the discriminating powers of the mind, and reduces it to state of almost savage torpor; and they only who lead a life akin to mine, can ever acquire that organic sensibility which imparts a genuine relish for the beauties of Nature and Poetry. The unsophisticated "RECLUSE," habituated to solitary meditation, will, by tracing in all things the primary laws of nature, engraft the most interesting emotions upon the most ordinary occurrences: he will delight to contemplate the marvels manifested in the goings-on of the Universe, or to create them where he does not find them. The sight of the meanest object—of a wheel-barrow or a washing tub, of a gooseberry pie or a sucking pig—will suggest to his mind a train of lofty, tender, and impassioned conceptions; and, if such a man be a poet, he will necessarily produce a species of poetry which will be genuine poetry,—describing, in the humblest language of daily life, things as they really *are,* not as they transitorily *appear;* as they exist in themselves, not as they seem to exist to the *imagination* and to the *passions.* For the object of poetry is truth, of which knowledge is the result. And therefore Aristotle, as I have been told, hath said that poetry is the most philosophic of all writing; and a still greater philosopher than

Aristotle, Mr. Hazlitt—by the bye, I reckon Mr. Hazlitt among the number of my pupils, for the Cockney school is nothing more than an affiliation from mine—has demonstratively proved, in his Lectures on the English Poets, that there is nothing which is not poetry, and that poetry is every thing;[5] that the child is a poet when he plays at hide-and-seek, or repeats the story of Jack the Giant-killer; that the city-apprentice is a poet, when he gazes after the Lord Mayor's show; the pedagogue who lifts a rod, and the dunce who smarts under its application; the cripple who leans on a crutch; the clown who whistles for want of thought; the Bedlamite who fancies himself a king, and the king who behaves like a Bedlamite.

Age and infirmity (even if the limits of a preface would permit me) prevent me from undertaking a systematic defence of my theory; but, I trust, that what has been already said, and a perusal of my poem, will convince the reader, if his ideas are in a healthful state of association, that a very needless and senseless outcry has been raised against it. And if, justified by a recollection of the insults which the Ignorant, the Incapable, and the Presumptuous have heaped upon my writings, I may venture to anticipate the judgment of posterity upon myself; I shall declare that I have given, in these unfavourable times, evidences of the "Vision and the Faculty divine,"[6] worthy to be holden in undying remembrance.

W. W.

NOTE, BY THE EDITOR

The Poem of The Nose-Drop, the last of Mr. W.'s literary labours, will be read with interest by the admirers of that highly-gifted man: for, though it may hardly be found to possess, in the same abundance as his other pieces, those details of minute description, and of innocent and infantine simplicity, which its author reckoned the surest proofs of poetic excellence; yet it is sprinkled throughout with many happy examples of his peculiar style. The presentiment which he had of his approaching death, probably led him to write it with a degree of rapidity which precluded that steady and elaborate attention which he would otherwise have bestowed: and, in fact, the many cancels, interlineations, and marginal marks which he had made in the MS. prove that he was himself aware of its imperfections, and wishful to correct them. It may be worth while also to remark, that I have found among his papers several small fragments, containing lines, or parts of lines, to be wrought at some future period of revision into the text; and, among them, the following fag-end of an unfinished stanza,—much too beautiful to be lost,— which he evidently meant to introduce into the description of the poverty of his hero's person:—

> "————one foot had on
> "A worsted stocking—only one,
> "The other had a shoe."

Mr. W's death took place in the following mysterious manner:—On Monday the 18th of last month, he left his home at break of day, and did not return by nightfall. His absence, however, created little or no uneasiness, as he frequently protracted it to a late hour for the purpose of composing, or reciting his verses aloud in the open air. But when morning came, and Mr. W. came not with it; and when the shepherds declared that they had not seen him during their night-watches, or heard his voice among the hills, his family became considerably alarmed. It was justly conjectured that some accident had befallen him; and, in the course of the search which was immediately undertaken throughout the neighbourhood, his footmarks were discovered,[7] and gradually tracked, until they terminated at the small pond, which he has noticed, with the loco-description precision of a land-surveyor, in his exquisite poem, THE THORN:—

> "—to the left, three yards beyond,
> "You see a little muddy pond
>   "Of water, never dry;
> "I've measured it from side to side,
> " 'Tis three feet long, and two feet wide."[8]

and there, alas! in the middle of it, his body was discovered in an inverted perpendicular position, his head stuck fast in the mud, and his feet erect and elevated, like a couple of water-lilies, a few inches above the level of the "green-grown"[9] surface. The usual means to restore suspended animation were employed—but in vain: the vital spark had fled for ever. From the marks of heavy pressure upon the grass near the bank, it was supposed by some that he had lain down and fallen asleep there; and that in his sleep he had walked to the margin of the pond, fallen headlong into it, and so perished. Others again affected to believe what was still more improbable, that he had met with his fate while in the act of leaning forward to lay his hands on the image of a star which was gleaming on the bosom of the water.[10] These opinions, however, were chiefly confined to the circle of his own friends and family; while most persons persisted in attributing his death to suicide, as the Ninth Volume of the Edinburgh Review—containing that cruel critique on his youthful poems, which (though he professed never to have read it) embittered the whole of his after-life—was found lying on the bank beside him.

In presenting the present Poem to the public, the Editor begs to disclaim all view of private emolument. The profits (if any) arising from its sale, will be religiously appropriated to the fulfillment of different testamentary bequests of the deceased to the most prominent personages of his poems—e.g. a cloak of duffle grey to Alice Fell, a pair of breeches to Little Dan, and a pet-lamb to Barbara Lewthwaite; item, a night-mare to the Idiot Boy, and a noggin of rum to Benjamin the Waggoner.

January 10, 1821.

———————

THE NOSE-DROP

———————

"Thou com'st in such a questionable shape,
"That I will speak to thee.————"

Hamlet

———————

One summer morn I chanced to meet,
Not twenty paces from my door,
—It was the thirty-first of May—
Upon the solitary way
That leads to Wrynose Moor,*

A gray old man.—He looked so old,
In truth you'd find it hard to say
How he could ever have been young,
Or how he could have lived so long,
He looked so old and gray.

And he was poorest of the poor.
His clothes were hardly worth a farthing—
Such weather-beaten rags as those
You hang, to scare away the crows,
Right in the middle of your garden.

A noticeable man was he,
This poor old man—so poor and old—
(You never looked upon the like)
The squint of his "moist eye"** would strike
And thick your blood with cold.

His nose was sharp as any scythe
That cuts the summer harvest down:
And at its end there hung a drop,
In colour like a mutton chop,
So very, very brown.

———————

*Wrynose Moor is situate on the confines of Cumberland, Westmorland, and Lancashire: the RIVER DUDDON, "of which I sung one song that will not die," rises upon it.   W. W.
**"Have you not a *moist eye?* a dry hand? a yellow cheek? a decreasing leg? an increasing belly? Is not your voice broken? your wind short? your chin double? your wit single? and every part about you blasted with antiquity?"

Part II. Henry IV.

Why this is strange![11] this drop! thought I;
And rubbed and tweaked my nose,—in doubt
That it might be some common-place
Of feature fixed on *every* face,—
But mine was quite without.

And forthwith came into my head
Some wayward questionings: as, whether,
By Nature fashioned or by Art,
The nose and it were things apart,
Or they had grown together.

Or if it were a gaudy gem,—
A ruby,—such as Indians wear:
Or living thing, endued with sense:
And how it thither came, and whence:
And what 'twas doing there.*

I racked my brain—'twas all in vain—
I could not tell; I wished I could.
I looked again; I scanned it o'er:
The more I looked I wondered more:—
My wits were thick as mud.

At length I ceased to think,—and then
I had an instinct what to do.—
"What drop is that?" said I, "old man:
"I pray you tell me, if you can;
"And mind you tell me true."
The old man raised his head, amazed,
And said, "What's that to you?"

There was a smile about his lips,
A smile of scorn:—I liked it not;
And fiercely by the arm I took him,

---

*Here, Mr. W. originally inserted a stanza, which he afterwards (and, in my opinion, very unjustly) rejected. The lines, both in thought and expression, are exceedingly beautiful, and highly claim preservation:—

> "Or might it be some fiend of hell,
> "Who led, as keeper leads a bear,
> "The old man thither by the nose.
> "Gramercy! when that thought arose,
> "I gaped for wonderment and fear."
>   Editor

And fiercely by the arm I shook him:
—He staggered like a sot.

And all in stately speech, I cried,
With voice as loud as any mill:
"Old gray-beard! tell me all you wist,
"Or by the cudgel in my fist!
"I'll bang your bones, I will."

Eftsoons, quite flurried and a-feared,
He answered, "It's a drop of snuff!"
And, bending forward from his place,
He sneezed it full into my face,
And wiped his nose upon his gray coat cuff.

Oh! happy, happy, happy me!
The outward shews of earth and sky
Are fair—and very fair: but they
Have never made me half so gay
As did that brief reply.

At once it made the matter plain.—
My limbs they were alive with glee:
I danced and ran about in joy,
And chattered like my Idiot Boy,
As like as like could be.

Now thanks to heaven! that of its grace
Hath given me large gray eyes to see,
And, with them, sense to comprehend
All things,—their being, use, and end,—
That in this strange world be.

32
William Hone, "A New Vision" (1821)

Like Byron, William Hone wrote a parody, in 1821, of Southey's *A Vision of Judgement*. He had earlier (1817) reprinted *Wat Tyler,* Southey's republican poem of 1794, to embarrass the poet laureate for his rejection of reformist values. Southey was unable to prevent this or other piracies, because his work was considered seditious and therefore outside the protection of the law [see Edgell Rickwood, *Radical Squibs & Loyal Ripostes: Satirical Pamphlets of the Regency Period 1819–1821* (Bath, Somerset: Adams & Dart, 1971), 10]. Hone's parody attacks Southey together with the vast horde of other sycophants and hangers-on who gained profits by aligning themselves with those in political power. The parody appeared in a broadsheet which was itself a parody of the conservative newspaper, *New Times,* begun in 1817 by John Stoddart (Dr. Slop) after he was dismissed as editor of *The Times* in 1816 for his tirades against Buonaparte. Hone despised Stoddart's paper, which received a regular government subsidy in exchange for voicing opinions identical with government policies. Hone also hated Stoddart because the latter had falsely issued a story at the time of Hone's trials that said that someone who had published parodies had been convicted and sentenced.

A *NEW* VISION, BY ROBERT SOUTHEY, ESQ.! LL.D.!! POET LAUREATE!!! &C.!!!! &C.!!!! &C.!!!!!!

'Twas at that sober hour when the light of day is receding,
I alone in SLOP's Office was left; and, in trouble of spirit,
I mused on old times, till my comfort of heart had departed.[1]
Pensile at least I shall be, methought—*sus. per coll.*[2] surely!
And therewithal felt I my neckcloth; when lo! on a sudden,
There came on my eyes, hanging mid-way 'twixt heav'n and St. James's,
The book call'd the *Pension list*. There did I see my name written,
Yea ev'n in that great book of life! It was sweet to my eyelids,
As dew from a tax! and *Infinity* seem'd to be open,
And I said to myself, "Now a blessing be on thee, my Robert!
And a blessing on thee too my Pen! and on thee too my Sack-but!"[3]

Now, as thus I was standing, mine ear heard a rap at the street-door,
Ev'n such as a man might make bold with, half gentle, half footman,
And lo! up the stairs, dotting one, one, after the other,
Came the leg of a wonder, hop! hop! through the silence of evening,
And then a voice snarling from the throat of the him they call MURRAY,[4]
Who said, as he hopp'd, "Must the *Muck Times* be mournful at *all* times?
Lo, SLOP, I've a sop, for your mop; yes—hop! hop! I've a *story*,
With which I'll light *you* up, if you'll light me, Slop, up another."
          "Don't be so *bold!*" methought a *larking* voice from the skylight
Answer'd, and therewithal I felt fear as of frightening;
Knowing not why, or how, my soul seem'd night-cap to my body.
Then came again the voice, but then with a louder squalling—
"Go to HELL," said the voice. "What *I*," said I, inwardly, "*I* go!"
When lo, and behold, a great wonder!—I, I, ROBERT SOUTHEY,
Even I, ROBERT SOUTHEY, *Esquire,* LL.D. POET LAUREATE,
Member of the Royal Spanish Academy, of the
Ditto of history too, of the Institute Royal
Of Dutchland, and eke of the Welch Cymmodorion wonder,
Author of Joan of Arc, of much Jacobin Verse, and Wat Tyler,[5]
Et caetera, et caetera, et caetera, et caetera, et caetera,
(For it's unknown all the things that I am and have written),
I, as I said before, ev'n I, by myself, *I,*
Unlike, in that single respect, to my great master Dante,
(For Virgil went with him to help him), but like in all others,
Rush'd up into PARADISE boldly, which angels themselves don't,
Yea ev'n into Paradise rush'd I, through showers of *flimsies,*[6]
All as good as the bank, and for hailstones I found there were *Sovereigns,*
Spick and span new; and anon was a body all glorified,
Even all the great HOST both of CHURCH and STATE, Crosses, Grand
     Crosses,
Commanders, Companions, and Knights of all possible orders,
Commons and Peers, the souls of the sold, whom Pensions made perfect,
Flocking on either hand, a multitudinous army,
Coronet, Crosier, and Mitre, in grand semicircle inclining,
Tier over tier they took their place, aloft in the distance,
Far as the sight could pierce, Stars, Garters, and Gold Sticks.
From among the throng bless'd, all full dress'd, in a Field Marshal's uniform,
Rose one, with a bow serene, who, aloft, took his station[7];
Before him the others crouch'd down, all inclining in concert,
Bent like a bull-rush sea, with a wide and a manifold motion:
There he stood in the midst alone; and in front was the presence,
With periwig curling and gay, and a swallow-cut coat-tail.
          Hear ye of long ears! Lo! in that place was *Canning,*
He who strengthens the Church and State, with his Manton's hair-triggers,

And sneers on his lips, and eyes leering, and *rupturous speeches*[8];
With him *Fletcher Franklin* I saw, and *Sir Robert,* my namesake,
Worthy the name! even *Baker,* Sir Robert, of Bow-street[9];
And *Gifford,* with face made of lachrymose, savage and feeble,
Who delighteth with *Croker* to cut up men, women, and young men,
And therefore did *Hazlitt* cut *him* up, and so he stood mangled.[10]
There, too, brocaded and satin'd, stood smiling and bowing,
With Court-mask'd appearance, *the Fearful One,* him of *Triangle!*
And there, too, the *Foolish* one, *circular*-conscienced, the *Doctor!*[11]
And I saw in the vision, the *Generals, Sol.* and *Attorney*[12];
And *Sacchi,* was there too, and him surnamed *Non mi Ricordo*;
And Mad'moiselle *Daemon,* and *Barbard Kress,* and *Rastelli;*
And *Mister,* and *Mister-ess Jessop,* and eke the *Miss Jessops;*
And *Mar——ss Il——d,* and *M——ss C——m,* also;
And Mrs. *Fitz—t,* and *C——ch*[13]; and in sooth all the *Beauties*
Of the "GEORGIAN *age,*" except *Robinson Mary,*
Whom great G. first sent to the D——, and *little* G. after,
(Namely *Gifford,* who smote at her sorely, yea, ev'n at her crutches,
So that she fell in her grave, and said, "Cover me kind earth!")[14]
And the great minded Cl—— was there, looking like to Behemoth;
And the *Lauderdale* disinterested, great Scotch standard-bearer,
And there, too, the king's much-conspired-against-stationer, *King,* stood,
The Lord Mayor of Dublin, who sendeth his Majesty's whiskey[15];
And the Members of *Orange Clubs* all, anti-Irish shillelahs;
And a heav'nly assembly of *parsons,* some, lately, expectant,
Parson *Hey?* Parson B called, otherwise, Parson *Black-cow,* divine brute!
Parson *C.* alias *Croly,* or *Crawley,* or *Coronaroly,*[16]
Who putteth forth innocent pamphlets on pure coronations,
Expecteth Milleniums, and laudeth the *Blackguard* of Blackwood's,
And looketh both lofty and slavish, a dreariness high-nosed,
As if he had, under the chin been, by worshipful men, chuck'd;
And great Parson *Eat-all-stone,* who'd swallow *any* thing surely;
And the *Manchester Yeomanry Cavalry,* riding down women[17];
And *Alderman Atkins,* with *Curtis,* that *big belly*-gerent,
And *Flower,* and *Bridges, C. Smith,* and the rest of the BRIDGE GANG,
All clothed for the heav'nly occasion in their *best* Indictments![18]
And there all the *Lottery-contractors,* and such like, were also;
And there Mr. *Strong-i-the'-arm,* his Majesty's Seal-Engraver, was also;
And they all, who *forged,* lo! the French Assignats, were there also[19];
And the *Court-newsman* also was there——
(The Spirit now bids me write *prose,* but that, you know's all the same thing)
And *Colburn* with his *Muck Monthly Magazine* was there;

And *Ward,* the Animal Painter, with a piece of spoil'd canvas, 35 feet wide
    by 21, was there[20];
But *Bird* who, most disloyally, died of a broken heart, was not there[21];
And the *Duke of Wellington,* with the Sword of State, was there;
And *Sir John Silvester,* the Recorder of London, and his *assistant,* were
    there;
And Messrs. *Rundell and Bridge,* the Jewellers who repair'd the Crown, were
    there[22];
And the *Pigtails* cut off from his Majesty's guards were there;
And the *Guards* themselves in their *next* uniforms, and new white gaiters,
    were there;
And the *State Coach and Coachmen and Horses* were there;
And the *other Ministers of State* in their new State Liveries were there;
And the *Clerks of the Council* and the *two Silver Inkstands* were there;
And all the Gentlemen of the *Stock Exchange* were there;
And all the Gentlemen of the *Shipping Interest* were there;
And all the Gentlemen of the *Landed Interest* were there;
But all the people *without Interest* were not there;
And all the *Peers* who voted the Queen of England *guilty* were there;
And all the *Ministerial Members* of the House of Commons were there;
And Dr. *Slop* with "*fresh* fig-leaves for *Adam* and *Eve*" was there[23];
And the *Royal Proclamation* against Vice and Immorality was pasted up
    there;
And behold, while I read it, thinking to put it, excellent as it was, into
    language still better,
Methought, in my vision, I dreamt—dream within dream intercircled—
And seem'd to be hurried away, by a vehement whirlwind,
To FLAMES and SULPHUROUS DARKNESS, where certain of my *Minor
    Poems* were scorching,
Yet unconsumed, in penal fire; and *so* was *I* purified
For deeds done in the flesh, being, through them, burnt by proxy!
There, too, roasted the Bishop of Osnaburgh's *Doxy,*[24]
But the Righteous-one, *the Prince Bishop himself,* was in Heaven[25];
And *two Boots* were there, as a burnt-offering for *peccadillo,*
But the *Owner* thereof was a glorified spirit above,
Where, as in duty bound, I had sung to him Twang-a-dillo,
He that loves a pretty girl, is a hearty good fellow!
And in *Torment* (but here the blest rage of the bard returns on me)
And in torment was *she,* who, on earth, had been also tormented
By him who is never, nor can be accused, of aught *vicious;*
With her were the friends of my childhood—not leaving out *Coleridge;*
And they who were *kill'd* by the Manchester Yeomanry also;
And *Truth,* the whole Truth, nothing *but* the Truth, suffered the burning.

Then I turn'd my meek eyes, in their gladness, to Heaven, and my *place* there,
And ascending, I flew back to Paradise, singing of Justice;
Where, fill'd, with divine expectation, of merited favour,
The gathering host look'd to him, in whom all their hopes center'd,
As the *everlasting* hand; and I, too, press'd forward to obtain—
But old recollections withheld me;—down, down, dropp'd my Sack-but,
And my feet, methought, slid, and I fell precipitate. Starting,
Then I awoke, with my hair up, and lo! my young days were before me,
Dark yet distinct; but instead of the voice of the honest,
I heard only Murray's *yap! yap!* and *hop! hop!* through the silence of evening:—
Yap! hop! and *hop! yap!*—and hence came the hop, step, and jump, of my verses.

33
Eyre Evans Crowe, "Characters of Living Authors, By Themselves" (1821)

This prose parody was published in *Blackwood's,* no. 1, pt. 2 (August 1821). Attributed to Eyre Evans Crowe by Alan Strout [*A Bibliography of Articles in 'Blackwood's Magazine,' Volumes I through XVIII, 1817–1825* (Lubbock, Texas: Texas Technological College, 1959), 83], the parody of Hazlitt's style of writing, his sentiments, and his ideas is ruthless and clever. Cast appropriately in the form of a personal essay, it ridicules Hazlitt's Rousseauistic self-obsession and his lame rationalizations for such self-centeredness. Crowe catches the impudent, disdainful tone of Hazlitt's prose and turns him into, by his own confession, a hack journalist whose "wisdom" is shallow and whose ideas are commonplace, however original they are presented as being.

CHARACTERS OF LIVING AUTHORS, BY THEMSELVES.

NO. I.

> "Dans ce siècle de petits talens et de grands succès, mes chefs-d'oeuvre auront cent éditions, *s'il le faut.* Par-tout les sots crieront que je suis un grand homme, et si je n'ai contre moi que les gens de lettres et les gens de goût, j'arriverai peut-être à l'Académie."
>
> LOUVET.[1]

I'm a philosopher of no philosophy, and know not where the deuce my wisdom came from, unless it was inborn or "connatural," as Shaftesbury will have it.[2] I have studied neither the heavens, nor the earth, nor man, nor books; but I have studied myself, have turned over the leaves of my own heart, and read the cabalistic characters of self-knowledge. Nor without success, for truth, I trust, has been no stranger to my pen. If all the world followed my example, there would be some sense in it.—But they do not. They have not courage and alacrity enough to catch wisdom and folly "as they fly."[3] They ponder and weigh—wind about a vacuum, like the steps of a geometrical stair-case. They do not "pluck bright knowledge from the pale-faced moon."[4] They do not dare to look from the table land of their own genius,—their own perceptions, nor sweep boldly over the regions of philosophy, "knowing nothing, caring nothing." They do not expatiate over literature with the step of freemen,—they are shackled, and have not the spirit to be truly vagabond. They are not elevated to a just idea of themselves, their own feelings are not hallowed, and they put forth their thought "fearfully, and in the dark."[5] This is not the way to be wise;—there is confidence required for wisdom as well as for war. We are all of one kind; the feelings of nature are universal, and he that can turn his eye in upon himself,—that has mental squint enough to look behind his nose, may read there the irrefragable laws and principles of humanity. This is the difficulty,—the bar between man and knowledge, as is observed by Mr Locke, (who, by the bye, is an author I despise,—a philosopher who reasoned without feeling, and felt without reason). If a person can once enter into the receptacles of his own feelings, muse upon himself, watch the formation and progress of his opinions, he will then have studied the best primer of philosophy. If he can once lay hold of the end of that web, he can unravel it *ad infinitum*. With his pen in his fingers, and his glass before him, he no sooner begins, than he is at the bottom of the page; and the Indian jugglers, with their brazen balls, were nothing to the style in which he can fling sentences about.[6] I can speak but from my own experience: I have found it so; and though there is a degree of excellence, which all persons cannot arrive at, yet the fabrication of essays is a *double* employment, and I here record the principle by which I arrived at its perfection, as a bequest and lesson to posterity.—Despise learning; never mind books, but to borrow. Let the ideas play around self, and that is the way to please the selfish reader—other readers there are not in the world.

It is vulgarly supposed, that a man, who is always thinking and talking of himself, is an egotist. He is no such thing; he is the least egotistical of all men.[7] It is the world he is studying all the time, and self is but the glass through which he views and speculates upon nature. People call me egotist; they don't know what they say. I never think of myself, but as one among the many—a drop in the ocean of life. If I anatomize my own heart, 'tis that I can lay hands on no other so conveniently; and when I do even make use of the letter *I,* I merely mean by it any highly-gifted and originally-minded individual. I have always thought myself very like Rousseau, except in one thing, that I hate 'the womankind,'—I have reason—he had not.[8] Nevertheless, had he hung up his shield in a temple, I'm sure I should recognize it. I feel within me a kindred spirit,—the same expansive intellect that strays over the bounds of speculation, and has grasped nothing, because it met nothing worthy,—the same yearning after what the soul can never attain,—the same eloquent and restless thought, whose trains are ropes of sand, undone as soon as done,—the same feverish thirst to gulp up knowledge, with a stomach in which no knowledge can rest. If a fortuitous congregation of atoms ever formed any thing, it formed us, for truly we are a tesselated pair, each of a disposition curiously dovetailed, as Burke said of Lord Chatham's ministry,[9]—of faculties put together so higgledy piggledy, that however excellent each is in its kind, the union is an abortion,—a worse than nothing—but the anagrams of intellect, as Donne would say.[10] The world, too, has treated us similarly; with the most patriotic feelings, our countries have laughed at us; with the most philanthropic pens, we have become the buts and bye words of criticism; and with the warmest hearts, we never had a friend. He despised poetry—so do I; he despised book-learning—I know nothing about it; he did not care for the great—the great do not care for me. What further traits of resemblance would you have?—his breeches hung about his heels.

The author of a *mighty fine* review of Childe Harold compares the author, my friend's friend, to Rousseau, and ekes out the similarity in poetic prose.[11] I have no fault to find with the Review, it being *buon camarado* of mine, but they might have made out a better comparison. It was L. H. first suggested to me my resemblance to the author of Eloisa; it is one of those obligations I can never forget. He said, at the same time, that he himself was like Tasso, and added, in his waggery, he would prove that bard a Cockney. This is neither wit nor good sense in my friend, who, finding he cannot shake off the title, wishes to convert it into a crown;—it won't do, the 'brave public' will have it a fool's cap.

As for me, I care not; they will have me Cockney—they're welcome; they will have me pimpled in soul and in body—they're welcome; I know what they will not have me—but no matter; I wander from my theme—myself, but I cannot help it.[12] The thoughts of what I have suffered from envenomed pens come thick upon me; but posterity will do me justice, and there will yet be "sweet sad tears" shed over the tombs of me and of my tribe.[13] Nevertheless, let me not give up the ghost before my time—I am worth two dead men yet; nor let it be here on record that I could be moved by my hard-hearted and hard-headed persecutors. But "what is writ is writ"—it goes to my heart to blot one quarter of a page. My thoughts walk forth upon the street, like malefactors on the drop, with their irons knocked off.[14] They come unshackled, unquestioned, unconcocted; and if I have uttered heaps of folly in my day, I trust there was some leaven—good or bad, which I care not—to save it from being utterly insipid.

There have been few great authors who took from the beginning to writing as a profession—it is too appalling—I doubt if it would require half so much courage to lead a forlorn hope. They are, for the most part, men against whom all other avenues were shut,—who have been pushed from their stools,

> "And being for all other trades unfit,
> Only t' avoid being idle, set up wit."[15]

And this not for lack of capacity, but for want of will; none of them could give a reason for being what they are—I could not, I know, for one. Yet mine was a natural course. It is an easy transition from the pencil to the pen, only the *handling* of the first must be the result of long practice, and unwearied assiduity. The latter goes more glibly, and is the engine of greater power. We long to grasp it, as if it were Jove's thunderbolt, and "hot and heavy" we find it. The study of the arts, too, is a terrible provocative to criticism—to canting and unmeaning criticism. I must confess, I tremble to think what literature is likely to suffer from the encroachments of that superficial and conceited tribe. I was myself one of them, and may own it, though they be to me the first 'aneath the sun.'[16] They leap to taste, without laying any foundation of knowledge—with their eyes stuck into the subject matter of their work; their notions of things are too apt to resemble those of the "fly upon the well-proportioned dome"; their overstrained idea of the all-importance of their art, may be a very useful feeling to themselves, and to their own exertions, but to the world, it is pedantry and impudence. There are other things besides painting, and of this truth they do not seem enough aware. There are exceptions, however—I am one, H—another. And I take this opportunity of weighing a little into the opposite scale, since I perceive they hold up their heads more than ordinary (especially the Cockney artists) on the strength of my former essays. I have heard a dauber speak of me, 'yes, he writes about the art,' in much the same tone as if he were recommending Milton to a divine for having treated of the Deity. They shall no more such essays, nor shall they again lay such flattering unction to their souls.[17]

I must needs be an honest man, for I speak hard always of what I love best;—it is upon points nearest our own hearts that we are most apt to feel spleen. Downright foes never come within arm's length of one,—one cannot get a blow at them; and we must fall foul of our friends, were it but for practice sake, to keep our pugnacity in tune. People, with whom I have been in habits of intimacy, have complained that I make free with their names, borrow my best things from their conversation, and afterwards abuse them. It is all very likely; but why do they talk so much? If they throw their knowledge into one's hands, how can we help making use of it? Let them enter their tongues at Stationer's Hall, if they would preserve the copyright of speech, nor be bringing their action of trover to regain what they have carelessly squandered.[18]

He that writes much, must necessarily write a great deal of bad, and a great deal of borrowed. The gentleman author, that takes up the pen once in three months, to fabricate a pet essay for his favourite miscellany or review, may keep up his character as a tasteful and fastidious penman. But let him be like me, scribbling from one end of the year to the other—obliged to it, at all hours and in all humours—and let's see what a mixture will be his warp and woof?—Let him, in an evil moment, be compelled to "set himself doggedly about it," as Johnson says, and he'll be glad to prop himself up with the gossip of his acquaintances, and the amusing peculiarities of his friends.[19] Let him stick in his working clothes, hammering away all weathers, like Lord

Castlereagh in the House, and he'll have little time for display and got up speeches. He'll soon learn to despise which word comes foremost, and which comes fittest, and, in the way of diction, he'll soon cry out with myself—"all's grist that comes to the mill." Grammarians and verbal critics may cry out against us for corrupting the language—they may collate, and talk with Mr Blair[20] of purity, propriety, and precision; but we own no such rules to our craft;—with us, words are

"Winds, whose ways we know not of."[21]

All we have to do is, to take the first that offers, and sail wherever it may blow;—all parts are alike, so as the voyage be effected—all subjects alike, so the page be concluded.

Talking of subjects—I have been often accused of a fondness for paradox. I am not ashamed of the predilection. Truth, in my mind, is a bull, and the only way to seize it is by the horns. This bold method of attack the startled reader calls paradox. He had rather spend hours in hunting it into a corner, with but a poor chance of noosing it after all, and is envious of him that has the courage to grasp it at once. I like the Irish for this, they blunder upon truth so heartily, and knock it out of circumstances, as if these were made of flint, and their hands of iron. I blunder on it myself often, but the worst of this method is, that one is so apt to mistake common-place for a new discovery. We light upon it so suddenly, that there is no time to examine its features, and thus often send forth an old worn-out maxim as a spic and span-new precept. But 'tis the same thing,—half the world won't recognize it, and the other half won't take the trouble of exposing it. All the didactic prosing of the age— prosing, be it in verse or not, is but the *his crambe repetita*—the old sirloin done up into kickshaws and fritters.[22] Gravity and sense are out of tune—the stock is exhausted to the knowing—the only vein unworked is humour. Waggery is always original; and there is more genuine inspiration in comic humour, than in the mighty-mouthed sublime. Madame de Stael, that eloquent writer,—whom I know but in translation by the bye—has anticipated these observations of mine in her Essay on Fiction:[23]—"Nature and thought are inexhaustible in producing sentiment and meditation; but in humour or pleasantry, there is a certain felicity of expression, or perception, of which it is impossible to calculate the return. Every idea which excites laughter may be considered as a discovery; but this opens no track to the future adventurer. To this eccentric power there lies no path,—of this poignant pleasure there is no perennial source. That it exists, we are persuaded, since we see it constantly renewed; but we are as little able to explain the course as to direct the means. The gift of pleasantry more truly partakes of inspiration than the most exalted enthusiasm." The world are beginning to be of the same opinion,—they are finding out this truth more and more every day. Natural humour, lightness of heart, and *brio,* it begins to think the best philosophy,—

and it is right. Doubtless this is the great cause of the popularity of that confounded Northern Magazine,[24] which seems to have taken out a patent for laughing at all the world. Like the spear of Achilles, however, its point can convey pleasure as well as pain—a balm as well as a wound. It is a wicked wag, yet one cannot help laughing with it at times, even against one's-self. I shall never forget the look of L.H. when he read himself described in it, as a turkey-cock coquetting with the hostile number newly come out. There was more good nature in the article than he had met any where for a long time, and he grinned with a quantum of glee that would have suffocated a monkey.

I would that Heaven had endowed me with more of the risible faculty, or more of the serious; that I had been decidedly one or the other, instead of being of that mongrel humour, which deals out philosophy with flippant air, and cracks jests with coffin visage. I can't enrol myself under any banner; and cannot, for the life of me, be either serious or merry. I've tried both; but my gravity was doggedness, and my mirth most uncouth gambolling. So I must e'en remain as I am,—up or down, as stimuli make or leave me. It is a sorry look-out, though, to be dependent on these,—to owe every bright thought to "mine host," or mine apothecary. I am not an admirer of "the sober berry's juice;" it generates more wind than ideas.[25] Johnson's favourite beverage is better, but it is not that I worship. "Tell me what company you keep," says the adage; a more pertinent query would be, "Tell me what liquor you drink." I would undertake to tell any character upon this data. There is a manifest "compromise between wine and water" in Mr Octavius Gilchrist[26]; 'tis easy to discover sour beer in Mr Gifford's pen: and brisk toddy in North's—equally easy in mine, to descry the dizziness of spirit, or the washiness of water, whichever at the time be the reigning potion.

This hurried sketch will not see the light till I am no more. 'Twill be found among my papers, affixed to my Memoirs, and my executors will give it to the world with pomp. Then will I, uncoated, unbreeched, and uncravatted, look down from the empyreal on the scatteration of my foes. A life of drudgery—of "hubble, bubble, toil, and trouble"[27]—will be repaid with ages of fame; and, enthroned between Addison and Bacon, my spirit shall wield the sceptre of Cockney philosophy.—Yet let me not be discontented; I am not all forsaken. From Winterston[28] to Hampstead my name is known—at least, with respect. I am in literature the lord-mayor of the city—the Wood of Parnassus[29] (what an idea!). The apprentices of Cockaigne point at me, as towards the highest grade of their ambition. I am the prefect of all city critical gazettes; and L.H. for all his huffing and strutting, is but my deputy—my proconsul.—Said I not well, Bully Rock?[30] I blew into his nostrils all the genius he possesses, and introduced him to the honourable fraternity of washerwomen and the round-table; since which auspicious day, he lacked never a beef-steak, or a clean shirt. But of him, and of all my acquaintances, I have left valuable memorials throughout my writings. This observation, and that anecdote, have always come *pat* into my sentences[31]; so that, with my mixture of gossip and philosophy, I shall be the half-Boswell, half-Johnson, of my age.—Not that I deign to compare myself with the first in dignity, or with the last in "that fine tact, that airy intuitive faculty," that purchases at half-price ready-made wisdom.[32] As to my politics, it would be a difficult matter to say what they were. I know not myself; so that we will treat them as a country schoolmaster gets over a hard word, "It's Greek, Bill, read on."—As to my temper, it is of the *genus irritabile prosaicorum* (if that be good Latin.)[33] I am very willing to give, but little able to return a blow. I weep under the lash, and, in truth, am too innocent for the world. After attacking private character and public virtue,—endeavouring to sap all principles of religion and government,—uttering whatever slander or blasphemy caprice suggested, or malice spurred me to,—yet am I surprised, and unable to discover, how or why any one can be angry with me. I own, it is a puzzle to me to find out how I have made enemies. Yet, such is the world, that I am belaboured on all sides;—friends and foes alike fall foul of me;—and often am I tempted to cry out, in the language of that book I have neglected, "There is no peace for me, but in the grave."[34.]

34
Lord Byron, *The Vision of Judgment* (1821)

The quarrel between Byron and Southey is long and complex, but Byron's *Vision of Judgment* is one of the most decisive salvos in this intense battle of personalities and beliefs. Begun in May 1821 at Ravenna and completed the following October, Byron's *Vision* was his response to Southey's *A Vision of Judgement* (published April 1821) and to the Preface in which Southey, thinking partly of Byron and the first two cantos of *Don Juan,* attacks a "Satanic school" [*The Works of Robert Southey,* 10 vols. (London: Longmans, 1837–1838), 10.206] of poets and condemns their "lewdness and impiety" (203).

The laureate's funeral ode in honor of George III (who died 29 January 1820) takes the form of a dream vision in which the poet witnesses the entry of the King into heaven. His accusers (such as Wilkes) are summoned but remain silent, and he is seen to be joined with earlier English kings and various "Worthies" and family members who appear to welcome him. Byron's rejoinder is a "true dream" (106.2 below) in contrast to what he would have seen as Southey's royalist hallucination. Byron's poem, so full of wit and lively dramatic interchanges, completely overshadows the egocentric, static pageantry of Southey's propaganda and throws into relief the laureate's stubborn efforts to introduce metrical rhythms into English verse "in imitation of the ancient hexameter" (Preface, 195). Byron's *Vision* was first published in *The Liberal,* first number (15 October 1822), and that poetic text is used here. The controversy about the Preface to the poem is described in William H. Marshall, *Byron, Shelley, Hunt, and 'The Liberal'* (Philadelphia: University of Pennsylvania Press, 1960); see especially 72–73, 90–91, and 130–33. The text of the Preface is from its first printing in January 1823 when the second edition of the first number of *The Liberal* was published.

THE VISION OF JUDGMENT.
BY
QUEVEDO REDIVIVUS.[1]

SUGGESTED BY THE COMPOSITION SO ENTITLED BY THE AUTHOR OF "WAT TYLER."[2]

"A Daniel come to judgment! yea, a Daniel!
I thank thee, Jew, for teaching me that word."[3]

PREFACE.

It hath been wisely said, that "One fool makes many;" and it hath been poetically observed,

"That fools rush in where angels fear to tread."—*Pope*[4]

If Mr. Southey had not rushed in where he had no business, and where he never was before, and never will be again, the following poem would not have been written. It is not impossible that it may be as good as his own, seeing that it cannot, by any species of stupidity, natural or acquired, be *worse*. The gross flattery, the dull impudence, the renegado intolerance and impious cant of the poem by the author of Wat Tyler, are something so stupendous as to form the sublime of himself—containing the quintessence of his own attributes.

So much for his poem—a word on his preface. In this preface it has pleased the magnanimous Laureate to draw the picture of a supposed "Satanic School," the which he doth recommend to the notice of the legislature, thereby adding to his other laurels the ambition of those of an informer.[5] If there exists anywhere, excepting in his imagination, such a school, is he not sufficiently armed against it by his own intense vanity? The truth is, that there are certain writers whom Mr. S. imagines, like Scrub, to have "talked to *him;* for they laughed consumedly."[6]

I think I know enough of most of the writers to whom he is supposed to allude, to assert, that they, in their individual capacities, have done more good in the charities of life to their fellow-creatures in any one year, than Mr. Southey has done harm to himself by his absurdities in his whole life; and this is saying a great deal. But I have a few questions to ask.

1stly. Is Mr. Southey the author of Wat Tyler?

2ndly. Was he not refused a remedy at law by the highest Judge of his beloved England, because it was a blasphemous and seditious publication?

3dly. Was he not entitled by William Smith, in full Parliament, "a rancorous Renegado?"[7]

4thly. Is he not Poet Laureate, with his own lines on Martin the Regicide staring him in the face?[8]

And, 5thly. Putting the four preceding items together, with what conscience dare *he* call the attention of the laws to the publications of others, be they what they may?

I say nothing of the cowardice of such a proceeding; its meanness speaks for itself; but I wish to touch upon the *motive*, which is neither more nor less, than that Mr. S. has been laughed at a little in some recent publications, as he was of yore in the "Anti-jacobin" by his present patrons. Hence all this "skimble scamble stuff" and "Satanic," and so forth. However, it is worthy of him—*"Qualis ab incepto."*[9]

If there is any thing obnoxious to the political opinions of a portion of the public, in the following poem, they may thank Mr. Southey. He might have written hexameters, as he has written every thing else, for aught that the writer cared—had they been upon another subject. But to attempt to canonize a Monarch, who, whatever were his household virtues, was neither a successful nor a patriot king,—inasmuch as several years of his reign passed in war with America and Ireland, to say nothing of the aggression upon France,—like all other exaggeration, necessarily begets opposition. In whatever manner he may be spoken of in this new "Vision," his *public* career will not be more favourably transmitted by history. Of his private virtues (although a little expensive to the nation) there can be no doubt.

With regard to the supernatural personages treated of, I can only say that I know as much about them, and (as an honest man) have a better right to talk of them than Robert Southey. I have also treated them more tolerantly. The way in which that poor insane creature, the Laureate, deals about his judgments in the next world, is like his own judgment in this. If it was not completely ludicrous, it would be something worse. I don't think that there is much more to say at present.

Quevedo Redivivus.

P.S.—It is possible that some readers may object, in these objectionable times, to the freedom with which saints, angels, and spiritual persons, discourse in this "Vision." But for precedents upon such points I must refer him to Fielding's "Journey from this World to the next," and to the Visions of myself, the said Quevedo, in Spanish or translated. The reader is also requested to observe, that no doctrinal tenets are insisted upon or discussed; that the person of the Deity is carefully withheld from sight, which is more than can be said for the Laureate, who hath thought proper to make him talk, not "like a school-divine," but like the unscholarlike Mr. Southey. The whole action passes on the outside of Heaven; and Chaucer's Wife of Bath, Pulci's Morgante Maggiore,[10] Swift's Tale of a Tub, and the other works above referred to, are cases in point of the freedom with which saints, &c. may be permitted to converse in works not intended to be serious.

Q. R.

[**Mr. Southey, being, as he says, a good Christian and vindictive, threatens, I understand, a reply to this our answer. It is to be hoped that his visionary faculties will in the mean time have acquired a little more judgment, properly so called: otherwise he will get himself into new dilemmas. These apostate jacobins furnish rich rejoinders. Let him take a specimen. Mr. Southey laudeth grievously "one Mr. Lander,"[11] who cultivates much private renown in the shape of Latin verses; and not long ago, the Poet Laureate dedicated to him, it appeareth, one of his fugitive lyrics, upon the strength of a poem called *Gebir.* Who would suppose, that in this same Gebir, the aforesaid Savage Landor (for such is his grim cognomen) putteth into the infernal regions no less a person that the hero of his friend Mr. Southey's heaven,—yea, even George the Third! See also how personal Savage becometh, when he hath a mind. The following is his portrait of our late gracious Sovereign:—

Prince Gebir having descended into the infernal regions,
 the shades of his royal ancestors are, at his request,
 called up to his view, and he exclaims to his ghostly
 guide)—

"Aroar, what wretch that nearest us? what wretch
Is that with eyebrows white and slanting brow?
Listen! him yonder, who, bound down supine,
Shrinks yelling from that sword there, engine-hung.
He too amongst my ancestors! I hate
The despot, but the dastard I despise.
Was he our countryman?"

"Alas, O King!

Iberia bore him, but the breed accurst
Inclement winds blew blighting from north-east."
"He was a warrior then, nor fear'd the gods?"
"Gebir, he fear'd the Demons, not the Gods,
Though them indeed his daily face ador'd;
And was no warrior, yet the thousand lives
Squander'd, as stones to exercise a sling!
And the tame cruelty and cold caprice—
Of madness of mankind! addrest, adored!"—*Gebir,* p. 28.

I omit noticing some edifying Ithyphallics of Savagius,[12] wishing to keep the proper veil over them, if his grave but somewhat indiscreet worshipper will suffer it; but certainly these teachers of "great moral lessons" are apt to be found in strange company.]

THE VISION OF JUDGMENT

I

SAINT PETER sat by the celestial gate:
    His keys were rusty, and the lock was dull,
So little trouble had been given of late;
    Not that the place by any means was full,
But since the Gallic era "eighty-eight,"[13]
    The devils had ta'en a longer, stronger pull,
And "a pull altogether," as they say
At sea—which drew most souls another way.

II

The angels all were singing out of tune,
And hoarse with having little else to do,   10
Excepting to wind up the sun and moon,
    Or curb a runaway young star or two,
Or wild colt of a comet, which too soon
    Broke out of bounds o'er the ethereal blue,
Splitting some planet with its playful tail,
As boats are sometimes by a wanton whale.

III

The guardian seraphs had retired on high,
Finding their charges past all care below;
Terrestrial business fill'd nought in the sky
    Save the recording angel's black bureau;   20
Who found, indeed, the facts to multiply
    With such rapidity of vice and woe,
That he had stripp'd off both his wings in quills,
And yet was in arrear of human ills.

IV

His business so augmented of late years,
    That he was forced against his will, no doubt,
(Just like those cherubs, earthly ministers,)
    For some resource to turn himself about,
And claim the help of his celestial peers,
    To aid him ere he should be quite worn out   30
By the increased demand for his remarks;
Six angels and twelve saints were named his clerks.

V

This was a handsome board—at least for heaven;
  And yet they had even then enough to do,
So many conquerors' cars were daily driven,
  So many kingdoms fitted up anew;
Each day too slew its thousands six or seven,
  Till at the crowning carnage, Waterloo,
They threw their pens down in divine disgust—
The page was so besmear'd with blood and dust.   40

VI

This by the way; 'tis not mine to record
  What angels shrink from: even the very devil
On this occasion his own work abhorr'd,
  So surfeited with the infernal revel;
Though he himself had sharpen'd every sword,
  It almost quench'd his innate thirst of evil.
(Here Satan's sole good work deserves insertion—
'Tis, that he has both generals in reversion.)14

VII

Let's skip a few short years of hollow peace,
  Which peopled earth no better, hell was wont,   50
And heaven none—they form the tyrant's lease
  With nothing but new names subscribed upon 't;
'Twill one day finish: meantime they increase,
  "With seven heads and ten horns," and all in front,
Like Saint John's foretold beast15; but ours are born
Less formidable in the head than horn.

VIII

In the first year of freedom's second dawn
  Died George the Third16; although no tyrant, one
Who shielded tyrants, till each sense withdrawn
  Left him nor mental nor external sun: 60
A better farmer ne'er brushed dew from lawn,17
  A weaker king ne'er left a realm undone!
He died—but left his subjects still behind,
One half as mad—and t'other no less blind.

IX

He died! his death made no great stir on earth;
  His burial made some pomp; there was profusion
Of velvet, gilding, brass, and no great dearth

Of aught but tears—save those shed by collusion;
For these things may be bought at their true worth:
  Of elegy there was the due infusion—   70
Bought also; and the torches, cloaks, and banners,
Heralds, and relics of old Gothic manners,

X

Form'd a sepulchral melo-drame. Of all
  The fools who flock'd to swell or see the show,
Who cared about the corpse? The funeral
  Made the attraction, and the black the woe.
There throbb'd not there a thought which pierced the pall;
  And when the gorgeous coffin was laid low,
It seem'd the mockery of hell to fold
The rottenness of eighty years in gold.   80

XI

So mix his body with the dust! It might
  Return to what it *must* far sooner, were
The natural compound left alone to fight
  Its way back into earth, and fire, and air;
But the unnatural balsams merely blight
  What nature made him at his birth, as bare
As the mere million's base unmummied clay—
Yet all his spices but prolong decay.

XII

He's dead—and upper earth with him has done:
  He's buried; save the undertaker's bill,   90
Or lapidary scrawl, the world is gone
  For him, unless he left a German will;
But where's the proctor who will ask his son?[18]
  In whom his qualities are reigning still,
Except that household virtue, most uncommon,
Of constancy to an unhandsome woman.[19]

XIII

"God save the king!" It is a large economy
  In God to save the like; but if he will
Be saving, all the better; for not one am I
  Of those who think damnation better still: 100
I hardly know too if not quite alone am I
  In this small hope of bettering future ill

By circumscribing, with some slight restriction,
The eternity of hell's hot jurisdiction.

XIV

I know this is unpopular; I know
   'Tis blasphemous; I know one may be damn'd
For hoping no one else may e'er be so;
   I know my catechism; I know we are cramm'd
With the best doctrines till we quite o'erflow;
   I know that all save England's Church have shamm'd.   110
And that the other twice two hundred churches
And synagogues have made a *damn'd* bad purchase.

XV

God help us all! God help me too! I am,
   God knows, as helpless as the devil can wish,
And not a whit more difficult to damn,
   Than is to bring to land a late-hook'd fish,
Or to the butcher to purvey the lamb;
   Not that I'm fit for such a noble dish
As one day will be that immortal fry
Of almost every body born to die.   120

XVI

Saint Peter sat by the celestial gate,
   And nodded o'er his keys; when lo! there came
A wond'rous noise he had not heard of late—
   A rushing sound of wind, and stream, and flame;
In short, a roar of things extremely great,
   Which would have made aught save a saint exclaim;
But he, with first a start and then a wink,
Said, "There's another star gone out, I think!"

XVII

But ere he could return to his repose,
   A Cherub flapp'd his right wing o'er his eyes—   130
At which Saint Peter yawn'd, and rubb'd his nose:
   "Saint porter," said the Angel, "prithee rise!"
Waving a goodly wing, which glow'd, as glows
   An earthly peacock's tail, with heavenly dyes;
To which the Saint replied, "Well, what's the matter?
"Is Lucifer come back with all this clatter?"

XVIII

"No," quoth the Cherub: "George the Third is dead."
   "And who *is* George the Third?" replied the Apostle:
"*What George? What Third?*" "The King of England," said
   The Angel. "Well! he won't find kings to jostle   140
Him on his way; but does he wear his head?
   Because the last we saw here had a tussle,
And ne'er would have got into heaven's good graces,
Had he not flung his head in all our faces.[20]

XIX

"He was, if I remember, king of France;
   That head of his, which could not keep a crown
On earth, yet ventured in my face to advance
   A claim to those of martyrs—like my own:
If I had had my sword, as I had once
   When I cut ears off, I had cut him down[21];   150
But having but my *keys,* and not my brand,
I only knock'd his head from out his hand.

XX

"And then he set up such a headless howl,
   That all the saints came out, and took him in;
And there he sits by St Paul, cheek by jowl;
   That fellow Paul—the parvenu! The skin
Of Saint Bartholomew, which makes his cowl
   In heaven, and upon earth redeem'd his sin,
So as to make a martyr, never sped
Better than did this weak and wooden head.   160

XXI

"But had it come up here upon its shoulders
   There would have been a different tale to tell:
The fellow feeling in the saint's beholders
   Seems to have acted on them like a spell,
And so this very foolish head heaven solders
   Back on its trunk: it may be very well,
And seems the custom here to overthrow
   Whatever has been wisely done below."

XXII

The Angel answer'd, "Peter! do not pout;
   The King who comes has head and all entire,   170
And never knew much what it was about—

He did as doth the puppet—by its wire,
And will be judged like all the rest, no doubt:
  My business and your own is not to inquire
Into such matters, but to mind our cue—
Which is to act as we are bid to do."

XXIII

While thus they spake, the angelic caravan,
  Arriving like a rush of mighty wind,
Cleaving the fields of space, as doth the swan
  Some silver stream (say Ganges, Nile, or Inde,   180
Or Thames, or Tweed) and midst them an old man
  With an old soul, and both extremely blind,
Halted before the gate, and in his shroud
Seated their fellow-traveller on a cloud.

XXIV

But bringing up the rear of this bright host
  A Spirit of a different aspect waved
His wings, like thunder-clouds above some coast
  Whose barren beach with frequent wrecks is paved;
His brow was like the deep when tempest-tost;
  Fierce and unfathomable thoughts engraved   190
Eternal wrath on his immortal face,
And *where* he gazed a gloom pervaded space.

XXV

As he drew near, he gazed upon the gate
  Ne'er to be entered more by him or sin,
With such a glance of supernatural hate,
  As made Saint Peter wish himself within;
He potter'd with his keys at a great rate,
  And sweated through his apostolic skin:
Of course his perspiration was but ichor,[22]
Or some such other spiritual liquor.   200

XXVI

The very cherubs huddled altogether,
  Like birds when soars the falcon; and they felt
A tingling to the tip of every feather,
  And form'd a circle like Orion's belt
Around their poor old charge; who scarce knew whither
  His guards had led him, though they gently dealt

With royal manes[23] (for by many stories,
And true, we learn the angels all are Tories).

XXVII

As things were in this posture, the gate flew
  Asunder, and the flashing of its hinges   210
Flung over space an universal hue
  Of many-coloured flame, until its tinges
Reach'd even our speck of earth, and made a new
  Aurora borealis spread its fringes
O'er the North Pole; the same seen, when ice-bound,
By Captain Parry's crew, in "Melville's Sound."[24]

XXVIII

And from the gate thrown open issued beaming
  A beautiful and mighty Thing of Light,
Radiant with glory, like a banner streaming
  Victorious from some world-o'erthrowing fight: 220
My poor comparisons must needs be teeming
  With earthly likenesses, for her the night
Of clay obscures our best conceptions, saving
Johanna Southcote,[25] or Bob Southey raving.

XXIX

'Twas the archangel Michael: all men know
  The make of angels and archangels, since
There's scarce a scribbler has not one to show,
  From the friends' leader to the angels' prince.
There also are some altar-pieces, though
  I really can't say that they much evince   230
One's inner notions of immortal spirits;
But let the connoisseurs explain *their* merits.

XXX

Michael flew forth in glory and in good;
  A goodly work of him from whom all glory
And good arise; the portal past—he stood;
  Before him the young cherubs and saint hoary—
(I say *young,* begging to be understood
  By looks, not years; and should be very sorry
To state, they were not older than St. Peter,
But merely that they seem'd a little sweeter).   240

XXXI

The cherubs and the saints bow'd down before
   That arch-angelic Hierarch, the first
Of Essences angelical, who wore
   The aspect of a god; but this ne'er nurst
Pride in his heavenly bosom, in whose core
   No thought, save for his Maker's service, durst
Interlude, however glorified and high;
He knew him but the viceroy of the sky.

XXXII

He and the sombre silent Spirit met—
   They knew each other both for good and ill;   250
Such was their power, that neither could forget
   His former friend and future foe; but still
There was a high, immortal, proud regret
   In either's eye, as if 'twere less their will
Than destiny to make the eternal years
Their date of war, and their "Champ Clos" the spheres.[26]

XXXIII

But here they were in neutral space: we know
   From Job, that Satan hath the power to pay
A heavenly visit thrice a year or so[27];
   And that "the Sons of God," like those of clay.   260
Must keep him company; and we might show,
   From the same book, in how polite a way
The dialogue is held between the Powers
Of Good and Evil—but t'would take up hours.

XXXIV

And this is not a theologic tract,
   To prove with Hebrew and with Arabic,
If Job be allegory or a fact,
   But a true narrative; and thus I pick
From out the whole but such and such an act
   As sets aside the slightest thought of trick.   270
'Tis every little true, beyond suspicion,
And accurate as any other vision.[28]

XXXV

The spirits were in neutral space, before
   The gate of heaven; like eastern thresholds is

The place where Death's grand cause is argued o'er,
   And souls despatched to that world or to this;
And therefore Michael and the other wore
   A civil aspect: though they did not kiss,
Yet still between his Darkness and his Brightness
There passed a mutual glance of great politeness.   280

XXXVI

The Archangel bowed, not like a modern beau,
   But with a graceful Oriental bend,
Pressing one radiant arm just where below
   The heart in good men is supposed to tend.
He turned as to an equal, not too low,
   But kindly; Satan met his ancient friend
With more hauteur, as might an old Castilian
Poor noble meet a mushroom rich civilian.

XXXVII

He merely bent his diabolic brow
   An instant; and then raising it, he stood   290
In act to assert his right or wrong, and show
   Cause why King George by no means could or should
Make out a case to be exempt from woe
   Eternal, more than other kings endued
With better sense and hearts, whom history mentions,
Who long have "paved Hell with their good intentions."

XXXVIII

Michael began: "What wouldst thou with this man,
   Now dead, and brought before the Lord? What ill
Hath he wrought since his mortal race began,
   That thou can'st claim him? Speak! And do thy will,   300
If it be just: if in this earthly span
   He hath been greatly failing to fulfil
His duties as a king and mortal, say,
And he is thine; if not, let him have way."

XXXIX

"Michael!" replied the Prince of Air, "even here
   Before the gate of him thou servest, must
I claim my subject; and I will make appear
   That as he was my worshipper in dust,
So shall he be in spirit, although dear
   To thee and thine, because nor wine nor lust   310

Were of his weaknesses; yet on the throne
He reigned o'er millions to serve me alone.

XL

"Look to *our* earth, or rather *mine;* it was,
   Once, more thy master's: but I triumph not
In this poor planet's conquest, nor, alas!
   Need he thou servest envy me my lot:
With all the myriads of bright worlds which pass
   In worship round him, he may have forgot
Yon weak creation of such paltry things;
I think few worth damnation save their kings.   320

XLI

"And these but as a kind of quit-rent,[29] to
   Assault my right as lord: and even had
I such an inclination, 'twere (as you
   Well know) superfluous; they are grown so bad,
That Hell has nothing better left to do
   Than leave them to themselves: so much more mad
And evil by their own internal curse,
Heaven cannot make them better, nor I worse.

XLII

"Look to the earth, I said, and say again:
   When this old, blind, man, helpless, weak, poor worm,   330
Began in youth's first bloom and flush to reign,
   The world and he both wore a different form,
And much of earth and all the watery plain
   Of Ocean call'd him king: through many a storm
His isles had floated on the abyss of Time;
For the rough virtues chose them for their clime.

XLIII

"He came to his sceptre, young; he leaves it, old[30];
   Look to the state in which he found his realm,
And left it; and his annals too behold,
   How to a minion first he gave the helm[31];   340
How great upon his heart a thirst for gold,
   The beggar's vice, which can but overwhelm
The meanest hearts; and for the rest, but glance
   Thine eye along America and France!

XLIV

" 'Tis true, he was a tool from first to last
    (I have the workmen safe); but as a tool
So let him be consumed! From out the past
    Of ages, since mankind have known the rule
Of monarch—from the blood rolls amass'd
    Of sin and slaughter—from the Caesars' school.   350
Take the worst pupil; and produce a reign
More drench'd with gore, more cumber'd with the slain!

XLV

"He ever warr'd with freedom and the free:
    Nations as men, home subjects, foreign foes,
So that they utter'd the word 'Liberty!'
    Found George the Third their first opponent. Whose
History was ever stain'd as his will be
    With national and individual woes?
I grant his household abstinence; I grant
His neutral virtues, which most monarchs want;   360

XLVI

"I know he was a constant consort; own
    He was a decent sire, and middling lord.
All this is much, and most upon a throne;
    As temperance, if at Apicius'³² board,
Is more than at an anchorite's supper shown.
    I grant him all the kindest can accord;
And this was well for him, but not for those
Millions who found him what oppression chose.

XLVII

"The new world shook him off; the old yet groans
    Beneath what he and his prepared, if not   370
Completed: he leaves heirs on many thrones
    To all his vices, without what begot
Compassion for him—his tame virtues; drones
    Who sleep, or despots who have now forgot
A lesson which shall be re-taught them, wake
Upon the thrones of earth; but let them quake!

XLVIII

"Five millions of the primitive, who hold
    The faith which makes ye great on earth, implored
A *part* of that vast *all* they held of old,—

Freedom to worship—not alone your Lord,   380
Michael, but you, and you, Saint Peter! Cold
   Must be your souls, if you have not abhorr'd
The foe to Catholic participation
In all the license of a Christian nation.[33]

XLIX

"True! he allow'd them to pray God; but as
   A consequence of prayer, refused the law
Which would have placed them upon the same base
   With those who did not hold the saints in awe."
But here Saint Peter started from his place,
   And cried, "You may the prisoner withdraw: 390
Ere Heaven shall ope her portals to this Gulf,[34]
While I am on guard, may I be damn'd myself!

L

"Sooner will I with Cerberus exchange
   My office (and *his* is no sinecure)
Than see this royal Bedlam bigot range
   The azure fields of heaven, of that be sure!"
"Saint!" replied Satan, "you do well to avenge
   The wrongs he made your satellites endure;
And if to this exchange you should be given,
I'll try to coax *our* Cerberus up to Heaven!"   400

LI

Here Michael interposed: "Good saint! and devil!
   Pray not so fast; you both out-run discretion.
Saint Peter ! you were wont to be more civil:
   Satan! excuse this warmth of his expression,
And condescension to the vulgar's level:
   Even saints sometimes forget themselves in session.
Have you got more to say?"—"No!"—"If you please,
I'll trouble you to call your witnesses."

LII

Then Satan turned and wav'd his swarthy hand,
   Which stirr'd with its electric qualities   410
Clouds farther off than we can understand,
   Although we find him sometimes in our skies;
Infernal thunder shook both sea and land
   In all the planets, and hell's batteries

Let off the artillery, which Milton mentions
As one of Satan's most sublime inventions.[35]

LIII

This was a signal unto such damn'd souls
   As have the privilege of their damnation
Extended far beyond the mere controls
   Of worlds past, present, or to come; no station   420
Is theirs particularly in the rolls
   Of hell assigned; but where their inclination
Or business carries them in search of game,
They may range freely—being damn'd the same.

LIV

They are proud of this—as very well they may.
   It being a sort of knighthood, or gilt key[36]
Stuck in their loins; or like to an "entré"
   Up in the brick stairs, or such free-masonry.
I borrow my comparisons from clay,
   Being clay myself. Let not those spirits be   430
Offended with such base low likenesses;
We know their posts are nobler far than these.

LV

When the great signal ran from heaven to hell—
   About ten million times the distance reckon'd
From our sun to its earth, as we can tell
   How much time it takes up, even to a second,
For every ray that travels to dispel
   The fogs of London; through which, dimly beacon'd,
The weathercocks are gilt, some thrice a year,
If that the *summer* is not too severe:—   440

LVI

I say that I can tell—'twas half a minute;
   I know the solar beams take up more time
Ere, pack'd up for their journey, they begin it;
   But then their telegraph is less sublime,
And if they ran a race, they would not win it
   'Gainst Satan's couriers bound for their own clime.
The sun takes up some years for every ray
To reach its goal—the devil not half a day.

LVII

Upon the verge of space, about the size
    Of half-a-crown, a little speck appear'd   450
(I've seen a something like it in the skies
    In the Aegean, ere a squall); it near'd,
And, growing bigger, took another guise;
    Like an aerial ship it tack'd, and steer'd,
Or *was* steer'd (I am doubtful of the grammar
Of the last phrase, which makes the stanza stammer;—

LVIII

But take your choice); and then it grew a cloud,
    And so it was—a cloud of witnesses.
But such a cloud! No land ere saw a crowd
    Of locusts numerous as the heavens saw these;   460
They shadow'd with their myriads space; their loud
    And varied cries were like those of wild-geese,
(If nations may be liken'd to a goose),
And realised the phrase of "hell broke loose."[37]

LIX

Here crash'd a sturdy oath of stout John Bull,
    Who damn'd away his eyes as heretofore:
There Paddy brogued "by Jasus!"—"What's your wull?"
    The temperate Scot exclaim'd: the French ghost swore
In certain terms I shan't translate in full,
    As the first coachman will; and amidst the roar,   470
The voice of Jonathan was heard to express
"*Our* President is going to war, I guess."[38]

LX

Besides there were the Spaniard, Dutch, and Dane;
    In short, an universal shoal of shades
From Otaheite's isle to Salisbury Plain,
    Of all climes and professions, years and trades,
Ready to swear against the good king's reign,
    Bitter as clubs in cards are against spades:
All summon'd by this grand "subpoena," to
Try if kings mayn't be damn'd, like me or you.   480

LXI

When Michael saw this host, he first grew pale,
    As angels can; next, like Italian twilight,
He turned all colours—as a peacock's tail,

Or sunset streaming through a Gothic skylight
In some old abbey, or a trout not stale,
    Or distant lightning on the horizon *by* night,
Or a fresh rainbow, or a grand review
Of thirty regiments in red, green, and blue.

LXII

Then he address'd himself to Satan: "Why—
    My good old friend, for such I deem you, though   490
Our different parties make us fight so shy,
    I ne'er mistake you for a *personal* foe;
Our difference is *political,* and I
    Trust that, whatever may occur below,
You know my great respect for you; and this
Makes me regret whate'er you do amiss—

LXIII

"Why, my dear Lucifer, would you abuse
    My call for witnesses? I did not mean
That you should half of earth and hell produce;
    " 'Tis even superfluous, since two honest, clean,   500
True testimonies are enough: we lose
    Our time, nay, our eternity, between
The accusation and defence: if we
Hear both, 'twill stretch our immortality."

LXIV

Satan replied, "To me the matter is
    Indifferent, in a personal point of view:
I can have fifty better souls than this
    With far less trouble than we have gone through
Already; and I merely argued his
    Late Majesty of Britain's case with you   510
Upon a point of form: you may dispose
Of him, I've kings enough below, God knows!"

LXV

Thus spoke the Demon (late called "multifaced"
    By multo-scribbling Southey).[39] "Then we'll call
One or two persons of the myriads placed
    Around our congress, and dispense with all
The rest," quoth Michael: "Who may be so graced
    As to speak first? there's choice enough—who shall

It be?" Then Satan answered, "There are many;
But you may choose Jack Wilkes as well as any."[40]   520

LXVI

A merry, cock-eyed, curious looking Sprite
    Upon the instant started from the throng,
Dressed in a fashion now forgotten quite;
    For all the fashions of the flesh stick long
By people in the next world; where unite
    All the costumes since Adam's, right or wrong,
From Eve's fig-leaf down to the petticoat,
Almost as scanty, of days less remote.

LXVII

The Spirit look'd around upon the crowds
    Assembled, and exclaim'd, "My friends of all   530
The spheres, we shall catch cold amongst these clouds;
    So let's to business: why this general call?
If those are freeholders I see in shrouds,
    And 'tis for an election that they bawl,
Behold a candidate with unturn'd-coat!
Saint Peter, may I count upon your vote?"

LXVIII

"Sir," replied Michael, "you mistake: these things
    Are of a former life, and what we do
Above is more august; to judge of kings
    Is the tribunal met; so now you know."   540
"Then I presume those gentlemen with wings,"
    Said Wilkes, "are cherubs; and that soul below
Looks much like George the Third; but to my mind
A good deal older—Bless me! is he blind?"

LXIX

"He is what you behold him, and his doom
    Depends upon his deeds," the Angel said.
"If you have ought to arraign in him, the tomb
    Gives license to the humblest beggar's head
To lift itself against the loftiest."—"Some,"
    Said Wilkes, "don't wait to see them laid in lead,   550
For such a liberty—and I, for one,
Have told them what I thought beneath the sun."

LXX

"*Above* the sun repeat, then, what thou hast
  To urge against him," said the Archangel. "Why,"
Replied the Spirit, "since old scores are past,
  Must I turn evidence? In faith, not I.
Besides, I beat him hollow at the last,
  With all his Lords and Commons: in the sky
I don't like ripping up old stories, since
His conduct was but natural in a prince.   560

LXXI

"Foolish, no doubt, and wicked, to oppress
  A poor unlucky devil without a shilling;
But then I blame the man himself much less
  Than Bute and Grafton,[41] and shall be unwilling
To see him punish'd here for their excess,
  Since they were both damn'd long ago, and still in
Their place below; for me, I have forgiven,
And vote his 'habeas corpus' into Heaven."

LXXII

"Wilkes," said the Devil, "I understand all this;
  You turn'd to half a courtier ere you died,   570
And seem to think it would not be amiss
  To grow a whole one on the other side
Of Charon's ferry; you forget that *his*
  Reign is concluded; whatsoe'er betide,
He won't be sovereign more: you've lost your labour,
For at the best he will but be your neighbour.

LXXIII

"However, I knew what to think of it,
  When I beheld you in your jesting way,
Flitting and whispering round about the spit
  Where Belial, upon duty for the day,   580
With Fox's lard was basting William Pitt,
  His pupil; I knew what to think, I say:
That fellow even in hell breeds farther ills;
I'll have him *gagg'd*—'twas one of his own bills.[42]

LXXIV

"Call Junius!"[43] From the crowd a Shadow stalk'd,
  And at the name there was a general squeeze,
So that the very ghosts no longer walk'd

In comfort, at their own aerial ease,
But were all ramm'd, and jamm'd (but to be balk'd,
  As we shall see) and jostled hands and knees, 590
Like wind compress'd and pent within a bladder,
Or like a human cholic, which is sadder.

LXXV

The Shadow came! a tall, thin, gray-hair'd figure,
  That look'd as it had been a shade on earth;
Quick in its motions, with an air of vigour,
  But nought to mark its breeding or its birth:
Now it wax'd little, then grew bigger,
  With now an aim of gloom, or savage mirth;
But as you gazed upon its features, they
Changed every instant—to *what,* none could say. 600

LXXVI

The more intently the ghosts gazed, the less
  Could they distinguish whose the features were;
The Devil himself seem'd puzzled even to guess;
  They varied like a dream—now here, now there;
And several people swore from out the press,
  They knew him perfectly; and one could swear
He was his father; upon which another
Was sure he was his mother's cousin's brother:

LXXVII

Another, that he was a duke, or knight,
  An orator, a lawyer, or a priest, 610
A nabob, a man-midwife; but the wight
  Mysterious changed his countenance at least
As often as they their minds: though in full sight
  He stood, the puzzle only was increased;
The man was a phantasmagoria in
Himself—he was so volatile and thin!

LXXVII

The moment that you had pronounced him *one,*
  Presto! his face changed, and he was another;
And when that change was hardly well put on,
  It varied, till I don't think his own mother 620
(If that he had a mother) would her son
  Have known, he shifted so from one to t'other,

Till guessing from a pleasure grew a task,
At this epistolary "iron mask."[44]

LXXIX

For sometimes he like Cerberus would seem—
    "Three gentlemen at once," (as sagely says
Good Mrs. Malaprop); then you might deem
    That he was not even *one;* how many rays
Were flashing round him; and now a thick steam
    Hid him from sight—like fogs on London days: 630
Now Burke, now Tooke, he grew to people's fancies,
    And certes often like Sir Philip Francis.[45]

LXXX

I've an hypothesis—'tis quite my own;
    I never let it out till now, for fear
Of doing people harm about the throne,
    And injuring some minister or peer
On whom the stigma might perhaps be blown;
    It is—my gentle public, lend thine ear!
'Tis, that what Junius we are wont to call,
Was *really, truly,* nobody at all.   640

LXXXI

I don't see wherefore letters should not be
    Written without hands, since we daily view
Them written without heads; and books we see
    Are fill'd as well without the latter too:
And really till we fix on somebody
    For certain sure to claim them as his due,
Their author, like the Niger's mouth, will bother
    The world to say if *there* be mouth or author.[46]

LXXXII

"And who and what art thou?" the Archangel said.
    "For *that,* you may consult my title-page,"   650
Replied this mighty Shadow of a Shade:
    "If I have kept my secret half an age,
I scarce shall tell it now."—"Canst thou upbraid,"
    Continued Michael, "George Rex, or allege
Aught further?" Junius answer'd, "You had better
First ask him for *his* answer to my letter:

LXXXIII

"My charges upon record will outlast
 The brass of both his epitaph and tomb."
"Repent'st thou not," said Michael, "of some past
 Exaggeration? something which may doom   660
Thyself, if false, as him if true? Thou wast
 Too bitter—is it not so? in thy gloom
Of passion?" "Passion!" cried the Phantom dim,
"I loved my country, and I hated him.

LXXXIV

"What I have written, I have written: let
 The rest be on his head or mine!" So spoke
Old "Nominis Umbra;"⁴⁷ and while speaking yet,
 Away he melted in celestial smoke.
Then Satan said to Michael, "Don't forget
 To call George Washington, and John Horne Tooke,   670
And Franklin:"—but at this time there was heard
A cry for room, though not a phantom stirr'd.

LXXXV

At length with jostling, elbowing, and the aid
 Of cherubim appointed to that post,
The devil Asmodeus to the circle made
 His way, and looked as if his journey cost
Some trouble. When his burden down he laid,
 "What's this?" cried Michael; "why, 'tis not a ghost?"
"I know it," quoth the incubus; "but he
Shall be one, if you leave the affair to me.   680

LXXXVI

"Confound the Renegado! I have sprain'd
 My left wing, he's so heavy; one would think
Some of his works about his neck were chain'd.
 But to the point: while hovering o'er the brink
Of Skiddaw (where as usual it still rained),
 I saw a taper, far below me, wink,
And stooping, caught this fellow at a libel—
No less on History than the Holy Bible.

LXXXVII

"The former is the devil's scripture, and
 The latter yours, good Michael; so the affair   690

Belongs to all of us, you understand.
   I snatch'd him up just as you see him there,
And brought him off for sentence out of hand:
   I've scarcely been ten minutes in the air—
At least a quarter it can hardly be:
I dare say that his wife is still at tea.''

LXXXVIII

Here Satan said, ''I know this man of old,
   And have expected him for some time here:
A sillier fellow you will scarce behold,
   Or more conceited in his petty sphere: 700
But surely it was not worth while to fold
   Such trash below your wing, Asmodeus dear!
We had the poor wretch safe (without being bored
With carriage) coming of his own accord.

LXXXIX

''But since he's here, let's see what he has done.''
   ''Done!'' cried Asmodeus, ''he anticipates
The very business you are now upon,
   And scribbles as if head clerk to the Fates.
Who knows to what his ribaldry may run,
   When such an ass as this, like Balaam's, prates?''[48]   710
''Let's hear,'' quoth Michael, ''what he has to say;
You know we're bound to that in every way.''

XC

Now the Bard, glad to get an audience, which
   By no means often was his case below,
Began to cough, and hawk, and hem, and pitch
   His voice into that awful note of woe
To all unhappy hearers within reach
   Of poets when the tide of rhyme's in flow;
But stuck fast with his first hexameter,
Not one of all whose gouty feet would stir.   720

XCI

But ere the spavin'd dactyls could be spurr'd
   Into recitative, in great dismay
Both cherubim and seraphim were heard
   To murmur loudly through their long array;
And Michael rose ere he could get a word
   Of all his founder'd verses under way,

And cried, "For God's sake stop, my friend! 'twere best—
'*Non Di, non homines*—' you know the rest."[49]

XCII

A general bustle spread throughout the throng,
  Which seem'd to hold all verse in detestation;   730
The angels had of course enough of song
  When upon service; and the generation
Of ghosts had heard too much in life, not long
  Before, to profit by a new occasion;
The Monarch, mute till then, exclaim'd, "What! what!
Pye come again? No more—no more of that!"[50]

XCIII

The tumult grew, an universal cough
  Convulsed the skies, as during a debate,
When Castlereagh has been up long enough
  (Before he was first minister of state,   740
I mean—the *slaves hear now*); some cried "off, off,"
  As at a farce; till grown quite desperate,
The Bard Saint Peter pray'd to interpose
(Himself an author) only for his prose.

XCIV

The varlet was not an ill-favour'd knave;
  A good deal like a vulture in the face,
With a hook nose and a hawk's eye, which gave
  A smart and sharper looking sort of grace
To his whole aspect, which, though rather grave,
  Was by no means so ugly as his case[51];   750
But that indeed was hopeless as can be,
Quite a poetic felony *"de se."*[52]

XCV

Then Michael blew his trump, and still'd the noise
  With one still greater, as is yet the mode
On earth besides; except some grumbling voice,
  Which now and then will make a slight inroad
Upon decorous silence, few will twice
  Lift up their lungs when fairly overcrowd'd;
And now the Bard could plead his own bad cause,
With all the attitudes of self-applause.   760

XCVI

He said—(I only give the heads)—he said,
  He meant no harm in scribbling; 'twas his way
Upon all topics; 'twas, besides, his bread,
  Of which he butter'd both sides; 'twould delay
Too long the assembly (he was pleased to dread)
  And take up rather more time than a day,
To name his works—he would but cite a few—
  Wat Tyler—Rhymes on Blenheim—Waterloo.

XCVII

He had written praises of a regicide[53];
  He had written praises of all kings whatever;   770
He had written for republics far and wide,
  And then against them bitterer than ever;
For pantisocracy he once had cried
  Aloud, a scheme less moral than 'twas clever;
Then grew a hearty anti jacobin—
Had turn'd his coat—and would have turn'd his skin.

XCVIII

He had sung against all battles, and again
  In their high praise and glory; he had call'd
Reviewing "the ungentle craft,"[54] and then
  Became as base a critic as e'er crawl'd—   780
Fed, paid, and pamper'd by the very men
  By whom his muse and morals had been maul'd:
He had written much blank verse, and blanker prose,
And more of both than any body knows.

XCIX

He had written Wesley's life:—here, turning round
  To Satan, "Sir, I'm ready to write yours,
In two octavo volumes, nicely bound,
  With notes and preface, all that most allures
The pious purchaser; and there's no ground
  For fear, for I can choose my own reviewers: 790
So let me have the proper documents,
That I may add you to my other saints."

C

Satan bowed, and was silent. "Well, if you,
  With amiable modesty, decline
My offer, what says Michael? There are few

Whose memoirs could be render'd more divine.
Mine is a pen of all work; not so new
   As it was once, but I would make you shine
Like your own trumpet: by the way, my own
Has more of brass in it, and is as well as blown.   800

CI

"But talking about trumpets, here's my Vision!
   Now you shall judge, all people; yes, you shall
Judge with my judgment! and by my decision
   Be guided who shall enter heaven or fall!
I settle all these things by intuition,
   Times present, past, to come, heaven, hell, and all,
Like King Alfonso![55] When I thus see double,
I save the Deity some worlds of trouble."

CII

He ceased, and drew forth an MS.; and no
   Persuasion on the part of devils, or saints,   810
Or angels, now could stop the torrent; so
   He read the first three lines of the contents;
But at the fourth, the whole spiritual show
   Had vanish'd, with variety of scents,
Ambrosial and sulphureous, as they sprang,
Like lightning, off from his "melodious twang."[56]

CIII

Those grand heroics acted as a spell:
   The angels stopp'd their ears and plied their pinions;
The devils ran howling, deafen'd, down to hell;
   The ghosts fled, gibbering, for their own dominions—   820
(For 'tis not yet decided where they dwell,
   And I leave every man to his opinions);
Michael took refuge in his trump—but lo!
His teeth were set on edge, he could not blow!

CIV

Saint Peter, who has hitherto been known
   For an impetuous saint, upraised his keys,
And at the fifth line knock'd the Poet down;
   Who fell like Phaeton,[57] but more at ease,
Into his lake, for there he did not drown,
   A different web being by the Destinies   830

Woven for the Laureate's final wreath, whene'er
Reform shall happen either here or there.

CV
He first sunk to the bottom—like his works,
    But soon rose to the surface—like himself;
For all corrupted things are buoy'd like corks,[58]
    By their own rottenness, light as an elf,
Or wisp that flits o'er a morass: he lurks,
    It may be, still, like dull books on a shelf,
In his own den, to scrawl some "Life" or "Vision,"
As Wellborn says—"the devil turned precisian."[59]   840

CVI
As for the rest, to come to the conclusion
    Of this true dream, the telescope is gone
Which kept my optics free from all delusion,
    And show'd me what I in my turn have shown:
All I saw farther in the last confusion,
    Was, that King George slipp'd into heaven for one;
And when the tumult dwindled to a calm,
I left him practising the hundredth psalm.[60]

35
Anonymous, "To the Veiled Magician" (1822)

"To the Veiled Magician" was published in *Blackwood's* (January 1822; 113) as one of the "New-Year's Day Congratulations." This parody of Leigh Hunt is addressed to Christopher North in a supposed gesture of self-admiring magnanimity. North was the pseudonym for John Wilson, who had written some of the attacks on Hunt and others in the *Blackwood's* series "The Cockney School of Poetry" initiated in 1817. Hunt—"The Jupiter of the Olympus of Cockaigne" according to the prose gloss to the poem—is made to appear conciliatory toward his critical enemy. Nevertheless, the proffered sonnet is skillfully characterized by the effeminate, dilettantish manner Wilson had always ascribed to Hunt and his "school." The Cockneys' amateurish knowledge of classical mythology, Hunt's paganizing of Hampstead, and his fatal weakness for certain words (e.g., "leafiness" and "fountain" but elsewhere "spot," "gush," and "delicious") all receive the parodist's scorn. Hunt's love of things Italian may be alluded to not simply because of his earlier *Story of Rimini* but because he was very soon to join two other expatriates, Shelley and Byron, in Italy and help them to launch attacks on England through *The Liberal;* certainly other periodicals made announcements about the proposed new periodical that same January [see William H. Marshall, *Byron, Shelley, Hunt, and 'The Liberal'* (Philadelphia: University of Pennsylvania Press, 1960), 45]. The sonnet compactly summarizes the *Blackwood* view of this group of young liberals: Cockneys were ill-bred, they were idle escapists who preferred romance and pastoral, and they lasciviously consorted with milk-maids (or at least imagined nymphs).

TO THE VEILED MAGICIAN

NORTH! many a time upon thy glory musing,
    Mid leafiness, I roam up Hampstead Hill,
When through white clouds Apollo is infusing
    Brightness, and milk-maids kneel their pails to fill,
Beside the meek cow ruminant. I feel

That thou hast beat and buffeted me about,
    More than the cook-maid doth an old dish-clout,[1]
Yet I must still admire thee;—ribs of steel,
Like Spenser's man,[2] are thine; thou carest not
    For blows from soft Italian palms like mine.
    Since it must be so, brightly mayst thou shine,
And long. I came to curse, but I cannot;
    Therefore, may thy bright fountain never fail,
    And Wisdom's long-jerk'd feather o'er thee swale![3]

36
Anonymous, "Lyrical Ballad" (1822)

Published in the *County Constitutional Guardian and Literary Magazine* [Liverpool], no. 1 (April 1822): 367–68, this parody provides yet another version of Wordsworth's encounter with the leech-gatherer, although it also makes reference to several others of his poems (including *Peter Bell*). The anonymous parodist portrays Wordsworth as introspective yet noticeably naive. The poet cannot see any contradiction between his all-consuming egoism and a genuine sympathy for others, or between a "fellow feeling" for the poor and the acceptance of a sinecure from a government of strictly conservative principles. The poem dramatically repudiates Wordsworth's vision of a joyful, innocent, and benign nature. In so doing, the leech-gatherer does ironically give the poet something to think about.

LYRICAL BALLAD

———————

'TWAS a March morning, about nine o'clock,[1]
   The Lark sung clear from an iron-grey cloud,
I past an old man on an Upping-stock,*[2]
   And, as I passed him, he sneez'd aloud.[3]

———————

*The upping-stock is, I believe, an image new to poetry; and to many readers its name and uses may, perhaps, be unknown. It is simply a flight of steps, formed of wood, brick, or stone, built near the door of most inns and farm-houses in this part of the country, to assist the aged and infirm in mounting their horses. It forms at times a convenient seat for old women to converse on, and sun themselves in the open air; and children often amuse themselves by running up the steps, and jumping off from the platform on the top. To minds formed for profound and sympathetic association, the idea of an upping-stock will therefore afford much food for deep thought and poetical interest. A fine youth about seven years and a fort-night old, Habbakuk Crakenthorpe, broke one of his fore teeth in jumping from one of the oldest upping-stocks in my neighborhood, his foot having slipped (when in the act of springing) on an old quid of Tobacco, accidentally left on the stock by his grandfather. The incident was striking, and I have commemorated it, with the name of the youth in a lyrical effusion of some length, which will soon appear annexed to the work announced in the concluding stanza of the above poem. This work may be considered to be, in some sort, a continuation of Peter Bell, but, for sufficing reasons, its title will be Job Ramsbottom.

In pious courtesy I blessed him,
Whilst he, with penetrating eye and keen,
Held forth a bottle, tied down round the rim
With an old rag of thread-bare velveteen.
And in my lonely thought I did surmise,
That the same velveteen had clothed his thighs.

Much musing on the change that could reduce
A pair of breeches to that bottle's use,
And why that aged man did stand
Holding that tied-down bottle in his hand;
And why, with twang that rattled through the trees,
That aged man so lustily did sneeze;
Deep in my mind I cast about
To make the matter out:

And to myself I said, that grey-beard crone
    Is human, and as much alive as I;
No sneezing 'mongst the dead, nor bottles blown,
    Nor scrap of velveteen their mouths to tie.
And as I travail'd in this birth of thought,
    A gust of fellow feeling thrill'd my soul,
When out he spake and ask'd me, if I bought
    Good Leeches—for he thought me Doctor Pole.[4]
In simple verity I answered him—
    He raising then the bottle to mine eye,
I saw the living leeches, sleek and slim,
    Wriggling their tails as if in very joy.

    In water pure they swam;—quoth I, " 'tis good,
Man hath not taught them yet to thirst for blood:"—
With that a harden'd smile gleam'd in his eye,
And, leering on me, this was his reply;—
"They don't lack teaching. Put your hand and try!"—
I turn'd me from that leering grey-beard crone[5]
And, marvelling deeply, sate me all alone
Upon a stone.

And though that flinty stone was ridged and bare,
    No moss nor lichen made a cushion on it,
Though it most sharply gall'd my kerseymere.[6]
Doing a rude stamp-office duty there,
    I'll take my oath upon it,
The rugged surface of that flinty stone

Hurt not my bone,
Nor to my outward self caus'd such deep smart,
As that old man's harsh leer smote on my inmost heart.

     That man was Peter Bell—alas, alas!
     Yea, though he kissed his own ass,
     Yet unredeem'd! But I will once again
     Try to reclaim him in some future strain.[7]
     —Amen.

                ****

37
Thomas Colley Grattan, "Confessions of an English Glutton" (1823)

This prose parody was published in *Blackwood's* (January 1823). Alan Strout [*A Bibliography of Articles in 'Blackwood's Magazine,' Volumes I Through XVIII, 1817–1825* (Lubbock, Texas: Texas Technological College, 1959), 104] attributes its authorship to Thomas Colley Grattan (1782–1864).

"Confessions" is nominally aimed at Thomas De Quincey's *Confessions of an English Opium Eater,* which had been published as a small volume in 1822 after appearing in the *London Magazine* in 1821. Although Grattan, evidently a very accomplished prose stylist, captures many features of De Quincey's elaborate style, the scope of the indictment extends beyond De Quincey to the egoism and egotism that seemed to characterize so much contemporary writing. For example, the autobiographical details about the glutton's childhood development look back unmistakably to the major source of contemporary self-scrutiny, the *Confessions* (1781) of Jean-Jacques Rousseau. Regarding this general development, Ian Jack has observed: "No feature of the literature of the early nineteenth century is more striking than the prominence of the element of autobiography" [*English Literature 1815–1832* (London: Oxford University Press, 1963), 363–64]. For the parodist, the solipsistic predilection has reached a point of excess imaged in the glutton's nightmarish account. Grattan was probably aware of another fact that immediately put this prose parody into a larger perspective: the Greek satirist Hipponax (ca. 540 B.C.), considered by many the inventor of parody, had portrayed Achilles as a glutton in his parody of the *Iliad.*

THE CONFESSIONS OF AN ENGLISH GLUTTON

> Puisque les choses sont ainsi, je pretend aussi avoir mon franc-parler.
>
> D'Alembert.[1]

This is confessedly the age of confession,—the era of individuality—the triumphant reign of the first person singular. Writers no longer talk in generals. All their observations are bound in the narrow compass of self. They think only of number one. *Ego sum* is on the tip of every tongue and the nib of every pen, but the remainder of the sentence is unuttered and unwritten.[2] The rest of his species is now nothing to any one individual. There are no longer any idiosyncrasies in the understanding of our essayists, for one common characteristic runs through the whole range. Egotism has become as endemical to English literature as the plague to Egypt, or the scurvy to the northern climes. Every thing is involved in the simple possessives *me* and *mine*—and we all cry out in common chorus,

> What shall I do to be for ever known,
> And make the age to come mine own?[3]

Since, then, the whole tribe of which I am an unworthy member, have one by one poured out their souls into the confiding and capacious bosom of the public; since the goodly list of scribblers, great and small, from the author of Eloise to the inventor of Vortigern[4]—since the Wine-drinker, the Opium-eater, the Hypochondriac, and the Hypercritic, have in due succession "told their fatal stories out,"[5] I cannot, in justice to my own importance, or honesty to the world, leave the blank unfilled, which stands gaping to receive the Confessions of a Glutton, and thus put the last leaf on this branch of periodical personality.

I have one appalling disadvantage beside my contemporaries, in that want of sympathy which I am sure to experience from readers in general. Many a man will be too happy to acknowledge himself hypochondriacal—it is the fashion. Others are to be found in great abundance who will bravely boast of their spungy intemperance, and be proud of their brotherhood with the drunkard. Even opium-eating, like snuff-taking, may come into vogue, and find unblushing proselytes—but who will profess himself a slave to gluttony—the commonest failing of all! Nevertheless, with all the chances of public odium and private reprobation impending over me, I hasten to the performance of my duty, and I am proud to consider myself a kind of literary Curtius, leaping willingly into the gulf, to save my fellow-citizens by my own sacrifice.[6]

The earliest date which I am able to affix to the development of *my* propensity is the month of August 1764, at which period, being then precisely two years and two months old, I remember well my aunt Griselda having surprised me in an infantine but desperate excess, for which she punished me with a very laudable severity. This circumstance made a great impression on me; and without at all lessening my *propensity,* added considerably to my prudence. My voracity was infinite, and my cunning ran quite in a parallel line. I was

> "Fox in stealth, wolf in greediness."[7]

I certainly eat more than any six children, yet I was the very picture of starvation. Lank, sallow, and sorrow-stricken, I seemed the butt against which stinginess had been shooting its shafts. I attacked every one I met with the most clamorous cries for cakes or bread. I watched for visitors, and thrust my hands into their pockets with most piteous solicitings, while aunt Griselda bit her lips for anger, and my poor mother, who was a different sort of person, used to blush to the eyes for shame, or sit silently weeping, as she contemplated the symptoms of my disgraceful and incurable disease. In the mean time every thing was essayed, every effort had recourse to, to soften down the savageness of my rage for food, or at least to turn what I eat to good account. I was pampered and crammed, with my increasing years, like a Norfolk turkey—I had an unlimited credit at the pastry-cook's shop, and the run of the kitchen at home, but in vain. The machinery of my stomach refused to perform its functions. I think I must have swallowed every thing the wrong way, or have been unconsciously the prey of an interminable intestine war; for every article of sustenance took, as it were, a peculiar and perpendicular growth, but never turned into those lateral folds of flesh, which produce the comfortable clothing of men's ribs in general. At fourteen years of age I was five feet ten inches high, covered almost entirely with the long hair that boys come home with at the Christmas holidays from a Yorkshire cheap academy—my bones forcing their way through my skin—and my whole appearance the fac-simile of famine and disease—yet I never had a complaint except not getting enough to eat.

I am thus particular as to my appearance at this period, in the hope, that by this exposure of an unvarnished portrait, I may excite some commiseration for sufferings, which did not proceed from my own wicked will. I was constitutionally a glutton: nature had stamped the impress of greediness upon me at my birth, or before it. In the sucking tenderness of infancy, and the upshooting of boyhood, it was the preponderating characteristic of my nature—no self-begot habit, growing on by little and little, fostered by indulgence, and swelled out, until it became too large for the constitution that shrined it, like these geese-livers which are expanded by a particular preparation, until they become, as a body might say, bigger than the unhappy animals to which they belong. Will you not then, reader, grant me your compassion for my inadvertent enormities? Must I look in vain for the sympathising tear of sensibility falling to wash out the scorching errors of invincible appetite— as forcible at least as the invincible ignorance of heresy, for which even there is hope in the semi-benignant bosom of the church? To you I appeal, ye cooks by profession—ye gormandizers by privilege—to the whole board of Aldermen—to the shade of Mrs. Glass,—to Mrs. Rundell, Doctor Kitchener, and the rest of the list of gastronomical literati, who, in teaching the world the science of good living, must have some yearnings, one would think, for those victims whom ye lead into the way of temptation.[8]

But lest this unsupported appeal to the melting charities of mankind might be ineffectual in its naked exhibition, I shall proceed to cover it with a short detail of some of the particular horrors to which I have been a prey for upwards of half a century, and I think it must be a hard heart that will then refuse me its pity, and a ravenous maw that will not involuntarily close, to shut out the possibility of sufferings like mine.

Up to the age of fifteen, when I presented the appearance faintly sketched above, I may be considered to have gone on mechanically gormandizing, with nothing to distinguish my way of doing so from that common animal appetite which is given, in different proportions, to all that creep, or walk, or swim, or fly. Those vulgar gluttonies, thus eating for eating-sake, unconnected with mental associations, have no interest and no dignity. A man who supplies instinctively his want of food, without choice or taste, is truly *Epicuri de grege porcus,* or may be compared rather to the *Porcus Trojanus* of the ancients, a wild-boar stuffed with the flesh of other animals—a savoury, punning parody upon the Trojan horse.[9] Such a man is no better than a digesting automaton—a living mass of forced meat—an animated sausage.

I was sent home from six successive schools, on various pretences; but the true reason was, that inordinate craving which no indulgence could satisfy. I eat out of all proportion; and my father was obliged to take me entirely to himself. My mother was miserable, but of inexhaustible generosity; my aunt Griselda was dead, and I had no check upon me. Doctors from all parts were consulted on my case. Innumerable councils and consultations were held, ineffectually, to ascertain whether that refrigeration of stomach, which they all agreed was the primal cause of my malady, was joined with dryness, contraction, vellication, or abstersion.[10] They tried every remedy and every regimen, without success. The fact was, I wanted nothing but food, for which they would have substituted physic. So that between my mother and my physicians, I had both in abundance—and for the mind as well as the body. The ψυχης ιατρειον[11] was plentifully supplied me by my father, for I had natural parts, and loved reading. But the whole turn of my studies was bent towards descriptions of feasts and festivals. I devoured all authors, ancient or modern, who bore at all upon my pursuit. Appetite, mental as well as bodily, grew by what it fed on; and I continually chewed, as it were, the cud of my culinary knowledge. I rummaged Aristophanes for the Grecian repasts, and thumbed over Macrobius and Martial for the Roman.[12] While seizing on every delicacy within my reach, I feasted my imagination with dainties not to be got at,—the Phrygian attigan, Ambracian kid, and Melian crane.[13] I revered the memory of Sergius Arata, who, we are told by Pliny, was the inventor of oyster-beds[14]; of Hortensius the orator, who first used peacock at supper[15]; of Vitellius, Apicius,[16] and other illustrious Romans,

Their sumptuous gluttonies and gorgeous feasts.[17]

These classical associations refined my taste, and seemed to impart a more acute and accurate power to my palate. As I began to feel their influence, I blushed for the former grossness of my nature, and shrunk from the common gratification to which I had been addicted. I felt an involuntary loathing towards edibles of a mean and low-lived nature. I turned with disgust from the common casualties of a family dinner, and began to view with unutterable abhorrence shoulders of mutton, beef, and cabbage, and the like. A feeling, I should rather say a *passion,* (the technical phrase at present for every sensation a little stronger than ordinary,) a passion seemed to have taken possession of my mind for culinary refinements, dietetic dainties—the *delicata fercula,*[18] fit only for superior tastes, but incomprehensible to the profane. A new light seemed breaking on me; a new sense, or at least a considerable improvement on my old sense of tasting, seemed imparted to me by miracle. My notions of the dignity of appetite became expanded; I no longer looked on man as a mere masticating machine—the butcher and sepulchre of the animal world. I took a more elevated view of his powers and properties, and I felt as though imbued with an essence of pure and ethereal epicurism, if I may so express myself—and why may I not?—my contemporaries would not flinch from the phrase.

My father was a plain sort of man—liked plain speaking, plain feeding, and so on. But he had his antipathies,—and among them was roast-pig. Had he lived to our times, he might probably have been won over by a popular essay on the subject, which describes, in pathetic phrase, the manifold delights attending on that dish—the fat, which is no fat—the lean which is not lean— the eyes melting from their sockets, and other tender touches of description.[19] Be this as it may, my unenlightened parent would never suffer roast-pig upon his table, and so it happened, that, at sixteen years of age, I had never seen one. But on the arrival of that anniversary, I was indulged by my mother with a most exquisite and tender two-months porker, in all its sucking innocence, and succulent delight, as the prime dish in that annual birth-day feast, to which I was accustomed, in my own apartment—all doors closed— no ingress allowed—no intruding domestics—no greedy companions to divide my indulgencies—no eyes to stare at me, or rob me of a portion of the pleasure with which I eat in, as it were, in vision, the spirit of every anticipated preparation, while savoury fragrance was wafted to my brain, and seemed to float over my imagination in clouds of incense, at once voluptuous and invigorating. Ah, this is the true enjoyment of a feast! On the present occasion, I sat in the full glory of my solitude—sublimely individual, as the Grand Lama of Thibet, or the Brother of the Sun and Moon.[20] The door was fastened—the servant evaporated; a fair proportion of preparatory foundation—soup, fish, &c.—had been laid in *secundum artem*—the *mensa prima,*[21] in short, was just dispatched, when I gently raised the cover from the dish, where the beautiful porker lay smoking in his rich brown symmetry of form and hue, enveloped in a vapour of such deliciousness, and floating in a gravy of indescribable perfection! After those delightful moments of dalliance (almost dearer to the epicure than the very fullness of actual indulgence) were well over—after my palate was prepared by preliminary inhalements of the odorous essence—I seized my knife and fork, and plunged in *medias res.* Never shall I forget the flavour of the first morsel—it was sublime! But oh! it was, as I may say, the last; for losing, in the excess of over-enjoyment, all presence of mind and management of mouth, I attacked, without economy or method, my inanimate victim. It was one of my boyish extravagancies to conform myself in these my solitary feasts to the strict regulations of Roman custom. I began with an egg, and ended with an apple, and flung into the fire-place (as there was no fire, it being the summer season) a little morsel, as an offering to the *dii patellarii.*[22] On this occasion, however, I forgot myself and my habits—I rushed, as it were, upon my prey—slashed right and left, through crackling, stuffing, body, and bones. I flung aside the knife and fork—seized in my hands the passive animal with indiscriminate voracity—thrust whole ribs and limbs at once into my mouth—crammed the delicious ruin by wholesale down my throat, until at last my head began to swim—my eyes seemed starting from their sockets—a suffocating thickness seemed gathering (no wonder) in my throat—a fullness of brain seemed bursting through my skull—my veins seemed swelled into gigantic magnitude—I lost all reason and remembrance, and fell, in that state, fairly under the table.

This, reader, is what we call, in common phrase, a surfeit. But what language may describe its consequences, or give a just expression to the sufferings it leaves behind? The first awakening from the apoplectic trance, as the lancet of the surgeon gives you a hint that you are alive, when the only taste upon the tongue—the only object in the eye—the only flavour in the nostril, is the once-loved, but now deep-loathed dish! The deadly sickening with which one turns, and twists, and closes one's lids, and holds one's nose, and smacks one's lips—to shut out, and stifle, and shake off the detested sight, and smell, and taste:—but in vain, in vain, in vain! But let me not press the point. Forty-two years have passed since that memorable day—forty thousand recollections of that infernal pig have flashed across my brain, and fastened on my palate, and fumigated my olfactories; and there they are, every one, as fresh—What do I say? a million times more fresh and more intolerable than ever. Faugh!—It comes again.[23]

But if such were some of the local and particular waking miseries of my excess, what, oh what tongue may give utterance to, what pen pourtray, the intolerable terrors of my *dreaming* hours! For many months of my protracted and painful re-establishment, I dreamt every night—not one respite for at least three hundred weary and wasting days—quotidian repetitions of visions, each one more hideous than the former. I dreamt, and dreamt, and dreamt—of what? Of pig—pig—pig—nothing but pig. Pork, in all its multiplied and multiform modifications, was ever before me. Every possible form or preparation into which imagination could convert the hated animal, was everlastingly dangling in my sight, running around me, pursuing and persecuting me, in all the aggravation of the most exaggerated monstruosities. The scenery which accompanied these animal illustrations was always in keeping with the sickening subject. Sometimes, as I began to doze away in the mellow twilight of an autumn evening, or the frosty rarefaction of a winter's day, or a day in spring, it was all one—a sudden expansion of vision has begun to open upon me; and be it remembered that I always fancied myself of Hebrew extraction, Abraham, or Joseph, or Isaac—a Rabanite or a Caraite, as the case might be—the high-priest of the synagogue, or an old clothes-man; but in all cases a Jew, with every religious predilection and antipathy strong fixed in my breast.[24] A sudden expansion of vision, I say, began to open upon me—vast wildernesses spread far around—rocks of tremendous aspect seemed toppling from mountains of the most terrific elevation. The forms of the former were of the strangest fantasy, but all presented some resemblance of a boar's head; while the hills shewed invariably, in their naked and barren acclivities, an everlasting sameness of strata, that presented the resemblance of veiny layers of pickled pork, and the monstrous flowers with which the earth was bespread were never-ending representations of rashers and eggs! A sickness and faintness always began to seize upon me at these sights; and, turning my glances upwards, I was sure to see the clouds impregnated with fantastic objects, all arising out of associations connected with my antipathy and loathing. Gigantic hams were impending over my head, and threatening to crush me with their weight. My eyes sunk, and I caught the peaks of the horrid hills frizzled with the grinning heads, and pointed with the tusks of the detested animal.[25] The branches of the trees were all at once converted to twisted and curling pig-tails. Atoms then seemed springing from the sand; they were soon made manifest in all the caperings and gambols of a litter of sucking gruntlings. They began to multiply—with what frightful celerity! The whole earth was in a moment covered with them, of all possible varieties of colours. They began to grow bigger, and instantaneously they gained dimensions that no *waking* eye can bring into any possible admeasurement. I attempted to run from them: They galloped after me in myriads, grunting in friendly discord, while magical knives and forks seemed stuck in their hams, as they vociferated in *their* way, "Come eat me, come eat me!" At other times I pursued them, in the frenzy of my despair, endeavouring to catch them, but in vain; every tail was soaped, and as they slipped through my fingers they sent forth screams of the most excruciating sharpness, and a laugh of hideous mockery, crying, in damnable chorus, "What a *bore*, what a *bore*! Bubble and squeak! Bubble and squeak!" with other punning and piggish impertinencies of the same cut and pattern.[26] Then, again, an individual wretch would contract himself to a common-sized hog, and, rushing from behind between my legs, scamper off with me whole leagues across the desert; then, gradually expanding to his former monstrous magnitude, rise up with me into the skies, that seemed always receding from our approach, and stretching out to an interminable immensity; when the horrid brute on which I was mounted would give a sudden kick and grunt, and fling me off, and I tumbled headlong down thousands of thousands of fathoms, till I was at length landed in a pig-stye, at the very bottom of all bottomless pits.

At other times I used to imagine myself suddenly placed in the heart of a pork-shop. In a moment I was assailed by the most overpowering steams of terrible perfume, the gravy of the fatal dish floating round my feet, and clouds of suffocating fragrance almost smothering me as I stood. On a sudden every thing began to move, immense Westphalian hams flapped to and fro, banged against my head, and beat me from one side of the shop to the other—huge flitchets of bacon fell upon me, and pressed me to the ground, while a sea of the detestable gravy flowed in upon me, and over me. Then frightful pigs' faces joined themselves together, and caught me in their jaws, when, called in by my shriek, which was the expected signal for their operations, three or four horrid-looking butchers rushed upon me, and, as a couple of them pinioned and held me down on my back, another stuffed me to choking with pork-pies, until I awoke more dead than alive.

Once, and once only, I had a vision connected with this series of suffering, which I must relate, from its peculiar nature, and as the origin of a popular hoax long afterwards put upon the world. I dreamt one night, that preparations were making, on a most splendid scale, for my marriage with a very beautiful girl of our neighbourhood, to whom I was (whatever my readers may think) very tenderly attached. The ceremony was to take place, me thought, in Canterbury Cathedral. I was all at once seized with a desire to examine the silent solemnity of the Gothic pile. I entered, I forget how. A rich strain of music was poured from the organ-loft. A mellow stream of light flowed in through the stained glass of the windows. I was quite alone, and the most voluptuous tide of thought stole upon my mind. While I stood thus in the middle of the aisle, a distant door opened, and the bridal party entered. My affianced spouse, surrounded by a clustre of friends, glittering with brilliant ornaments, and glowing in beauty, approached me. I advanced to meet her, in unutterable delight; when, as I drew near, I saw that the appearance of every thing began to change. The pillars seemed suddenly converted to huge Bologna sausages; the various figures of saints and angels, painted on the windows, were altered into portraits of black porkers; the railings of the different enclosures took the curved form of spare ribs; the walls were hung with pig-skin tapestry; the beautiful melody just before played on the organ, was followed by a lively and familiar tune, and a confusion of voices sung,

"The pigs they lie," &c.[27]

while a discordant chorus of diabolical grunting, wound up each stanza. In the meantime the bride approached; but what horror accompanied her! The wreath of roses braided round her head, was all at once a twisted band of black-puddings. Hog's bristles shot out from the roots of what was so lately her golden hair; a thin string of sausages took place of her diamond necklace; her bosom was a piece of brawn; her muslin robe became a piebald covering of ham-sandwiches; her white satin shoes were kicked, oh, horror! off a pair of pettitoes[28]; and her beautiful countenance—swallow me, ye wild boars!—presented but the hideous spectacle, since made familiar to the public, under the figure of THE PIG-FACED LADY!!![29] Hurried on by an irresistible and terrible impulse, I rushed forward, though with loathing, to embrace her; when instantly the detested odour of the hateful gravy came upon me once more; the pillars of the Cathedral swelled out to an enormous circumference, and burst in upon me with a loud explosion; the roof fell down with a fearful crash, and overwhelmed me with a shower of legs of pork, and pease-pudding; while, in the agony of my desperation, I caught in my arms my hideous bride, whose deep-brown skin crackled in my embrace, as I pressed to my bursting bosom the everlasting fac-simile of a *roast pig!*—In after years I took a fit of melancholy enjoyment in setting afloat the humbug of the Pig-faced Lady.

I will not press upon the reader the manifold miseries that attended upon subsequent surfeits, for a period of more than five-and-twenty years. From what I have feebly sketched, some notion may be conceived of the nature and extent of my disorder. I need not, therefore, dwell on the consequences of my second memorable excess, which took place on the occasion of my eating turtle-soup for the first time. The misery in this matter was more from fright than from repletion; for when, after the sacrifice of repeated helpings of calipash and calipee,[30] I found my teeth immoveably stuck together—in the style which my city readers well understand—I was seized with the horrible conviction that I had got a locked-jaw. Imagination worked so powerfully on this occasion, that when I had pulled my mouth wide-open, beyond even its natural capacity, (which is not trifling, believe me, reader,) I sat for hours, roaring out for a dentist to punch in two or three of my front teeth, that I might get some sustenance introduced through a quill. Even when I perfectly recovered my senses, I was long before I could bear to sit a moment with my mouth shut, from the dread of a return of my imagined danger. Then came the *dreaming* again—the crawling tortoises; the clammy glutinous liquid; the green fat—but enough of this!

Repeated sufferings like these broke in upon the crust of my constitution, if I may use the trope; so that when I became of age, and possessed of a good fortune without incumbrance, by the demise of my father, and the second marriage of my mother, (who by that step forfeited her jointure, and with *it* every claim on my regard,) I was in appearance a middle-aged man, and in mind a septuagenary, of the *common sort* I mean—I, like old Burton, had "neither wife nor children"[31]—my early attachment—my beautiful neighbour—the prototype spare me the repetition, reader!—but *she,* you know, *she*—the LADY was lost to me forever! She had but one failing, poor girl—nervousness, just then coming first into fashion; and she took it strongly into her head, that if she married me, I should play the part of the wolf with the Little Red Riding-hood, and eat her up one night in bed. To avoid this unusual and uncomfortable consummation of our nuptials, she discarded my suit altogether, and I lost her forever. To get over the effects of this blow, I resolved to look for consolation in the joys of foreign cookery. I determined to travel, and I did travel, in pursuit of what I never have been able to discover—the art of allaying an uncontrolable appetite. As for the love affair, I soon swallowed my grief.

I shall not enumerate my adventures in distant countries, nor detail my observations on objects foreign to my purpose. *Ne sutor ultra crepidam.*[32] I shall therefore merely say, that having eaten frogs in France, macaroni at Naples, ollapodrida in Spain,[33] opium in Turkey, camel's-flesh in Egypt, horse-flesh in Arabia, elephant-flesh in India, cat's-flesh in China, and hog's flesh—no, never never after the affair of the pig—it was a slip of the pen—I returned to England to sit down to plain beef and mutton; convinced that I had come back to the real, healthy, honest standard of good taste. In the broad interval, however, which I have jumped over so rapidly, I had many and many a visiting of direful consequence. At one time I fancied that I was doomed to die of starvation, and the excruciating agonies then endured from cholics and indigestions (proceeding from my even more than natural efforts to eat up to the standard of sufficiency) beggar all description. On another occasion a horrid apprehension oppressed me, that I should one day—but how express myself in English? I cannot; and I should have been silent perforce, did not the *delicacies* of the French language come in to my aid— that I should one day, *me crever le ventre!*[34] To guard against this expected calamity, I had a pair of stays made—yes, reader, I was the first of the dandies—the lacing and unlacing of which, before and after meals, was attended with torments more horrible than those pelting and pitiless showers, imagined by Dante for the Gluttons of *his* Inferno.[35]

I forget precisely how many years have elapsed since the exhibition of fat Lambert.[36] It is enough to know, that I went to see the show. I saw him.— Would that I never had! Oh, Heavens! what agonies has that sight cost me! The by-standers who observed me as I entered the room, burst into a loud and involuntary laugh—and no blame to them; for never was there a more ludicrous contrast than Lambert was to me, and I to Lambert. I am six feet five inches and a half high in my stockings; extremely like Justice Shallow, only taller, "like to a man made after supper of cheese-parings, for whom the case of a treble hautboy would make a mansion;"[37] and I will venture to say that the skeleton of the Irish giant, dressed in my habiliments, and its back turned, might be taken for my figure by my nearest acquaintance. You all remember, readers, what Lambert's figure was. I do, alas! at any rate! The very instant I saw him, the notion struck me that I had become his second-self—his ditto—his palpable echo—his substantial shadow—that the observ-ers laughed at our "double transformation," for he was become me at the same time—that I was exhibiting as he then was,—and, finally, that I was dying of excessive fat. The idea was like an electric shock, and in one moment I felt that the double identity was completed—that the metamorphosis of Salamis and her lover was acted over again in the persons of myself and the fat man[38]—that I, in short, was Lambert, and Lambert me!—I shot out of the exhibition-room—rushed into the street—quitted the confines of the city—ran up towards Hampstead-hill—tried back again, and made off in the direction of the river, endeavouring in vain to shake off the horrid phantasm that had seized upon my mind. I darted along with lightning-speed, my long legs seemed to fling themselves out spontaneously, as if they no more belonged to me than Grimaldi's do to him, yet I fancied that I crept with the pace of a tortoise—that my fat totally prevented my quicker motion—that I should be crushed to death between the hedges, the turnpikes, or the carriages that passed me—and thus I ran in the middle of the road, vociferating for assistance, fighting against the foul fiend, and followed by a crowd of draggle-tailed blackguards, till I reached the banks of the river, and saw myself reflected in the stream. Oh, Heavens! what a delightful sight was that!

"Then like Narcissus—"[39]

But I must leave the quotation unfinished, and come at last to a full stop; for I fear I am trenching upon the privilege—poaching upon the preserve—of some contemporary hypochondriac. If so, if any may have led the way in giving to the world, like me, their *real unexaggerated* Confessions, I can only complain, with the modern poet who accused Shakespeare of forestalling his thoughts, that they, be they who they may, have very unhandsomely and plagiaristically anticipated my own original lucubrations. And now having fairly unbosomed my sins, if they are sins, I trust to receive from a grateful public, in whose interest alone have I compiled these sheets, the absolution which should always follow confession. Then, as is usual in these cases, that having disgorged my over-loaded conscience, I may be allowed to return to my *old courses*—following in this the example of Caesar, who, according to Cicero, *post caenam vomere volebat, ideoque largius edebat.*[40] Should any harsh hearer or rigorous reader be inclined to constrain the bowels of his compassion, and still deny me pardon, to him I beg to propose a question in the words of our immortal Bard, which he may answer the next time we meet at dinner,—

> "_____ If little faults
> Shall not be wink'd at, how shall we stretch our eye,
> When capital crimes, shew'd, swallow'd, and digested,
> Appear before us!"[41]

38
Caroline Bowles Southey, "Letter from a Washerwoman" and "Fragments" (1823)

This attack on the Cockneys—principally Hunt and Hazlitt, but Shelley is also implicated (especially in the poetic "fragments")—appeared anonymously in *Blackwood's* in February 1823. The lengthy letter attempts to capture the characteristics of the Cockney manner and pronunciation. The two men about whom Patience Lilywhite complains to Christopher North are clearly guilty of the charges normally brought against the "Cockney school" (pretension, paganism, and so on). Alan Strout [*A Bibliography of Articles in 'Blackwood's Magazine,' Volumes I Through XVIII, 1817–1825* (Lubbock, Texas: Texas Technological College, 1959), 105] has identified Patience as Caroline Bowles Southey, daughter of William Lisle Bowles (1762–1850) and wife of Southey.

The poetic fragments that follow the letter alternate between parodies of Hunt and parodies of Shelley. The Hunt pieces are, as usual, escapist and self-indulgent. The first of two closing fragments features a curious mixture of paternal affection and lasciviousness ("Pretty little playful Patty!"), while the second is virtual nonsense. Syntactically and grammatically, the poem collapses under a burden of sexual fantasy and the multiplication of trivial details. In Hunt's hands, it seems every subject—even sea turtles—becomes a matter of leers and titters. The two parodies of Shelley are assertively anti-Christian, expressing belief in universal love, humanitarianism, and vegetarianism. In fact, the parodist manages to indicate that this high-minded rhetoric only rationalizes adultery as well as to suggest that Shelley's inspiration is actually from the gutter. The mystical love for all things, in turn, is cleverly juxtaposed with a brutal contempt for parts of the creation (his former wife, for example).

Shelley was also the target of an earlier *Blackwood's* article, "Remarks on Shelley's *Adonais*," published in December 1821. George Croly, author of about 300 contributions to that magazine between 1820 and 1860, singles out "licentiousness," peculiar "private habits," "servile slang," "triviality," and atheism as some of the Cockney characteristics. The article concludes with a brief parody, "Elegy on My Tom Cat," and both serve as a good introduction to the "Letter" and "Fragments."

LETTER FROM A WASHERWOMAN.

Puddleditch-Corner, Islington, January 30, 1823.

WORSHIPFUL SUR,

I'm a lone widder woman, left with five fatherless children to purvide for in a wicked world, where simple folks is shure to be putt upon, as ive larnt to my sorrow; but i'm not one to sit down content, if there's la or gustice to be had above ground. My good man used to say, rest his sole, Patience, you've a sperrit, says he, and so i have, thank God, for what shuld a pore lone widder do without in such a world as this where honnor goes afore honesty. Well, sur, how i comes to rite you these few lines, is this. You must know i'm a washer-woman, an' lives at Islington, and takes in loddgers; but i ant come to that yet; only i must say summut about it, by way of beginnin to let you know how i've got a new loddger; for i takes in single gentlemen; an' i was telling of he, what oudacious treetment id met with from they; he, i would say, the other was as bad as he, as hockipied my apartments last, how i was flammed over tho' i mid a known fine words buttered no passenips, to give em trust, an' let em turn evry thing topsy turvy, so long as it sarved their turn to stay, and then they takes French leave, an' walks off, without paying so much as a brass farden, and what's warse, wi' Nance; but i ant come to that yet. Only, sir, the long and the short's this; i was gust telling of these here purceedins to my new loddger, and how they'd a sarved me, an habsconded, as the gustice called it, and left nothin to pay my rent, an' all the power o' mischif they'd done me, with all their outlandish heethen fancies, but a room full of dryd weeds, peeble stones, cracked chalk images, an' bits of crumpled paper, all over blots, an' ritin stuff that no Criscteun can make head nor tale on. Well, i was a tellin of all my misfortins to Mr Perkins, who seems a civil, pretty behaved sort of a gentleman, only he's allways att his books and his pen, an' at first i was rather huffed, for he sniggered and sniggered, but it want att me, only at them graceless chapps i was telling about, an' att last he says, says he, when i told him how Gustice Dosy could get me no redress nor cumpinsashun, i tell you what Mrs Lilywhite says he, tell your story to the larned Kristophur North, an maybe hel gif you cumfurt an' cumpinsation besides. Att first i thot how he was a hummin me, tho he's a grave godly lookin gentleman, not much given to vain talkin an' gestin; butt at last i found he was in downrite earnest, an' thatt you was a friend of his, a sort of a Scotch gustice, an' rites a book every month, an' mite maybe take up the cawse of hingured hinnocence, as we said to the late Queen of blessed memory, and put in mi pittiful story to shame their parjury willains, an' mite moreover make me a hansome present into the bargain, an' he promissd if id rite a letter, hed send it safe to you, and so worshippfull sir, tho' i never heard youre name before i makes bold to tell you how i've been put upon.

Well, sur, you must know then my name is Patience Lilywhite, an' i'm a washerwoman, an' lives att Islington, at Puddleditch corner, a pretty rural spott, where i letts loddgins to single gentlemen as wants a little country hair and quiett, after the noise an' smoke of Lunnon. Well, sir, the 20th of last July was twelvemouth, i minds the day peticklar, bein that after the crownashun day, comes a thin spindle shanked gentleman to look at my loddgins, bein, as he said, ordered into the country for change of hair, and shure enuff he looked as yoller as a kite's foot.[1] The rooms seemed to please him mitily, and well they mought; two prettier, pleasanter, more convenienter, a king need'nt covet, for the parlour winder looks out into our garden, thats very private an' rural; for 'tis parted off by a ditch an' an elder hedge from the backs of the sope manifactory, an' Mr Bullock's slawtur-house, so there bent no unpleasant hop-jacks ner it, an't overlookd by nobody. An' the parlor was just fresh painted very illigent, sky-blue in the pannells with yollor moldins; an' the corner cupbord was chock full of illigant chaney, an' id a just bought a spick an' span new gappan tea-tray, an' a spontious hurn, whereof he took peticklar notice, an' axed how much it constrained; and when i told him two gallons, that seemed to settle his mind at once, an' he agreed with me at haff a ginnee a week, little enough of all conshince; but he said how he was a very quiett body, an' shuld give but little trubbel, so i was agreeabel to take him in.— Well, rivrend sir, he comed shure enuff the very next eveenin off wun of the stages, an' brought all his luggadge in his hand, witch was no more than a smaal porkmanky, an' an ould earthen ware crate wi sum chalk himmiges.

He had nothin for supper, but some tea an' bread-an-butter, an' sett up haff the nite, rummadgin about the rooms, an' stickin up they himmiges as comed in the crate, an' sum books, an' bitts of broken stones, an' craked shells, out of the porkmanky, witch was crammed three parts full of sich rubbish, instead of good holland shurts an' warin apparrel. Well, i seed there woodnt be many gobbs for me, in my way; but the gentleman seemed quiett an' civill, an' spoke verry goodnaturd to the childern, an' i rather bepitteed him, for he seemd in a pore weak way.

Next day, about aternoon, a frind cawled in to see him, a shamblin sort of a chapp, with grate thick lipps, an' littel piggs eyes, an' a puffy unholesum lookin face, as yoller as tother; but he spoke verry soft an' civil too, an' took peticklar notice of Nance, as was mi eldest, an' just turned fifteen.[2] Well, this here wun, i cant never mind his name, for they calld him bi too att wunce, seemed verry thik with my loddger, Mr Pennyfeather, an' hardly missd a day cummin to see him, to mi sorrow; for i do think 'twas he put sich wild vagarys into tother's head, an' pswaided him at last to run off in mi dett, like a shabbroon as he was. Youd niver beleeve me, wurshippfull sur, if i was to tell you haff the goins on of they two rapscallions, an' watt wurk they maid in mi pore littel garden, an' with mi Nance, but i ant cum to that yet; the moore foole i, not to cutt em short in there heethenish doins; but sum how they comed over me wi thur fine hard words and palaverin spitches, tho i beleeve, o mi conshince, twant nothin ater all butt a pack of nonsenciccle jabber. So, sur, you must no, they gott mi leeve to halter or transmoggrify our bitt of garden, that was a sweet spott they said, only they wanted to lay it out classy cully. Tho, for my part, i thot twas classed out rigglar enuff, wi beds of cabbadges an' iniuns, an sich like sensibel stuff. To work they fell, an' routed out all they pore innocent things; an' watt do they think they sett in in the room of em? As im an honnest woman, if yule beleeve me, worshippfull sur, nothin but a pack o rubbitch i woodnt a piled in mi faggit stakk. Wun blessed day they cums home loded lik jack asses, wi grate bundels of long scragglin green bows off the chesnut an' lime trees, an' never beleeve me, if they didnt stick them up an end all about the garden, in the room of mi fine guseberri bushes, the rite hairy sort, thatt theyd grubbd up bi the roots, the moore fowl i to lett em. But they wanted to convert it into a grove, they sedd. Lord bless ye, gemmen, says i, why them sticks 'll all be dead in a weak; butt they only nidged their heads, as mutch as to say, i spose weel be off bi that time. An so when they bows was stuck about like pee-sticks, they brings a parsel of daysys, nothin but common field daysys, primroses an' gilty cupps, and sich like trumpery, guodd for nothin weeds, and sets em in all amongst tothers; an' wenn thatt was done to their minds, whatt maggots shuld bite next, butt they falls to wurk, nockin up of our ould piggsty. So then, thinks i, they be gott about some good att last; for, to be shure, theyre goin to mend itt upp tidy, an' prapps make mee a present of a fattin pigg, or a pritty littel chany sow. But no sich things was in there noddels, gud sur. Furst of all they piled up a sort of a mount, with peat an' bricks, an' rubbitch, an' rite upon top on it, they setts about bildin up o the piggsty, as i thot; so says i, "Lawk, gemmen, how shall wee ever clamber up there wi the piggs vittels; an' watt for shuld ye perch un upp so hy, pore dumb beestesses." So they seemd quite huffed. A piggsty, says they. Why, woman—Mi names Lilywhite, says i.—So, says they, Mrs Lilywhite, were recktin a tempel to Pollar.—*Pollards* they must meen,[3] thinks i, for thatts piggs vittels; so they be goin to by me one ater all, only they thinks to sprize me: so i wont take no more notiss. But thatt was all mi innocence. They no more thot of bilding up mi sty, than i didd of bildin the tempel of Geruzleum. Well, they cobbled upp a sort of a queer lookin fore cornerd shed, and coverd it over wi a round bitt of oil cloth, paneted wi yoller stripes, all round from the middel, for all the world like a sunflower; an' then they made a kind of paath upp the mount, wi broken briks an' oyster shells, stikin out here an' thare, to look like rokks, they sedd: an' ater thatt, they stuck it full of grene lawrel bows, by the same token that Mr Deppity Doughnut, of Wellintun Willa, thretened to persecute em for tarin down all his lawrel heddges. But they didn't care for la nor gosple, not they. An next there was a grand confab atwixt em, about makin of a fowntane; for witch there didn't seem, to me thinkin, no manner of need, when there was a good pump, with beautiffull soft water, not ten steps from our own dore. But a fowntane they must have; nothin else would serve em: so they take an' diggs out the ditch up to the bottum of thatt new fangled mount, an' damms upp the water, that was nothing but sope sudds an' kennel stuff ater all, an' then setts it a running thro a cows horn, as they beggd of the buttchur, trickel, trickel, trickel over some pebbel stons an' bitts of broken bottels as theyd strood along the bottum of the drain. Then, to sea how they rubbd there hans, an' chuckeld an' capurd about wen they seed the dirty water com spurtin out. For mi part i begun to think they was craasy, butt my yung wuns likd the sport well enuff, for 'twas summut in thur one way. Well, then, they seemd to think 'twas all parfict, an' two or three more chapps of there one sort comd in, an' they all lade thur hedds togethur, an' setteld to have a feest at the diddicashun of the Tempel, as they cawld it. Most of whatt they tawkd was Greak to me; but i prikkd upp mi years wen i hurd of a feest. Mortall pore livin theyd kept since id had to do for em. Mi loddger most times rambbeld away, lord nos were, wen he shuld hav bin enjoyin hisself in my comfurtabel parlor, over a good beef stake or a pork chopp, an' a pott of porter, wereby a body mite a gott sum smaal mattur now an then, in an onest way, for wuns toilin and moilin; butt itts mi belief, he fedd like the varment and the Frinch, upon froggs an' tods, an' ditch sallat. Howsumdever, wen tother cumd, as he did most aternoons, they two stowd in a mortal site of tea an' bread-an'-buttur. Oshuns an' oshuns of tea didd they sett an' swil, to be shure, till i sedd to owr Nance, says i, for sartain theyl go droppsicul.[4]

Well, wen i hurd em tawk of a feest, i makes bold to putt in mi ore. "An," says i, "there's sum butifull ducks just fatt in owr coup, and noo grin pees is cum in;" butt lawk, they cutt me short in a giffy. "Ducks!" says Mr Pennyfeather; an' then he runned on sich a pak of stuff, as i couldn't mak hedd nor tale on, only thatt there was to be no vittels bot, but Nektur an' Hambrowsy, two things i'd never hurd on, only i found out afterwards, them names was Greak for tea, an' butter an' bread. Furst of awl, they sett about kristenin awl there fine wurks. But sich names they sett em, it's amost a shame for a Kriscteun to tell agen; for they sedd how the mownt was to be cawld Hellycome. Lawk, sur, sich blasphemy wickedness; and the fowntane was Hagganipper.[5] Wat that ment i culdn't tell for sartin, only i nod well enuff 'twas no gud; so i told mi yung uns, if ever i ketched em sayin sich awfull wurds, i'd hang em up hyer than ever bakon was hung. Then there was a deel of gabberin about Pollar an' Pollar, whoever he was, for i found out bi them 'twas a man's name, no sponsibel parson im sure, summut of a Jack Ketch,[6] most lik, for they tawked about his halter; an' sum sedd that was upon Mownt Parnassus, an' how he oft to bide there; butt att last they agreed he shuld be had down too Hellycome; and then they fixed how that there commicle place a top of the Mownt was to be the Tempel of the Mooses. O Gemminnes! if i didn't think upon thatt, thatt they wer a goin to lugg over thatt ere grate beest as is showed in Lunnon, an' hoist em up for a site to the Islington fokes, att so mutch a hedd; but i culdn't abide the thot on it; so says i, awl in a flurry an' a combustion, "Lord's sake, gemmin!" says i, "wat be ye goin about? you mite as well go for to cram a cow in a coffee-pott, as thatt ere rampagus wild beest upp in thatt poppett-show place." Upon thatt they showted, an' fleerd, an' geerd att me, an' sedd how Mooses was yung ladys, an' how they was goin to hackd a play, an' how my Nance, an' Sal, an' littel Hannermarier shuld pessonify the Mooses; only, as there was nine, neether more nor less, there must be six othur gurls to hact the tothers, an' them they soon pickd out. Then mi littel billy begun fur to cry, an' ax why he midn't be a Moose too, as well as the rest, for he was a cute littel feller, an' always foremost when there was annything to be larnd; but they passyfide him, and sedd, he shuld be Cubit, an' stan by Nance's side wi' a flambo, an' she was to be cawld Hairytoe—a fritefull name to my thinking—wun of they Misses—Mooses, i wood say; an' Buttchur Bullocks wench was to be Polly summut, i forget wat[7]; "but howsumdever," says i, "that av gott more of a Kriscteun sound with it, an' the gurls raal name is Mary." I forgets the rest of they heethenish names, fit for none but Turks an Hottenpots; butt there was a fine to do, wen evry thing was gott in order, as they cawled it. 'Twas rare funn to the gurls, and to awl the naburs too, for the mattur of that; and they broke down awl my butifull hedge, wi' clamberrin over to get a peep at the show. There was owr Nance stuk upp, who butt she, more foole i to wink att sich doins, dressed out, nott in her Sunday gownd an' spenser, and beever hatt an' fethers, thatt she used to be so proud on; butt rolled up for awl the wurld lik a corps in a wite tabel cloth, skiverd together, as if there wus no pins to be had, over wun sholder; an awl mi cabbidge roses, wat i used to save for dryin, an' for to sell for popery's an' sich lik, was pulld, an' plukkd, and stringd lik a rope of inions round her hedd, insted of a decent cap and top nott. Then they borried Tim Whippy's fiddle for she to hold, tho i told em sheed never larnd a toone; an' little Billy was strippt amost nakid, qwite nakid they wanted im, butt thatt i wasn't to be hargufied into; an' they put a lited link in his hand, an' stuk him up close bi Nance; an' awl the tother wenches wus figgerd up much the same, lik hidols an' himages, more than Kriscteun craturs; and then they strikes out all of a hurry, as how he wi' the two names as comd every day to see my loddger, should hackt Pollar. So they pulls off his shoos and stockins, pure and ragged they was; an' for the matter of thatt, they wanted to do the same bi the girls; but no—"D'ye think," says i, "mi hoffspring shall tramp about, barefoot, like begger-wenches?" Butt they off wi hisn howsumdeever, and strippt down his nekcloth an' shirt collars, and tyed wun of mi aperns round his neck, an' figured his head up wi lawrel bows, till he looked for all the wurld like a Jack in the Greene, only not haff so funny[8]; and then they gave him hold of the ould base vial that theyd got the lone of from our parish clark, Old Mumps,—more sheame he to lend un, for to mi mind 'twas heethen sakerlidge. Well, then, the rest sett up sich a showt, and begun dancin an singin lik propper beddlamites, an' skreechin owt, "Hail, Pollar! Gloryows Pollar! Hail! Hail!"

Lord gif me patience to think o sich hardend wikkedness as cawlin down hail in the very middle of hay harvest, and the deppitys cropps a carryin; but they owd he a gruddge about threttenin to take the law on em. Then the feest was to begin. "Sich a feest," i says; an' the Mooses was to serve em wi necktur, meenin nothin else, your honor, then a power o wishy-washy tea thatt was made in owr grate hurn; an' wen i was a goin to fettch owt the best chany cups an' saasurs wi the goold rims, for i liks to see every thing hansom, they axed me if so be i hadn't a got anny antik vessells; an' afor i culd puzzel owt the meenin o that, they goes an' rummages owt sum owld crackd butter-botes, an' squatt bottles, an' emty oil flaskks, an' for wat wuld yur worshipp think?—why to drink tea owt on, ass i'm a livin woman, an' mi name's Patience; becawse, they sedd, the heethen Turks, that mi best cupps an' saasurs wasn't classycull. I don't know wat ware that is—not i; but i'll tak mi Bibel othe, mi chany was the best Darby sheer. Well, they swiggd an' sung, an' sung an' swiggd, till he as hackted Pollar turned ass sik ass a dogg, for hed a bin sukkin out of an oil flaskk, sarvd im rite too; an' i wishd the tother hadd bin ass badd, for turning up their noses at mi best chany. But wurse than thatt was brewin, for owr Bill an' the gurls hadd gott to rompps, an' stuffin of bred an' butter, an' the link as sarved for Cubit's flambo, sett fire to Nance's tabel-cloth, an' she in her frite rund up agen Pollar, so his apern ketchd all in a blaaze, an' he tares it off, an' flares it away into the middel of the garden, where mi linnens was hangin on the lines, an' afore you culd say Jack Robbison, it was awl in a conflarashun.

Thatt ever i shuld liv to sea sich ruinn brot upon my honest cawlin, bi sich a pakk of——; but that wern't the wurst. Well, Nance unskiverd the tabel-cloth sumhow an' rund away in her flannell dicky. But sum of the other wenches raggs took fire, an' then fine fuzion there was. They put it owt among em, howsomdever, butt not afore the tempel pigsty, i says, ketched awl of a flame, an' the owld rotten postesses blaazed owt lik tutchwood, an' the oil cloth top blowed off rite agen the faggit pile, an' sett fire to thatt too. There was a kettel of fish. I speckted to sea house an' awl burnt to the ground, an' awl Islington too, for wat wun culd tell; but the naburs cumd porin in, an' the hengins was brot owt; an' att last, bi the marcy of Heeven, the flames was got under, butt nott till i'd bin dammadged an' hinjurd, pownds an' pownds.

Well, honnurabel sur, mayhap you taks it for sartain thatt they rantipate chapps as maid awl the misschiff, lended a hand to get it under, for the best amens they culd mak. No sich a thing, yur wurshipp. They sneekt off att the first owtcry, lik cowwardly currs, with there tales betwene there leggs; an' from that ower to thisn—O, wurshippful sur, that such proffelgate villains shuld walk this blessed erth!—i've niver sett eyes upon a muther's sunn of em; an' ass if it weren't enuff to diddel me owt of haff mi subbstance, an' leeve me a ruinated undun widder, they ticed away mi Nance along wi em, tho for the matter o thatt, no feer butt watt she was willin enuff, for they'd turnd her poor foolish hedd among them; an' wun of owr naburs seed her thatt same blissed aternoon, purch'd up, who but she, from top o wun o the Lunnon stages between Pollar an' Mr Pennyfeather.[9]

So there's the long an' the shortt of mi true story, an' a pittyfull wun it is surely, thof i niver shuld a thot of ritin it to yur wurshipp, but for Mr Perkinses pswasions, an' the considderashions be putt into mi hedd; an wun thing that maid me more timmersome abowt trubbelling yur honour, is, thatt it awl happnd so long aggo, an' thatt i heers them parjury willains is gon beyond sees, butt Mr Perkins says how they be playin off their owld pranks there; and thatt there's no place so far off butt wat yur wurshipps book getts there; an' that mi story oft to be deserted in it, if 'twas only only for the porposs of putting pore hinnocent parsons like miself upon their offensive agen the hartfull magnations of them divels in scarlett. Moore over, he devises me to send you they scrapps of writin, ass they left to pay mi rent. To my thinkin, they bant worth rappin up a varden rushlite wi[10]; butt he says, heve gott his reesons for giffin me this device; so i've a pickkd owt the best on em, an' bad they be, not a hole sheat among em. So, hoppin yore wurship will scuse awl fawts, an' tak mi pittyfull case into considderashun, no more at present from

Your wurshipps misfortunate an' obleegin sarvant,
PATIENCE LILYWHITE.

FRAGMENTS

* * * * * * * * * * * *

I never saw a more delightful spot!—
One might have lain there, when the days were hot,
Hours and hours—hark'ning to the sweet singers
Up in the leaves—twiddling one's thumbs and fingers—
Watching the sun-beams in that quiet scenery,
Spangling about the jaunty greenery,
And the small flies and gnats—that sort called midges,
Bite one confoundedly, raising long ridges
Upon one's skin.—Oh! it were sweet, most sweet,
As I before said, in the summer heat,
To lie there sprawling flat upon one's back,
Dozing and dreaming of one's—Zounds! what's that?—
Pshaw! a cockchafers[11]—what was I saying?—
Oh! that would be delicious, thus a laying,
To dream of * * * * * * * * * *

* * * * * * * * * * * * * * *

They were not married by a mutt'ring priest,
With superstitious rites, and senseless words,
Out-snuffled from an old worm-eaten book
In a dark corner (railed off like a sheep-pen,)

Of an old house, that fools do call *a Church!*
Their altar was the flowery lap of earth—
The starry empyreum their vast temple—
Their book, each other's eyes—and Love himself,
Parson, and Clerk, and Father to the bride!—
Holy espousals! whereat wept with joy
The spirit of the Universe.—In sooth
There was a sort of drizzling rain that day,
For I remember (having left at home
My parapluie, a name than *umbrella*
Far more expressive,) that I stood for shelter
Under an entry not twelve paces off,
(It *might* be ten,) from sheriff Waithman's shop,[12]
For half an hour or more, and there I mused,
(Mine eyes upon the running kennel fixed,
That hurried on a het'rogenous mass
To th' common-sewer, its dark reservoir,)
I mused upon the running stream of *life.*

But that's not much to th' purpose—I was telling
Of those most pure espousals.—Innocent pair!
Ye were not shackled by the vulgar chains
About the yielding mind of credulous youth,
Wound by the nurse and priest,—*your* energies,
Your unsophisticated impulses,
Taught ye to soar above their "settled rules
Of Vice and Virtue."[13]—Fairest creature! He
Whom the world called thy husband, was in truth
Unworthy of thee.—A dull plodding wretch!
With whose ignoble nature, *thy free spirit*
Held no communion.—'Twas well done, fair creature!
T' assert the independence of a mind
Created—generated I would say—
Free as "that chartered libertine, the air."[14]
Joy to thy chosen partner!—blest exchange!
Work of mysterious sympathy! that drew
Your kindred souls by * * * * * * * *

* * * * * * * * * * * * * * * *

Come, and you'll find the muffins hot,
And fragrant tea in the tea-pot,
And she, you know, with the taper fingers,
Shall pour it out for you—Wherefore lingers

My friend so long? where can he be?
Didn't he promise he'd come to tea?
Ah! there's his knock—the very cat knows 'tis—
Now we'll be snug and toast our noses,[15]
Now we * * * * * * * * * * * * * *

              * * * * * * * * * * * * * * *

There fled the noblest spirit!—the most pure,
Most sublimated essence that e'er dwelt
In earthly tabernacle. Gone thou art,
Exhaled, dissolved, diffused, commingled now
Into and *with* the all-absorbing frame
Of Nature the great mother. Ev'n in life,
While still pent up in flesh and skin, and bones,
My thoughts and feelings like electric flame
Shot through the solid mass, towards their source,
And blended with the general elements,
When thy young star o'er life's horizon hung
Far from its zenith yet, low lagging clouds
(Vapours of earth) obscured its heav'n-born rays—
Dull fogs of prejudice and superstition,
And vulgar decencies begirt thee round;
And thou didst wear awhile th' unholy bonds
Of "holy matrimony!"—and didst vail
Awhile thy lofty spirit to the cheat.—
But reason came—and firm philosophy,
And mild philanthropy, and pointed out
The shame it was—the crying, crushing shame,
To curb within a little paltry pale
The love that over *all* created things
Should be diffusive as the atmosphere.[16]
Then did thy boundless tenderness expand
Over all space—all animated things,
And things inanimate. Thou hadst a heart,
A ready tear for *all*—The dying whale,
Stranded and gasping—ripped up for his blubber,
By Man, the tyrant—The small sucking pig
Slain for his riot—The down-trampled flower,
Crushed by his cruel foot—*All, each* and *all*
Shared in thy boundless sympathies, and then—
(Sublime perfection of perfect *love*)
Then didst thou spurn the whimp'ring wailing thing
That dared to call *thee* "husband," and to claim,

As her just right, support and love from *thee*,—
Then didst thou * * * * * * * * * * *

* * * * * * * * * * * * * *

Pretty little playful Patty!
Daddy's darling! fubsy[17] fatty!
Come and kiss me, come and sip,
Little bee upon my lip—
Come, and bring the pretty ship,
Little brother Johnny made ye,
Come, ye little cunning jade ye,[18]
Come and see what I've got here,
In my pocket, pretty dear!
What! and won't ye come no higher?
Want to go to aunt Marier?
Want to go to * * * * * *

* * * * * * * * * * *

Oh! lay me when I die
     Hard by
That little babbling brook, where you
     and I
Have sat, and sauntered many a sum-
     mer's day,

Scenting the sweet soft hay;
There let me lay,
For there young mincing May
Comes first with mouth so meek,
And pale peach-coloured cheek,
And little naked feet,
That go pit pat,
     And all that,
Tripping among the sweet
     Daisies and violets,
And pale primroses;
     And there she comes and sits
A tying up of posies
Fit for immortal noses
To sniff unto, and there
With silky, swaling[19] pair,
And iv'ry hands that wring it,
And to the zephyrs fling it,

Up from that babbling brook
The little Naiad's look,

Heaving up round white shoulders,
That dazzle all beholders,
And then so graceful glide they,
Some crablike (sidling) sideway;
Then on the bank I mention,
Like turtles at Ascension,[20]
In heaps they're all a laying,
And then with pretty playing,
One, like a frightened otter,
Flops down into the water;
The rest they flounce in a'ter—
Then some, with pea-green blushes,
Hide in amongst the rushes,
And one lies shamming sleep,
And one squeaks out "bo peep!"
And one raised head doth peer
Out with a laughing leer;
And then pops up another;
Another and another,
Then they pretend to smother,
A titt'ring talk coquettish,
Then with affected wonder,
    And feigned frowns so pettish,
Like ducks they dive down under,
Then through the gurgling water,
To look and see * * * * * * *

39
Catherine Maria Fanshawe, "Fragment in Imitation of Wordsworth" (n.d.)

The date of this parody of Wordsworth by Catherine Maria Fanshawe (1765–1834) is not known, but it contains allusions to a number of the well-known lyrical ballads. Her poems were seldom published and were known by her contemporaries, such as Scott, only in manuscript. With the exception of those poems she included in Joanna Baillie's *Collection of Poems* (1823), her poems first appeared as a group in the privately printed *Memorials of Miss Catherine Maria Fanshawe* (1865), edited by William Harness. On the Fanshawe circle of acquaintances, see Mary Russell Mitford, *Recollections of a Literary Life or, Books, Places, and People* (New York: Harper & Brothers, 1852), 158–59.

"Fragment" primarily mocks the poet-speaker for his homely images, poeticizing on the commonplace, and obsession with nature. Fanshawe's mastery of the Wordsworth idiom and rhythm also helps to portray the speaker as simple-minded and naive. He is so enamored of nature that, in the poem's witty conclusion, he fantasizes about his son's metamorphosis into a tree—strictly speaking, a literalizing both of the earlier personification of the trees and of his son's status as a child of nature.

FRAGMENT IN IMITATION OF WORDSWORTH

> THERE is a river clear and fair,
> 'Tis neither broad nor narrow;
> It winds a little here and there—
> It winds about like any hare;
> And then it takes as straight a course
> As on the turnpike road a horse,
> Or through the air an arrow.
> The trees that grow upon the shore
> Have grown a hundred years or more;
> So long there is no knowing.
> Old Daniel Dobson does not know
> When first those trees began to grow;

But still they grew, and grew, and grew,
As if they'd nothing else to do,
   But ever to be growing.

The impulses of air and sky
Have reared their stately stems so high,
   And clothed their boughs with green;
Their leaves the dews of evening quaff,—
   And when the wind blows loud and keen,
I've seen the jolly timbers laugh,
   And shake their sides with merry glee—
   Wagging their heads in mockery.

Fix'd are their feet in solid earth,
   Where winds can never blow;
But visitings of deeper birth
   Have reached their roots below.
For they have gained the river's brink,
And of the living waters drink.

There's little Will, a five years' child—
   He is my youngest boy;
To look on eyes so fair and wild,
   It is a very joy:
He hath conversed with sun and shower,
And dwelt with every idle flower,
   As fresh and gay as them.
He loiters with the briar rose,—
The blue-belles are his play-fellows,
   That dance upon their slender stem.

And I have said, my little Will,
Why should not he continue still
   A thing of Nature's rearing?
A thing beyond the world's control—
A living vegetable soul,—
   No human sorrow fearing.

It were a blessed sight to see
That child become a willow tree,
   His brother trees among.
He'd be four times as tall as me,
   And live three times as long.

40

William Hay Forbes, "Cockney Contributions for the First of April" (1824)

This combination of parodies on Leigh Hunt and William Hazlitt was published in *Blackwood's* (July 1824). It has been attributed to William Hay Forbes, probably the eldest of four sons of Sir William Forbes (1739–1806), banker and author.

Forbes's is yet another attack in the tradition of Cockney-bashing initiated by the "Cockney School of Poetry" series (1817). Cockneys (here, Hunt and Hazlitt) are portrayed as intellectually pretentious (e.g., their use of classical mythology without having been to one of the universities) and as cloyingly familiar (e.g., their use of the editorial, even royal, "we" in personal essays). Slurs are again made about the Cockney accent, their relatively lower class origins, and their taste in women (as noted earlier, Hunt wrote essays such as "On Washer-women" or "The Maid-Servant"; Hazlitt's notorious *Liber Amoris* describes his pursuit of a young servant girl).

In these clever parodies, Forbes transforms Hunt's geniality into a scatter-brained instability, a giggly silliness, and a tiresome chattiness. He makes Hunt's domestic asides (in repeated references to his "table") and confessions about a toothache into the embarrassingly indecorous remarks they were felt by Forbes to be. The obsession with "green" things probably glances at Hunt's *Foliage* (1818) with its two sections of poems: "Green-woods" (original poems) and "Evergreens" (translations from poets of antiquity).

While Hunt is a rhymester seeking a cozy escape in nature, the theater, or things Italian, Forbes suggests that Hazlitt, in his adulation of nursery rhymes, is a critic of severely confused standards. Moreover, as a mere journalist, his Latin and Greek are very faulty and his knowledge of Shakespeare piecemeal. In *Hazlitt: The Mind of a Critic* (London: Oxford University Press, 1983), David Bromwich notes that Hazlitt often quoted from memory and that De Quincey termed it "dealing in borrowed tinsel" (275, 276). Forbes seizes on this habit and has Hazlitt indiscriminately mix quotations (often misquotations) with proverbial bits of wisdom or clichés of the most lifeless kind. The Cockney writers, in short, are street-smart upstarts, sentimental and self-indulgent, and not to be taken seriously by individuals of refined taste.

COCKNEY CONTRIBUTIONS FOR THE FIRST OF APRIL

[The following articles were intended for our April Number, but unfortunately have only now reached us. We print them, however, for the amazement of our readers. We had certainly appointed Leigh Hunt our Vicelaureat, but we gave him the place merely as a kind of sinecure. However, as Leigh hates all sinecures, he has taken up his pen crisply, and has not only sent us a complimentary letter, accompanied by a contribution of his own, written in a fine Italian hand, but has moreover ordered one of his gentlemen of the press—Billingsgate,[1] *alias* Billy Hazlitt, Esquire,—to furnish an article, which he has done. HUNT AND HAZLITT BECOME CONTRIBUTORS TO BLACKWOOD'S MAGAZINE!!! *The Aristotle and Longinus of the Cockneys joining the "Crew of mischievous Critics in Edinburgh!"*— !!—!!!—"Vy, this is vonders above vonders!" as Mr Coleridge says—and as all Cockneys *must* say—compelled by the same eternal and immutable law which obliges them to superadd an R to every word, of which the final letter has the misfortune to be a vowel.]

I think we do know the sweet Roman hand.
                                        —*Twelfth Night.*
'Tis extant—and written in very choice Italian.
                                        —*Hamlet.*
A very, very—peacock.
                    —*Hamlet.*[2]

I. LETTER FROM LEIGH HUNT TO CHRISTOPHER NORTH, ESQ.
(INCLOSING AN ARTICLE.)

Florence, 1st April, 1824.

MY DEAR NORTH,

(What a jauntiness there is in beginning a letter in this way!) *We* (for we are still so conscious of the critical, that we are apt to slide into these sorts of contradictions to personal identity) began the dedication of "The Story of Rimini" with an address to "my dear Byron," for which a certain base and reviewatory person had an uncongenial fling at us in the Quarterly.[3] This awakened in our spirits a mild surprise; for we thought we were only engrafting upon the passionate, and breathing of our rhymes some natural and hushing gentilities—too fine to be apprehended by the person aforesaid. But we are sure that you, Mr Christopher North, (we find ourselves unconsciously writing these words in a better hand than the rest,) feel too well what is social and off-hand, to be offended at this kind-of-sort-of kind-of-thing, or to rate us very clerically about it; and though you have often a touch of the minaceous or so about you, one may easily see that it proceeds only from an excess of the jovial, and that there are always handsome laughs ready to sparkle out over the deep and sweet gravity of your face. We like a charming nature of all things; and there is a kind of sufficing and enjoying naturalness about all you write, that convinces us that you love all true and fine humanities, and that you are an admirer of all sorts of green leafinesses in your heart. We have therefore determined (ourselves and some more) to send you certain liberalities of ours, in the shape of articles, which we are sure will give you a lift in the world. Indeed, though we feel that we have been great and calumniated spirits, we are just now in such good humour with every possible thing and body, that we could go rhyme on the grass, or stand upon our heads, or drink tea out of an absolute rain-spout. But we will do none of these nice and graceful things; but sit down at our piano, and put forth our whole gentle strength in composing an elaborate harmony to that handsome and genteel lyric—

> Hey, Johnny, Johnny,
> Looking blithe and bonny,
> And singing nonny, nonny,
> With hat just thrown upon ye, &c.

—which seems as if it would warble itself into chromatics. Music is always sure to float us into a fine kind-spiritedness; and it is for this reason we are coy of a science which was Mozart's, and is now ours.[4] This will give us a little inspiring to effect what is to follow; and we shall then go into the most agreeable-looking corner of our library, which pierces out upon the youngest green of a garden, powdered all over with flowers, that are perking up their beauty in your face, in spite of you—together with all sorts of jauntinesses in general—and then we will write a deep and lively article for Blackwood's Magazine. What shall be the subject? Let us poke about and see. There is Croly's new Comedy *laying* on the table, like a petition to the House of Commons; let us notice it, which the House never does the other.[5] The comedy will, no doubt, have been already reviewed by some of the great and pleasant men who write for that oddic and periodic miscellany; for in this spot of spots ("sitting by the sweet shores Italian," as that most lovely and fearful spirit Barry Cornwall* says) we do not hear as often as we wish of

---

*We have been promised an article—a fragment of a poem—by Barry Cornwall. It is to be called "The Skiey Immortals (those who peopled Greece"), and will be about "Apollar, and Mercurius, and the rest."—C.N.

what is going on in the one we have left.[6] But we must try our hand at plumping up an article upon it, notwithstanding. We shall no doubt have something abundant and sweet-natured to say about it, which the readers of that apex and tenderest top of Magazines could not afford to go without. We have no rhymes upon table at present, not having put on our mild singing clothes this morning; but we must try to set some a-flowing before your next Number. We could easily send you a good savage assortment of blank verse; but as to having it said that we could not do anything better and more rimatory, we had as lief be told that we never had an old aunt, or that we were our grandmother. However, to make up for our lack of verse, we have sent our commands to Mr. W. Hazlitt, to furnish you with an article before he writes any more for Mr Jeffrey, or Mr Campbell,[7] or *The London;* and we inclose you a copy of our royal orders to Mr. H., which will be like a thump to make him jump, and give a sort of twitch to his memory like a dun, or any other dull stumbling-block to orthodox fancies. We are sure you will print our contributions (as Mr Jeffrey does) without even looking at them, a custom for which we have no light esteem—

(Black, but such as in esteem, &c.)[8]

We have got a *Wishing Cap* of our own, as good as new, though not quite so good as Fortunatus's:[9] if it were, we would put it on, and wish you could be brought to our gate some day or other, just as we were sitting at our writing of an evening: And some one of our two maid-servants, with their worsted graces, should conduct you hushing to our library-door, which opening, should shew a kind face reflected in our own graceful and social looks. Our wife should make tea and hot buttered toast, (a thing of taste "not inelegant," as Milton says—especially in July, and under Italian heavens;)[10] we would then go out and taste the lawns and trees, and returning at night through the green leaves, we would have a booze of gin and water sociable together. We, however, never take more than one weak glass—for we are fonder of nice health and quiet sleeps, than of all sorts of contradictions to both. But we must make an end of this, for fear of sliding off into something which would make us forget our promised article, which would be a dull mistake. So, to finish our letter, pleasantly and grandly, as we like to do everything, we add only our *sign manual.*[11]

(COPY OF HIS MAJESTY'S LETTER TO MR HAZLITT.)

We, Leigh the First, Autocrat of all the Cockneys, command our trusty and well-beloved cousin and counsellor, William Hazlitt, Gentleman of the Press, &c. &c. &c., to furnish forthwith, in virtue* of his allegiance, an article for

---

*In the original MS. *wartue*.

Blackwood's Magazine—in which there shall be nothing taken out of the Edinburgh Review, or other Periodicals for which the said William Hazlitt scribbleth, and in which there shall be as little as may be possible to the Gentleman of the Press aforesaid, about "candied coats of the auricula,"—"a fine paste of poetic diction encrusting" something or another—"clear waters, dews, moonlit bowers, Sally L—," &c. &c.[12] As witness our hand.

> LIUNTO, *Imperatore e Re
> di Cocagna*.[13]

PART OF AN ARTICLE BY LEIGH HUNT.
(ADDRESSED TO C. NORTH, ESQ.)

We are always unwilling to speak of ourselves: but as your readers will otherwise see no reason upon table for the delay of our article promised on the First of April, we are obliged to afflict them by saying, that we have had for the last fortnight an aggravating (as the old women say) toothache, in the fourth tooth of our critical under-jaw. The said toothache has not only shut us out from such in-door amusements as theatres and books, but even from relishing as finely and deeply as we do at other times the green and glad world without them, which is invidious. We are not even yet quite as we should be, and are afraid that instead of saying natural and lively things, as usual, we may slide into a melancholy hilarity, amounting to the ponderous. However, as everybody told us, that folks would be impatient to know what those at the top of the critical in these matters thought of the new comedy, we contrived to fortify ourselves with flannel and fortitude, (things not to be lightly praised,) and sat down to our desk. The evening was most bird-like and sparkling—and was just such a one as we once described in a distich of our own,[14] written long before a sense of wars and debts had taken place in our minds of all sorts of amenities and merry graces—

> The climbing trees were sleeping in that
> > colour
> Which richly trembles out crisp-hair'd
> > Apollo.

What a contrast there is now to those days when we used to go to town of an evening to see plays, and write our Theatrical Examiner![15] Oh, the sweet morning-time of these evenings! If the wind was now and then thundering without doors, we had an inside place, and could enjoy it; and thinking of all sorts of natural pieties, we used to get snugly into the theatre, which to us had always a frank and agreeable-looking feel about it. There is nothing that draws us to such a fine and true humanity, as finding ourselves together at the theatre. There are people in the City, we are told, who know so little of the glad and flowering world about their very ears, that if they ever do exchange their ledgers for nature they do nothing but grumble at the blackness of the green leaves, and hasten back to the world of brick and mortar, and money getting. To us, now, a tree or so is an absolute god-send; and as to seeing even a flower-pot without a certain freshening-up, we could just as soon think of shattering the benignity of the summer-heavens. We have never lived in the city, which is perhaps the reason why we have always had a high taste for gracefulness of living: We love to have the flowers in season put upon our table along with the mutton—whereas these folks, if care and common-places do not prevent any addition whatever, make it a sorry business of a pudding or so extra. But though such people can scarcely relish anything but their own forlorn money-makings, (which are much less to the purpose than the Christmas merry-makings we have done so much to revive,)[16] there is always something enjoying even to them about the Theatre. Play-houses are the most social of houses; and one feels more sociable together at Covent-Garden, than at any of the others, (our old pit-and-box-hand-shaking favourite, the Haymarket, excepted). Indeed, when one sits in the pit, (as we always used to do,) one feels a certain frank cordiality about one, which is quite delicious, at the sight of so many pleasant faces sparkling all round you; and the most intellectual and graceful-spirited may there enjoy humanity even in its very common-places. You shall have on the same bench a high and dark far-thoughted, inward-looking aspect, worthy of the finest times of Italy, (if anything English, except perhaps Mr Hazlitt and one or two more, may be compared to the great and pleasant men whom Raphael has painted,) con-trasted with the pale and perking-up face of a city clerk, just escaped from his ledger, and glad to be for an hour or two out of the common-place sphere of realities, and to get into the less material world of poetry and the drama—those eternal stumbling-blocks to square-toes. In this way, those whose natures are not fine enough to relish fields and flowers as we do, are drawn into a kindly sympathy by apprehending along with us the passionate of a play—or starting off into a bench-and-side-shaking merriment at a comedy—a thing which is (to our idea at least) much more devout and thankful than the unhappy sounds that one hears of a Sunday, from churches, in as forlorn a taste as their music[17]* * *

* * *

[Here our Vice-laureat gets so very* * * * * * * * * * * and imperti-nent, that we dare not print the rest of his article. Indeed, a Second Review of Croly's admirable comedy, even by Hunt, would be a work of supererogation, after the excellent article that has already been written upon it in this Magazine—especially as Leigh says very little that we had not already said.[18] His criticism is, upon the whole, "kind-natured" and indulgent; though he says that the fine imitations of Shakespeare, which occur in the comedy, "are as unlike as imitations are apt to be, yet not ill felt in the general." He finds fault, indeed, with the title, *(Pride shall have a Fall,)* which he says, "we are sure we have often written for a copy when a boy at school;" and he adds, what must have been no doubt suggested by his own personal experience, that "it smacks too much of a truism." He praises, in general, "the lovely and fearful beauty" of the verse, which he thinks "resembles Beaumont and Fletcher in its swalings and undulations;" but he thinks it too ambitious—or, as he phrases it, "the verse is always wanting to be great and grand, as the maid-servants say." Of course, we must not dispute with Leigh about maid-servants or char-women, with whose ways and opinions he is much better acquainted than we can pretend to be; and, for the same reason, we must agree with his criticism on the *Suivantes*[19] of the piece, who, he says, "talk wilful blank verse just as well as their mistresses—which is a thing not to be thought of." The exquisite and polite critic finds "a good deal of raffishness" in the scenes with the Hussars, and says there is "some ill-worded expressing" in the dialogue. However, he assures us, that he has "prodigiously felt and admired the comedy in general,"—a fact, of which the knowledge must be infinitely delightful to Mr Croly. But we must now come to Mr Hazlitt's article. We print his Latin and French quotations as we find them in the MS., and as our readers will always find them printed in the Edinburgh Review, &c. &c.]

2. TABLE TALK. A NEW SERIES
NO. I

On Nursery Rhymes in general.

To me the meanest flower that blows can give
Thoughts, that do often lie too deep for tears.[20]

Sweet are the dreams of childhood, but sweeter the strains that delight its early ears!* We would give anything to recall those pleasant times, when we thought Jack Horner finer than anything in Shakespeare. And sometimes we think so still! What a poet was he who composed all these sweet nursery verses—the violet bed not sweeter! Yet he died "without a name!"[21] How unintelligible they are, and yet how easily understood! They are like Wordsworth, (but oh, how unlike!) and we admire them for the same reason that we do him. How many young lips have breathed out these "snatches of old songs," making the breeze about them "discourse most eloquent music!"[22] Wherever these rhymes "do love to haunt, the air is delicate." Let us try to make them "as palpable to the feeling" of others, as they are to our own.[23]

We once said in Constable's Magazine, that, "to be an Edinburgh reviewer, was the highest distinction in literary society;" because, about that time, we began to write in the Edinburgh Review.[24] We were proud of it then, and we

---

*Quaere, *years*.—Printer's devil.

are so yet!—But it is a finer thing now. One could not then be radical, if one would. Now it is *tout au contraire*—Whigs and Radicals have met together—Jeffrey and Hunt have embraced each other. And it is right they should. Jeffrey is the "Prince of Critics and King of Men;" just as Leigh Hunt is King of Cockaigne, by divine right.[25] They are your only true legitimates.* They are like the two kings of Brentford![26] There they sit upon their thrones—the Examiner and the Edinburgh Review—*sedet, eternumque sedebit*—"both warbling of one note, both in one key." Each "doth bestride his little world like a Colossus"—(little, but oh! how great!)[27] *There* they are *teres et rotundus;* while Universal Suffrage, like "Universal Pan, knit with the graces" of Whiggism, leads on the eternal dance![28] We have said in *The London,* that "to assume a certain signature, and write essays and criticisms in THE LONDON MAGAZINE, was a consummation of felicity hardly to be believed."[29] But what is writing in the Edinburgh Review, or the New Monthly, or the London, compared to writing in Blackwood's Magazine? That, after all, is your only true passport to Fame.

We thought otherwise once—but we were wrong!—Well, *better late than never.* But we must get to our subject.

What admirable pictures of duty (finer than Mr Wordsworth's Ode to Duty) are now and then presented to us in these rhymes!—what powerful exhortations to morality (stronger and briefer than Hannah More's) do we find in them![30] What can be more strenuous, in its way, than the detestation of slovenliness inspired by the following example? The rhyme itself seems "to have caught the trick" of carelessness, and to wanton in the inspiration of the subject!

> See saw, Margery Daw, sold her bed, and lay in the straw;
> Was not she a dirty *slut,* to sell her bed, and lie in the
>   *dirt?*

Look at the paternal affection (regardless of danger) so beautifully exemplified in this sweet lullaby:—

> Bye, baby bunting! papa's gone a-hunting,
> To catch a little rabbit-skin, to wrap the baby bunting in.

There is a beautiful spirit of humanity and a delicate gallantry in this one. The long sweep of the verse reminds one of the ladies' trains in Watteau's pictures:—[31]

---

*Mr. Hazlitt here omits the name of *another* sovereign, of whom he thus speaketh in the Edinburgh Review—"The Scotsman is an excellent paper, with but one subject—*Political Economy*—but the Editor may be said to be *King* of it!" But perhaps he bethought him afterwards, that, to be "King of one subject," was no very brilliant sovereignty.

> One a penny, two a penny, hot cross-buns,
> If your daughters do not like them, give them to your sons;
> But if you should have none of these pretty little elves,
> You cannot do better than to eat them yourselves.

Economy is the moral of the next. It is worth all the Tracts of the Cheap Repository!—

> When I was a little boy, I lived by myself,
> All the bread and cheese I got, I put it on the shelf.

What can be more exquisite than the way in which the most abstruse sciences are conveyed to the infant understanding? Here is an illustration of the law of gravitation, which all Sir Richard Phillips's writings against Newton will never overthrow!—[32]

> Rock a bye, baby, on the tree top,
> When the wind blows, the cradle will rock:
> If the bough breaks, the cradle will fall,
> Then down tumbles baby and cradle, and all.

The theories of the Political Economists are also finely explained in this verse, which very properly begins with an address to *J.B. Say,* who has said the same thing in prose:—[33]

> See, *Say,* a penny a-day, Tommy must have a new master—
> Why must he have but a penny a-day? *Because he can work
> no faster.*

This is better than the Templar's Dialogues on Political Economy in The London, and plainer and shorter than the Scotsman. It is as good as the Ricardo Lecture. Mr M'Culloch could not have said anything more profound![34]

There is often a fine kind of pictured poetry about them. In this verse, for instance, you seem to hear the merry merry ring of the bells, and you see the tall white steed go glancing by:—

> Ride a cock-horse to Bamborough Cross,
> To see a fair lady sit on a white horse;
> With rings on her fingers, and bells on her toes,
> That she may have music wherever she goes.

There is also a rich imagination about the "four-and-twenty blackbirds, baked in a pye;" it is quite oriental, and carries you back to the Crusades. But, upon the whole, we prefer this lay, with its fearful and tragic close:—

> Bye, baby bumpkin, where's Tony Lumpkin?
> My lady's on her death-bed, with eating half a pumpkin.

No wonder!—for we have seen pumpkins in France, that would "make Ossa like a wart!" There is a wildness of fancy about this one, like the nightmare.[35] What an overwhelming idea in the last line!—

> We're all in the dumps, for Diamonds is trumps,
>   And the kittens are gone to St. Paul's:
> And the babies are bit, and the moon's in a fit,
>   And the houses are built without walls!

But there is yet another, finer than all, of which we can only recollect a few words. The rest is gone with other visions of our youth! We often sit and think of these lines by the hour together, till our hearts melt with their beauty, and our eyes fill with tears. We could probably find the rest in some of Mr Godwin's twopenny books; but we would not for worlds dissolve the charm that is round the mysterious words.[36] The "gay ladye" is more gorgeous to our fancy than Mr Coleridge's "dark ladye!"

> London bridge is broken down—
> How shall we build it up again?
> ———With a gay ladye.

The following is "perplexed in the extreme"—a pantomime of confusion![37]

> Cock-a-doodle-do, my dame has lost her shoe;
> The cat has lost her fiddle-stick—I know not what to do.

There is "infinite variety" in this one:[38] the rush in the first line is like the burst of an overture at the Philharmonic Society.[39] Who can read the second line without thinking of Sancho and his celestial goats—"skytinctured?"[40]

> Hey diddle, diddle, a cat and a fiddle,
>   The goats jump'd over the moon;
> And the little dogs bark'd to see such sport,
>   And the cat ran away with the spoon.

But if what we have quoted is fine, the next is still finer. What are all these things to Jack Horner and his Christmas-pye? What infinite keeping and *gusto* there is in it!—(we use keeping and *gusto* in the sense of painters, and not merely to mean that he kept all the pye to himself, (like a Tory,) or that he liked the *taste* of it—which Mr Hunt tells us is the meaning of *gusto*.) What quiet enjoyment! what serene repose! There he sits, *teres et rotundus,* in the *chiar-oscuro,* with his finger in the pye! All is satisfying, delicious, secure from intrusion, "solitary bliss!"

> Little Jack Horner sat in a corner,
>   Eating his Christmas-pye:
> He put in his thumb, and he pull'd out a plumb,
>   And said, "What a good boy am I!"

What a pity that Rembrandt did not paint this subject! But perhaps he did not know it. If he had painted it, the picture would have been worth any money. He would have smeared all the canvass over with some rich, honeyed, dark, bright, unctuous oil-colour; and, in the corner, you would have seen, (obscurely radiant) the figure of Jack; then there would have been the pye, flashing out of the picture in a blaze of golden light, and the green plum held up over it, dropping sweets!—We think we could paint it ourselves!

We are unwilling that anything from our friend C. P., *Esquire,** should come in at the fag-end of an article; but for the sake of enriching this one, we add a few lines from one of the *Early French Poets,* communicated to C.P., by his friend *Victoire, Vicomte de Soligny,* whom he met in Paris at the *Caffée des Milles Colonnes.*[41] The translation is by Mr Hunt; it is like Mr Frere's translations from the *Poema del Cid,* but is infinitely more easy, graceful, and antique:** [42]

> C'est le Roy Dagobert,
> Qui met sa culotte a l'envers;
> Le bon Saint Eloy
> Lui dit: "Mon bon Roy,
> Votre Majesté
> Est mal culottée."
> "Eh bien," lui dit le bon Roy,
> "Je vais la remettre a l'endroit."

It was King Dagobert who poking on his yellow breeches,
Whisk'd out the lining with a fling, and most elaborate stretches;
Kind Saint Eloi perk'd crisply up, and said with frankliest air,
"Your majesty's most touching legs are got one don't know where."
"Well," (with his best astonishment hush'd out the kindly king,)
"We'll swale them over jauntily, and that's the very thing."

W. H.

---

*Alias *Wictoire, Wicomte de Soligny.* This Cockney wrote (as few but Mr. Colburn the bookseller have the misfortune to remember) *Letters on England,* under this title, which we demolished. We had then occasion to shew that this imposter did not even know how French noblemen signed their names; and we might have added, that his title-page proved he did not know a man's name from a woman's—*Victor,* being evidently the name which *C.P. Esq.* was vainly endeavouring to spell. *Victoire, Vicomte de Soligny,* sounds to a French ear just as *Sally, Lord Holland,* would to an English one. Besides, *Victoire* is, everybody knows, a name given in France (almost exclusively) to females of this *Wicomte's* own rank—*maid-servants;* and when he was in PARIS, he had no doubt, often occasion to violate propriety, by calling out from his room on the ninth floor, *Wictoire, woulez wous wenir wite awec du win.*—C. N.

**Quaere, *antic*. Printer's devil.

41

William Frederick Deacon, from
Warreniana (1824)

Warreniana was published in 1824. William Frederick Deacon (1799–1845), journalist and author, was troubled all his life by ill health. He wrote for newspapers and *Blackwood's* and, in addition to publishing volumes of essays and "Tales," a novel *(Annette)* appeared posthumously. In *Warreniana* Deacon uses the successful business man Robert Warren and his well-known blacking firm as the framework for this collection of parodies. Warren's boot polish was widely advertised both in England and in Europe. The advertisements that were placed in daily newspapers in England such as the *Star, Post, Globe, Courier,* and *Times* ("The Triumph of Warren," in *Warreniana,* 53) often featured rhythmical rhymes. This idea of "puffing" a product to increase its sales is cleverly applied to contemporary writers who, Deacon seems to assert, are so preoccupied by commercial considerations that they unashamedly engage in all forms of self-promotion.

In the Wordsworth parody, for example, the lengthy and occasionally mistaken "Summary" is itself a kind of incongruous and misleading "puff" for the empty rhetoric that follows. Southey, of course, had the platform of laureate to promote himself and did so by puffing the establishment in lame epic manner. Even the reviewers and critics, feeding on contemporary writers, manage to promote themselves by inventing "schools" of poetry. In hailing Warren as the founder of a new group of writers who unite aspects of both Lake and Cockney schools, the review is demonstrating the poverty of existing critical "discourse." Finally, in using Childe Harold's pilgrimage as a way of satirizing the entire London scene, the Byron parody reveals how the "self-eulogistic" impulse has infected all areas of life from the Stock Exchange to the law courts.

OLD CUMBERLAND PEDLAR
BY W. W.

SUMMARY OF CONTENTS

A summer afternoon. The Solitary (i.e. author) seats himself on a bank of buttercups with Johanna, Goody Blake, Tims, Stokes, and some others beside him[1]; informs them that he shall not drink tea till half past eight, and that as it is now only seven o'clock, he has got one hour and a half left for conversation. Solitary accordingly describes his EXCURSION some years ago among the mountains, where he saw Warren's name engraved upon the rocks.[2] Philosophical reflections upon Warren's Blacking. Solitary then commences the tale of Peter Bell; describes how he blew his nose among the mountains, and how the mountains sent back an echo—Catalogue of mountains engaged in the chorus. Solitary proceeds to detail the particulars of his interview with Bell, who, it seems, was a travelling pedlar to the firm of Robert Warren, 30, Strand. Eulogium on Robert and his Blacking. Solitary goes on to say that Bell and himself walked together towards Rydal, but that on the road he was bitten on the nose by a gnat. Meditations on a gnat-bite. Solitary closes his account of the Pedlar, and gives good advice to his little friends, Goody Blake, Johanna, Stokes & Co. Stokes indecent. Solitary admonishes him to tie up the knee-strings of his breeches, and informs him that Goody Blake has been peeping for the last half-hour. Stokes ties up his knee-strings, and the poem is concluded by the Solitary exhorting his juvenile audience to "BUY WARREN'S BLACKING."

George Fisher, Goody Blake, and Betty Foy,[3]
Johanna, Matthew, Tims, and you too, Stokes,
Come, sit ye down upon this bank of fresh
But bilious buttercups: 'tis scarcely seven,
And I shall not drink tea till half-past eight,
Or peradventure nine, so that one hour,
One sober hour remains for converse sweet.
You all knew Peter Bell, the pedlar, he
Was a hale man and honest, and each spring
What time the cuckoo carolled in the hedge,
Would seek our simple villages, to vend
His patron's wares—of him I now would speak;
And while yon grave, 'neath which his ashes sleep,
Feeds in the fattening twilight, I will tell

An incident that once befell us both
Among the rocks by steep Helvellyn's side.

It chanced one summer morn I passed the clefts
Of Silver-How,[4] and turning to the left,
Fast by the blacksmith's shop, two doors beyond
Old Stubb's, the tart-woman's, approached a glen
Secluded as a coy nun from the world.
Beauteous it was but lonesome, and while I
Leaped up for joy to think that earth was good
And lusty in her boyhood, I beheld
Graven on the tawny rock these magic words,
"BUY WARREN'S BLACKING;" then in thought I
        said,
My stars, how we improve! Amid these scenes
Where hermit nature, jealous of the world,
Guards from profane approach her solitude;
E'en here, despite each fence, adventurous art
Thrusts her intrusive puffs; as though the rocks
And waterfalls were mortals, and wore shoes.

That morn I lost my breakfast, but returning
Home through the New Cut by Charles Fleming's field
Westward of Rydal Common, and below
The horse-pond, where our sturdy villagers
Duck all detected vagrants, I espied
A solitary stranger; like a snail
He wound along his narrow course with slow
But certain step, and lightly as he paced,
Drew from the deep Charybdis of his coat,
What seemed to my dim eyes a handkerchief,
And forthwith blew his nose: the adjacent rocks,
Like something starting from a hurried sleep,
Took up the snuffling twang and blew again.
That ancient woman seated on Helm-crag
Was ready with her cavern; Hammar-scar,
And the tall steep of Silver-How sent back
Their nasal contributions; Loughrigg heard,
And Fair-field answered with a mountain tone.[5]

The old man paused to listen, but when ceased
This mountainous bravura, on his staff
He bowed his palsied head in compliment
To my approach; "Dear God! 'tis Peter Bell,"

I cried aloud; "how fare you, my good friend?"
Then thus the pedlar spake: "Oddsniggers, sir,"
I use his very words, "full twenty years
Have past since you and I held talk together,
So now let's chat a bit." With that he spake
Familiarly of me and of old times,
And of grand sights that he had seen since last
We roved through Hammar-scar; how he had dwelt
Long with a mighty merchant in the Strand,
Hight Warren, and was travelling to grave
His name upon each rock, that when the hinds[6]
Passed by that way, their speculative eyes
Might linger on the carved advertisement.
He added, that this merchant was a man,
Like those of Tyre and Sidon, glorified
By the wide universe, and that his name
Was honoured among nations; he was one
Who sprang from nothing, like a mountain rill,
Till widening in its course the ambitious stream
Of his good fortune poured a tide of wealth
Into the sea of Number thirty, Strand.

When Peter ended, I proposed a walk
To Rydal, for the day was fresh with youth,
And thousand burnished insects on the wing,
The bee, the butterfly, and humming gnat,
Flew swift as years of childhood o'er our heads.
Touching these gnats, I could not choose but feel,[7]
When I had walked, perhaps, some minutes' space,
The venomous superficies of a pimple,
On the left side my nose: 'twas streaked with hues
Of varied richness, like a summer eve;
And edged, as is the thunder-cloud, with tints
Albescent, and alarming to the eye.—
It was a gnat-bite!! On the previous eve,
When, rapt in thought by lone Helvellyn's side,
My fancy slept; this unrelenting insect
Marking his hour, had borne me company,
And tweaked a memorandum on my nose.

Thus nature warns her sons, and when their thoughts[8]
Aspire too boldly, or their soaring minds
Elope with truant fancy from the flesh,
Their lawful spouse, she spurns the gross affront,

And sends a gnat to tell them they are clay.
My spirit owned her chastening hand, and gazed
On heath and hill, and sunless glen and rock,
In lowliness of heart, while pitying heaven,
As it approved th' offender's penitence,
Looked down upon me with an eye of love—
An eye of love it was, but Peter Bell,
(Antique pedestrian,) felt the gracious charm
O'erflow his soul no longer; he was clad
In thick buff waistcoat, cotton pantaloons
I' th' autumn of their life, and wore beside
A drab great coat, on whose pearl buttons beamed
The beauty of the morning; as we strolled,
I could not choose but ask his age, assured
That he was seventy-five at least, and though
He did not own it, I'm convinced he was.

That hour hath long since past, and the old man
Peter is with his fathers; but at eve,
When mid the deepening hush of winds I rove
Along that mountain glen, where erst he blew
His vocal nose, the memory of his talk
Floodeth my spirit with a freshening stream
Of bygone thoughts; then too I call to mind
The fame of Warren, and reflect how wit,
Albeit in commerce, will attain respect
And glory from the nations; therefore, friends—
(Tie up the knee-strings of your breeches, Stokes,
For shocked am I that Betty Foy should see
Coy nature peeping through your ragged hose)—[9]
Still be the name of Warren in your mouths,
His blacking in your cottages, and still
Let the example of his industry
Fall, like a genial shadow from the West,
Upon your minds; and when in after years
You strive to prison Mammon in your purse
By various traffic, think how Warren rose
By punctual payments; for believe me, friends,
That in commercial contact with the world,
A tradesman's TICK, is a TIC-DOULOUREUX,[10]
Incurable by all, save those who bear,
Like Henry Hase, a SOVEREIGN remedy.[11]

CARMEN TRIUMPHALE[1]
BY R. S.

Last eve as I sate in my room that looks o'er the church of Saint Clement,
(*Nota Bene:* I had but of late arrived in town upon business,)
I ordered my boots for a walk, my boots that polished and pointed,
Bright on their surface display the beauty of Warren's jet blacking:
Now you must know that my man, in his speed to reply to my summons,
Brought me my Wellington boots, but never once thought of the boot-hooks;
So to allay my spleen by calm and ennobling reflections,
Such as might wile the time disturb'd by my valet's omission,
I sate me down in a chair, and thus apostrophised Warren.
"Pontiff of modern art! whose name is as noted as mine is,
Noted for talent and skill, and the cardinal virtues of manhood,
Receive this tribute of praise from one whose applause is an honour.
I am he who sang of Roderick, the last of the Goths, and
Gothic enough it was, I'm told, in metre and meaning;
Thalaba too was mine, that wild and wondrous effusion,
Madoc and Joan of Arc, and the splendid curse of Kehama;
If I then, the author of these and other miraculous volumes,
And a laurell'd bard to boot, laud thee, oh my Warren, in epic
Verse, both peasant and peer will echo thy name o'er the West end,
And thus shall it be with the man whom S—y delighteth to honour.—
Already I hear thy puffs discussed in the circle at Almack's,
Dusking with sable shade the light of the Scotch Ariosto[2];
Already I hear them arranged for the violoncello by Smart, and
Melting on syren lips in lieu of Italian bravuras:
Braham at Drury Lane, the Stephens at proud Covent Garden,[3]
Dwell on each soul-stirring rhyme as a lover dwells on the moonlight,
When by its virgin beam his nymph hurries onward to kiss him.

"Through thee in the season of spring, oh pride of the modern creation!!!
Beauty sets off by night each grace of her whirligig ankle,
When to the music of harps in dulcet symphonies sounding,
She waltzes with twinkling twirl, and butterfly bucks hover round her;
Thee she hails as a friend, while her pumps, in the pride of their polish,
Illumine the ball-room floor like the slippers of famed Cinderella.—
In Brighton thy name is known, and waxeth important at Cheltenham;
Travels *per coach* to Bath, that exceedingly beautiful city;
Thence crossing the channel to Wales, it stirs up attention at Swansea;
Or flees with the speed of a dove o'er the mountainous ridges of Snowden,
Till valley, and rock, and glen, ring aloud with 'Buy Warren's Blacking.'

"But not unto Britain alone is thy fame, Robert Warren, confined: o'er
The civilised regions of Europe, believe me, 'tis equally honoured;
For when, as proof of the fact, I rambled through Switzerland lately,
And, spent with the labour of travel, put up in the vale of Chamouny,
My boots by the waiter were bathed in the luminous dew of thy blacking:
This, as you well may guess, astonished my nerves not a little;
So, flaming with zeal, I said, 'Now tell me, oh waiter, I pray thee,
Th' extent of this tradesman's fame in the vales of the Switzer, that straight I
May note it down as a hint for some future edition of travels?'
Then blythe the waiter assured me, that thorough Chamouny, the splendour
Of Warren's name beamed joy, as the snow on the summit of Jura,
Tinged by the occident ray, sheds glory and gladness around it,
While villages bask in its smiles:—meantime I continue my carmen.—
Thrice honoured artist, who hast a minstrel like me to commend thee!
Year upon year may roll, but you never will get such another;
For I am the bard of time, the puffer of peer or of peasant,
Whether Russ, German, or French, Whig, Radical, Ultra, or Tory,
Provided my *sack-butt* is paid with a *butt of sack* for each bouncer.
Hence, nobles are proud to bow to my laurelled head at Saint James's,[4]
Deeming his Majesty's grace dispensed through me, for they well know
His Majesty loves in his heart my political creed. *(Nota Bene,*
I will not swear that he does; but is it not likely, oh Europe?)"

Here I concluded my stave, for my valet return'd with my boot-hooks;
So taking my hat in my hand, a remarkably requisite practice,
I sought that widening gulf where the Strand with a murmur susurrous[5]
Flows into Pall Mall east, like Thames at the Nore into ocean:
Here I stood rapt awhile, commending the buildings around me,
Especially Waterloo Place, with which I was highly delighted;
Till hearing the clock strike eight, I returned to my Strand habitation,
And heard the bell from Saint Clement's toll, toll through the silence of
    evening.

THE SABLE SCHOOL OF POETRY
BY B. M.[1]

We are desirous, my public, of talking with you on two subjects of infinite
national importance, to wit, ourselves and Warren's Blacking. As our rheumatism (thanks to the Odontist) is somewhat abated, and we are now seated
at Ambrose's, with a jug of hot toddy on one side of us, and our beloved
O'Doherty[2] on the other, we intend to be exceedingly amiable, eloquent, and

communicative. But by the bye, when were we ever otherwise? Our disposi-
tions, like our alimentary organs, are always gently open; and though some
pluckless flutterlings of Cockaigne may wince at the occasional efferves-
cence of our Tory bile, yet the majority of the civilised world will bear
witness to our benevolent genius. And well, indeed, may they do so, for with
our sweeping besom of reform we have stirred up a revolution not only in
periodical literature, but in every department of science. Sir Humphrey Davy
and Sir Thomas Lawrence owe their reputation especially to us.[3] We and
Buonaparte were among the first to point out the talents of the one, and we
introduced the other to the notice of his present Majesty.

Standing then as we do upon the very pinnacle of popularity, and aware
that every man of talent we encourage is immediately received at court, we
are cautious in disseminating our patronage. But when such scientific characters as Pierce Egan,[4] regius professor of pugilism, or Robert Warren, poet and
manufacturer, solicit our aid, we are nervously alive to their interests. The
latter gentleman in particular we have long marked, as Doctor Johnson
observed of Milton, "stealing his way in a sort of subterranean current
through fear and silence,"[5] and we determined to take the earliest opportunity of encouraging his virtuous perseverance. This intention we communicated to him last year, but as month after month rolled on without a notice, he
resolved to remind us of it in the following delicate manner. It seems that Mr.
Blackwood is in the daily habit of opening his own shop-windows, and on
going the other morning for that express purpose, he was astonished to see
chalked up on the left-hand shutter, "Buy Warren's Blacking." Now could
any hint, my public, be more modestly characteristic than this? Not "Puff
Warren's Blacking," or "Write an article on Warren's Blacking," but simply
and negatively, "Buy Warren's Blacking;" thus connecting us in exhortation
with the uninterested majority of his patrons. And this delicate re-
membrancer is a Cockney! One who makes use of his grandmother's shin-
bone for a switch, bedecks himself in yellow breeches, and dispenses with
the luxury of a cravat. But no, we beg his pardon, Robert Warren is no
Cockney; he is of the land of William Wallace[6] and Christopher North; and
for any man to assert that he is not, is about as ridiculous as to assert that
Doctor Parr performed Harlequin in the late pantomime.[7]

In directing, then, the attention of the universe to Mr. Warren, we are
anxious that it should consider him not merely as a manufacturer of blacking,
but as the FOUNDER OF A NEW SCHOOL OF VERSE, an opinion which
we boldly rest on the ground of his poetical advertisements. With the exception of ourselves, and a few of the Lake writers, he is the most accomplished
versifier of his day. Byron may, perhaps, be more gloomily magnificent, but
Warren has a purer invention, full even to overflowing, of those fanciful
humanities which shed a sweet and holy charm over the poetry of Wordsworth and Wilson. In opening a subject, he steps into it as he would into his
shoes, with the familiarity of an acquaintance; and whatever character or

feeling he may describe, whether it be a cock mistaking a pair of boots for a looking glass, or a gentleman adrasing his beard by the same sort of luminous dumb-waiter, still you feel that the mighty minstrel draws his every charm from the intense sensibility of self. But it is in delineating the soberer feelings of humanity, that Mr. Warren is more immediately successful; he is the Wordsworth of commerce, and revolts from scenes of horror to dwell with affectionate interest on subjects of familiar nature. In this respect he resembles the Lake writers; but as their characters and descriptions are all drawn from the country, while those of Warren are confined in their localities to the Strand, and in their incidents to commerce, a sufficient difference exists to warrant us in holding him out as the founder of a new school.

In the poetry of *things in general,* his genius is equally felicitous. Even a pair of boots become in his eye creatures of loveliness and life, like the consecrated white doe of Rylstone. Thus, too, in walking the Strand, if he comes in sudden contact with a gutter, he does not vulgarly avoid it for its capacity of bespattering his pantaloons, but connects it with the streams of his native land, where the rivers glide "at their own sweet will," unless, like the Caledonian canal,[8] they are taught to glide at the "will" of others. On the same ideal principle a sow is not to him a mere guttling porker; it is either the "savage of the wild," or the "sovereign of the stye." In the latter case he associates it in thought with images of royal magnificence. Its bristles are the sceptres of its majesty, its grunt the thunders of its voice, and even its salt bacon recalls the attic *salt* of the philosophic *Verulam.*[9]

This is the true secret of imagination, of that "divine faculty," which enables its owner to see deeper into things in general than the less gifted majority of mankind; to discover philosophy in a pedlar, poetry in a traveling tinker, and in the intestines of the buttercup, "thoughts that do often lie too deep for tears."[10] In a word, this is the sole secret of genius, and hence it follows that many of our most imaginative but neglected authors have been enabled by its exercise to detect a bailiff in every stranger that accosts them.

The only fault we have to find with Mr. Warren consists in his excessive egotism. Though his genius, like some coy maid, loves to wander among scenes of congenial gentleness, amid the groves of Lisson, and the umbrageous walls of Kensington and London, yet he would have his walls inscribed with exhortations to "Buy Warren's Blacking," and teach his groves to lisp its praise.[11] In spite, however, of this defect, which he shares in common with the choicest spirits of the age, his advertisements are peculiarly popular; and knowing, as we do, the sympathetic sensibilities of their minds, we can conceive nothing more pregnant with advantage to literature, than a matrimonial alliance between the rival schools of Warren and Wordsworth. Of Byron we say nothing, he is decidedly inferior to both; but it is clear that the suburban fancy of Warren would blend beautifully with the sylvan imagination of Wordsworth; their homely dialect would meet in exact accordance, and the pedlars and jack-asses of the one prove an interesting counterpart to the cock and boots of the other.

We must now suspend our criticism, and say a few words upon Robert in his well-known capacity of manufacturer. His blacking, then, upon which he principally plumes himself, merits every commendation that his poetry has so eloquently bestowed on it. To boots, shoes, and all the family of the leathers, it answers the purpose of aqua-vitae, by strengthening them with a spirit of rejuvenescence that it is *truly refreshing* to behold. It would suit Saint Leon to a T.[12] With the alchymist's elixir for himself in one pocket, and Warren's elixir for his boots in the other, he might still wear imperishable apparel. Even Africa is now becoming sensible of its merits, for O'Doherty assures us, that when he was with his regiment at the Cape, he messed with a corps of Hottentots, who were all dressed in Hessian-boots, and solemnly assured him, that they needed no better looking-glasses.[13]

In Europe, we are happy to observe, that its circulation is equally marvellous. Wherever Blackwood's Magazine goes, *(et quoe carent nostro ora libro?)*[14] Warren's blacking accompanies it; and our kind Cossack correspondent, who dates from the Wolga, informs us, that he saw them both slumbering in peaceful fellowship together on the borders of Crim Tartary. Conceive, then, its enormous circulation! We sell about 30,000 magazines monthly, and Warren must be hard at our heels. So astonishing indeed is his present popularity, that at Holland House he is said to be the GREAT UNKNOWN. This, however, is a falsehood of the whigs, for we have every reason to believe, that Sir William Curtis is the author of the Scotch novels.[15]

Thus much by way of eulogium on Warren; but before we conclude, we cannot help reverting to ourselves in the instance of a recent calumny, which was evidently intended to ruin us in the eyes of Europe. It has been whispered in the upper circles, that we have accepted the offices of prime minister, on condition of colleaguing with Lord Grey.[16] This blood-thirsty bouncer we have traced to the same wretches who accused his Majesty of being a sylph, and can only say in answer, that like Caesar we have *three several times* refused the seals[17] for after the back-sliding of our once honoured contributor Tims,[18] who (we are shocked to say) has married his grandmother, we have felt little inclination to enter into public life. But could we ever do so without compromising our principles, Robert Warren should be our poet-laureate.

THE CHILDE'S PILGRIMAGE
BY LORD B—

—————

1.

WHILOME in Limehouse docks there dwelt a
    youth,[1]
Childe Higgins hight, the child of curst ennui,
Despair, shame, sin, with aye assailing tooth,
Had worn his beauty to the bone.—Ah me!
A lone unloving libertine was he;
For reft of health and hope's delusive wiles,
And tossed in youth on passion's stormy sea,
He stood a wreck 'mid its deserted isles,
Where vainly pleasure wooes and syren woman smiles.

2.

He was a merchant, 'till ennui'd with toil[2]
Of counting house turned but to small account,
Sated of home, and Limehouse' leaden soil,
Nee more to his dried heart a freshening fount
Of kindly feelings; he aspired to mount
To intellectual fame, for when the brain
Is dulled by thoughts aye fearful to surmount,
When youth, hope, love, essay their charms in vain,
The rake-hell turns as blue as doth his sky again.

3.

Thus turned the Childe, when in the Morning Post,
The Herald, Chronicle, and eke the Times,
He read with tasteful glee a daily host
Of the Strand bard's self-eulogistic rhymes;
He read, and fired with zeal, resolv'd betimes
A pilgrim to that minstrel's shrine to move,
As Allah's votaries in Arabian climes
To far Medina's hallowed altar rove,[3]
There low to bend before the idol of their love.

4.

He left his home, his wife without a sigh,
And trod with pilgrim-pace the Limehouse road;
The morn beamed laughing in the dark blue sky,
And warm the sun on post and pavement glowed;

Each varied mile new charms and churches showed,
But sceptic Higgins jeered the sacred band;
For his full tide of thought with scorn o'erflowed,
Or deep immersed in objects grave and grand,
Dwelt on the Warren's fame, at Number Thirty, Strand.

5.

He passed Whitechapel in such ireful mood,[4]
Where murdered muttons bob to every wind;
He saw the runnels red with bestial blood,
Their lazy streams through street and alley wind:
He saw and sickened in his inmost mind,
Felt how the heart with savage spleen ycrammed,
In blood alone can strange endearment find;
But such is man, (each pure affection shammed,)
Mean, heartless, lawless, dull, detestable, and damned.

6.

A truce to thought, for attic Billingsgate[5]
Already lures the pilgrim from his road;
Awe-struck he sees each naiad and her mate,
Haggling for halfpence with some river god,
Her Doric dialect, beautiful as broad,
Her plump cheek redolent of *ancient grease,*
Her *fleecy* hose with yellow worsted sewed,
Recall proud Athen's days, its *golden fleece,*
Its academic wits, and fame that nee shall cease.

7.

Not so thy street, Boeotian Leadenhall!
Famed for new novels, *leaden all* and dull;
Though wags thy library "Minerva" call,
Yet very British is Minerva's skull.—[6]
Her brainless books seem'd doom'd to gather wool,
Or sold to vile cheesemongers by the pound,
To scour the soulless sculleries of John Bull,
While pots and pans (not sylvan) aye surround
Each panic-stricken tome, despite its lore profound.

8.

And this is fame, that covetous cooks' shops
Should form the graves of every martyr'd work,
That Southey's strains should wrap up mutton chops,
Or Cheshire cheese anoint the leaves of Burke.—

That Theodore Ducas[7]—Catiline—should lurk
'Mid Granger's sweets,[8] with Wordsworth's Peter Bell,
Or Chalmers's Lecture on the Scottish kirk[9]
Sleep with its fathers in some London hell,
Some fruiterer's fruitful shelf where dirt and dulness dwell.

9.

But, lo, th' Exchange; a busy world is here,—
A world of knaves in wide confusion blent;
Here beams the smile,—there falls th' unheeded tear,
For stock well-purchased, or for gold ill-spent.
All are on one fool's errand madly bent,
And Turk and Christian pass unnoticed by,
While Israel's sons nee more to discontent
A prey,—the new Jerusalem espy,
In this barbaric booth, this fair of vanity.

10.

Ah me! how grovelling is the mind of man!
How fixed on perishable hopes, and mean!
Wealth, honor, pride, engross his paltry span
Of life,—then leave him scathed in heart as
        mien.—
Here where I stand, the spirit of the scene
Enchains all hearts with talismanic spell,
In vain aspiring youth with blossoms green,
Bedeck'd domes forth;—here Mammon tolls
        his knell,—
And round him weaves the chain of avarice and of
        hell.

11.

Th' Exchange is past, the Mansion House[10]
        appears,
Surpris'd the Childe surveys its portly site,
Dim dreams assail him of convivial years,
And keener waxes his blunt appetite.—
Luxurious visions whelm his fancy quite,
Of calipash and eke of calipee,[11]
While sylphs of twenty stone steal o'er his sight,
Smiting their thighs with blythe Apician glee,[12]
And licking each his lips right beautiful to see.

12.

'Twas here they tucked,—these unctuous
 city sprites,—
'Twas here like geese they fattened and they
 died,
Here turtle reared for them her keen delights,
And forests yielded their cornuted pride.—[13]
But all was vain, 'mid daintiest feasts they sighed;
Gout trod in anger on each hapless toe;
Stern apoplexy pummelled each fat side,
And dropsy seconded his deadly blow,
'Till floored by fate they sunk to endless sleep below.

13.

But hark, the hum of multitudes, the roar
Of carts and coaches, and the various squalls
Or cries, that pierce the ear-drum's inmost core,
Have roused the Childe's attention at Saint Paul's.
Cheapside to near Guildhall in thunder calls,
Guildhall replies, of lungs with justice proud;
Milk-street and Lothbury, glad to join the brawls,
Have found a tongue, while Wood-street from
 her shroud
Rebellows to Lad-lane, who calls to her aloud.

14.

And in the midst, as leader of the band,
Stands the magnificent Saint Paul's;—he towers
Sublime to heaven, by winnowing breezes fanned,
Unknown on lower earth;—the rattling showers,
The storm, the whirlwind that in vengeance lowers,
Pass him unharm'd;—he lifts his giant brow,
As if in mockery of their puny powers,
Or rapt in clouds like conscious guilt in woe,
Soars from the vulgar ken a mystery as now.

15.

Something too much of this; but now 'tis past,[14]
And Fleet-street spreads her busy vale below:
Lo! proud ambitious gutters hurry past,
To rival Thames in full continuous flow;
The Inner Temple claims attention now,
That Golgotha of thick and thread-bare skulls,
Where modest merit pines in chambers low,

And impudence his oar in triumph pulls
Along the stream of wealth, and snares its rich
        sea-gulls.

16.

Hail to this shrine of barristers and brass!
Of wigs and wags of learning and of lead!
Solomon's brazen temple—but alas!
With old king Log, king Solomon instead.[15]
Ye gifted spirits of the legal dead,
Will none arise to grace degraded law?
Vain hope, despite the lore of each long head,
Satan hath found their lives a moral flaw,
And on them, bailiff-like, hath laid his ebon paw.

17.

And thus the world is rife alone with fools,
Who clank in chains while fashion holds the noose;
Court, camp, and church,—what are they but the tools
Of sin, shame, slang, buffoonery, and abuse?
Momus with man has made a lasting truce.[16]
And hence our patriots puff,—our warriors bray,—
Hence critics flood us with a muddy sluice
Of maudlin prose,—hence cant holds sovereign sway,
And sinless saints are spurn'd, while sainted sinners pray.

18.

Our life is one fierce fever—death the leech
Who lulls each throb;—the has been, and to be;—
The sole divine whose welcome aid can teach
The mysteries of a dread futurity.—
Come when he may, his advent will to me
Be spring and sunshine, for my soul is dark,
And o'er the billows of life's shoreless sea,
A sea uncheer'd by hope's celestial ark,
Cradled in storms and winds floats lone my little
        bark.

19.

Thus mused the Childe, as thoughtful he drew near
The sacred shrine of Number Thirty, Strand,
And saw bright glittering in the hemisphere—
Like stars on moony nights—a sacred band
Of words that formed the bard's cognomen—grand
Each letter shone beneath the eye of day,

And the proud sign-boot, by spring breezes fanned,
Shot its deep brass reflections o'er the way,
As shoots the tropic morn o'er meads of Paraguay.

20.

Childe Higgins hied him to this bless'd abode—
Not forked Parnassus—Crete's Olympian hill—
Not Ilium's plain—by kings and warriors trod—
Calypso's cavern, Aganippe's rill,
Or Circe's isle famed for enchantment still—
Ere thrilled his soul with such intense delight
As thrilled it now when Warren's magic till
Thro' each shop-window gleamed upon his sight,
Clear as Italian dawn that gilds the brow of night.

21.

But I forget—my pilgrim's shrine is won—
And he himself—the lone unloving Childe—
His Limehouse-birth, his name, his sandal-shoon,
And scallop shell, are dreams by fancy piled:
His dull despairing thoughts alone—once mild
As love—now dark as fable's darkest hell,
Are stern realities;—but o'er the wild
Drear desert of their blight the soothing spell
Of Warren's verse flits rare as sun-beams o'er
        Pall Mall.

22.

Farewell—a word that must be and hath
        been—[17]
Ye dolphin dames who turn from blue to grey,
Ye dandy drones who charm each festive scene
With brainless buzz, and frolic in your May,
Ye ball-room bards who live your little day,
And ye who flushed in purse parade the town,
Booted or shod—to you my Muse would say,
"Buy WARREN'S BLACKING," as ye hope to crown
Your senseless souls or soulless senses with renown.

42

Thomas Hood, "Ode to Mr. Graham," from *Odes and Addresses to Great People* (1825)

Odes and Addresses to Great People was co-authored by Thomas Hood and John Hamilton Reynolds. The text for Hood's "Ode to Mr. Graham, The Aeronaut" is from the third edition (1826) as reprinted in *The Works of Thomas Hood* (London: Moxon, 1862), vol. 1. Hood (1799–1845) was best known as a humorous writer and as the editor of a number of periodicals. The volume, a popular success, was probably Hood's idea, although Reynolds did claim a share in the Graham ode and others.

Odes and the ascent of balloons had been associated with one another as early as 1785 when, in *Probationary Odes for the Laureateship,* Thomas Warton was described as having ascended with James Sadler in a balloon at Oxford. Warton's purpose was to compose a "sublime" ode for the king's birthday. Sadler was, in fact, the first English balloonist in 1784, following quickly upon the French pioneers of 1783. Graham made his flight in 1823.

The parody is modeled on the introduction to *Peter Bell* and Hood literalizes the notion of a flight of fancy found in the "ethereal height" (152) reached in *Peter Bell*. The Wordsworthian tone of moralistic condescension some readers found tedious is here given body; Wordsworth is above, looking down, making demeaning comments on all things contemporary, from fellow writers to St. Paul's.

ODE TO MR. GRAHAM, THE AERONAUT.

——*——

"Up with me!—up with me into the sky!"
                              Wordsworth—on a Lark![1]

Dear Graham, whilst the busy crowd,
The vain, the wealthy, and the proud,

Their meaner flights pursue,
Let us cast off the foolish ties
That bind us to the earth, and rise
    And take a bird's-eye view!—

A few more whiffs of my cigar
And then, in Fancy's airy car,
    Have with thee for the skies:—
How oft this fragrant smoke upcurl'd
Hath borne me from this little world,
    And all that in it lies!—

Away!—away!—the bubble fills—
Farewell to earth and all its hills!—
    We seem to cut the wind!—
So high we mount, so swift we go,
The chimney tops are far below,
    The Eagle's left behind!—

Ah me! my brain begins to swim!—
The world is growing rather dim;
    The steeples and the trees—
My wife is getting very small!
I cannot see my babe at all!—
    The Dollond, if you please!—[2]

Do, Graham, let me have a quiz,
Lord! what a Lilliput it is,
    That little world of Moggs!—[3]
Are those the London docks?—that channel,
The mighty Thames?—a proper kennel
    For that small Isle of Dogs!—

What is that seeming tea-urn there?
That fairy dome, St. Paul's!—I swear,
    Wren must have been a Wren!—
And that small stripe?—it cannot be
The City Road!—Good lack! to see
    The little ways of men!

Little, indeed!—my eyeballs ache
To find a turnpike.—I must take
    Their tolls upon my trust!—
And where is mortal labour gone?

Look, Graham, for a little stone
  Mac Adamized to dust![4]

Look at the horses!—less than flies!—
Oh, what a waste it was of sighs
  To wish to be a Mayor!
What is the honour?—none at all,
One's honour must be very small
  For such a civic chair!—

And there's Guildhall!—'tis far aloof—
Methinks, I fancy through the roof
  Its little guardian Gogs[5]
Like penny dolls—a tiny show!—
Well,—I must say they're ruled below
  By very little logs!—

Oh! Graham, how the upper air
Alters the standards of compare;
  One of our silken flags
Would cover London all about—
Nay then—let's even empty out
  Another brace of bags!

Now for a glass of bright champagne
Above the clouds!—Come, let us drain
  A bumper as we go!—
But hold!—for God's sake do not cant[6]
The cork away—unless you want
  To brain your friends below.

Think! what a mob of little men
Are crawling just within our ken,
  Like mites upon a cheese!—
Pshaw!—how the foolish sight rebukes
Ambitious thoughts!—can there be *Dukes*
  Of *Gloster* such as these!—[7]

Oh! what is glory!—what is fame?
Hark to the little mob's acclaim,
  'Tis nothing but a hum!—
A few near gnats would trump as loud
As all the shouting of a crowd
  That has so far to come!—

Well—they are wise that choose the near,
A few small buzzards in the ear,
    To organs ages hence!—
Ah me, how distance touches all;
It makes the true look rather small,
    But murders poor pretence.

"The world recedes!—it disappears!
Heav'n opens on my eyes—my ears
    With buzzing noises ring!"—
A fig for Southey's Laureat lore!—
What's Rogers here?—Who cares for Moore
    That hears the Angels sing!—[8]

A fig for earth, and all its minions!—[9]
We are above the world's opinions,
    Graham! we'll have our own!—
Look what advantage height we've got!—
Now——do you think Sir Walter Scott
    Is such a Great Unknown?

Speak up,—or hath he hid his name
To crawl through "subways" unto fame,
    Like Williams of Cornhill?—[10]
Speak up, my lad!—when men run small
We'll show what's little in them all,
    Receive it how they will!—

Think now of Irving!—shall he preach[11]
The princes down,—shall he impeach
    The potent and the rich,
Merely on ethic stilts,—and I
Not moralize at two miles high
    The true didactic pitch!

Come:—what d'ye think of Jeffrey, sir?
Is Gifford such a Gulliver
    In Lilliput's Review,[12]
That like Colossus he should stride
Certain small brazen inches wide
    For poets to pass through?

Look down! the world is but a spot.
Now say—Is Blackwood's *low* or not,

For all the Scottish tone?
It shall not weigh us here—not where
The sandy burden's lost in air—
    Our lading—where is't flown?[13]

Now,—like you Croly's verse indeed—
In heaven—where one cannot read
    The "Warren" on a wall?
What think you here of that man's fame?
Though Jerdan magnified his name,[14]
    To me 'tis very small!

And, truly is there such a spell
In those three letters, L.E.L.,
    To witch a world with song?
On clouds the Byron did not sit,
Yet dared on Shakespeare's head to spit,
    And say the world was wrong![15]

And shall not we? Let's think aloud!
Thus being couch'd upon a cloud,
    Graham, we'll have our eyes!
We felt the great when we were less,
But we'll retort on littleness
    Now we are in the skies.

O Graham, Graham, how I blame
The bastard blush,—the petty shame,
    That used to fret me quite,—
The little sores I cover'd then,
No sores on earth, nor sorrows when
    The world is out of sight!

My name is Tims.—I am the man
That North's unseen diminish'd clan
    So scurvily abused!
I am the very P.A.Z.
The London's Lion's small pin's head[16]
    So often hath refused!

Campbell—(you cannot see him here)—
Hath scorn'd my *lays:*—do his appear
    Such great eggs from the sky?—
And Longman, and his lengthy Co.[17]

Long only in a little Row,
  Have thrust my poems by!

What else?—I'm poor, and much beset
With damn'd small duns—that is—in debt
  Some grains of golden dust!
But only worth above, is worth.—
What's all the credit of the earth?
  An inch of cloth on trust!

What's Rothschild here, that wealthy man!
Nay, worlds of wealth?—Oh, if you can
  Spy out,—the *Golden Ball!*[18]
Sure as we rose, all money sank:
What's gold or silver now?—the Bank
  Is gone—the 'Change and all!

What's all the ground-rent of the globe?—
Oh, Graham, it would worry Job
  To hear its landlords prate!
But after this survey, I think
I'll ne'er be bullied more, nor shrink
  From men of large estate!

And less, still less, will I submit
To poor mean acres' worth of wit—
  I that have heaven's span—
I that like Shakespeare's self may dream
Beyond the very clouds, and seem
  An Universal Man!

Mark, Graham, mark those gorgeous crowds!
Like Birds of Paradise the Clouds
  Are winging on the wind!
But what is grander than their range?
More lovely than their sun-set change?—
  The free creative mind!

Well! the Adults' School's in the air!
The greatest men are lesson'd there
  As well as the Lessee!
Oh could Earth's Ellistons thus small[19]
Behold the greatest stage of all,
  How humbled they would be!

"Oh would some Power the giftie gie 'em
To see themselves as others see 'em,"[20]
   'Twould much abate their fuss!
If they could think that from the skies
They are as little in our eyes
   As they can think of us!

Of us! are *we* gone out of sight?
Lessen'd! diminish'd! vanish'd quite!
   Lost to the tiny town!
Beyond the Eagle's ken—the grope
Of Dollond's longest telescope!
   Graham! we're going down!

Ah me! I've touch'd a string that opes
The airy valve!—the gas elopes—
   Down goes our bright Balloon!—
Farewell the skies! the clouds! I smell
The lower world! Graham, farewell,
   Man of the silken moon!

The earth is close! the City nears—
Like a burnt paper it appears,
   Studded with tiny sparks!
Methinks I hear the distant rout
Of coaches rumbling all about—
   We're close above the Parks!

I hear the watchmen on their beats,
Hawking the hour about the streets.
   Lord! what a cruel jar
It is upon the earth to light!
Well—there's the finish of our flight!
   I've smoked my last cigar!

43

Thomas Love Peacock, "Proemium of an Epic," from *Paper Money Lyrics* (1825)

The satiric aims of Thomas Love Peacock's *Paper Money Lyrics* (written ca. 1825; published 1837) are divided. The poems ridicule the economic theories that brought paper money into being and also parody the contemporary poets Peacock had already attacked in, for example, *Nightmare Abbey* (1818). As Carl Dawson suggests [*His Fine Wit: A Study of Thomas Love Peacock* (Berkeley: University of California Press, 1970), 63], the collection may also be an ironic glance back to William Cobbett's tract *Paper Against Gold* (first published 1810–1811 in *The Political Register;* collected edition in 1815).

The parody of Southey is the poem in Peacock's collection probably least disturbed by diggressive comments on the Smith-Malthus-Ricardo line of laissez-faire economists. As William Walling observes [" 'On Fishing Up the Moon': In Search of Thomas Love Peacock" in *The Evidence of Imagination: Studies of Interactions Between Life and Art in English Romantic Literature,* ed. Donald H. Reiman, Michael C. Jaye, and Betty J. Bennett (New York: New York University Press, 1978), 347, 350], Peacock objected to aspects of utilitarianism, particularly some of its "unfortunate social consequences." Certain contemporary poets, Peacock thought, bore marks of a similarly dangerous self-preoccupation. In the following parody Peacock portrays Southey as a Proteus, a turncoat, a "Fly-By-Night" operator who has prostituted his poetic gifts. The plot elements of the projected "Epic" are typical of Southey (pathetic, emotive, even hysterical), and Peacock aptly has them dissipate quickly into nursery rhyme materials.

PROEMIUM OF AN EPIC WHICH WILL SHORTLY APPEAR IN QUARTO, UNDER THE TITLE OF

"F L Y - B Y - N I G H T,"
BY R— S— ESQ., POET LAUREATE.

———

"His promises were, as he once was, mighty;
And his performance, as he is now, nothing."

—*Hen. VIII.*[1]

———

How troublesome is day!
It calls us from our sleep away;
It bids us from our pleasant dreams awake,
And sends us forth to keep or break
      Our promises to pay.
      How troublesome is day![2]

Now listen to my lay;
      Much have I said,
      Which few have heard or read,
And much have I to say,
Which hear ye while ye may.
Come listen to my lay,
      Come, for ye know me, as a man
      Who always praises, as he can,
All promisers to pay.
So they and I on terms agree,
And they but keep their faith with me,
Whate'er their deeds to others be,
They may to the minutest particle
Command my fingers for an ode or article.

Come listen while I strike the Epic string,
And, as a changeful song I sing,
      Before my eyes
      Bid changeful Proteus rise,
Turning his coat and skin in countless forms
      and dyes.

Come listen to my lay,
While I the wild and wondrous tale array,
How Fly-by-Night went down,
And set a bank up in a country town;
How like a king his head he reared;
And how the Coast of Cash he cleared;
And how one night he disappeared,
When many a scoffer jibed and jeered;
And many an old man rent his beard;
And many a young man cursed and railed;
And many a woman wept and wailed;
And many a mighty heart was quailed;
And many a wretch was caged and gaoled:
Because great Fly-by-Night had failed.
And many a miserable sinner

Went without his Sunday dinner,
Because he had not metal bright,
And waved in vain before the butcher's sight,
The promises of Fly-by-Night.

And little Jackey Horner
Sate sulking in the corner,
And in default of Christmas pie
Whereon his little thumb to try,
He put his finger in his eye,
And blubbered long and lustily.

Come listen to my lay,
And ye shall say,
That never tale of errant knight,
Or captive damsel bright,
Demon, or elf, or goblin sprite,
Fierce crusade, or feudal fight,
Or cloistral phantom all in white,
Or castle on accessless height,
Upreared by necromantic might,
Was half so full of rare delight,
As this whereof I now prolong,[3]
The memory in immortal song—
The wild and wondrous tale of Fly-by-Night.

44

Hartley Coleridge, "He Lived Amidst Th' Untrodden Ways" (1827)

This is a close parody by Hartley Coleridge of Wordsworth's "She dwelt among the untrodden ways" and was published in the *Inspector, Literary Review and Magazine* 2 (1827): 40. Hartley Coleridge's opinions of Wordsworth were well-balanced, as a letter to his brother Derwent in 1826 shows. He is highly critical of the poet's prose, his "gasconading prefaces, and that illtimed blundering supplement" with their "sophistry and unfounded assertion." Yet he goes on to exclaim: "What a mighty genius is the Poet Wordsworth!" [See *Letters of Hartley Coleridge*, ed. Grace Evelyn Griggs and Earl Leslie Griggs (London: Oxford University Press, 1936), 92–93]. Hartley's admiration for Wordsworth can also be seen in such poems as "To Wordsworth" and "To William Wordsworth on his Seventy-fifth Birthday" [in Hartley Coleridge, *New Poems,* ed. Earl Leslie Griggs (London: Oxford University Press, 1942)]. Another fragment of a satirical poem on Wordsworth, titled "Peter Bell," appears in *New Poems* (99–100) for the first time. Here we reprint the text from Griggs.

HE LIVED AMIDST
TH' UNTRODDEN WAYS

He lived amidst th' untrodden ways
    To Rydal Lake that lead:——
A bard whom there were none to praise,
    And very few to read.[1]

Behind a cloud his mystic sense,
    Deep-hidden, who can spy?
Bright as the night, when not a star
    Is shining in the sky.

Unread his works—his 'Milk white Doe'[2]
    With dust is dark and dim;
It's still in Longman's shop, and Oh!
    The difference to him!

45
James Hogg, "Ode to a Highland Bee" (1829)

This parody by James Hogg was published in the *Edinburgh Literary Journal*, 2 (1829): 199. Together with "Andrew the Packman" in volume 3 (1830): 179–80, of the same periodical, "Ode to a Highland Bee" features Hogg's return to the subject of his most successful parodies in *The Poetic Mirror* of 1816. This meditation on a bee, with its allusions to such Wordsworth lyrics as "The Solitary Reaper" and the "Immortality Ode," delightfully demonstrates the idea that every experience for Wordsworth seems to become a revelation of self and of personal evolution. This evolution, the parody hints, would eventually place Wordsworth in the angelic chorus. We are grateful to David Groves for alerting us to this parody [see his "James Hogg, Leigh Hunt, and the 'New Poetic Mirror'," *Wordsworth Circle* 17 (1986): 249–50].

A NEW POETIC MIRROR
BY THE ETTRICK SHEPHERD

NO. I—MR. W. W.

ODE TO A HIGHLAND BEE

Astounding creature, what are thou,
Descending from the mountain's brow
With such a boom, and passing by
Like spirit of the nether sky?
While all around this mountain reign
I look for thee, but look in vain;
Thee I shall never behold again!
And it is painful thus to sever
From trumpeter of heaven for ever.
   Thou art a wonder, I confess,
Thou journeyer of the wilderness;
Yet a holy thing art thou to me,
As emblem of pure industry—
And as an emblem higher still,

Which made my heart and spirit thrill;
For I bethought me thou mightst be
The angel of eternity,
Sent down, with trumpet's awful boom,
To summon nature to her doom,
And make the churchyards heave and groan,
With flesh to flesh, and bone to bone:
I choose not say the wild emotion
Of my moved soul, and its devotion,
At thy astounding locomotion.
   Blest be thy heart, sweet Highland bee,
That thou pass'd by, and changed not me;[1]
For though I know what I am now,
(The world knows not, I must allow,)
Yet the wild wonder strikes me dumb,
What I shall be in time to come!
Whether a zephyr of the cloud,
A moving and mysterious shroud,
A living thing without a frame,
A glory without sound or aim,
Or a creature like thee of a thousand years,
Booming through everlasting spheres!
Such bolt of bold sublimity,
Man never has seen, and never shall see,
As the great W. a bumbee!
   Therefore, blest creature of thy kind,
I laud thy speed upon the wind,
And, dream or spirit as thou art,
I bless thee with a human heart—
God speed thee to thy latest years;
I neither know thee nor thy peers,
And yet mine eyes are fill'd with tears.
   For, as a bee, if thou hadst been
As perilous as some I've seen,
When my rash boyhood's hands were given
(Hands made to strike the harp of heaven)
To feel the poignancy and smart
Of thy empoison'd ruthless dart,
How with that dart of ebony
Mightst thou have wrong'd my friend and me;
And dreadful damage mightst have done
To our beloved Miss Hutchison![2]
Therefore, it doth behove me well
To bless thee and thy little cell.

And now, again, sweet bee, I say,
With earnest feeling I shall pray
For thee when I am far away.
    Again I hear thy voice devout,
About—about—and all about,
As stretch'd recumbent on the grass—
From hill to hill it seems to pass,
Sounding to me like trump of death,
Far o'er the brown astonish'd heath;
I look to cloud, to sky, and tree,
A thousand ways, yet cannot see
Thy faery path of mystery.
    'Tis thus the high poetic mind
Can trace, with energy refined,
The slightest atom on the wind
To its high source; and to the goal,
Where perishes its tiny soul,
Then step by step ascend on high,
From dunghill to the yielding sky:
And thus shall I ambitious be,
When inquest is perform'd on me,
So rise above my grovelling race,
Bounding, like thee, and one day trace
My path on high, like heavenly dove,
Which none dare challenge or reprove,
A path all human walks above!
    * * * * * * * * * * * * * * * *

46
Anonymous, "A Driver of a Rattling Cab" (1831)

"A Driver of a Rattling Cab" was published in the *National Omnibus* (London) 1 (4 November 1831): 157. This parody, based on Wordsworth's "We Are Seven," makes Wordsworth the spokesman for the newer writers who are petitioning the King (here the driver of an omnibus) so that they all might be made peers. In short, they wish to join the aristocracy of English poetry in which the House of Lords figures as a kind of Pantheon or Parnassus. The King, however, quickly spurns the petition and Wordsworth is left "in a furious rage."

A DRIVER OF A RATTLING CAB

A driver of a rattling Cab,
    Or gorgeous Omnibus,[1]
That passeth every great man by,
    What could he know of us?

I met a driver such as this,
    And I knew that he was king,
For his steeds trod over classic ground,
    And they made its echoes ring.

He bore a thousand books along,
    The best their authors had,
And his praise was fair, and very fair,
    But his censure made me mad.

'Why come you here, why come you here,
    And how many may you be?'
'We each come here to be made a peer,'
    I said, 'and Seven are we.'

'And where are the seven—I see but one?'
  I answered 'Seven are we;
But Rogers is digging up some old pun,[2]
  And Southey is gone to see:

Tom Campbell is shaking Bentley's hands,
  And Croly a sermon giving,[3]
In praise of the good Lord Chancellor,
  Who popt him into his living.

Coleridge is now expounding why
  The Latin for 'fish' is pisces,
While Moore has lunched on one lady's sigh,
  And will dine on another's kisses.[4]

Then did the mighty king reply,
  'Seven are ye, I see,
But the devil a peer in all the lot
  Shall ever be made by me.'

With a rolling eye, and a visage sage,[5]
  I gazed on the glorious heaven,
Then turned away in a furious rage,
  And shouted *We are Seven.*'

Notes

FOREWORD: PARODY AND ROMANTIC IDEOLOGY

1. See, for example, Homi K. Bhabha, "Of Mimicry and Man: The Ambivalence of Colonial Discourse," *October* 28 (1984): 125–33.
2. Jerome J. McGann, *The Romantic Ideology: A Critical Investigation* (Chicago: University of Chicago Press, 1983), 1.
3. Michel Foucault, *The History of Sexuality: Volume 1: An Introduction*, trans. Robert Hurley (New York: Pantheon, 1980), 101.
4. Edward Said, *The World, the Text, and the Critic* (Cambridge, Mass: Harvard University Press, 1983), 139.

INTRODUCTION

1. Malcolm Bradbury, "An Age of Parody: Style in the Modern Arts," *Encounter* 55, 1 (July 1980): 44.
2. Carolyn Wells, ed. *A Parody Anthology* (New York: Blue Ribbon Books, Inc., 1904), xxi.
3. Margaret Rose, *Parody/Meta-Fiction* (London: Croom Helm, 1979), 155. Elsewhere she puts the matter as follows: "In focusing on problems specifically associated with the interpretation of texts, and on the role of the reader outside the text, as well as on the role of the parodist as reader of the text parodied, the parodist raises questions about the role of the reception of literary texts played in both the formation of the author's expectations of the reader and of theirs for his work" (107).
4. Linda Hutcheon, *A Theory of Parody: The Teachings of Twentieth-Century Art Forms* (New York: Methuen, 1985), 2, 6, 77.
5. J. L. Smeall, *English Satire, Parody and Burlesque* (Exeter: A. Wheaton & Co. Ltd., 1952), 21.
6. Christopher Stone, *Parody* (London: Martin, Secker, 1914?), 8.
7. Quoted by Robert Gittings, *The Mask of Keats* (Cambridge, Mass.: Harvard University Press, 1956), 132–33.
8. *The Works of Robert Southey*, 10 vols. (London: Longmans, 1837–1838), 10.206. In Southey's notes to *A Vision of Judgement* are the following related comments: "The reader will so surely think of the admirable passage of Dante, which was in the writer's mind when these lines were composed, that I should not think it necessary to notice the imitation, were it not that we live in an age of plagiarism; when not our jackdaws only, but some of our swans also, trick themselves in borrowed plumage." (*Works,* 10.221)
9. See Jerome J. McGann, *The Romantic Ideology: A Critical Investigation* (Chicago: University of Chicago Press, 1983).
10. See the important article by N. Stephen Bauer, "Early Burlesques and Parodies of Wordsworth," *Journal of English and Germanic Philology* 74 (1975): 553–69.
11. *The Poetical Works of Wordsworth*, rev. ed. Ernest de Selincourt (London: Oxford University Press, 1950), 740.
12. Norman Fruman, "Originality, Plagiarism, Forgery, and Romanticism," *Centrum* 4 (1976): 47. See also Hutcheon, 4.
13. William Hone, preface to *Wat Tyler: A Dramatic Poem* (London: W. Hone, 1817), xv–xvi.
14. Donald A. Low, *Thieves' Kitchen: The Regency Underworld* (London: J. M. Dent & Sons Ltd., 1982), 183.

15. J. B. Priestley, *The Prince of Pleasure* (New York: Harper & Row, 1969), 291, 58.
16. Marilyn Gaull, "Romantic Humour: The Horse of Knowledge and The Learned Pig," *Mosaic* 9.4 (Summer 1976): 44, 52.
17. Isaac Disraeli, *Curiosities of Literature* (Boston: William Veazie, 1858 [14th ed.]), 213, 220.
18. See Jerold Savory and Patricia Marks, *The Smiling Muse: Victoriana in the Comic Press* (Philadelphia: The Art Alliance Press, 1985), 68. See also Patrick Scott, "From Bon Gaultier to *Fly Leaves:* Context and Canon in Victorian Parody," *Victorian Poetry* 26, no. 3 (Autumn 1988): 249–66.
19. J. G. Riewald, "Parody as Criticism," *Neophilologus* 50 (1966): 128.
20. G. D. Kiremidjean, "The Aesthetics of Parody," *Journal of Aesthetics and Art Criticism* 28 (1969): 234.

1. GEORGE CANNING AND JOHN HOOKHAM FRERE, FROM *THE ANTI-JACOBIN* (1797)

1. *Mrs. Brownrigg:* notorious for sadistic cruelty toward young female apprentices while she was employed as a midwife to pregnant women in the workhouse of St. Dunstan's parish. Her torturings, described in the Newgate Calendar, are said to have "roused the indignation of the populace more than any criminal occurrence in the whole course of our melancholy narratives." See *The Newgate Calendar,* ed. Edwin Valentine Mitchell (New York: Garden City Publishing Co., 1926), 171. She was executed on 14 September 1767.
2. *Geneva:* a spirit distilled from grain and made in Holland.
3. *Tothill:* Tothill Fields, where the fair of Westminster was established in 1257, was well known in the eighteenth century for bear and bull baiting. *St. Giles* was synonymous with disease, crime, and squalor. During its worst period (1720–1750), this north London parish reported three deaths for every two baptisms; one quarter of its houses were gin shops that attracted the destitute. See John Lehmann, *Holborn: An Historical Portrait of a London Borough* (London: Macmillan, 1970), 79–92.
4. *Lycurgus:* Thracian king famous for his persecution of Dionysus and his followers. He was driven mad by the gods and killed.
5. *Orthyan Goddess:* surname of Artemis at whose altar the Spartan boys had to undergo flogging.
6. *Sapphics:* a meter used by Sappho.
7. *Dactylics:* metrical foot consisting of a long foot followed by two short. Both Southey and the *Anti-Jacobin* parodies are cited by the *O.E.D.* under "dactylics."
8. In late 1794 and 1795 there were incidents of mutiny in the fleet at Spithead which even spread to units at sea. These mutinies "were not a revolt against authority" but a demand for improvements in the crews' "wretched conditions." See Jacques Mordal, *25 Centuries of Naval Warfare* (London, 1965), 164.
9. *Fasces:* Roman emblem of authority carried before magistrates (a bundle of rods bound together around an axe with the blade projecting).
10. *Dilworth* and *Dyche:* Thomas Dilworth (d. 1780), among other books, wrote *A new guide to the English tongue,* which went through dozens of editions in the eighteenth century. It was for instructing young people. Thomas Dyche (died between 1731 and 1735) was author of the earlier *A Guide to the English Tongue, in two parts* (London, 1709). Dyche's volume (which contains sections on grammar and common and proper words) went through more than 100 editions by 1800.

6. ANONYMOUS, "BARHAM DOWNS; OR GOODY GRIZZLE AND HER ASS" (1801)

1. *Barham Downs:* between Canterbury and Dover in Kent. After 1778, and during the threat of French invasion, troops were stationed here and elsewhere in southeastern England.

7. PETER BAYLEY, "THE FISHERMAN'S WIFE" (1803)

1. *Absit invidia dicto:* said without ill will.
2. Possibly "And from about her shot Darts of desire" (*Paradise Lost* 8.62). For the Cowley reference, see "Davideis," book 3, 57–58.

8. EDWARD COPLESTON, "L'ALLEGRO, A POEM" (1807)

1. See *Henry IV, Part 1,* 3.1.53.
2. Pathetically garrulous old acquaintance of Falstaff in *Henry IV.*
3. Legal terms. For example, "force and arms" in law means a particular act or instance of unlawful violence.
4. From Edmund Burke, *Reflections on the Revolution in France* (1790).
5. From Ben Jonson's *Bartholomew Fair* 5.4.116–21. Leatherhead's commentary on the puppet show is a debased conflation of Marlowe's *Hero and Leander* and the *Damon and Pithias* (1571) of Richard Edwards. The point seems to be that Milton might be accused (by an unqualified reader) of forcing his poem to fit the rhymes as crudely as Leatherhead does. And the same reader might consider Milton's use of bits of classical myth as "debauching" the originals (as Leatherhead does).
6. Far from knowing nothing of evil, I knew how to come to the aid of those who suffer from it.
7. Macheath's song about the difficulty of choosing between his two sweethearts in act 3 of *The Beggar's Opera.*
8. *Democritus* (460–370 B.C.) was known as the "Laughing Philosopher." His teachings rested on the importance of pleasure and self-control. He is said to have blinded himself to facilitate mental concentration.
9. James 5:13.
10. *Mr. Newbury:* probably Francis Newbery (1743–1818), son of the well-known publisher of St. Paul's Churchyard, John Newbery (1713–1767), who was famous for publishing children's books.
11. *Mrs. Sarah Trimmer* (1741–1810) wrote books for charity-school children and servants and edited the *Guardian of Education.*
12. *Thomas Sternhold* (d. 1549) was, with John Hopkins (d. 1570), joint versifier of the Psalms.
13. *Edward Cocker* (1631–1675), best known for *Cocker's arithmetic* (1678), which was reprinted many times throughout the eighteenth century. The reference here, however, is more likely to one of his texts on penmanship: *England's pen-man* (1670), *The Guide to penmanship* (1664), *The London writing-master* (1676?), *The pen's celerity* (1673), etc.
14. John Milton, the elder, was admitted to the Company of Scriveners in 1600.

9. GEORGE MANNERS, "THE BARDS OF THE LAKE" (1809)

1. Wordsworth, of course.
2. Coleridge fits all the biographical details. He wrote "To a Young Ass" (1794), entered Jesus College, Cambridge, in 1791, and enlisted (December 1793) in the 15th Light Dragoons as Silas Tomkyn Comberbache (discharged April 1794).
3. "Lectures on Poetry and Principles of Taste" at The Royal Institution in 1808.
4. Milton's "On the morning of Christ's Nativity," 64.
5. *Charles Lamb* (1775–1834) and *Charles Lloyd* (1775–1839). Lloyd met Coleridge in 1796 and offered him £80 a year to instruct him for three hours each morning. At Lloyd's insistence, his own poems were published, together with Lamb's, as an appendage to Coleridge's (1797). Lloyd's *Edmund Oliver* (1798) attacks Godwin's view of marriage. He later went insane and eventually died in France.

6. *Par nobile fratrum* is from Horace, *Satires* 2.3, 243: "a fine fraternal pair / in spending and fooling, / in love of the perverse, true twins. . . ." *Arcades ambo, cantare pares* are from Virgil, *Eclogues* 7, 5: "They [Corydon and Thyrsis] were both in the flower of their youth, Arcadians, / Both ready to sing at the drop of a hat, or take a tune up. . . ."

7. Southey wrote a witch poem ("The Witch")—as did Lamb ("The Witch")—and also a ballad titled "The Old Woman of Berkeley."

8. Southey is critical of epic poems in, for example, his original preface to *Joan of Arc* (1795) [*The Works of Robert Southey*, 10 vols. (London: Longmans, 1837–1838), 1.xxiii–xxvi *passim*]. And later, in his preface to *Madoc in Wales* (1805), he remarks: "It assumes not the degraded title of Epic" (*Works*, 5.xxi).

9. Not traced.

10. Dithyramb: Greek choric hymn in honor of Dionysus or Bacchus and thus wild, vehement, and irregular in style.

11. Southey's reaction to a horse's fate here does not seem so exaggerated when we recall his poem "The Pig": "Jacob! I do not like to see thy nose / Turned up in scornful curve at yonder pig." The parody also echoes Southey's "The Soldier's Wife," earlier mocked in *The Anti-Jacobin*.

12. The article simply breaks off.

10. ANONYMOUS, "LINES ORIGINALLY INTENDED TO HAVE BEEN INSERTED IN THE LAST EDITION OF WORDSWORTH'S POEMS" (1811)

1. The name seems to combine allusions to Robert Southey (whose own poems of a similar nature had already been parodied in *The Anti-Jacobin*) and to the so-called "Lake School of Poets" to which both he and Wordsworth supposedly belonged.

11. ANONYMOUS, "REVIEW EXTRAORDINARY" (1812)

1. *Pedestribus historiis:* "storied prose" (from Horace, *Odes* 2.12, 9).

2. A common phrase from chivalric romances.

3. The use of stationary here suggests a play on words to do with book-sellers and paper makers. There is a Mr. Hoffman, author of a *Treatise on Paper-making*, listed in the bibliography of A. Dykes Spicer, *The Paper Trade* (London: Methuen, 1907), 264.

12. JAMES AND HORACE SMITH, FROM *REJECTED ADDRESSES* (1812)

"THE BABY'S DEBUT"

1. *Richard Cumberland* (1732–1811): the author of a number of sentimental comedies. Acquainted with the Smiths, he also contributed to the *Pic-Nic* newspaper and *The Cabinet* (into which it merged) early in the nineteenth century. He later persuaded James Smith to become a contributor to the *London Review*.

2. *Peg top:* a pear-shaped wooden spinning top.

3. Cf. "Alice Fell," 7. For Pentonville, see note 8 to *Leaves of Laurel* below.

4. *Flags:* flagged paving stones.

5. *William Henry West Betty* (1791–1874) first appeared on stage at age 12 and was able to retire with a fortune by the time he was 17.

"CUI BONO?"

1. "Who benefits?" Cicero, *Pro Milone*, 12.32.

2. *Columbine:* a character in pantomime.

3. Cf. *Childe Harold* 1.82.

4. *James Wyatt* (1746–1813): architect of the rebuilt Drury Lane Theatre.

5. *Holland House:* built by John Thorp in 1606 and a chief salon of Lord Byron's. *fleet:* evanescent.

6. *Lemnos:* Greek island between Greece and Turkey sacred to Hephaestus, the lame god of fire (and therefore possibly an indirect reference to Byron; cf. p. 142 of 18th edition of *Rejected Addresses* with the comments on the late Byron's "deformed foot").

7. Cf. *Childe Harold* 1.56.

8. *Smithfield:* NW of City of London and the grisly scene of public executions (such as boiling alive or burning at the stake) up to the seventeenth century. Bartholomew's Fair was also held there—hence the reference to St. Bartholomew, flayed alive and crucified by heathens. His emblem is a large knife, instrument of his martyrdom, and he is usually portrayed bearing a human skin over one arm to indicate his flaying. Ironically enough, Smithfield was later to become a well-known meat market.

9. *Tunbridge toy:* Tunbridge was known for its hard-wood wares, including toys. An etching by Thomas Rowlandson, "Miseries of Social Life" (9 April 1807), has a "Tunbridge toy" (here a small covered wagon) in the foreground.

10. *Unbelieving tooth:* obscure expression for Jew's harp.

11. *Hare:* i.e., mad hare. *Rolla:* one of the commanders of the army of Ataliba, King of Quito, in Sheridan's adaptation (1799) of Kotzebue's *Die Spanier in Peru* (1790) and one of Kemble's most famous roles. *steep'd:* possibly from to steep, to frame a discourse in formal or pretentious terms. *Orlando:* a character in *The Cabinet,* a play by Thomas Dibdin (1771–1841).

12. *Macbeth,* e.g., 1.1.11.

13. *John Braham* (1774–1856): a famous tenor who assisted Isaac Nathan in the arrangement of the music for Byron's *Hebrew Melodies* and who wrote the music for his own role as Orlando in Dibdin's *The Cabinet.*

14. Cf. *Childe Harold* 1.60.

15. *Thespis:* ancient Greek tragedian who introduced an actor in addition to the chorus.

16. *Lignum vitae:* hard wood. Quintus Roscius Gallus (d. 62 B.C.), the most celebrated of Roman comic actors. On Byron's view of British theatre see, for example, "English Bards and Scotch Reviewers," 575ff.

"THE REBUILDING"

1. Horace, *Odes* 4.2, 10: "He rolls new words through daring dithyramb and is carried along in numbers freed from rule."

2. *Glendoveer:* blessed spirit.

3. *Indra:* Hindu god of the elements.

4. "This rhyme was inserted here to demonstrate the fact that, contrary to the received opinion, there was a passable rhyme to the word 'chimney' " (Smith 1833).

5. Compare this opening stanza with Southey's "The Curse of Kehama," I.i.1–13. *Brentford:* a suburb of West London.

6. *Surya:* a gigantic wooden figure of Apollo had been erected on the roof of Drury Lane Theatre.

7. A description of fire-fighters from the insurance companies rushing to put out the fire.

8. *O.P.:* "Old Prices" was the shout of the theater patrons who protested increased ticket prices when the new Covent Garden Theatre opened 18 September 1809. After several weeks of tumult, a compromise was reached; the new price of seven shillings was to be restricted to the boxes.

9. *Kemble:* John Philip Kemble (1757–1823). His first appearance in London was as Hamlet at Drury Lane (September 1783). He became manager in 1788 and then manager of Covent Garden in 1803.

10. *Veshnoo:* the Preserver, one of the Brahmin trinity, perhaps representing Mr. Whitbread (1785–1815), brewer and politician, M.P. for Bedford, and Chairman of the committee for the rebuilding of Drury Lane Theatre.

11. *Ithaca's Queen:* Penelope.

12. "At the top of Arundel Street, Strand, well known meeting-place for political and other gatherings." (Smith 1833)

13. *Himakoot book:* Hemakoot (Southey's spelling) in book 10.4.70 of *The Curse,* the holy mount. *Baly:* judge of the dead in Kehama. *Swerga:* one of the Hindu heavens sacred to Indra.

14. *Meru:* central mountain of the earth.

15. *Levi:* committed suicide 18 January 1810 by jumping off the Monument's top.

16. *Carisbrooke Well:* one hundred and sixty foot well at ancient castle on Isle of Wight where Charles I was confined.

"A TALE OF DRURY LANE"

1. See *Don Quixote* by Cervantes, pt. 1, ch.ii.

2. *Augusta:* old name for London.

3. *Henry's chapel:* Henry VIII's Lady Chapel in Westminster Abbey (completed 1519). *Rufus' hall:* the Great Hall of the Palace of Westminster was completed in 1097 during the reign of William Rufus (who held Christmas celebrations there in 1099). The subsequent places are west, north, and east; the impression meant is "all over town."

4. Cf. *Marmion* II, xxxii, 597.

5. Remains of the tower were still visible in the late eighteenth century; it was situated between Aldersgate Street and Golden Lane or Red Cross Street.

6. Watt's Shot Factory (erected 1789 near Waterloo Bridge).

7. Which stood in the Old Bailey.

8. Narrow passage adjoining Drury Lane (named after the vineyard once attached to Covent Garden).

9. Various fire insurance companies are named here.

10. *Hockley in the Hole:* neighboring district to Clerkenwell; *St Giles's Pound:* in the eighteenth century it was at the corner of Tottenham Court Road and Oxford Street. *Chick Lane:* later West Street, Clerkenwell (pulled down in 1857). These were all places of disrepute.

11. *plug:* or fire-plug, the cock on public water pipe.

12. Cf. *Marmion* VI, xxix, 897, 901.

13. Cf. Marmion's last words in *Marmion,* VI, xxxii.

14. Kinds of cake.

15. Cf. *Marmion* VI, xxvi, 786.

16. *King Lear* 4.6 12ff.

17. The portico was vetoed by Whitbread because of cost, but it was later erected under Elliston.

"PLAYHOUSE MUSINGS"

1. Horace, *Satires* 2.1, 30–32: "He long ago regarded books as his faithful companions and, in bad times or good, resorted to no other."

2. Cf. Coleridge's "To a Young Ass."

3. Rev. Rowland Hill preached, apparently, on the "happy" occasion of the fire.

4. *Solyma:* ancient name for Jerusalem.

5. *Regency Theatre:* formerly The Tottenham Theatre (opened 1810), reopened as the Regency after renovations in 1815 by Harry Beverly, but closed again in 1819. Besides the smaller *Olympic* theater (built in 1806 with timbers from an old dismantled warship), Philip Astley also founded Astley's *Royal Amphitheatre* in Lambeth (1768). The latter was known for its spectacular entertainments based on equestrian displays. The *Sans Pareil Theatre* was built in 1806 by John Scott. It was sold in 1819 and renamed the *Adelphi.*

6. *Grimaldi:* Joseph Grimaldi (1779–1837), actor and pantomimist of Italian descent. As a boy he acted in Drury Lane and Sadler's Wells "on the same night, and had to run from one to the other" (D.N.B.). His greatest success was as the clown in "Mother Goose." His memoirs were edited by Dickens and published in 1838. Although he did perform elsewhere, his main association was with Sadler's Wells. *Laurent* made his first appearance at Covent Garden on 28 May 1799. *Robert Bradbury* (1774–1831) became known as the "Brummell of Clowns" because of his dandyism. He was also acrobatic and sported a tame bear as a pet. See Dickens's *Memoirs of Joseph Grimaldi,* ed. Richard Findlater (London: MacGibbon and Kee, 1968), 180–84, for Grimaldi's relationship with Bradbury.

7. *Johnson:* Alexander Johnston (d. 1810) was a carpenter, painter, costume and scene

designer, dancer, and actor. He was celebrated for the creation of special effects. *proboscis:* cf. *Paradise Lost* 4.345. *Padmanaba:* elephant in pantomine.

13. FRANCIS HODGSON, FROM *LEAVES OF LAUREL* (1813)

1. *Old Saul, S—y:* William Sotheby (1757–1833) was acquainted with the leading authors of his time and took an interest in struggling younger writers. His first publication was *Poems* (1790) and in 1807 he wrote an ambitious epic poem, *Saul.* He wrote at least six tragedies, of which only one *(Julian and Agnes)* was ever staged and that for a single performance (25 April 1800) which dissolved in laughter when Mrs. Siddons struck the head of an infant dummy she was carrying against a door post.

2. *Mr. Banks:* perhaps Thomas Banks (1765–1854), genealogist and expert in disputed inheritances. "None of the cases he undertook possessed more than the very flimsiest claims, and there was scarcely any genealogical will-o'-the-wisp which he was not ready, if the fancy struck him, to adopt as a reality" (D. N. B.). By 1813 he had published six books, the most recent being a pamphlet demanding the restoration of a lapsed peerage to a Mr. Walter Howard.

3. From "A Pastoral Ballad" (part ii, Hope, i) by Shenstone (1714–1763).

4. In return for two odes a year (at New Year's and on the monarch's birthday), the laureate annually received a cash payment and a cask of sweet wine.

5. *Grimaldi:* Joseph Grimaldi (1779–1837).

6. *Delpini:* Carlo Antonio Delpini (?–1828), pantomimist and manager of private theatricals (he arranged entertainments for George IV at Brighton). He was associated primarily with the Haymarket Theatre. He was seriously injured in 1789 while acting in the "Death of Captain Cook," a serious ballet from the French, and in later years fell into poverty. In *Probationary Odes for the Laureateship* (1785), the Lord Chamberlain (Lord Salisbury) appoints Mr. Delpini as judge of the compositions.

7. *Old Sadler:* Sadler's Wells was originally a hydropathic establishment at a mineral spring. It was developed in 1683 by a Mr. Sadler and a theater was opened there in 1765.

8. *Pentonville:* area of North London, immediately east of Islington. "Still a village" in 1800, when Charles Lamb lived there [George Rude, *Hanoverian London 1714–1808* (Berkeley: University of California Press, 1971), 61].

9. *Stanmore:* residential town in the greater London borough of Harrow.

10. In 1813 Pye died at a villa in Pinner (which was also in Harrow).

11. The title is from Robert Burns's poem "Man was Made to Mourn: A Dirge."

12. The well-known Gloucester epitaph reads as follows: "Beneath this dust lies the smouldering crust / Of Eleanor Batchelor Shoven, / Well versed in the arts of pies, puddings, and tarts / And the lucrative trade of the oven. / When she'd lived long enough / She made her last puff, / A puff by her husband much praised, / And now she doth lie and makes a dirt pie / And hopes that her crust will be raised." In *Epitaphs: Graveyard Humour & Eulogy,* comp. W. H. Beable (London, 1925), 184.

13. *Rhamazan* (Ramadan) is the annual fast (from sunrise to sunset) of Moslems and lasts one lunar month. Ramadan Bairam is the three-day "breakfast" that follows.

14. *Elkanah Settle* (1648–1724): see *The Dunciad,* iii, 285. Author of "a series of bombastic dramas, the scenario of which was discreetly laid in Persia or Morocco" (D. N. B.). Encouraged as a dramatist by Rochester (who wished to humiliate Dryden), Settle is ridiculed in the second part of *Absalom and Achitophel* (1682). *Bayes:* the name under which Dryden is ridiculed in *The Rehearsal* (1671) by George Villiers, second Duke of Buckingham. The name is taken from the bay laurel, traditional wreath of the poet.

15. According to a Concordance, "dust" (more than 100 times), "weak" (more than 60), and "wander" (with its cognates, more than 100) are three of Byron's favorite words. That Hodgson was also ridiculing Byron's use of alliteration and "obselete words and phrases" in this parody, see Rev. James T. Hodgson, *Memoir of the Rev. Francis Hodgson, B.D.: Scholar, Poet, and Divine* (1878; rpt. New York: AMS Press, 1977), 1: 264.

16. *Donellan, Boughton:* John Donnellan was convicted in 1781 of murdering the twenty-year-old Sir Theodosius Boughton. The method was poisoning with laurel water. Evidently Donnellan wanted to ensure that the Boughton estate would pass to the young heir's sister, Donnellan's

wife. *The Trial of John Donnellan* (London, 1781) gives a close account of the trial and shows how the defendant was convicted on the basis of overwhelming circumstantial evidence. The publication of *The Theory of Presumptive Proof; or, An Inquiry in to the Nature of Circumstantial evidence: including an examination of the evidence on the trial of Captain Donnellan* (London, 1815) suggests the trial continued to be an important legal precedent.

17. *Remorse:* blank verse tragedy by Coleridge, produced at Drury Lane in 1813. Richard Brinsley Sheridan (1751–1816) was the author of *The Rivals* and became a member of Parliament when elected in 1780.

18. *Remorse* features a centipede in act V, i. Aposiopesis, the figure of speech illustrated here, indicates a sudden halt as if the speaker is unable or unwilling to proceed.

19. *Mighty-One:* The Duke of Wellington, commander of the British forces in the Peninsular War in Spain (1809–1813).

20. *Wyndham:* Captain Wymondham of the 14th Light Dragoons. During the pursuit of the retreating French at the Battle of Vittoria (1813), Wymondham and a Lieutenant Worster captured state papers, oil canvases, and King Joseph's silver chamber pot in the carriage from which the King had only moments before fled. See *An Ensign in the Peninsular War: The Letters of John Aitchison,* ed. W. F. K. Thompson (London: M. Joseph, 1981), 247–48.

21. At the battle of Vittoria, the baton of French Marshall Jourdain was captured. It was sent to England under the simple label of the staff of a Marshall of France.

22. *Fontarabia:* Fuenterrabia, a Spanish town where Wellington crossed the Bidassou in 1813. *Soult:* Marshall Nicholas Soult, Duke of Dalmatia, assumed command of French forces in Spain from Joseph Napoleon on 12 July 1813. He soon lost major battles with Wellington at Nivelle and Pamplona. *Jean Pied de Port:* fortified town on River Nive.

23. *17, 28 July:* Wellington's counterattack and the defeat of Soult at the Battles of Sorauen. *Abisbal's Conde:* Enrique José O'Donnell, Count of La Bisbal (1769–1834). *Rowland Hill:* Sir Rowland Hill (1774–1842), British army commander whose forces were initially defeated at Pamplona.

14. EATON STANNARD BARRETT, FROM *THE HEROINE, OR ADVENTURES OF CHERUBINA* (1813)

1. *The Delicate Distress* by Mrs. Griffiths.

2. Some of these references include *Evelina* by Fanny Burney (1752–1840); Emily from *The Mysteries of Udolpho* by Mrs. Ann Radcliffe (1764–1823); and *Pamela* by Samuel Richardson (1689–1761).

3. *Pantheon:* opened 1772 in Oxford Street. It was used for masquerades, concerts, theater, and opera.

4. *Possets:* a drink composed of hot milk curdled with ale, wine, or other liquor.

5. All are from *The Mysteries of Udolpho.*

6. Byron and Grandison are from Samuel Richardson's *Sir Charles Grandison;* Delville is from Fanny Burney's *Cecilia;* Amanda and Mortimer are from *The Children of the Abbey* by Mrs. Roche.

7. Cecilia from a novel of same name by Fanny Burney (1782); *Colebs: In Search of a Wife* (1809) by Hannah More (1745–1833); *The Bravo of Venice* by Matthew Lewis (1775–1818).

8. In *La Nouvelle Heloise* (1761) by Jean-Jacques Rousseau, Saint-Preux is the man with whom Julie has a love affair.

9. *Rasselas* by Samuel Johnson; *A Picture of Society; or the Misanthropist* (London: T. Hookham, Jun. and E. T. Hookham, 1813).

15. ANONYMOUS, "THE UNIVERSAL BELIEVER" (1815)

1. *Lady Jersey,* whom Byron met in 1812 just after *Childe Harold's Pilgrimage* made him famous, acted as his protectoress and confidante until he left England.

2. *Rascals in France:* presumably Voltaire and other Enlightenment skeptics whom Byron read while at Cambridge.

3. *Trowsers:* pantaloons worn in Islamic countries.

4. *Mufti's:* holy men. *Houries:* a houri is a seductive nymph, always young and beautiful, of the Moslem Paradise. *salam:* greeting of peace. *harams:* the haram, or harem, is the part of a Moslem house appropriated to the women.

5. *Nathan:* Isaac Nathan (1792–1864), Jewish muscial composer, adapted ancient Hebrew melodies and persuaded Byron to compose lyrics for them. *Hebrew Melodies* (with Nathan's music) was published in April 1815. See *Byron's Letters and Journals,* ed. Leslie A. Marchand (London: John Murray, 1973), vol. 4, 1814–1815, 187.

16. JAMES HOGG, FROM *THE POETIC MIRROR* (1816)

"THE FLYING TAILOR"

1. Although "The Recluse" is mentioned in the title, Hogg uses material drawn largely from Books 6 and 7 of *The Excursion* ("The Churchyard Among the Mountains") during which the Solitary and the Vicar speak about the graves before them and sketch the biographies of people in the cemetery.

2. An echo of *Lycidas,* 64.

3. *Tinchel's chain:* wide circle of hunters driving the deer together into a smaller and smaller circle.

4. Presumably Hogg's parodic version of the "many hardships to endure" ("Resolution and Independence," 102) of the leech-gatherer.

5. *Diuretic:* increasing the secretion and flow of urine.

6. *Hugh Thwaites:* a thwaite is a piece of land, especially one reclaimed. The word is frequently suffixed to place names in the Lake District: e.g., Tiberthwaite, Schoulthwaite, Legberthwaite, Bassenthwaite. Another delightful use of this joke is in "James Rigg" below when Gilbert Ormathwaite appears (Ormathwaite is actually near Keswick).

7. *John Wilson* (1785–1854), or "Christopher North," published *The Isle of Palms* in 1812.

8. *Cassimere:* lamb's wool.

9. Cf. "To the Daisy," 70.

"JAMES RIGG"

1. Cf. "Michael," 34–36.

2. *Stickle-Tarn:* the first of several place names in this passage associated with the Lake District. *Coniston* is south of Grasmere; *Yewdale* is near Coniston; *Lowood* is on the northeast corner of Lake Windermere. In 1814 Hogg visited and dined with Wordsworth several times while staying with James Wilson. The "trembling rocks" are presumably the Langdale Pikes. See Wordsworth's *Guide to the Lakes* in *The Prose Works of William Wordsworth,* eds. W.J.B. Owen and Jane Worthington Smyser (London: Oxford University Press, 1974), 2.160–63.

3. *Gor-cock:* Scottish and northern dialect for male red grouse.

4. *Bold Russ:* perhaps the 1812 repulse of invading French troops by the Russians. *Blucher:* Prussian general who, with Britain's Wellington, defeated Napoleon at Waterloo (18 June 1815).

5. *Gavelock:* dialect for iron cross bar or lever.

6. Cf. "Resolution and Independence," stanza ix.

7. Cf. "Tintern Abbey," 41.

8. The Cheviot-hills are in Scotland. Here the parodic point seems to be that the poet cannot resist indulging in a simile even when it is wildly inappropriate.

9. Cf. "Intimations of Immortality," 204–5.

10. Cf "Tintern Abbey," 110.

11. *Yean'd:* dialect for bring forth.

12. A glance at "Christabel," 45–49, and possibly an anticipation of the subsequent parody "Isabelle."

"ISABELLE"

1. However attentive Isabelle appears to be, she has miscalculated the total.
2. Cf. *Hamlet,* 3.2. 346 ff.
3. Echo of Burns's "Holy Willie's Prayer," 3: "God sends one to heaven and ten to hell."
4. *Weird:* fate or destiny. By this point, Hogg's taste for the macabre almost controls the poem. This preoccupation is described by Maurice Lindsay in *History of Scottish Literature* (London: Robert Hale, 1977):

> Hogg's natural element was that old Scottish pagan world of the supernatural, and the dark legends surrounding the early men of the reformed religion who routed these older superstitions to make way for their own grimmer mythology. (285)

5. Cf. "Christabel," 2.359.

"THE CURSE OF THE LAUREATE: CARMEN JUDICIALE"

1. "Song of Judgement": Southey became Poet Laureate in October 1813.
2. *Thirlmere:* lake between Grasmere and Keswick.
3. *Joan of Arc* (1796).
4. *Thalaba the Destroyer* (1801).
5. *Bested:* beset.
6. *Francis Jeffrey* of the *Edinburgh Review,* a lawyer turned literary judge, criticized *Thalaba* for its experimental meter and for its remoteness from ordinary experience (i.e., its source is Arabian legend).
7. *Madoc* (1805) and *The Curse of Kehama* (1810).
8. *Roderick, The Last of the Goths* (1814).
9. *Reave:* rob, steal.
10. *Aristarch:* severe Greek critic of the Homeric poetry.
11. Cf. the curse in *The Curse of Kehama,* book 2, stanza 14, 144–69.
12. Possibly *Joseph Cottle,* publisher and Southey's friend.

17. WILLIAM HONE, FROM HIS PARODIES ON *THE BOOK OF COMMON PRAYER* (1817)

"THE BULLET TE DEUM" AND "THE CANTICLE OF THE STONE"

1. On 28 January 1817 a window of the Prince Regent's coach was broken by a stone thrown at it as he returned from the opening of Parliament. The parodies suggest that the government took the opportunity of this attack to transform the stone into a bullet and thereby justify harsh, repressive legislation.
2. *Courier:* a Tory newspaper.
3. In 1802 the Prince of Wales installed a Chinese Gallery in Brighton Pavilion and he continued to elaborate the Oriental aspects of the Pavilion thereafter.
4. *Stannaries:* tin mines of Cornwall and Devon, the revenues from which were the privilege of the Prince of Wales.
5. *Hertford:* Isabella, Marchioness of Hertford (1760–1834) with whom the Prince of Wales became infatuated in 1807. *Jersey:* Frances, Countess of Jersey (1753–1821) with whom the Prince of Wales fell in love in 1793. *St. Ursula:* fourth-century virgin martyr of Cologne; the companions murdered with her were sometimes said to have numbered 11,000.
6. *George Canning* (1770–1827).
7. The Bank of England.
8. *Louis Phillippe:* Louis XVIII (1755–1824). Very popular with the public during his exile in England, 1807–1814. Before his return to France in April 1814, he made the Prince Regent a Chevalier du Saint Esprit, and the Prince Regent made Louis a Knight of the Garter. He always claimed that "la nation toute entière" desired his restoration, which finally took place after

Napoleon's abdication on 22 June 1815. *Ferdinand VII:* King of Spain briefly in 1808 before being deposed by Napoleon, but restored to the throne in 1814.

9. *Lord Ellenborough:* Edward Law, 1st Baron Ellenborough (1750–1818), Lord Chief Justice of England, 1802–1818. Presided at Hone's second and third trials in 1817 and was so enraged by the jury's verdict of not guilty that he proposed resigning his office. Perhaps coincidentally, his health broke after Hone's acquittal. *Sir John Silvester* (1745–1822) was chosen common serjeant by the corporation of London (1790) and succeeded Sir John William Rose as recorder in 1803. *Mr. Justice Hicks:* not traced.

"THE LATE JOHN WILKES'S CATECHISM OF A MINISTERIAL MEMBER"

1. *John Wilkes* (1727–1797): a journalist who began the *North Briton* in 1762 and who supported popular causes (e.g., parliamentary reform) by which he could attack the government. With respect to the subtitle of this "Catechism," Wilkes wanted to introduce a bill into Parliament specifically to get rid of "placemen."

2. *Sureties:* sponsors, backers.

3. John Nash, with the Prince's approval, in 1810 proposed a "New Street" that would join Marylebone Park (now Regent's Park) to the Regent's residence, Carlton House, reducing the traveling time to central London and improving the architectural appearance of the capital, thought to be somewhat provincial in comparison with European capitals. The construction of Regent Street, begun in 1813, greatly disrupted the entire area. *Knights of the Bath:* a medieval order of merit revived in 1725 and expanded significantly in 1815 from 35 Companions to 72 Knights Grand Cross, 180 Knight Commanders, and an unspecified number of Companions.

4. *Lord Liverpool:* prime minister from 1812 to 1827.

5. *Lord James Murray:* 1782–1837, second son of the fourth Duke of Atholl, was in the carriage with the Prince Regent when stones were thrown at it. Lord James alleged a pistol had been fired, but no bullet was found. *Betty Martin:* "All my eye and Betty Martin"—slang phrase repudiating as nonsense any attempt to impose a deception.

6. *Lord Cochrane* (1775–1860) played an independent, radical role in Parliament and often attacked the admiralty administration. He was expelled from Parliament after being unjustly accused of a stock-exchange fraud. He was reinstated as a rear admiral in the British navy in 1832.

7. *Levee:* from French *lever,* to rise. A reception or assembly held by a monarch during the morning or early afternoon. Under Louis XIV the stages of the ceremonial reception coincided with the stages of the king's rising, ablutions, and dressing, culminating in the donning of his wig. Hone of course means that government ministers demand the fawning subservience formerly accorded absolute monarchs.

8. *Sir William Turtle:* In *A Slap at Slop,* Turtle is described as "the patron of knavish-traders, biscuit bakers, contractors, loan-jobbers, and other third-rate thieves" [William Hone, *Facetiae and Miscellanies,* 2d ed. (London: Hunt & Clarke, 1827), 26]. *Sinking Fund:* sinking funds were funds specifically directed to the extinction of a debt, especially a national debt. The British national debt consisted in large part of "floating debts"—very short-term treasury bills—an expensive mode of state borrowing which the "sinking funds" were intended to eliminate.

9. *Lord Castlereagh:* Viscount Robert Stewart Castlereagh (1769–1822) was British Foreign Secretary from 1812 to 1822. *Sir Matthew Wood* (1768–1843): a radical who was alderman in 1807, sheriff in 1809, and Lord Mayor of London in 1815 and 1816, the first such re-election in hundreds of years. *Mr. John Langley:* not traced.

19. ANONYMOUS, "THE OLD TOLBOOTH" (1818)

1. *Tolbooth:* the old prison on High Street in Edinburgh.

2. *Excursion* 8:216–18. The sound of the bell in the Cathedral of St. Giles beginning the poem may also be ironically related to the factory in *The Excursion,* 8:170.

3. *Schists:* metamorphic rock whose component flaky metals are visible to the eye. *Humboldt,* Friedrich Heinrich Alexander, Baron von (1769–1859): German naturalist, scientist, and

traveler whose expedition to South America (1799–1804) was important to the emerging sciences of physical geography and meteorology.

4. *Werner,* Abraham Gottlob (1750–1817): famous German geologist who believed that all rocks are water-formed accumulations and that volcanoes are coal-fired. His "Nepturnist" theories prompted great geological controversies and were opposed to, for example, the uniformitarianism of the Scottish geologist, *James Hutton* (1726–1797). Hutton was the originator of this basic principle of geology which proposed that the same forces now operating on and within the earth have been operating in the same general manner throughout geological time. He defended his view in *Theory of the Earth* (2 vols. 1795) after it was attacked in 1793.

5. *Constable,* Archibald (1774–1827): Scottish publisher (based on High Street, Edinburgh) of the *Edinburgh Review* and Walter Scott. He went bankrupt in 1826. *Francis Jeffrey* (1773–1850) was known for his harsh criticism of the Lake poets.

6. *Sauded:* sanded.

7. *Mr. Thomson:* James Thomson (1700–1748), Scottish poet and author of *The Seasons* (1726–1730).

8. *Belcher:* a blue kerchief with white spots, named after Jim Belcher, a pugilist (first used in 1812, *O.E.D.*). *Leathern stock:* a kind of stiff, close-fitting neck cloth worn by soldiers.

9. *Lavater,* Johann K. (1741–1801): Swiss divine and poet, student of physiognomy (how the spirit is reflected in one's physical features).

10. *Sir John Carr* (1772–1832): writer of "tours" in a "light, gossipy style" (D.N.B.): e.g., *The Stranger in Ireland,* 1806; *Caledonian Sketches,* 1808.

11. *Baxter:* a baker, living among ovens and fires.

12. *Excursion* 4.75.

13. *Cuisse:* the front thigh-piece of scarlet breeches. *Spatterdash:* protective garter.

14. *Joseph Bonaparte* (1768–1844): Napoleon's eldest surviving brother, King of Naples (1806–08) and King of Spain (1808–13).

15. Cf. Wordsworth's poem about a pile of rocks, "Lines Written with a slate-pencil upon a Stone, the largest of a heap lying near a deserted Quarry, upon one of the Islands at Rydale."

16. *As Shakespeare says:* see *King John* 4.2.149. *Craigleith* and *Ravelston:* sandstone quarries northwest of Edinburgh. Much of the stone used in building the New Town of Edinburgh came from these places.

17. Aristophanes satirized Socrates and the Sophists in *The Clouds.* Socrates' father, Sophrinicus, was a statuary and his mother, Phaenarete, was a midwife. In his youth Socrates followed his father's profession and executed the group of clothed Graces which was preserved in the Acropolis.

18. The old Tolbooth was near Calton Hill.

19. See *Excursion* 1.324 and 108 (where the Wanderer is described as having been born "Among the hills of Athol").

20. *Immanuel Kant* (1724–1804): German philosopher. *Jakob Boehme* (1575–1624): German religious mystic.

20. THOMAS LOVE PEACOCK, FROM *NIGHTMARE ABBEY* (1818)

1. See Shelley, preface to *Prometheus Unbound* (1818).

2. Novel by P. Will, 1796.

3. Leaders of secret societies.

4. See chapter 5 of Godwin's *Political Justice.*

5. See Shelley's *Declaration of Rights* (Dublin 1812).

6. Godwin's *Mandeville,* 1816.

7. *Paul Jones:* Scottish-born American pirate (1747–1792). Byron's *The Corsair* was published in 1814.

8. Book listing state officials and pensioners.

9. Robert Southey. "Roderick" from his poem of that name, and "Sackbut" from his annual stipend as Poet Laureate of a butt of sack.

10. Coleridge named his first son after the philosopher Hartley. (See *Biographia Literaria,* chapter 10.)

11. Coleridge's phrase from *The Statesman's Manual, Lay Sermons,* ed. R. J. White [*The Collected Works of Samuel Taylor Coleridge,* 6 (Princeton: Princeton University Press, 1972), 36].

12. An exaggerated example of Coleridge's habit of coining inflated neologisms.

13. See *Biographia Literaria,* chapter 13.

14. *The Tempest,* 4.1.156.

15. Cf. preface to *Kubla Khan.*

16. *A Midsummer Night's Dream,* 4.1.215.

17. *All-blasting upas:* the upas was a fabulous poison tree said to exist in Java. See *Childe Harold,* 4.126: also 4.124–125.

18. See *Childe Harold,* 1.83.

19. Lamp reputedly found still alight in tomb of Cicero's daughter when it was opened in the 16th century.

21. D. M. MOIR, "THE RIME OF THE AUNCIENT WAGGONERE" (1819)

1. *Nine tailors make a man:* "An old expression of contempt at the expense of tailors signifying that a tailor is so much more feeble than anyone else that it would take nine of them to make a man of average stature and strength . . . tailor is probably a facetious transformation of *teller,* a teller being a stroke on the bell at a funeral, three being given for a child, six for a woman, and nine for a man." From *The Reader's Encyclopedia: An Encyclopedia of World Literature and the Arts,* ed. William Rose Benét (New York: Thomas Y. Cromwell, 1948), 1095.

2. *Boreas:* the north wind.

3. *Prog:* slang or colloquial for food (especially for eating on a journey or excursion). *Choppines:* Scotch half-pint. *Usquebaugh:* whisky (Gaelic).

4. *Bumbailiffe:* lowest type of bailiff.

5. *Glyffe:* scare, or sudden fright.

6. *Mendoza:* Daniel Mendoza (1764–1836) developed a new style of boxing; it was named after him and described in *The Art of Boxing* (1789).

7. *Crichtown:* James Crichtown (1560–1585?), surnamed "The Admirable," was extraordinarily accomplished as a philosopher, linguist, poet, fencer, and horseman. He went to France in 1577 and later to Italy where he was probably murdered. The most complete account of his life is by P. F. Tytler, first published in 1819.

8. *Fandango:* lively Spanish dance.

9. *Gardyloo:* the warning shout in Edinburgh given when emptying chamber pots out of the window.

10. *Shoan Dhu:* dagger (Gaelic)

11. *Dilettanti Society:* founded ca. 1734 to cultivate conviviality and artistic knowledge.

22. ANONYMOUS, "PLEASANT WALKS: A COCKNEY PASTORAL" (1819)

1. Cf. Hunt's "To John Keats" (1818): "Lo! for the love of leaves / I'll quote myself!" And in the same poem, apropos the opening line of the parody, are the following lines: "Tis well you think me truly one of those, / Whose sense discerns the loveliness of things."

2. Cf. Keats's "Sleep and Poetry," 181–206, and also "The Feast of the Poets" (1815) for the following comment by Hunt on Pope: "But ever since Pope spoiled the ears of the town / With his cuckoo-song verses, half up and half down. . . ."

3. *Loo:* a card game.

4. For echoes, cf. Keats's "Woman! when I behold thee flippant, vain" and *Endymion* I. 153.

5. The springs on Mount Parnassus, home of the Muses.

6. Cf. the abrupt halt by Keats, "Sleep and Poetry," 85.

7. Name evidently borrowed from Byron's poem of the same name (1818), a poem conspicuous for its own violent rhyming.

23. JOHN HAMILTON REYNOLDS, *PETER BELL* (1819)

1. The footnote parodies Wordsworth's footnote in "To The Daisy" in which he implies that he is the poet to revive a tradition associated with Chaucer. The quotation is from "To The Same Flower," 25.
2. *King Lear* 3.4.142.
3. Cf. "The Sparrow's Nest" and "To A Sexton" by Wordsworth.
4. As a political reward, Wordsworth was made Stamp Distributor for Westmorland in 1813.
5. Cf. "The Thorn" and "The Waterfall and the Eglantine" by Wordsworth.
6. Presumably Francis Jeffrey and the *Edinburgh Review*.
7. *Vansittart* (1766–1851): Chancellor of the Exchequer 1812–1823.
8. Bacon is quoted in Wordsworth's epigraph to "The White Doe."
9. *Macbeth* 5.12.71.
10. "To The Same Flower," 25–28.
11. Cf. Wordsworth's "Rob Roy's Grave."
12. Cf. opening of "To My Sister" ("It is the first mild day of March") or "The Idiot Boy."
13. *Christabel,* 1.61.
14. *Bugles:* creeping plants with small, dark blue flowers.
15. Cf. "Stanzas Written in my pocket copy of Thomson's 'Castle of Indolence'."
16. In act 3, scene i of Sheridan's *The Critic: or a Tragedy Rehearsed* (performed 1779; published 1781), the Justice reveals that all characters in the play within a play are relations of the "Son."
17. *Pent-house:* sloping roof.
18. From the 1807 version of "The Sparrow's Nest."
19. Cf. "Foresight," 10: "pull as many as you can."
20. *Medlar:* a fruit eaten only when decayed.
21. "To Sleep" (published 1807).
22. See the speaking vegetation in "The Oak and the Broom."
23. Cf. "Alice Fell," 57.
24. I.e., as opposed to Gothic lettering.
25. *Dr. Andrew Bell* (1753–1832) was founder of the Madras system of education. Based on the principle of mutual instruction, it eventually grew to become a system of national education superintended by the Church of England. Bell became embroiled in controversy with Joseph Lancaster, a Quaker who also claimed to be the originator. Southey, a personal friend, was left £1000 by Bell and requested to write the educator's biography (one volume was completed, the work completed by Southey's son Cuthbert).
26. See *The Poetical Works of Wordsworth,* rev. ed. Ernest de Selincourt (London: Oxford University Press, 1950), 748.
27. Collins's "The Passions: An Ode for Music," 20.
28. "Simon Lee," 1–8 (1798 version). Wordsworth subsequently altered lines 4–8 to:

> Full five-and-thirty years he lived
> A running huntsman merry;
> And still the centre of his cheek
> Is red as a ripe cherry.

29. "Andrew Jones" (1800), omitted in later collections.
30. Cf. "To a Sexton (with a wheelbarrow)" and "The Pet-Lamb. A Pastoral."
31. *Stephen Hill:* Martha Ray's unfaithful suitor in "The Thorn." For Reginald Shore and Giles (it should be Charles) Fleming, see "Rural Architecture."
32. *Dilly, Dilly:* a call to ducks.
33. The old man solves the riddle. Wordsworth has a poem "Poet's Epitaph" which Reynolds may be recalling. In "J.H. Reynolds' 'Peter Bell'," *Notes and Queries* 24 (1977): 323–24, Gerald Pyle has pointed out that the concluding rhyme first appeared in *Literary Gazette* (6 December 1817) in a letter from "Sexton" who suggests that English epitaphs should be serious, not humorous.
34. Cf. two descriptions in *The Faerie Queen:* I, viii, 30.2 (Ignaro) and II, ix, 55.5 (Eumnestes).

24. D. M. MOIR, "CHRISTABEL, PART THIRD" (1819)

1. *William Gifford* (1766–1826) became well-known as a satirist in the 1790's and was made editor of *The Anti-Jacobin* in 1797. In 1809 he became editor of *The Quarterly Review*. Gifford hated radicals and was known for his bitter reviews of authors who were not of his politically conservative principles. The prefatory comments reflect Coleridge's complaints in *Biographia Literaria* about contemporary reviewing practices.

2. *Francis Jeffrey* (1773–1850): founder (with Sydney Smith) and editor of *The Edinburgh Review*. His criticism of the Lake School was unsparing.

3. *Henry Colburn* (d. 1855) was, from 1817, publisher of *The Literary Gazette* as well as of other magazines and light literature. A skilled businessman, he amassed a considerable fortune. *Dr. John William Polidori* (1795–1821) was personal physician and travelling companion to Byron after 1816. The famous proposal that each visitor at the Villa Diodati should compose a ghost story resulted not only in Mary Shelley's *Frankenstein* but also in *The Vampyre* (the unfinished ghost story by Byron which Polidori completed and published). Polidori eventually died at the age of 25 in London, possibly from taking prussic acid. In *The Vampyre,* Lord Ruthwen traps the hero's sister into marriage by making her pregnant—hence the allusion to Christabel's illegitimate child in this parody.

4. *Joanna Baillie* (1762–1851): Scottish dramatist and poet. The first volume of her controversial *Plays on the Passions* (1798) was thought to be by Scott. In *Collection of Poems* (1823) she brought together poems by Scott, Catherine Fanshawe, Mrs. Hemans, and others for a charitable purpose. She continued to write until she was almost eighty.

5. *Macvey Napier* (1776–1847) succeeded Jeffrey in 1829 as editor of *The Edinburgh Review*. He had been previously active (with his friend Constable) in the sixth and seventh editions of the *Encyclopedia Britannica*.

6. *Bagman:* a commercial traveller who shows samples and solicits orders.

7. *Archie Cameron's College:* Archie Cameron was the janitor or porter at Glasgow College in the early nineteenth century. In the latter part of the eighteenth century a social club was established by the professors in the porter's lodge. Cameron held a license and sold liquor. The Faculty ended the selling of liquor in 1829. See David Murray, *Memories of the Old College of Glasgow: Some Chapters in the History of the University* (Glasgow: Jackson, Wylie & Co., 1927), 52–54.

8. *Ugsome:* horrible, loathsome.

9. *Eleusinian Mysteries* were the most famous of the secret religious rites of ancient Greece and were probably connected with beliefs about life after death.

10. *Lykewake:* a watch kept at night over a dead body.

25. JOHN WILSON LOCKHART, FROM *BENJAMIN THE WAGGONER* (1819)

1. *Simon Lee,* 65–72.

2. *Peter Bell,* 1–2.

3. *Gambado:* pseudonym for Henry William Bunbury (1750–1811), English caricaturist and author of *An Academy for grown horsemen* (1787) and *Annals of horsemanship* (1787?), both reprinted several times. The parodist's note at the foot of the page reads as follows: "See a likeness of that model of symmetry, in the frontispiece to Gambado's Horsemanship."

4. *Peter Bell,* 6: and here follows an aerial journey as in the model.

5. These lines were originally part of a stanza that appeared between lines 515 and 516 in *Peter Bell,* but Wordsworth later omitted them:

> Is it a party in a parlour?
> Cramm'd just as they on earth were cramm'd—
> Some sipping punch, some sipping tea,
> But, as you by their faces see,
> All silent and all damn'd!

For the subsequent lines ("Could Adam . . ."), see "The Redbreast Chasing the Butterfly," 12–14.

6. The moon and related forms (moonlight, moonshine, etc.) occur 26 times in *Peter Bell;* ass is mentioned 35 times in the same poem (and a further 7 times in *The Excursion* to make 42).

7. From "The Kitten and Falling Leaves," 41–44.

26. JOHN HAMILTON REYNOLDS, *THE DEAD ASSES* (1819)

1. Thomas Gray, "Elegy in a Country Churchyard," 81.

2. *George Morland* (1763–1804) was a popular painter of rustic scenery and animals (e.g., "Pigs in a fodder yard"). Morland was debauched and squandered large sums of money. His masterpiece is said to be "Interior of a Stable" (1791). For the reference in the latter part of this sentence, see Wordsworth's "Dedication to Robert Southey" of "Peter Bell: A Tale."

3. See the "Dedication to Robert Southey" cited in note 2.

4. In the same dedication, Wordsworth states that the imagination is more stimulated by "incidents within the compass of poetic probability, in the humblest departments of daily life" than it is by "supernatural agency." The parody, of course, literalizes Wordsworth's preference for the commonplace with a vengeance.

5. From chapter 34 of Walter Scott's *The Bride of Lammermoor.*

6. Cf. stanza 29 below and Wordsworth's supposed note.

7. Presumably Izaak Walton (1593–1683) who wrote *The Compleat Angler* (1653).

8. Cf. "She gave me eyes to see" ("The Sparrow's Nest").

9. Cf. Coleridge's "To a Young Ass," 30, a central pretext for this parody.

10. "To a Young Ass," 16–17.

11. *All-spice:* aromatic spice.

12. *Bess:* daughter of the squire in *Peter Bell,* 158.

13. Cf. "His shining hazel eye" (*Peter Bell,* 435).

14. Cf. "I hail thee brother" ("To a Young Ass," 26).

27. PERCY BYSSHE SHELLEY, *PETER BELL THE THIRD* (1819)

1. Wordsworth later omitted this stanza from his poem. The initials of the imputed author, Miching Mallecho, may playfully allude to Wordsworth (M. M. is like W. W. upside down), although the name also contains its own valuation of Wordsworth (bad echo or sound).

2. *Hamlet* 3.2. 136–37.

3. Thomas Moore (under the name of Thomas Brown the younger) was the author of *The Fudge Family in Paris* (1818); hence H. F. may refer to him as the "Historian of the Fudges."

4. I.e., Wordsworth and Southey. In July of 1818, Thomas Love Peacock had sent Shelley a box of books and magazines, including *The Fudge Family in Paris* [see Peacock's letter of 5 July 1818; rpt. in F. L. Jones, ed. *The Letters of Percy Bysshe Shelley* (Oxford: Clarendon Press, 1964), 2.24]. The "rat" appears in Moore's "Letter VI" [471, *The Poetical Works of Thomas Moore,* ed. A. D. Godfrey (Oxford, 1915)] and refers to a political opportunist and sycophant; in politics, to "rat" is to desert one's party: "Rat after rat, they graduate / Through job, red ribbon and silk gown, / To Chanc'llorship and Marquisate" (102–4). Shelley's attitude toward Wordsworth was divided between admiration for the poetry and revulsion from the political principles. For Shelley's scornful attitude to *Peter Bell* in particular, see the dedicatory poem to *The Witch of Atlas* ("To Mary," stanza iv, 25–32). Southey, of course, was often pictured as the prototypical turncoat. In his dedication of *Peter Bell* to Southey, Wordsworth described himself as "one with whose name yours has been often coupled (to use your own words) for evil and for good" (188).

5. The remainder of Shelley's paragraph (removed by Mrs. Shelley) actually reads as follows: "That murderous and smiling villain at the mere sound of whose voice our susceptible friend the *Quarterly* fell into a paroxysm of eleutherophobia [hatred of freedom] and foamed so much acrid gall that it burned the carpet in Mr. Murray's upper room, and eating a hole in the floor fell like

rain upon our poor friend's head, who was scampering from room to room like a bear with a swarm of bees on his nose:—it caused an incurable ulcer and our poor friend has worn a wig ever since. Well, this monkey suckled with tyger's milk, this odious thief, liar, scoundrel, coxcomb and monster presented me to two of the Mr. Bells. Seeing me in his presence they of course uttered very few words and those with much caution. I scarcely need observe that they only kept company with him—at least I can certainly answer for one of them—in order to observe whether they could not borrow colours from any particulars of his private life for the denunciation they mean to make of him, as the member of an "infamous and black conspiracy for diminishing the authority of that venerable canon, which forbids any man to mar his grandmother"; the effect of which in this on our moral and religious nation is likely to answer the purpose of the controversy. My intimacy with the younger Mr. Bell naturally sprung from this introduction to his brothers. And in presenting him to you, I have the satisfaction of being able to assure you that he is considerably the dullest of the three." Reprinted for the first time in *Shelley's Poetry and Prose*, ed. Donald H. Reiman and Sharon B. Powers (New York: Norton, 1977), 323–24. The above passage is reprinted with the permission of W.W. Norton & Company, Inc.

6. Christianity.

7. Prelude 9.142–44. First published in *The Friend* on 26 October 1809.

8. I.e., lunatic. See the many allusions to the moon and moonlight in *Peter Bell*.

9. In quoting from Wordsworth's preface to *Peter Bell*, Shelley pointedly removes the phrase "however humble."

10. No address is specified for Mallecho's lodgings. Moore gives the address of Thomas Brown as 245 Piccadilly.

11. John Hamilton Reynolds's parody *Peter Bell* was published just before Wordsworth's own poem appeared.

12. *Aldric:* Henry Aldrich (1647–1710), author of a standard text on logic, *Artis Logicae Compendium* (1619).

13. A disease marked by the formation of calculi in the bladder.

14. Here Shelley's storm silences the "sounding cataract" (1.76) of Wordsworth's "Tintern Abbey."

15. Part of the stipend paid to the poet laureate (then Southey).

16. A seller of cheap clothing to sailors at Wapping, a dock area.

17. *Benjamin:* an overcoat worn while driving.

18. Cf. Prefatory verses to *The Excursion*, 63–68.

19. *Phiz:* face.

20. *John Castle:* government spy.

21. *Caitiff:* villainous; *cozening:* cheating; *trepanning:* swindling.

22. Possibly the Lord Chancellor (i.e., Eldon who, as Donald Reiman and Sharon Powers suggest [eds., *Shelley's Poetry and Prose* (New York: Norton, 1977), p. 331, n. 9], appears as Fraud in *The Masque of Anarchy*, line 14).

23. *Amant misere:* love to be miserable.

24. I.e., mendacious.

25. *Flams:* falsehoods.

26. Cf. *Prometheus Unbound* 1.618–31.

27. "A mouth kissed does not lose its attraction. Instead, it renews itself like the moon." (Boccaccio, *Decameron*, second day, end of the seventh novella.)

28. S. T. Coleridge.

29. In *Nightmare Abbey* Peacock portrays Coleridge as Mr. Flosky and explains that the name is from the Greek word meaning "lover of shadows" (Peacock's notes to Chapter 1).

30. Cf. "Michael," line 33.

31. *Pipkin:* small earthenware pot or pan.

32. Joseph Cottle purchased the copyright to *Lyrical Ballads*.

33. Job 31:35.

34. A father and two sons of this name treated George III for mental illness.

35. F. G. Born's Latin translation of Kant's works was published in Leipzig in 1796–98.

36. *Furor verborum:* inspired frenzy of poets or prophets (Lewis and Short, *Latin Dictionary*).

37. *Sir William Drummond* (1770–1828) published *Academical Questions*, a critique of Kant, in 1805.

38. I.e., word-worthy.

39. *Ex luce praebens fumum:* an inversion of Horace, *Ars Poetica,* 143–44: "Not smoke after flame does he plan to give, / but after smoke the light."

40. *Subter humum:* under the ground.

41. *Flibbertigibbet:* name of a fiend (*King Lear* 3.4.120).

42. John Calvin (1509–1564); *Saint Dominic* (1170–1221).

43. Coleridge was born in Ottery St. Mary on the banks of the River Otter in Devonshire and wrote a sonnet "To the River Otter" (1793) concluding, "Ah! that once more I were a careless Child!"

44. Shelley's note cites *The Excursion* 8.568–71. Shelley has already alluded to books 7 and 8 of *The Excursion* in line 432.

45. *Sherry:* Richard Brinsley Sheridan (1751–1816), former crony of the Prince of Wales, allegedly abandoned when the Prince became Regent.

46. *George Colman* (1762–1836), dramatist.

47. *Molly:* milksop.

48. Cf. Wordsworth's "Ode: The Morning of the Day Appointed for a General Thanksgiving. January 18, 1816."

49. Shelley has turned Wordsworth's Waterloo into the Peterloo massacre in Manchester (16 August 1819), the subject of his "The Masque of Anarchy."

50. *Lord MacMurderchouse:* William Lowther, Earl of Lonsdale. *chouse:* swindle.

51. Through Lonsdale's influence, Wordsworth was appointed stamp distributor for Westmorland in 1813.

52. *Oliver:* W. J. Richards, government spy.

53. *Pelf:* profits.

54. Rydal Mount, much larger than Dove Cottage.

55. I.e., a Struldbrugg (*Gulliver's Travels,* part 3, chap. 10).

56. *Guatimozin:* Aztec hero tortured on grid by Cortez.

57. The seven sleepers of Ephesus.

28. WILLIAM MAGINN, "DON JUAN UNREAD" (1819)

1. *Constable's Magazine:* Archibald Constable (1774–1827) was one of the founders of the *Edinburgh Review* in 1802.

2. *Holland House:* major salon for prominent Whigs such as Byron and Wilberforce.

3. *Mary Shelley* (1797–1851) published *Frankenstein or the Modern Prometheus* in 1818.

4. *Peter Pindar* was the pseudonym for John Wolcot (1738–1819), a political satirist who, like *Thomas Paine,* opposed George III.

5. *Zanny:* Venetian form of Giovanni (in general, a buffoon).

6. *Henry Colburn* (?–1855), a publisher who began *The New Monthly Magazine* in 1814. *Lady Morgan* (1776–1859), whose *The Wild Irish Girl* (1806) established her reputation as a romance writer.

7. *Charles Robert Maturin* (1782–1824) was a principal writer of terror novels (e.g., *The Fatal Revenge,* 1807). His tragedy, *Bertram,* was produced in 1816 at Drury Lane on the recommendation of Byron and Scott.

8. *Henry Peter Brougham* (1776–1868): barrister and Whig politician associated with reformist causes. He instituted an inquiry into charity abuses in 1818 that extended to the universities, to Eton, and to Winchester and made scandalous revelations.

9. *William Cobbett* (1762–1835): the leading political journalist favoring parliamentary reform, founder of *The Political Register. Thomas Wooler* (?1786–1853): radical journalist best known for the weekly paper *The Black Dwarf* (1817–1824). *James Watson* (?1766–1838): follower of Thomas Spence (who held that private ownership was un-Christian) and acquitted of high treason in 1817 after being involved in the Spa Fields riots. *Henry Hunt* (1773–1835): radical politician who presided at the meeting in St. Peter's Fields, Manchester, subsequently known as Peterloo (August 1819).

10. *Mr. Percival:* Prime Minister Spencer Perceval was assassinated at the House of Commons by John Billingham on 11 May 1812. There were many who believed that this event was the signal for a revolution in England; it provoked some celebrations in Nottingham and Leicester.

11. An echo of Burns's "Gie the Lass her Fairin' " with its refrain of "The mair she bangs the less she squeals, / An' hey for houghmagandie."

29. DAVID CAREY, "THE WATER MELON" (1820)

1. A satirical sonnet published the same year furnishes yet another reference to this idea: "Coleridge! when you your dose of opium take, / And Southey drinks his sack, a happy fellow, / And I imbibe my water from the lake, / Though now with better stuff I might get mellow;" ["Sonnet II" in *The Battered Tar, or, The Waggoner's Companion: A Poem with Sonnets, etc.* (London: J. Johnston, 1820)].
2. Evidently a more dignified (and pastoral) form of Wordsworth's own Lucy. Cf. Thomson's "Spring," 932–45.

30. WILLIAM MAGINN AND OTHERS, FROM " 'LUCTUS' ON THE DEATH OF SIR DANIEL DONNELLY, LATE CHAMPION OF IRELAND" (1820)

1. *In rerum naturâ:* in the nature of things. Bacon's essays are liberally sprinkled with Latin tags and quotations.
2. "Lie like surfaces": not traced.
3. See *The Statesman's Manual, Lay Sermons,* ed. R. J. White [*The Collected Works of Samuel Taylor Coleridge,* 6 (Princeton: Princeton University Press, 1972)], 36.
4. The allusion may be to Spenser's Talus, the iron man representing power in Book 5 of *The Faerie Queene.*
5. Terms from boxing: *challenge* is the summons to fight; to *ruffian* is to strike without regard to rules; *fibbing* is the delivery of blows in quick succession.
6. *Agnize:* archaic for recognize.
7. Probably from "Expostulation and Reply," 17 (but also see *The Excursion* 2.429 or *Peter Bell,* 518).
8. *Grimalkin:* traditional name for a witch's cat.
9. *Timothy:* cf. Wordsworth, "The Childless Father" (1800).
10. *Courier:* a Tory newspaper to which Wordsworth contributed.
11. *Donnybrook:* a part of Southeast Dublin which was once a village famous for a disorderly fair first held under a license granted by King John in 1204.

31. ANONYMOUS, "THE NOSE-DROP: A PHYSIOLOGICAL BALLAD" (1821)

1. The epigraph to the first two volumes of Byron's *Don Juan.* Byron translated the Latin as "Tis no slight task to write on common things" (see note 3, 99, in the article by Mortenson cited in the headnote).
2. Not a humorous invention but an allusion to Wordsworth's thirty-two line lyric "To the Spade of a Friend" (published 1807), the first line of which is, "Spade! with which Wilkinson hath tilled his lands. . . ."
3. See *The Idiot Boy,* 112: "But then he is a horse that thinks." Also *Peter Bell,* 825–26: "The Ass turned round his head and *grinned.* / Appalling process!"
4. *Bulbul:* a kind of thrush. *Gul:* short for Gulistan (rose garden in Persian). Bulbuls were "said to be enamoured of the rose" (*OED,* 1797). The reference may be to Byron's *The Bride of Abydos. A Turkish Tale,* line 8, and the kind of orientalism it embodied.
5. "Fear is poetry, hope is poetry, love is poetry, hatred is poetry; contempt, jealousy, remorse, admiration, wonder, pity, despair, or madness, are all poetry." See "On Poetry in General," the first of the *Lectures on the English Poets* in *The Complete Works of William Hazlitt,* ed. P. P. Howe (London: Dent, 1930–1934), 5.2.

6. *The Excursion* 1.79.

7. As in "Lucy Gray," 46.

8. Apparently, after Coleridge objected to the final couplet in chapter 17 of *Biographia Literaria,* Wordsworth altered it to read, "Though but of compass small, and bare / To thirsty suns and parching air."

9. *The Idiot Boy,* 294, or *The Excursion* 1.904.

10. See *The Idiot Boy,* 320.

11. A phrase used both by Coleridge (*The Ancient Mariner,* 524) and by Wordsworth ("Anecdote for Fathers," 40).

32. WILLIAM HONE, "A NEW VISION" (1821)

1. *Slop, old times:* (Sir) John Stoddart (1776–1856) was an ultra-royalist who, when dismissed as editor of *The Times* in 1816, founded the *New Times* to promote government policies.

2. *Pensile:* hanging or suspended. *Sus. per coll:* hanged by the neck.

3. *Sack-but:* obsolete musical instrument, a pun on the butt of sack (part of the stipend of the post laureate).

4. *Murray:* publisher John Murray (1778–1843).

5. *Welch Cymmodorion:* The Cymmrodorian Society was founded in London (1751) by Richard Morris for the study and encouragement of Welsh literature and learning. On the title page of Southey's *History of the Peninsular War* (London: John Murray, 1823), the poet's honors are listed as follows: "Esq. LL.D. Poet Laureate, Honorary Member of the Royal Spanish Academy of History, of the Royal Institute of the Netherlands, of the Cymmrodorion, of the Massachusetts Historical Society, etc."

6. *Flimsies:* bank notes.

7. The Prince Regent, later George IV.

8. *George Canning* (1770–1827) was known as a witty and sarcastic speaker. He was wounded in a duel with Castlereagh in 1809. *Manton's hair-triggers:* Joseph Manton (1766–1835) was the inventor of various improvements in gun-making and had a shop in London.

9. *Fletcher Franklin:* William (alias Fletcher or Forbes) Franklin was a government spy apparently responsible for various inflammatory placards posted in London between 1818 and 1820. See J. Ann Hone, *For the Cause of Truth: Radicalism in London 1796–1821* (London: Oxford University Press, 1982), 349–50. *Sir Robert Baker:* a chief magistrate dismissed from office after public disturbances (and two deaths) when Queen Caroline's coffin was moved overland to Harwich, instead of by water as the King had requested.

10. *William Gifford* (1756–1826): first editor of the *Quarterly Review* in 1809. *John Croker* (1780–1857): prominent politician and contributor to the *Quarterly Review* and remembered now for his attack on Keats's *Endymion*. Hazlitt attacked Gifford in a pamphlet, "A Letter to William Gifford, Esq." [1819; in *The Complete Works of William Hazlitt*, ed. P. P. Howe (London: Dent, 1930–1934), vol. 9. 13–59]. An essay on Gifford also appeared in *The Spirit of the Age* (1825; in Howe, 11.114–26).

11. *him of the Triangle:* Robert Stewart, Viscount Castlereagh who vigorously suppressed the Irish rebellion of 1798. The reference to triangle is an allusion to cat o' nine tails used in floggings (see Edgell Rickwood, p. 48). Castlereagh committed suicide in 1822 by cutting his throat with a penknife; the verdict of the inquest was that he was of "unsound mind." *The Doctor:* the prime minister, Henry Addington, 1st Lord Sidmouth (so-called because his father was a doctor). Sidmouth was severe (under him fourteen Luddites were hanged in one day at York) and conservative (he voted against Catholic Emancipation and the Reform Bill).

12. I.e., the Solicitor-General and his superior, the Attorney-General. The subsequent references all concern the inquiry in the House of Lords (August 1820) into the behavior of Princess Caroline. *Sacchi:* Giuseppe Sacchi, a former cavalry captain, was for nine months courier to the Princess and then her equerry. *Non mi Ricordo:* "I do not remember," a flustered Teodoro Majocchi repeatedly answered to Brougham's cross-examination. *Daemon:* Louisa Demont, chambermaid in the Queen's service but a witness for the prosecution. *Barbara Kress:* a chambermaid at the inn at Karlsruhe where the Princess of Wales stayed (another prosecution witness). *Rastelli:* the Milan Commission's courier who tried to persuade reluctant Italian

witnesses to come to England to testify against the Princess. These witnesses had fled home after rumors of Englishmen attacking other Italian witnesses.

13. *Jessops:* untraced: perhaps members of the royal household staff. *Mar——s Il—d:* untraced, but possibly a disguised or inaccurate allusion to Isabella, Marchioness of Hertford (1760–1834), one of the more unpopular mistresses of George IV. *M—ss C—m:* Marchioness Elizabeth Conyngham, a motherly woman adored by the King. According to Christopher Hibbert, *George IV: Regent and King 1811–1830* (London: Allen Lane, 1973), 215, she was "excessively fond of clothes, money, and, above all, jewellery." *Mrs. Fitz——t:* Mrs. Fitzherbert (1756–1837) secretly married the Prince of Wales in 1785 despite her being a Roman Catholic; they separated permanently in 1809. *C——ch:* Mrs. Anna Maria Crouch (1763–1805), actress introduced to the Prince Regent by Charles James Fox in the presence of Mrs. Fitzherbert. Mrs. Crouch's influence with the Prince lasted three days.

14. *Mary Robinson* (1758–1800), "Perdita," because in this role at Drury Lane in 1779 she attracted the attention of the Prince of Wales. For a few months she became the Prince's mistress. She is sneered at by Gifford in his *The Baviad* (line 24). Toward the end of her life, while paralyzed from the waist down, she wrote both plays and poetry.

15. *Cl——:* William, Duke of Clarence (1776–1834). *Lauderdale:* James Maitland, 8th Earl of Lauderdale (1759–1839), a violent-tempered, eccentric Scots parliamentarian. He was first an ardent Whig but after 1821 an increasingly anti-reformist Tory. *King:* untraced.

16. *George Croly* (1780–1860): rector of St. Stephen's Walbrook, and a writer of narrative and romantic poems as well as of plays. *Crawley* and *Coronaroly:* word plays on Croly.

17. A reference to the "Peterloo Massacre" of 1819 in Manchester.

18. *Atkins:* both Atkins and Curtis (Tories) lost their seats as aldermen in 1818 because they supported the renewal of *habeas corpus*. *Curtis:* Sir William Curtis (1752–1829), M. P. for City of London, Lord Mayor of London (1795–1796), an active Tory and supporter of Pitt. *Flower:* Sir Charles Flower, Lord Mayor of London (1808). *Bridges:* George Bridges, Lord Mayor (1819). *C. Smith:* Christopher Smith, Lord Mayor (1817). The "Bridge Street Gang" was Hone's term for the Constitutional Society.

19. *French Assignats:* promissory notes issued by the French revolutionary government, 1790–1796.

20. *Henry Colburn* (d. 1855) founded the *New Monthly Magazine* in 1814 and the *Literary Gazette* in 1817. *James Ward* (1769–1859) was a painter and engraver attached to the household of the Prince of Wales and subsequently famous as a painter of cattle.

21. *Edward Bird* (1772–1819): court painter to Queen Charlotte. He had difficulty obtaining cooperation for contemporary portraits in his last large picture and then the death of his son and daughter further disheartened him. The D. N. B. states: "His spirits forsook him, and he died."

22. *Sir John Silvester* (1745–1822): Recorder of London, 1803–1822. *Rundell and Bridge:* jewelers favored by George IV. Between 1821 and 1829 the King purchased more than £100,000 worth of jewellery. In February and March 1820, he spent more than £2,000 alone, much of it for Lady Conyngham.

23. *Fresh fig-leaves for Adam and Eve:* apparently a reference to Dr. Slop's penchant for attacking obscenity in prints or caricatures (see p. 29 of the book by Rickwood cited in the headnote).

24. *Doxy:* girlfriend. As the ruler of Hanover, George III bestowed the Bishopric of Osnaburgh (Osnaburg is a town in northern Germany) on the Duke of York while he was still a child.

25. *Prince Bishop:* i.e., the Duke of York.

33. EYRE EVANS CROWE, "CHARACTERS OF LIVING AUTHORS, BY THEMSELVES" (1821)

1. *Jean-Baptiste Louvet* (1760–1797): a literary figure prominent as a Girondin during the French Revolution. He won fame as the author of a licentious novel, *Les Amours* (1786–1791). In 1795 a portion of his *Memoirs* was published; they were sentimental, hysterical, honest, and unbalanced. A second novel contained such radical notions as questioning priestly celibacy and affirming the right to divorce. He was a revolutionary philosopher. An English translation of the

untraced epigraph follows: "In this century of little talents and large successes, my masterpieces will run to 100 editions, if need be. Everywhere fools will cry out that I am a great man, and if no one opposes me but lettered people and people of taste, I shall perhaps attain the Academy."

2. The 3rd Earl of Shaftesbury (1671–1713) was the author of *Characteristics of Men, Manners, Opinions, Times* (1711).

3. Probably proverbial, but possibly from *The Merchant of Venice* 1.1.14.

4. *Henry IV*, part 1: 1.3.202.

5. *Fearfully, and in the dark:* not traced.

6. Hazlitt's "The Indian Jugglers" originally appeared in *Table-Talk; or, Original Essays* (1821).

7. See Hazlitt's "On Shakespeare and Milton," *Lectures on the English Poets* in *The Complete Works of William Hazlitt*, ed. P. P. Howe (London: Dent, 1930–1934), 5.47.

8. *Liber Amoris: Or, The New Pygmalion* (1823) autobiographically describes Hazlitt's tortured relationship with Sarah Walker, his landlady's daughter and his lodging-house servant-girl.

9. In *Thoughts on the Present Discontents* (1770) Edmund Burke attacked the secretive and opportunistic machinations of the government of the elder Pitt, Earl of Chatham. The phrase, "tessellated pavement without cement," was used four years later to characterize the same self-serving government. Quoted in J. Steven Watson, *The Reign of George III, 1760–1815* (Oxford: Clarendon Press, 1960), 125.

10. *anagrams of intellect:* the word *intellect* does not (surprisingly) appear in Donne's poetry and the word *anagram* only once.

11. *Review:* see *Edinburgh Review* 30 (June 1818): 87ff for a review of *Childe Harold* (fourth canto) which includes an extended comparison of Byron and Rousseau. Byron also praises Rousseau (and identifies with him) in *Childe Harold,* 3.77ff.

12. *But this is not my theme: Childe Harold,* 3.76.

13. *sweet sad tears:* not traced.

14. *what is writ is writ: Childe Harold,* 4.185. *drop . . . :* trap door in gallows. These "malefactors" are unshackled but condemned.

15. Oliver Goldsmith, "Retaliation," 37–38.

16. Hazlitt was the art critic for *The Champion* from 1814; he had earlier contributed art criticism to *The Morning Chronicle* (from 1812). *aneath the sun:* a pseudo-Scotticism which had a brief currency during the period.

17. *Fly upon the well-proportioned dome:* not traced. For "flattering unction," see *Hamlet* 3.4.145.

18. *Trover:* a legal term. An action to recover the value of personal property illegally converted by another to his own use.

19. Boswell's *Life of Johnson* (March 1750).

20. *Lord Castlereagh* (1769–1822) was foreign secretary after 1812. *Mr. Blair:* Hugh Blair (1718–1800), *Lectures on Rhetoric* (1777–1801), 5 vols.

21. *Winds, whose ways we know not of:* not traced.

22. *his crambe repetita:* "warmed over" (Juvenal, bk. 7, line 154). Cabbage, if eaten twice (i.e., warmed up), was fatal according to a proverb. *kickshaw:* fancy, frivolous dish. *fritters:* trifles.

23. Madame de Staël (1766–1817), *Essai sur les fictions* (1795).

24. I.e., *Blackwood's.*

25. *mine host:* a common expression in Shakespeare (e.g., used 20 times in *The Merry Wives of Windsor*) and playfully altered by Byron in a letter to Lady Melbourne (10 October 1818): "Mine guest (late host) has just . . ." *the sober berry's juice:* Byron, *Corsair,* 347.

26. *Octavius Gilchrist* (1799–1823): antiquary, editor of old plays, and friend of John Clare.

27. *Macbeth* 4.1.10.

28. *Winterston:* Winterslow, near Salisbury, was Hazlitt's home from 1808–1812. His wife, Sarah Stoddart, had property there. In later years he often visited a small inn outside the village ("the Hut") where he wrote.

29. *Wood:* Sir Matthew Wood (1768–1843), radical alderman and Lord Mayor of London (1815–1816, 1816–1817).

30. *Bully Rock:* the sense is "my fellow trickster." Cf. *The Merry Wives of Windsor* 1.3.2.

31. Cf. *Hamlet* 3.3.13.

32. *that fine tact, that airy intuitive faculty:* not traced.

33. *genus irritabile prosaicorum:* cf. Horace, *Epistolae* 2.2.102. Originally *vatum* (for "unstable tribe of bards"), here changed to prose writers.

34. A kind of conflation of Biblical texts: "there is no peace, saith the Lord, unto the wicked" (Isaiah 57:21) and "the wicked be silent in the grave" (Psalm 31.17). Cf. also *King Lear* 1.1.125.

34. LORD BYRON, *THE VISION OF JUDGMENT* (1821)

1. *Quevedo Redivivus:* Quevedo reborn. Francisco Gomez de Quevedo y Villegas (1580–1635) published his six satirical *Visions* in 1635 (English translation, 1745).

2. Southey wrote *Wat Tyler* when he was 19 but it remained unpublished for 22 years. However, some 60,000 copies were sold after it was published in pirated editions in 1817, much to the poet's consternation and embarrassment.

3. *The Merchant of Venice* 4.1.218, 336.

4. Pope, *Essay on Criticism,* 625.

5. In Southey's attack on Byron, Shelley, and Hunt (the "Satanic school," Preface, 206), he describes such poets (though unnamed) as "men of diseased hearts and depraved imaginations" and their works as "monstrous combinations of horror and mockery, lewdness and impiety, with which English poetry has . . . been polluted" (203).

6. *Scrub:* servant to Squire Sullen in George Farquhar's *The Beaux' Stratagem* (1707).

7. In the House of Commons on 14 March 1817, William Smith (the member for Norwich) attacked Southey as showing "the determined malignity of a renegade."

8. *Henry Marten:* one of the Parliamentary commissioners who tried and sentenced Charles I. When the surviving commissioners were themselves tried after the Restoration, Marten was treated with unexpected leniency and imprisoned for life in Chepstow Castle (situated in the mouth of the Wye Valley). The poem Byron refers to is Southey's "Inscription IV," printed above, p. 29.

9. *qualis ab incepto:* the same from the beginning.

10. *Pulci:* Luigi Pulci (1432–1484), Italian author of *Morgante Maggiore* (1483), a comic account of the adventures of Orlando and the giant Morgante. The first canto was translated by Byron in 1820 and published in the fourth number of *The Liberal* (July 1823).

11. *Walter Savage Landor* (1775–1864) is praised as a poet and friend by Southey in his Preface to *A Vision of Judgement* (p. 205n).

12. *Ithyphallics of Savagius:* the meter of the Bacchic hymns suggesting indecency.

13. I.e., the year of the Congress of the Estates General, which led to the French Revolution (1789).

14. Satan will recover possession of both generals, Napoleon and Wellington, on their deaths (reversion is legal terminology).

15. See *Revelation* 12:3.

16. George died in January 1820, the year in which revolutionary movements began in Italy.

17. George died blind and insane. He had been popularly known as "Farmer George" because of his conventional English habits.

18. It was rumored that George IV had hidden his father's will, as George II had hidden his father's will. *Proctor:* an official who examined the validity of wills and other legal documents.

19. The better known reading here is a "bad, ugly woman." George III was as well known for his marital fidelity to Queen Charlotte as his son was for his infidelity to Princess Caroline, herself notoriously unfaithful.

20. Louis XIV of France was guillotined in 1793.

21. See *Matthew* 26:50–52.

22. *ichor:* blood of the gods.

23. *Manes:* ancestral spirits.

24. In search of the Northwest Passage in 1819, Sir William Edward Parry and his crew wintered in Melville Sound, Greenland.

25. *Joanna Southcott* (1750–1814), a religious fanatic, prophesied that she would give birth to a new Messiah. Her pregnancy turned out to be dropsy, from which she died.

26. *Champ Clos:* tournament field.

27. Cf. *Job*, chap. 1 and 2.

28. It had been argued (by John Mason Good in *The Book of Job*, 1812) that the narrative of Job was based on historical and biographical facts. Good consulted Hebraic and Arabic versions for his study.

29. *quit-rent:* a token rent.

30. George III became king in 1760 (when he was 22 years old) and died in 1820.

31. John Bute, Prime Minister, 1762–1763.

32. Roman epicure of the first century A.D.

33. George III was a life-long opponent of Catholic emancipation.

34. *Guelph:* Family name of the Hanoverians.

35. Cf. *Paradise Lost* 6.469–536.

36. Insignia of certain court officials.

37. *Paradise Lost* 4.918.

38. *Jonathan Trumbull* (1710–1785), American statesman, represents the United States.

39. "Caitiffs, are ye dumb? cried the multifaced Demon in anger;" Southey's *A Vision of Judgement* 5.70 [*The Works of Robert Southey*, 10 vols. (London: Longman's 1837–1838), vol. 10].

40. *John Wilkes* (1727–1797), Whig Parliamentarian and journalist opposed to George III.

41. The 3rd Duke of Grafton (1735–1811) was Prime Minister 1768–1770.

42. *Charles James Fox* (1749–1806), leader of the Whig opposition and notoriously obese; *William Pitt the Younger* (1759–1806), Prime Minister (1783–1801, 1804–1806) and framer of repressive legislation, including the "gagging laws" (1795).

43. *Junius:* pseudonym of the unknown author of attacks in *The Public Advertiser* (1769–1772) on the government and George III.

44. Mysterious masked prisoner in the Bastille who died in 1703.

45. The quotation in line 626 is from R. B. Sheridan, *The Rivals*, 4.2. *Edmund Burke* (1727–1797), *John Horne Tooke* (1736–1812), *Sir Philip Francis* (1640–1818), each of whom had been proposed as the author of *The Junius Letters*.

46. The mouth of the Niger River was not discovered until 1830.

47. The title page of *The Letters of Junius* included the phrase *Stat Nominis Umbra* ("it is the shadow of a name").

48. Cf. *Numbers* 22:28.

49. Horace, *Ars Poetica*, 372–73: "Neither men nor gods can tolerate mediocre poets."

50. *Henry James Pye* (1745–1813), Southey's predecessor as Poet Laureate.

51. Byron did admire Southey's appearance. On 27 September 1813 he wrote to Thomas Moore: "Yesterday, at Holland-house, I was introduced to Southey—the best looking bard I have seen for some time. To have that poet's head and shoulders, I would almost have written his Sapphics" [Byron's *Letters and Journals*, ed. Leslie Marchand (London: John Murray, 1973) 3.122].

52. I.e., suicide.

53. See note 8 above.

54. Byron's note refers the reader to Southey's *Remains of Henry Kirke White* (1808; 1.23).

55. Byron's note reads: "had he been consulted at the creation of the world, he would have spared the Maker some absurdities." He is quoting King Alfonso X of Castille (1226?–84) speaking of the Ptolemean system.

56. Byron's note reads: "See Aubrey's account of the apparition which disappeared 'with a curious perfume and a melodious twang;' or see the Antiquary, Vol. I."

57. *Phaeton:* son of Apollo who attempted to drive the chariot of the sun across the sky but lost control and was thrown down to earth.

58. Byron's note reads: "A drowned body lies at the bottom till rotten; it then floats, as most people know."

59. *Wellborn* is a character of Philip Massinger's *A New Way to Pay Old Debts* (1633). *precisian:* Puritan.

60. 100th psalm: a psalm of praise, perhaps with special feeling for the verse "Enter into his gates with thanksgiving, and into his courts with praise: be thankful unto him, and bless his name."

35. ANONYMOUS, "TO THE VEILED MAGICIAN" (1822)

1. *Dish-clout:* dishcloth.
2. *Talus:* the man of iron in *The Faerie Queen,* book 5.
3. *Swale:* sway side to side, or move up and down.

36. ANONYMOUS, "LYRICAL BALLAD" (1822)

1. Cf. the opening of *The Excursion* (1.1), or of "The Idiot Boy": " 'Tis eight o'clock,—a clear March night"; or of "Lines" (in *Lyrical Ballads,* 1798): "It is the first mild day of March."
2. Wordsworth was sometimes a fussy note-maker. For example, in his Preface to *The Excursion,* he offers the following rationale before quoting from Heron's *Journey in Scotland:* "It may still, however, be satisfactory to have prose testimony how far a Character, employed for purposes of imagination, is founded upon general fact." The parodist's note suggests that Wordsworth intends to fulfill his principle of writing about "incidents and situations from common life" [*The Poetical Works of Wordsworth,* ed. Ernest de Selincourt (London: Oxford University Press, 1950), 734], however trivial or uninteresting the event may be.
3. Presumably, he has caught a cold from standing around in pools.
4. Probably a generic name. By a statute still in force, surgeons and barbers were to use a pole to designate their place of business.
5. Usually a withered old woman but occasionally applied to a man.
6. Fine, woollen trousers.
7. In *Peter Bell* the little orphan boy kisses the ass "a thousand times" (line 1115); Peter sees it and is redeemed. In the parody Peter remains unredeemed, irrespective of who kissed which ass.

37. THOMAS COLLEY GRATTAN, "CONFESSIONS OF AN ENGLISH GLUTTON" (1823)

1. *D'Alembert:* Jean Le Rond d'Alembert (1717–1783), French mathematician and philosopher known for his unorthodox views. The quotation from a letter to Voltaire written 27 February 1765 could be translated as follows: "Since things are as they are, I too claim my right to speak candidly."
2. Presumably a deliberate confusion of Descartes's *cogito, ergo sum* (I think, therefore I am) with *ego sum* (I am)
3. From Abraham Cowley (1618–1667), "The Motto."
4. *La Nouvelle Heloise* by Jean-Jacques Rousseau (1712–1778); William Henry Ireland (1777–1835) passed off the play *Vortigern and Rowena* as a hitherto undiscovered play by Shakespeare, but it was jeered in the Kemble production of 2 April 1796.
5. Possibly William Hickey (1749–1830), De Quincey, Robert Burton (quoted by the parodist below; see note 31), and Coleridge (for *Biographia Literaria*). We have been unable to trace the quotation. Hickey was the author of entertaining memoirs (1749–1809) in which he confesses his weakness for women and claret.
6. *Curtius:* legendary Roman hero who leapt into a chasm that appeared in the Forum. The name was apparently invented to explain the name of the *Lacus Curtius,* a pond in the Forum.
7. *King Lear* 3.4.93.
8. Authors of popular books on cooking. Mrs. Hannah Glasse, *The art of cookery, made plain and easy* (ca. 1747; reprinted frequently into the nineteenth century). Mrs. Maria Eliza Rundell (1745–1828), *A new system of domestic cookery* (1807). William Kitchiner (1775?–1827), *Redivivus; or, The Cook's Oracle* (1817).
9. *Epicuri de grege porcus:* a pig of the Epicurean herd. *Porcus Trojanus:* Trojan pig.
10. *Vellication:* irritation. *Abstersion:* purging.
11. Mental therapy.
12. *Aristophanes* (448–388 B.C.): Greek playwright. *Macrobius* (ca. 400 A.D.): Latin writer

and philosopher, author of *Saturnalia. Martial* (40–104 A.D.): Roman satirist and the first epigrammatist.

13. *Phrygian attigan:* Phrygia was an ancient region of Central Asia Minor (now Central Turkey). *Attigan:* he-goat. *Ambracian kid:* Ambracia was a city of ancient Greece (now Arta). *Melian crane:* Melos is an island in the Aegean Sea.

14. *Sergius Arata:* Arata was not only the inventor of oyster beds but also of showerbaths for country houses (Pliny, book 9, sec. 79). Pliny (23–79 A.D.) was a Roman naturalist and author of *Natural History* who died of asphyxiation near Vesuvius, having gone to investigate the eruption.

15. *Hortensius* (114–50 B.C.): wealthy Roman orator.

16. *Vitellius:* briefly Roman emperor (January–December, 69 A.D.), a glutton and epicure. His vices made him a favorite of Tiberius, Caligula, Claudius, and Nero. *Apicius:* the name of three notorious gluttons, the best known being the alleged author of a work on cookery.

17. *Paradise Regained,* 4.114.

18. *Delicata fercula:* voluptuous dishes.

19. Charles Lamb, "A Dissertation on Roast Pig" in *Essays of Elia* (1823).

20. Not traced.

21. *Secundum artem:* in keeping with the art. *Mensa prima:* first course.

22. *Dii patellarii:* platter gods.

23. *Hamlet* 1.1.126: "lo where it comes again!"

24. As Alethea Hayter notes in her edition of De Quincey's *Confessions* (Harmondsworth, Middlesex: Penguin, 1971), 218, "De Quincey always sympathized with Jews as a persecuted people, some of the 'pariahs' to whom he felt so psychologically akin."

25. The pig has replaced the crocodile of De Quincey's Oriental dreams, described in similar terms in "The Pains of Opium" section of the *Confessions.*

26. In this nightmare the pigs, in describing themselves, also pass judgment on their own author. *Bubble and squeak:* leftovers re-cooked noisily (hence the name).

27. Not traced.

28. *Brawn:* pickled pig's meat. *Pettitoes:* pig's trotters.

29. Although he does not mention a Pig-Faced Lady, in *The Shows of London* (Cambridge, Mass.: Harvard University Press, 1978), Richard Altick does refer to numerous human freaks on display in London during this period, including a Welsh female dwarf, a bearded lady from the Alps (251), various out-sized females (255), and a well-known "'fireproof female'" (264).

30. *Calipash:* green flesh of turtle inside upper shell. *Calipee:* yellow flesh of turtle inside lower shell.

31. "I have no wife nor children good or bad to provide for" is in the opening pages of the prefatory "Democritus to the Reader" (Robert Burton, *The Anatomy of Melancholy*).

32. *Ne sutor ultra crepidam:* "Let the cobbler stick to his last" (Pliny 35.36.12).

33. *Ollapodrida:* a dish of meat and vegetables.

34. *Me crever le ventre:* bust my belly.

35. Gluttony is the second of the sins of incontinence, and gluttons were to be found in the third circle of Hell (Canto VI of *The Inferno*).

36. *Daniel Lambert* put himself on display at 53 Piccadilly in 1806 and was visited by all of London society. At age 36 he is said to have weighed 700 lbs. He died in 1809 and it took 20 men half an hour to wedge his huge coffin into the grave. See p. 254 of Altick's book (note 29 above).

37. *Justice Shallow:* cf. *Henry IV,* part 2: 3.2.309.

38. *Salamis:* actually Salmacis. Cf. Ovid, *Metamorphoses,* book 4.375–379.

39. Not traced.

40. *Post caenam vomere volebat, ideoque largius edebat:* after dinner he liked to vomit so that he could eat still more.

41. *Henry V:* 2.2.56.

38. CAROLINE BOWLES SOUTHEY, "LETTER FROM A WASHERWOMAN" AND "FRAGMENTS" (1823)

1. Leigh Hunt as Mr. Pennyfeather. It should be noted that Hunt did publish an essay "On Washerwomen" in the *Examiner* for 15 September 1816.

2. William Hazlitt.

3. *Pollar:* Apollo. *Pollards:* bran.

4. "Like Dr. Johnson, he [Hazlitt] made himself a poor amends for the loss of wine by drinking tea, not so largely, indeed, as the hero of Boswell, but at least of equal potency. . ." Mr. Justice Talfourd quoted by A. Birrell, *William Hazlitt* (London: Macmillan, 1902), 210.

5. *Hellycome:* Helicon; *Hagganipper:* Aganippe; both fountains of the Muses.

6. *Jack Ketch* (d. 1686): executioner.

7. *Cubit:* Cupid, god of love. *Hairy-toe:* Erato, muse of erotic poetry. *Polly summut:* Polyhymnia, muse of the sublime hymn.

8. *Jack in the Greene:* "a man or boy enclosed in a wooden or wicker pyramidal framework covered in leaves in the May-day sports of chimney-sweepers, etc." *(O.E.D.).*

9. In his essay "On Great and Little Things," Hazlitt is boldly confessional of his admiration for "humble beauties, servant-maids and shepherd-girls."

10. *varden rushlite:* farthing rush-candle. A candle of feeble power made by dipping the pith of a rush in grease.

11. *cockchafers:* Maybug.

12. *Robert Waithman* (1764–1833) was an active liberal politician in London from 1794, sometimes as M.P. and at other times as alderman. He became sheriff of London and Middlesex in 1820 and was elected Lord Mayor in 1823. He also amassed a fortune from his linendraper's shop in Fleet Street.

13. Not traced.

14. *Henry V,* 1.1.47.

15. Hunt did write an essay entitled "Tea-Drinking." Also, cf. "A 'Now,' Descriptive of a Cold Day": "Now the muffin-bell soundeth sweetly in the streets, reminding us, not of the man, but his muffins . . ." Hunt was also fond of noses (see, for example, lines 11 and 39–40 in "To J.H., Four Years Old: A Nursery Song" [1816]).

16. Shelley married Harriet Westbrook in 1811 but ran off with Mary Godwin in 1814. This complex passage appears to have Shelley writing, in elegaic and *Adonais*-like fashion, about himself in the third person, as he does in *Adonais* (stanza 34).

17. *fubsy:* fat and squat.

18. Cf. again "To J.H.": "Ah little ranting Johnny, / Forever blithe and bonny, / And singing nonny, nonny, / With hat just thrown upon ye . . ." This fragment also anticipates the kind of osculatory banter of "Jenny" (published in 1838).

19. *swaling:* swaying (a new word at the time).

20. Ascension Island in the South Atlantic was a noted breeding ground for sea turtles.

40. WILLIAM HAY FORBES, "COCKNEY CONTRIBUTIONS FOR THE FIRST OF APRIL" (1824)

1. *Billingsgate:* synonym for ribald, abusive, and vituperative language.

2. Quotations from *Twelfth Night* 3.4.28; *Hamlet* 3.2.262–63; *Hamlet* 3.2.284. In the last quotation, "pajock" is Hamlet's substitution for the rhyme word "ass."

3. *The Story of Rimini* was published in 1815. It was reviewed in *The Quarterly* 14 (January 1816): 473–81.

4. Keats and Hunt were both acquainted with the musician and composer Vincent Novello (1781–1861). At Novello's Keats enjoyed listening to Mozart [see *The Letters of John Keats 1814–1821,* ed. Hyder E. Rollins, 2 vols. (Cambridge, Mass: Harvard University Press, 1958), 1.126, 225 and 2.8].

5. George Croly's *Pride Shall Have a Fall: A Comedy, in Five Acts—With Songs* was first performed at Covent Garden on 11 March 1824. It was favorably reviewed in *Blackwood's* 15 (March 1824): 343–50.

6. *Barry Cornwall* (Bryan Waller Procter, 1787–1874) wrote poetry under Hunt's inspiration, but in 1832 bid farewell to verse and became a metropolitan commissioner in lunacy. Hunt lived in Italy from 1821 to 1825.

7. *Thomas Campbell* (1777–1844) was editor of the *New Monthly Magazine* from 1820 to 1830. In 1824 Hunt was hired by Colburn to write for this periodical.

8. Milton, *Il Penseroso,* 17.

9. While in Florence from January to October 1824, Hunt wrote his "Wishing Cap Papers" for *The Examiner. Fortunatus* (1600) is a comedy by Dekker.

10. The quotation is an elliptical version of *Paradise Lost* 5.335 in which Eve prepares lunch for Raphael.

11. *sign manual:* autograph signature (especially of the sovereign) used to authenticate a document.

12. Not traced.

13. (In Italian) Leigh Hunt, Emperor and King of Cockaigne.

14. *distich:* a pair of lines usually rhymed but of uneven length and making complete sense.

15. Hunt had first written theater criticism for his brother John's newspaper the *News* in 1805. Some of these articles on the leading actors and actresses of the day were revised and issued as an appendix to *Critical Essays of the London Theatre* (1807). He initially continued with theatrical criticism when he and his brother began *The Examiner* in 1808.

16. In *The Months: Descriptive of the Successive Beauties of the Year* (London: C. & J. Ollier, 1821), reprinted from the *Literary Pocket-Book of 1819,* Hunt observes: "December has one circumstance in it, which turns it into the merriest month of the year,—Christmas." He also notes that the "Wassail-bowl" has "been a little revived of late" (130) and encourages his readers to enjoy themselves on holidays. Also typical of Hunt on the subject of Christmas is his later essay in the *Monthly Repository* (1837–38) titled "Inexhaustibility of the Subject of Christmas," in which he catalogues various associations of Christmas from goose pie and carols to gifts and cards and in which he again urges merry thoughts and enjoyment.

17. Hunt's ideas about Christianity were unorthodox, some might even say heretical. For example, for his rejection of eternal punishment, see *The Autobiography of Leigh Hunt,* ed. Roger Ingpen (New York: Dutton, 1903), 2.301.

18. Croly's *Pride Shall Have a Fall: A Comedy, in Five Acts—With Songs* was reviewed in *Blackwood's* (see note 5 above). It is a play, states the reviewer, "worth noticing even by us who have long since given up criticizing the Acted Drama of London" (343).

19. *Suivantes:* confidential maid (modish word; *O.E.D.* 1821).

20. The concluding two lines of Wordsworth's "Immortality Ode."

21. From Pope's "Elegy to the Memory of an Unfortunate Lady," 69.

22. *Hamlet* 4.7.178 and 3.2.381.

23. The first seems a misquotation of *Macbeth* 1.9.10. For the second, see *Macbeth* 2.1.36.

24. Hazlitt began contributing to the *Edinburgh Review* in 1814. His relations with Jeffrey are described in Herschel Baker, *William Hazlitt* (Cambridge, Mass.: Harvard University Press, 1962), 207–16.

25. Hazlitt has much praise for the former in "Mr. Jeffrey" in *Spirit of the Age.*

26. This reference is to the old saying "There cannot be two kings of Brentford."

27. *A Midsummer Night's Dream* 3.2.206; *Julius Caesar* 1.2.134–35.

28. *teres et rotundus:* Horace, *Satires* 2.7.86 (misquotation of *teres atque rotundus*): smooth and rounded. For the second quotation, see *Paradise Lost* 4.266–67.

29. See "The Dulwich Gallery" in *The Complete Works of William Hazlitt,* ed. P. P. Howe (London: Dent, 1930–1934), vol. 8.18.

30. *Hannah More* (1745–1833) published a series of cheap tracts (three a month for three years, each containing a tale, a ballad, and a tract for Sunday reading) whose circulation was two million in the first year. The *Cheap Repository Tracts* were collected in three volumes. The *Religious Tract Society* was formed in 1799; it had a strong evangelical bias and aimed at reformation of the poor.

31. *Antoine Watteau* (1684–1721): highly original French painter who created the *fête galante* painting, a few figures in a park setting or dancing in either contemporary or fancy dress. His work was based on subtle and close observation despite its sometimes other-worldly quality.

32. *Sir Richard Phillips* (1767–1840) became a stationer, bookseller, and patent medicine vendor in 1790. He developed radical political sympathies (Christopher North called him "a dirty little Jacobin" *DNB*) as well as a conviction that the theory of gravitation had no basis in fact. He published *The Proximate Causes of Material Phenomena* in 1821.

33. *Jean Baptiste Say* (1767–1832) was a French economist who disseminated the economic doctrines of Adam Smith throughout Europe.

34. *J. R. McCulloch* (1789–1864) was a political economist and follower of Smith and Ricardo.

He wrote the economics articles for *The Scotsman* (1817–1827) and in 1824 delivered the Ricardo Memorial Lectures.

35. *Hamlet* 5.1.306. *Henry Fuseli* (1741–1825) exhibited "The Nightmare" in 1782.

36. *William Godwin,* besides writing children's stories under the name of Baldwin, translated some children's books from French.

37. *Othello* 5.2.346.

38. *Antony and Cleopatra* 2.2.235.

39. The Philharmonic Society began in 1813 to encourage instrumental music. The Society used the Argyll Rooms, Regent Street, until their destruction by fire in 1830. As the Society of professional musicians, the Philharmonic had all the leading musicians of the period appear before it.

40. See chapter 11 of the first part of *Don Quixote.* For "sky-tinctured," see *Paradise Lost* 5.285.

41. See the review of *Letters on England* by Victoire, Count de Soligny (2 vols.: Henry Colburn, 1823) in *Blackwood's* 13 (May 1823): 558–66. See also P. G. Patmore, *My Friends and Acquaintances* (London, 1854), 1.116, where he describes the intial publication of the "Letters" in the *New Monthly Magazine* and the reason he used a pseudonym.

42. *John Hookham Frere* (1769–1846) made translations from *Poema del Cid;* three of them were printed as an appendix to Southey's *Chronicle of the Cid* (1808).

41. WILLIAM FREDERICK DEACON, FROM *WARRENIANA* (1824)

"OLD CUMBERLAND PEDLAR"

1. *Joanna Hutchinson* (1780–1843): younger sister to Mary Wordsworth and addressed in "To Joanna" (1800). *Tims:* possibly Timothy in "The Childless Father."

2. Wordsworth was interested in the Roman inscriptions on native rocks (cf. "Poems on the Naming of Places").

3. The names of other Wordsworth characters: for example, George Fisher, like Charles Fleming below, is a schoolboy in "Rural Architecture" and Betty Foy is the mother in "The Idiot Boy."

4. *Silver-How* is a mountain near Grasmere visible from Dove Cottage in Wordsworth's day.

5. The echoing mountains appear both in "To Joanna" and in *The Excursion* 2.706–07.

6. *hind:* rustic, boor.

7. Echo of *The Excursion* 2.429, *Peter Bell,* 518, and "Expostulation and Reply," 17.

8. Cf. moralizing in "The Old Cumberland Beggar," 73–77.

9. Cf. the "newly breeched" urchins in "The Old Cumberland Beggar," 65.

10. *Tick:* credit. Owing money to tradesmen gives you neuralgic pain.

11. *Henry Hase:* not traced.

"CARMEN TRIUMPHALE"

1. Southey's poem of this name was prompted by the defeat of Napoleon in 1814.

2. *Almack's:* Assembly Rooms in King Street. *Scotch Ariosto:* Byron called Scott "the Ariosto of the North," because both Scott and Ariosto as narrative poets enjoyed immense popularity outside their native countries. As a boy, Scott taught himself Italian so as to read the *Orlando Furioso.* See *Childe Harold* 4.40.

3. *Smart:* Sir George Thomas Smart (1776–1867) was a musician, conductor, violinist, and singing teacher. At the time of the parody, he had recently been appointed director of Covent Garden under Charles Kemble. *Braham:* John Braham (1774?–1856) was a popular tenor singer associated with Drury Lane where he began appearing in 1796. *The Stephens:* Catherine Stephens (1794–1882) was a popular singer who first appeared at Covent Garden on 23 September 1818. Jane Austen wrote to her sister Cassandra in March 1814: "Excepting Miss Stephens, I daresay *Artaxerxes* will be very tiresome."

4. *bouncer:* a thumping lie (1805). *Saint James's:* the scene of social functions.

5. *susurrous:* whispering.

"THE SABLE SCHOOL OF POETRY"

1. *B.M.: Blackwood's Magazine.*
2. *Ambrose's:* tavern, supposed scene of the "noctes Ambrosianae"; in fact, an imaginary location in Edinburgh off the east end of Princes Street. *Odontist:* extractor of teeth. In a note by Deacon, Doctor Scott the Odontist is identified as one of the contributors to *Blackwood's*. *O'Doherty:* Ensign O'Doherty, pseudonym of William Maginn (1793–1842), frequent contributor to *Blackwood's*.
3. *Besom:* broom. *Sir Humphrey Davy* (1778–1829): renowned experimental scientist, Professor of Chemistry with the Royal Institution and later President of the Royal Society. *Sir Thomas Lawrence* (1769–1830): principal portrait painter of the king and, in 1820, President of the Royal Academy.
4. *Pierce Egan* (1772–1849): sports journalist and author of "Boxiana; or Sketches of Modern Pugilism."
5. "stealing his way . . .:" In his *Life of Milton,* Johnson speaks of Milton's watching the reputation of *Paradise Lost* "stealing its way in a kind of subterranean current through fear and silence."
6. *William Wallace* (1272?–1305): Scottish general and patriot, executed for treason under Edward I.
7. *Doctor Samuel Parr* (1747–1825): schoolmaster and author with strong Whig principles; regarded as rather pompous.
8. "At their own sweet will": Wordsworth, "Sonnet Written on Westminster Bridge," 12. *Caledonian canal:* Opened in 1822 and completed in 1847. The canal is about 60 miles long, extending from Fort William in the south west to near Inverness in the north. Loch Ness is part of it.
9. In 1618 Francis Bacon was created Lord Chancellor and 1st Baron Verulam.
10. The concluding line in Wordsworth's "Immortality Ode."
11. *Lisson:* Lisson Grove in the Paddington area of London. In 1815, after his release from Horsemonger Lane Prison, Leigh Hunt went to reside at No. 13 Lisson Grove North.
12. *Saint Leon:* novel by William Godwin (published in 1799) in which the hero invents a potion conferring eternal youth.
13. *Hottentot:* native South African of low stature. *Hessian-boots:* high boot with tassels.
14. *et quoe carent nostro ora libro?:* "And what shores are devoid of our book?" A garbled version of Horace, *Odes,* 2.1, 36, "Quae caret ora cruore nostro: What shore is free of our spilled blood?"
15. *Sir William Curtis:* Lord Mayor of London, M.P., and friend of George IV. Curtis was much ridiculed for being a poor speaker and being poorly educated. Forbes includes a long note giving various arguments in support of identifying Curtis as the "Great Unknown," all spurious of course.
16. *Lord Grey:* Charles Grey, second Earl Grey (1764–1845), a reformist Whig, well-known orator and debater in Parliament.
17. Cf. *Julius Caesar* 1.2.228.
18. *Tims:* possibly Timothy Tickler in *Blackwood's* "Noctes Ambrosianae," pseudonym for Robert Sym (1750–1844), uncle to John Wilson.

"THE CHILDE'S PILGRIMAGE"

1. *Limehouse:* easterly part of the borough of Stepney on the Thames, a district which used to have lime kilns. The parodist is inverting the aristocratic lineage given Harold by Byron.
2. *ennui'd:* occurs nowhere in Byron, but ennui occurs only in *Don Juan* (8 times).
3. *Medina:* sacred city of Islam where Mohammed died and is buried.
4. *Whitechapel:* east of Aldgate, London, known for narrow, filthy streets and disreputable inhabitants.
5. *Billingsgate:* chief fish market of London, located just below London Bridge on the north bank of the Thames.
6. *Boeotian:* thick-headed, stupid. Minerva Press in Leadenhall Street published sentimental novels early in the nineteenth century.
7. *Theodore Ducas:* Ducas was the name of a Byzantine family that supplied several rulers

)

to the Eastern Empire. Theodore I Lascaris (1204–1222) organized the new Byzantine State in Western Asia Minor with Nicaea as its centre.

8. *Catiline:* infamous Roman conspirator (d. 62 A.D.). *Granger's sweets:* In 1769 James Granger (1723–1776) published *Biographical History of England,* with blank leaves available for inserting engraved portraits or other illustrations of the text. To "grangerize" came to mean to illustrate a book by the addition of prints or engravings cut out of other books.

9. *Thomas Chalmers* (1780–1847): founder of the Free Church of Scotland, professor of moral philosophy at St. Andrews, and later professor of divinity at Edinburgh.

10. *Mansion House:* first official home of the Lord Mayors of London.

11. *calipash, calipee:* upper and lower shell from which turtle soup, a traditional part of the Lord Mayor's banquet, was made.

12. *Apician:* pertaining to epicureans named after the Roman Apicius.

13. *cornuted:* horned, hence venison, another traditional dish of the banquet.

14. *Childe Harold* 3.64.

15. *Log:* Hiram, king of Tyre, sent cedar and other wood in the form of logs tied together as rafts by sea to Solomon for the building of the temple (1 Kings 5:8–9).

16. *Momus:* Greek god of ridicule.

17. *Childe Harold* 4.1666.

42. THOMAS HOOD, "ODE TO MR. GRAHAM," FROM *ODES AND ADDRESSES TO GREAT PEOPLE* (1825)

1. Wordsworth's "To a Skylark" (1802). The opening line in *Poems, in Two Volumes* (1807) correctly reads: "Up with me! up with me into the clouds!"

2. *Dollond:* a fine make of telescope manufactured by an established firm of opticians of the same name.

3. *Edward Moggs,* the editor of *Pocket Itinerary of the Roads of England and Wales.*

4. *John McAdam* (1756–1836) was the inventor of the macadam road surface. In 1827 he was appointed general surveyor of roads in Great Britain. He had already written *Remarks on the Present System of Road Making* (1819) and *Practical Essay on the Scientific Repair and Preservation of Roads* (1819).

5. Magog and Gog were statues guarding the entrance to the council chamber of the Guildhall.

6. *cant:* pitch, toss.

7. Cf. *King Lear* 4.6.11ff where Edgar pretends to describe the scene from a cliff top on which Gloucester believes he is standing.

8. *Samuel Rogers* (1763–1855): English poet, author of *The Pleasures of Memory,* who secured for Wordsworth the position as distributor of stamps for Westmorland. *Thomas Moore* (1779–1852): Irish poet, author of *Irish Melodies* (1808–34) and *Lalla Rookh* (1817), friend and biographer of Byron.

9. An echo of Burns's "Jolly Beggars": "A fig for those by law protected." Hood's stanza form is like the six line stanza used by Burns in several of his satires and epistles.

10. *subway:* underground passage for pipes or a tunnel for pedestrians. *John Williams* advocated in 1823 the provision of "subways" capable of housing gas and water mains and sewers. Williams had taken out a patent in 1822 and published a book on the subject in 1828. See Michael Harrison, *London Beneath The Pavement* (London: Peter Davies, 1961), 68, 191.

11. *Edward Irving* (1792–1834): Scottish preacher and popular orator under whose influence was founded the Catholic Apostolic Church.

12. *Francis Jeffrey* edited the *Edinburgh Review; William Gifford* (1756–1826) edited the *Quarterly Review* from 1809 to 1824.

13. *lading:* cargo (ballast of sand).

14. *George Croly* (1780–1860): minor poet, frequent contributor to *Blackwood's* and the *Literary Gazette.* He eventually secured the rectory of St. Stephen's, Walbrook, in 1835. *Warren's Blacking:* the boot polish manufactured in London by Robert Warren. *William Jerdan* (1782–1869): editor of the *Literary Gazette.*

15. *L.E.L.:* Letitia Elizabeth Landon (1802–1838), well-known poet and novelist. For Byron's

attitude to Shakespeare, see Jonathan Bate, *Shakespeare and the English Romantic Imagination* (London: Oxford University Press, 1986), 222–47.

16. *Tims:* See above note 18 to "The Sable School of Poetry" in *Warreniana. Christopher North:* the pseudonym of *Blackwood's* editor, John Wilson (1785–1854). *P.A.Z.:* De Quincey signed articles X.Y.Z. for the *London Magazine* (1821–1824), and an earlier article in *Blackwood's* (April 1818, 75) is signed A. Z. Evidently, this reference is to the practice of signing articles with initials, but the identity of the writer in question we have been unable to discover. *London Magazine:* its correspondence appeared under the title of the Lion's Head.

17. *Thomas Campbell* (1777–1844): editor of *New Monthly Magazine.* Longman, Wordsworth's publisher, had been established in Paternoster Row since 1724. By 1823 the full name of the firm had become Longman, Hurst, Rees, Orme, Brown, and Green.

18. *Nathan Meyer Rothschild* (1777–1836), British banker and powerful financier. *Golden Ball:* an apparent reference to the ornamental sign outside the House of Rothschild in London.

19. *Adults' School:* possibly the London Mechanics' Institute (which opened in 1824 and had nearly 2,000 students within a year), as opposed to the infant school opened by Henry Brougham and James Mill in 1818. *Robert Elliston* (1774–1831): extremely popular actor who began acting in London in 1796. He was praised as a tragedian but especially as a comedian and was associated with Drury Lane (1819–1826) at the time of this parody.

20. Burns, "To a Louse," 43–44.

43. THOMAS LOVE PEACOCK, "PROEMIUM OF AN EPIC," FROM *PAPER MONEY LYRICS* (1825)

1. *Henry VIII* 4.2.41–42.

2. Cf. the repetition of "how beautiful is night" in the opening lines of Southey's *Thalaba* (1801).

3. For Southey's professionalism as a working writer and for his interest in prolonging a poem, one might cite the final stanza of the poet's own "To A Spider":

> Thou busy labourer! one resemblance more
> May yet the verse prolong,
> For, Spider, thou art like the Poet poor,
> Whom thou hast help'd in song.
> Both busily our needful food to win,
> We work, as Nature taught, with
> ceaseless pains;
> Thy bowels thou dost spin,
> I spin my brains.

44. HARTLEY COLERIDGE, "HE LIVED AMIDST TH' UNTRODDEN WAYS" (1827)

1. From almost the beginning of his career (with the exception of *Lyrical Ballads*), Wordsworth's publisher was Longman of London. Unfortunately, the firm never had much financial success with Wordsworth's poetry. For example, it took six years to sell the 500 copies of *The Excursion* published in 1814 (probably because it was much too expensively priced at 2 guineas). See Harold Cox and John E. Chandler, *The House of Longman 1724–1924* (London: Longmans, Green & Co., 1925), 15–16. Wordsworth's dissatisfaction with Longman reached a crisis in 1825, but he failed to find another publisher willing to meet his terms. For an account of this dispute and his eventual return to Longman, see Mary Moorman, *William Wordsworth: A Biography. The Later Years 1803–1850* (Oxford: Clarendon Press, 1965), 444–48.

2. "The White Doe of Rylstone," 202, 972.

45. JAMES HOGG, "ODE TO A HIGHLAND BEE" (1829)

1. See "The Solitary Reaper," 30–32.
2. Possibly the "friend" is Coleridge; "Miss Hutchison" is presumably Wordsworth's future wife (they were married in 1802).

46. ANONYMOUS, "A DRIVER OF A RATTLING CAB" (1831)

1 On 4 July 1829 the first public vehicle (a horse-drawn omnibus) traveled on a fixed route— from Paddington to the city.
2. *Samuel Rogers* (1762–1855): best known for *The Pleasures of Memory* (1792).
3. *Thomas Campbell* (1777–1844): author of *The Pleasures of Hope* (1799). *Richard Bentley* (1794–1871) joined in partnership with Henry Colburn in 1829 for three years. Bentley's *Miscellany* began in 1837, a magazine edited for a time by Dickens; he was the publisher of such writers as Moore, Isaac and Benjamin Disraeli, Theodore Hook, Thomas Haliburton, and Dickens. *George Croly* (1780–1860), author and divine, contributor to *Blackwood's,* eventually secured a "living" (St. Stephen's, Walbrook) through Lord Lyndhurst in 1835.
4. *Thomas Moore* (1779–1852): a poet with notable musical gifts (*Irish Melodies,* 1807) and good friend of Byron. A lyric such as " 'Tis sweet to think," with the following lines, explains the kind of attitude here ascribed to Moore: " 'Tis sweet to think, that, where'er we rove, / We are sure to find something blissful and dear, / And that, when we're far from the lips we love, / We've but to make love to the lips we are near!" Moore, in a note to the poem, disavows his assertion of inconstancy.
5. Expression combines Shakespeare's lunatic poet in *A Midsummer Night's Dream* (5.1.7– 22) with Wordsworth's fondness for the word "sage" (which appears 14 times in *The Excursion* and nearly 50 times in other Wordsworth poems).

Selected Bibliography

Altick, Richard. *The Shows of London*. Cambridge, Mass.: Harvard University Press, 1978.

Baker, Herschel. *William Hazlitt*. Cambridge, Mass.: Harvard University Press, 1962.

Bate, Jonathan. *Shakespeare and the English Romantic Imagination*. Oxford: Clarendon Press, 1986.

Bauer, N. Stephen. "Early Burlesques and Parodies of Wordsworth." *Journal of English and Germanic Philology* 74 (1975): 553–69.

Beable, W.H., comp. *Epitaphs: Graveyard Humour & Eulogy*. London, 1925.

Benet, William Rose. *The Reader's Encyclopedia: An Encyclopedia of World Literature and the Arts*. New York: Thomas Y. Cromwell, 1948.

Bhabha, Homi K. "Of Mimicry and Man: The Ambivalence of Colonial Discourse." *October* 28 (1984): 125–33.

Birrell, A. *William Hazlitt*. London: Macmillan, 1902.

Bradbury, Malcolm. "An Age of Parody: Style in the Modern Arts." *Encounter* 55.1 (July 1980): 36–53.

Bromwich, David. *Hazlitt: The Mind of a Critic*. London: Oxford University Press, 1983.

Butler, Marilyn. *Romantics, Rebels and Reactionaries: English Literature and Its Background 1760–1830*. London: Oxford University Press, 1981.

Byron, Lord. *Byron's Letters and Journals*. Edited by Leslie A. Marchand. 12 vols. London: John Murray, 1973–1982.

Coleridge, Hartley. *Hartley Coleridge: New Poems*. Edited by Earl Leslie Griggs. London: Oxford University Press, 1942.

———. *Letters of Hartley Coleridge*. Edited by Grace Evelyn Griggs and Earl Leslie Griggs. London: Oxford University Press, 1936.

Coleridge, Samuel Taylor. *The Collected Works of Samuel Taylor Coleridge*. Princeton: Princeton University Press, 1969–.

Cox, Harold, and John E. Chandler. *The House of Longman 1724–1924*. London: Longmans, Green & Co., 1925.

Dawson, Carl. *His Fine Wit: A Study of Thomas Love Peacock*. Berkeley: University of California Press, 1970.

De Quincey, Thomas. *Confessions of an English Opium Eater*. Edited by Aletha Hayter. Harmondsworth: Penguin, 1971.

Dickens, Charles. *Memoirs of Joseph Grimaldi*. Edited by Richard Findlater. London: MacGibbon and Kee, 1968.

Disraeli, Isaac. *Curiosities of Literature*. Boston: William Veazie, 1858.

The Trial of John Donnellan. London, 1781.

The Theory of Presumptive Proof; or, an Inquiry in to the Nature of Circumstantial evidence: including an examination of the evidence on the trial of Captain Donnellan. London, 1815.

Erdman, David. "Coleridge as Nehemiah Higginbottom." *Modern Language Notes* 73 (1958): 569–80.

Fanshawe, Catherine Maria. *Memorials of Miss Catherine Maria Fanshawe.* Edited by William Harness. n.p. 1865.

Foucault, Michel. *The History of Sexuality: Volume I: An Introduction.* Translated by Robert Hurley. New York: Pantheon, 1980.

Fruman, Norman. "Originality, Plagiarism, Forgery, and Romanticism." *Centrum* 4 (1976): 44–49.

Garlitz, Barbara. "The Baby's Debut: The Contemporary Reaction to Wordsworth's Poetry of Childhood." *Boston University Studies in English* 4 (1960): 85–94.

Gaull, Marilyn. *English Romanticism: The Human Context.* New York: Norton, 1988.

———. "Romantic Humour: The Horse of Knowledge and The Learned Pig." *Mosaic* 9.4 (1976): 43–64.

Gifford, Douglas. *James Hogg.* Edinburgh: The Ramsay Head Press, 1976.

Gillray, James. *The Works of James Gillray, The Caricaturist.* Edited by Thomas Wright. 1874. Reprint. Amsterdam: Emmering, 1970.

Gittings, Robert. *The Mask of Keats.* Cambridge, Mass.: Harvard University Press, 1956.

Gohn, Jack. "Did Shelley Know Wordsworth's 'Peter Bell'?" *Keats-Shelley Journal* 28 (1979): 20–24.

———. "Who Wrote 'Benjamin the Waggoner'? An Inquiry." *Wordsworth Circle* 8 (1977): 69–74.

Groves, David. "James Hogg, Leigh Hunt, and the 'New Poetic Mirror'." *Wordsworth Circle* 17 (1986): 249–50.

Haller, William. *The Early Life of Robert Southey, 1774–1803.* 1917. Reprint. New York: Octagon Books, 1966.

Hamilton, Walter, comp. *Parodies of the Works of English & American Authors.* 6 vols. London: Reeves & Turner, 1884–89.

Harrison, Michael. *London Beneath the Pavement.* London: Peter Davies, 1961.

Hazlitt, William. *The Complete Works of William Hazlitt.* Edited by P. P. Howe. 21 vols. London: Dent, 1930–34.

Hibbert, Christopher. *George IV: Regent and King 1811–1830.* London: Allen Lane, 1973.

Hodgson, Rev. James T. *Memoir of the Rev. Francis Hodgson, B.D.: Scholar, Poet, and Divine.* 2 vols. 1878. Reprint. New York: AMS Press, 1977.

Hone, J. Ann. *For the Cause of Truth: Radicalism in London 1796–1821.* London: Oxford University Press, 1982.

Hone, William. *Facetiae and Miscellanies.* 2d ed. London: Hunt and Clarke, 1827.

———. Pref. *Wat Tyler: A Dramatic Poem.* London: W. Hone, 1817.

Hood, Thomas. *The Works of Thomas Hood.* Edited by T. Hood, Jr. 7 vols. London: Moxon, 1862. Volume 1.

Hopkins, Kenneth. *The Poets Laureate.* London: Bodley Head, 1954.

Hunt, Leigh. *The Autobiography of Leigh Hunt.* Edited by Roger Ingpen. 2 vols. New York: Dutton, 1903.

————. *The Months: Descriptive of the Successive Beauties of the Year.* London: C. & J. Ollier, 1821.

Hutcheon, Linda. "Ironie et parodie: stratégie et structure." *Poetique* 36 (1978): 367–77.

————. "Ironie, Parodie, Satire." *Poetique* 46 (1981): 13–28.

————. *A Theory of Parody: The Teachings of Twentieth-Century Art Forms.* New York: Methuen, 1985.

Jack, Ian. *English Literature 1815–1832.* London: Oxford University Press, 1963.

Jacobus, Mary. *Tradition and Experiment in Wordsworth's 'Lyrical Ballads' (1798).* Oxford: Clarendon Press, 1976.

Keats, John. *The Letters of John Keats 1814–1821.* Edited by Hyder E. Rollins. 2 vols. Cambridge, Mass.: Harvard University Press, 1958.

Kiremidjean, G. D. "The Aesthetics of Parody." *Journal of Aesthetics and Art Criticism* 28 (1969): 231–42.

Kitchin, George. *A Survey of Burlesque and Parody in English.* 1931. Reprint. New York: Russell & Russell, 1967.

Lee, Guy. *Allusion, Parody and Imitation.* Hull: University of Hull, 1971.

Lehmann, John. *Holborn: An Historical Portrait of a London Borough.* London: Macmillan, 1970.

Lewis, Paul. "Laughing at Fear: Two Versions of the Mock Gothic." *Studies in Short Fiction* 15 (1978): 411–14.

Lindsay, Maurice. *History of Scottish Literature.* London: Robert Hale, 1977.

Low, Donald A. *Thieves' Kitchen: The Regency Underworld.* London: J. M. Dent & Sons Ltd., 1982.

McCoy, Ralph. *Freedom of the Press: An Annotated Bibliography.* Evanston: Southern Illinois University Press, 1968.

Macdonald, Dwight, ed. *Parodies: An Anthology from Chaucer to Beerbohm—and After.* New York: Random House, 1960.

McGann, Jerome J. *The Romantic Ideology: A Critical Investigation.* Chicago: University of Chicago Press, 1983.

Maginn, William. *The Fraserian Papers of the late William Maginn.* Edited by R. Skelton Mackenzie. New York: Redfield, 1857.

Markiewicz, H. "On the Definitions of Literary Parody." *To Honour Roman Jacobson: Essays on the Occasion of His 70th Birthday.* Vol. 2. La Haye: Mouton, 1967.

Marsh, George. "The *Peter Bell* Parodies of 1819." *Modern Philology* 40 (1943): 267–74.

Marshall, William H. *Byron, Shelley, Hunt, and 'The Liberal'.* Philadelphia: University of Pennsylvania Press, 1960.

Mitchell, Edwin Valentine, ed. *The Newgate Calendar.* New York: Garden City Publishing Co., 1926.

Mitford, Mary Russell. *Recollections of a Literary Life or, Books, Places, and People.* New York: Harper & Brothers, 1852.

Moore, Thomas. *The Poetical Works of Thomas Moore.* Edited by A. D. Godfrey. London: Oxford University Press, 1915.

Moorman, Mary. *William Wordsworth: A Biography, The Later Years 1803–1850.* Oxford: Clarendon Press, 1965.

Mordal, Jacques. *25 Centuries of Naval Warfare.* London: Souvenir Press, 1965.

Mortenson, Robert. " 'The Nose-Drop': A Parody of Wordsworth." *Wordsworth Circle* 2.3 (1971): 91–100.

Murray, David. *Memories of the Old College of Glasgow: Some Chapters in the History of the University.* Glasgow: Jackson, Wylie and Co., 1927.

Nethercot, Arthur H. *The Road to Tryermaine.* 1939. Reprint. New York: Russell & Russell, 1962.

Patmore, P. G. *My Friends and Acquaintances.* 3 vols. London: Saunders & Otley, 1854.

Priestman, Donald G. "An Early Imitation and A Parody of Wordsworth." *Notes and Queries* N.S. 26 (1979): 229–31.

———. "Lyrical Ballads and Variant, Ashley 2250." *English Language Notes* 21 (1984): 41–48.

Priestley, J. B. *The Prince of Pleasure.* New York: Harper & Row, 1969.

Pyle, Jr., Gerald J. "J. H. Reynolds's 'Peter Bell.' " *Notes and Queries* N.S. 24 (1977): 323–24.

Quinn, Mary A. "Shelley's 'Verses on the Celandine': An Elegaic Parody of Wordsworth's Early Lyrics." *Keats-Shelley Journal* 36 (1987): 88–109.

Reiman, Donald H. "Christobell; or, The Case of the Sequel Preemptive." *Wordsworth Circle* 6 (1975): 283–89.

Reiman, Donald H., and Sharon B. Powers, eds. *Shelley's Poetry and Prose.* New York: Norton, 1977.

Reiman, Donald H., Michael C. Jaye, and Betty T. Bennett, eds. *The Evidence of Imagination: Studies of Interactions Between Life and Art in English Romantic Literature.* New York: New York University Press, 1978.

Rickwood, Edgell. *Radical Squibs and Loyal Ripostes: Satirical Pamphlets of the Regency Period 1819–1821.* Bath, Somerset: Adams & Dart, 1971.

Reiwald, J. G. "Parody as Criticism." *Neophilologus* 50 (1966): 125-48.

Rogers, Winfield H. "The Reaction Against Melodramatic Sentimentality in the English Novel, 1796–1830." *PMLA* 49 (1934): 98–122.

Rose, Margaret. *Parody/Meta-Fiction.* London: Croom Helm, 1979.

Rudé, George. *Hanoverian London 1714–1808.* Berkeley: University of California Press, 1971.

Ruszkiewicz, John J. "Parody and Pedagogy: Explorations in Imitative Literature." *College English* 40 (1979): 693–701.

Said, Edward. *The World, the Text, and the Critic.* Cambridge, Mass.: Harvard University Press, 1983.

Savory, Jerold, and Patricia Marks. *The Smiling Muse: Victoriana in the Comic Press.* Philadelphia: The Art Alliance Press, 1985.

Schwartz, Lewis M., ed. *Keats Reviewed By His Contemporaries.* Metuchen, N.J.: The Scarecrow Press, Inc., 1973.

Scott, Patrick. "From Bon Gaultier to *Fly Leaves:* Context and Canon in Victorian Parody." *Victorian Poetry* 26.3 (1988): 249–66.

Shelley, H. C. *Literary By-Paths in Old England.* Boston: Little, Brown, 1909.

Shelley, Percy Bysshe. *Letters of Percy Bysshe Shelley.* Edited by F. L. Jones. 2 vols. Oxford: Clarendon Press, 1964.

Shepperson, Archibald. *The Novel in Motley.* Cambridge, Mass.: Harvard University Press, 1936.

Sigmon, Dennis H. *"Rejected Addresses" and the Art of Poetic Parody. DAI* 37 (April 1977): 6514–A.

Smeall, J. L. *English Satire, Parody and Burlesque*. Exeter: A. Wheaton & Co. Ltd., 1952.

Smith, Nelson. *James Hogg*. Boston: Twayne, 1980.

Southey, Robert. *Poems by Robert Southey*. Bristol, 1797.

———. *The Works of Robert Southey*. 10 vols. London: Longmans, 1837–38.

Spicer, A. Dykes. *The Paper Trade: A Descriptive and Historical Survey of the Paper Trade from the Commencement of the Nineteenth Century*. London: Methuen & Co., 1907.

Stone, Christopher. *Parody*. London: Martin, Secker, 1914 (?).

Strout, Alan. *A Bibliography of Articles in 'Blackwood's Magazine,' Volumes I Through XVIII, 1817–1825*. Lubbock, Texas: Texas Technological College, 1959.

Teich, Nathaniel. "Wordsworth's Reception and Copleston's *Advice* to Romantic Reviewers." *Wordsworth Circle* 6 (1975): 280–82.

Thompson, W. F. K. *An Ensign in the Peninsular War: The Letters of John Aitchison*. London: M. Joseph, 1981.

Ward, William. "Some Aspects of the Conservative Attitude Toward Poetry: 1798–1820." *PMLA* 60 (1945): 386–98.

Watson, J. Steven. *The Reign of George III, 1760–1815*. Oxford: Clarendon Press, 1960.

Wells, Carolyn, ed. *A Parody Anthology*. New York: Blue Ribbon Books Inc., 1904.

Wordsworth, William. *The Poetical Works of Wordsworth*. Rev. ed. Ernest de Selincourt. London: Oxford University Press, 1950.

———. *The Letters of William and Dorothy Wordsworth*. Edited by Ernest de Selincourt. 2d ed. *I: The Early Years, 1787–1805*. Rev. ed. Chester L. Shaver. Oxford: Clarendon Press, 1967.

———. *The Letters of William and Dorothy Wordsworth*. Edited by Ernest de Selincourt. 2d ed. *III: The Middle Years, 1812–1820, Part 2*. Rev. ed. Mary Moorman and Alan G. Hill. Oxford: Clarendon Press, 1970.

———. *Guide to the Lakes*. 2 vols. In *The Prose Works of William Wordsworth*, edited by W. J. B. Owen and Jane Worthington Smyser. London: Oxford University Press, 1974.

Zall, P. M. "Sam Spitfire: or, Coleridge in *The Satirist*." *Bulletin of the New York Public Library* 71 (1967): 239–44.

Index